THE NEW NATURALI

A SURVEY OF BRITISH NAT'

WILDFOWL

THE NEW NATURALIST LIBRARY

WILDFOWL

DAVID CABOT

Collins

This edition published in 2009 by Collins,
An imprint of HarperCollins Publishers

HarperCollins Publishers
77–85 Fulham Palace Road
London W6 8JB
www.collins.co.uk

First published 2009

© David Cabot, 2009

A CIP catalogue record for this book is available
from the British Library.

Set in FF Nexus by
Martin Brown

Printed in Hong Kong by Printing Express

Hardback
ISBN 978-0-00-714658-1

Paperback
ISBN 978-0-00-714659-8

Contents

Editors' Preface

EW GROUPS OF BIRDS fire the imagination more broadly than wildfowl. Ducks, geese and swans are the subject of fable, serious poetry and nursery rhyme, music – especially ballet – and, above all, graphic art. Even those who profess little or no interest in birds can readily separate ducks, geese and swans, and across a broad range of habitats, wildfowl are popular with and fascinating to birdwatchers, researchers and conservationists alike.

Over the ages, wildfowl (and their eggs) have featured prominently in our diet, in earlier times including birds shot in bulk by punt gunners and those trapped in the network of duck decoys across lowland areas. Today ducks and geese are largely bred for the table and reared by specialist farmers. Wildfowl are also the subject of sometimes heated debate, not just between protectionists and those who see wildfowling as a legitimate sporting interest, but also over the apparent ease with which they escape from collections or are released by wildfowling interests to boost quarry availability.

Wildfowl are as spectacularly colourful as they are fascinating: some are daily familiars, while others, equally visually attractive, command attention and respect for the prodigious journeys they undertake to reach our shores. The Bewick's swans' annual journey from Arctic Russia in autumn has become a matter of sufficient public interest to feature regularly in the daily papers. Overall wildfowl behaviour, biology and ecology are so varied that their account makes a compelling read.

The author, ornithologist David Cabot, has had a passion for wildfowl since childhood. He has condensed a lifetime of dedicated enthusiasm, involvement and knowledge into this comprehensive and fascinating overview of the natural history of British and Irish wildfowl.

Author's Foreword and Acknowledgements

ORNITHOLOGY, AND ESPECIALLY THE STUDY OF WILDFOWL, has always been one of my great passions. For me, wildfowl are the most fascinating of all birds. More than five million of them that breed throughout the Arctic, from Canada to Siberia, and across northern Europe, visit Britain and Ireland each winter to join the half-million resident breeding swans, geese and ducks plus their progeny. Not only are wildfowl icons of our diminishing wilderness areas – marshlands, fens, coastal wetlands, lakes, river systems and offshore islands – but also their seasonal migrations evoke mystery and awe. A skein of white-fronted geese, high in the sky, accompanied by their wild, cackling calls; long wavering strings of barnacle geese flying over the sea towards a welcoming landfall, barking like a pack of terriers; a flock of wigeon, whistling and growling, wheeling over marshland; the rapid swerving and twisting flight of a pack of teal; or the October arrival of whooper swans, low across the sea, fresh from Iceland, and their excited displays as they touch down on the water and greet those that have already arrived – these are sights and sounds that raise the hairs on the back of my neck, and I am sure on many other necks.

Wildfowl also lay claim to a special grip on our psyche. Their romantic and aesthetic qualities have long been a source of inspiration to artists, from the earliest days of rock carvings some 20,000 years ago, to photographers, poets, painters and writers. Of all birds, wildfowl occupy an unrivalled position in our mythological fables and tales, a reflection of their large size, strength, power of flight, plumage, calls, and their often mysterious and surprising migrations. From a more practical viewpoint, they have provided us with important sources of food from the earliest times. Rather than waste our precious time and energy hunting them, we have domesticated many – from the Egyptian goose of the time of the Old Kingdom in Egypt (around 2300 BC) to more recent Roman times when the swan goose and the greylag goose, the mallard and the muscovy duck, were selectively bred to provide many of the races we know today. Not only were these birds useful for their flesh and eggs, but they were also sources of fat for ointments and burning in lamps, feathers for arrows and quill pens, and down for pillows, quilts and padded clothing.

While wildfowling is one of the most exacting and challenging field sports, increasing numbers of people have sublimated these activities to watching and photographing wildfowl in their natural habitats or visiting wildfowl collections, of which there are many fine examples throughout Britain – though, alas, fewer in Ireland. At these collections wildfowl can be observed and savoured at close quarters, at all stages of their life cycles. One ironic aspect of these collections is that while the conservation of rare and endangered wildfowl is often a prime objective, many collections have been a source of escapes of non-indigenous species such as the mandarin, ruddy and wood ducks, as well as Egyptian, Canada and barnacle geese. These escapees pose serious issues of genetic contamination through interbreeding with wild populations of the same or, worse still, closely related species. Some of our feral wildfowl populations, often introduced with good intentions, have become agricultural pests or threats to air safety, while others pose threats to the native species either through habitat competition or genetic contamination.

Wildfowl have been studied more intensely than any other group of birds. The quantity of published books and scientific papers is so vast that one may ask – why another book on them? In reply I will say what this book is not. It is not a wildfowl identification guide. In Chapter 3, which forms about half the book, while dealing with species accounts I have tried to avoid, as far as possible, traditional descriptions of plumage, moult, voice, field characteristics, habitats, displays and breeding behaviour. All these aspects are extremely well catered for in other major texts such as *Birds of the Western Palearctic* (Cramp & Simmons, 1977) and the recently published monograph *Ducks, Geese and Swans* (Kear, 2005). Nor is this book a strictly traditional approach to wildfowl, structured on a species by-species account. This work does, however, attempt to focus on some of the aspects of wildfowl ecology that appeal to me: their evolution and history; our long relationship with wildfowl; the fluctuations in numbers and changing distributions; breeding biology, productivity, mortality and survival, and finally migrations of the 56 species that are either native or occur as vagrants or in self-sustaining feral populations in these islands. Their social behaviour, feeding ecology, relationships with man, and population dynamics are examined in separate chapters. I have presented three case studies on the population dynamics of the mute swan, barnacle goose and mallard. Finally the conservation of wildfowl is considered.

My passion for wildfowl started 54 years ago when I cut my teeth as a wildfowl counter for the National Wildfowl Counts organised by the Wildfowl Trust, working the upper parts of the River Dart in south Devon. At the same time I sharpened my skills on Dawlish Warren at the mouth of the Exe Estuary, where I spent some time living alone in a house, amongst the birds, that was eventually gobbled up by the encroaching sea, studying the ducks, geese and waders. I expended much time and energy there trapping and ringing waders and a few duck. Later, in 1961, as a student at Trinity College, Dublin, I stumbled into a lifelong passion for the Greenland population of barnacle geese that winter in western Ireland and Scotland. While looking for an unstudied area to observe spring migration along the west coast of Ireland the late Major R. F. Ruttledge, doyen of Irish ornithology, suggested that I should go to the Inishkea Islands, off the coast of County Mayo. There I found some 2,500 barnacle geese wintering on the islands, and I immediately became intrigued by them. That addiction led me to northeast Greenland for three summers – first in 1984 with a Brathay Expedition, then on my own expeditions in 1985 and 1987 – where we tried to unravel barnacle goose breeding biology while also catching and ringing large numbers of moulting geese. Long before that I had my first low-Arctic tundra experience when in 1962 I joined, as film cameraman, the Cambridge Whooper Swan Expedition to Iceland, where we caught moulting whooper swans, ringing large numbers for the first time.

ACKNOWLEDGEMENTS

Like many other amateur naturalists, I have had to accommodate my ornithological obsessions into the more mundane world of working for a living – a difficult high-wire act but one that has a long and robust tradition among thousands of excellent amateur British and Irish naturalists. The victims of these pursuits are the partners and children left behind. However, I did try and encourage my own family along on many excursions and expeditions, and I like to think that they enjoyed their experiences. So, thank you Penny, Liam, Tim and Redmond for your forbearance and support over the many years as I set off on many trips into the wilds.

This book draws upon a huge reservoir of published information from a dedicated and highly professional community of wildfowl biologists. The book has greatly benefited from the enthusiastic counting and censusing carried out by an army of wildfowl counters – many of whom are amateurs, doing their work at their own expense – who annually contribute data to the British Wetland Bird Surveys (WeBS), a joint scheme of the British Trust for Ornithology (BTO), the Wildfowl & Wetlands Trust (WWT), the Royal Society for the Protection of Birds (RSPB) and the Joint Nature Conservation Committee (JNCC). In Ireland I-WeBS is a joint scheme between BirdWatch Ireland, the National Parks and Wildlife Service of the Department of Environment, Heritage and Local Government and the WWT, with support from the Heritage Council and the World Wide Fund for Nature.

There are many people I would like to thank for their help and assistance with this book. Firstly, Ken Kinsella provided a large number of the photographs, some of them especially commissioned. Nicholas Cottrell kindly supplied photographs of the WWT visitor centres, and Alyn Walsh provided photographs of Greenland white-fronted and other geese. Hugh Boyd, long-standing friend and mentor, kindly read the draft of Chapter 3 and provided valued comments and observations. Brian West, one of my earliest long-term collaborators, read Chapters 4, 5 and 6, and made many very helpful comments and provided good guidance and advice, as always. Andy Musgrove read Chapter 3 and made many helpful observations and corrections. Paul Milne very kindly checked Appendix 1. He also supplied information about rare wildfowl and mandarin duck in Ireland. Any errors that may endure, whether in these chapters or elsewhere in the book, are my sole responsibility.

Olivia Crowe helped with I-WeBS data. Ralph Sheppard provided information on breeding whooper swans and common mergansers (goosanders) in Co. Donegal. Alyn Walsh gave me information on snow and red-breasted geese observed on the Wexford Slobs, results from the March 2008 aerial survey of barnacle geese and information on the recovery of an American wigeon, as well as other general assistance. Tony Fox supplied me with information on the numbers of Greenland white-fronted geese in Ireland and Britain. Pat Smiddy gave me details of mandarin duck in Cork. Hugh Shiels dug out a copy of the relevant section of the report concerning archaeological excavations at Lagore, Co. Meath. The late William McDowell gave me information on breeding whooper swans in Ireland and permission to use information from a CD copy of his excellent but as yet unpublished *History of the Birds of Northern Ireland*. He also provided information on the mandarin duck and Egyptian goose in Northern Ireland.

Over the years I have received much help and assistance from an enthusiastic band of collaborators with my studies on the Greenland population of the barnacle goose, some results of which appear in the book. I would like to acknowledge with gratitude the help, both in the field and in other ways, of Brian

West, Maurice Cassidy, Michael Viney, Richard Nairn, Steve Newton and Roger Goodwillie. Alyn Walsh worked with me on the Inishkea Islands on several occasions while cannon netting geese there, while John Wilson and David Norriss made these visits possible. Larry Griffin and Richard Hesketh provided help both in the field and with the fitting of GPS satellite transmitters on barnacle geese during April 2008. Ross and Denise Parker kindly lent me a printer that was indispensable while I was finishing the final draft of the book in Vermont.

The irrepressible Myles Archibald of HarperCollins never lost faith in the book, nor in me, as it and I journeyed towards completion. I would also like to thank my editor, Hugh Brazier, who made most helpful contributions towards improving the text, way above what would normally be expected. Julia Koppitz, editor, provided invaluable support, both seen and unseen, towards the production of the book. Book jacket designers seldom get an acknowledgement, but Robert Gillmor has excelled again with his marvellous and evocative design.

I would also like to thank the following publishers for permission to use illustrations: Oxford University Press; the British Waterfowl Association; Blandford Press; Constable & Co. Ltd; the National Environmental Research Institute, Denmark; the National Geographic Magazine; and the British Trust for Ornithology. The sources of all illustrations are acknowledged in the captions.

And, finally, a big thank you to all the many thousands of wildfowl counters, researchers and enthusiasts, both amateur and professional, who provided much of the information upon which this book is based.

CHAPTER 1

Introduction

T
HE EARLIEST KNOWN BIRD, *Archaeopteryx lithographica*, was essentially a feathered, flying–gliding dinosaur that lived in the late Jurassic period, some 150 million years ago. It is known from a fossil record in southern Germany, and its discovery in the early 1860s was quickly taken as confirmation of the idea that birds evolved from reptiles. The skeletal structure of this half-bird, half-reptile suggested that it was probably more a glider than a flyer, but most significantly its rounded wings and tail were feathered. An even earlier bird-like fossil, *Protoavis*, has been found in late Triassic deposits in Texas, but its status is controversial. Because of the hollow structure of bird bones and their propensity for being crushed, very few early fossils remain, and the evolutionary trail that leads through the Cretaceous period, from dinosaurs to the birds we know today, is unknown.

During the past 25 years, however, knowledge of the evolutionary path of birds has undergone remarkable revision with the aid of cladistics – a method of classification in which organisms are grouped together on the basis of similarities due to recent origin from a common ancestor – and molecular phylogeny. These analytical tools now place birds not as evolving during the Triassic period (254–206 million years ago) from basal archosaur reptiles but directly from a subgroup of the Dinosauria, with their closest relatives being modest-sized dinosaurs such as the dromaeosaurids and troodontids. The evidence for the relationship between the birds and these theropod dinosaurs is based on the skeletal structures in the forelimbs, pelvis, hind limbs and skull.[1] Four of these meat-eating theropod dinosaurs, with bird-like bones and traces of feathers, were discovered in Liaoning Province, China, in the late 1990s. They had the forelimbs of a primitive bird and the tail of a dinosaur (Fig. 1).

FIG 1. Unnamed oviraptorosaur, one of the Chinese theropod dinosaurs that may be the ancestors of modern birds. (Image from an article by Christopher Sloan, *National Geographic Magazine*, November 1999. Reproduced with permission)

The true birds of the Cretaceous (145–65 million years ago) were the Neornithes (modern birds), flapping or running around the shallow tidal waters of the ancient oceans. They included the 'fish bird' or *Ichthyornis*, a small, tern-like seabird, some 20 cm in length and an efficient flying machine, and a large flightless diver called *Hesperornis*, up to 160 cm in length, that had a lower jaw resembling that of mosasaurs, the swimming reptiles (Fig. 2). Only the lower jaw had teeth. Its wings were vestigial but it was apparently a strong swimmer with powerful legs. *Hesperornis* was effectively a well-developed type of water bird. It is clear that by this point in geological history the avifauna was well diversified.

The earliest identifiable anseriform fossils, *Romainvillia stehlini* and *Eonessa anaticula*, representing two separate, distinct and extinct subfamilies, were discovered in two widely separated geographical areas – France and the United States – and date from the late Eocene period, some 40–35 million years ago. The first known fossils of wildfowl belonging to the present-day subfamilies Anserinae and Anatinae come from the Oligocene period, 34–24 million years ago. One of these fossils was of a waterfowl, *Cygnopterus affinis*, somewhat similar to the mute swan, discovered in Oligocene deposits in Belgium.[2] But it is not until the more recent Miocene period, 24–5 million years ago, that the fossil

Hesperornis

Ichthyornis

FIG 2. *Ichthyornis* and *Hesperornis,* true birds from the Cretaceous. From R. Freethy, *How Birds Work* (Blandford Press, 1982).

record reveals a total of 27 anseriform species, including goose bones that could be ascribed to the genera *Branta* (black geese) and *Anser* (grey geese).

During the Pliocene period, some 5–2 million years ago, the number of species representing each genus of wildfowl increases rapidly in the fossil record, so that by the start of the Pleistocene period, about 1.7 million years ago, most of today's wildfowl species had evolved as we know them today.

Wildfowl (ducks, geese and swans) all belong to a single large family, the Anatidae, which makes up the bulk of the order Anseriformes. According to the classification put forward by Jean Delacour and Ernst Mayr in 1945 and later modified by Paul Johnsgard in 1978, the Anatidae embrace some 151 species.[3] This is the classification adopted by the British Ornithologists' Union (BOU), and followed in Chapter 3. More recently Livezey proposed several changes to the classification of the order Anseriformes, based on cladistic analysis of morphological characters.[4] This classification recognises two small families – the screamers (Anhimidae) and the magpie goose (Anseranatidae) – alongside the Anatidae; the number of subfamilies within the Anatidae is increased from three to five; and a number of fossil species are included, making a total of 173 species in 55 genera.

Despite a great diversity of size, body shape, plumage coloration, ecology and behaviour, the Anatidae are united by certain common features in physical

FIG 3. Greenland white-fronted geese in flight. These geese fly approximately 5,800 km on a round trip from their wintering grounds in Ireland and Scotland to their breeding grounds in west Greenland and back again. The spring journey from Ireland/Scotland to their staging grounds in Iceland takes some 14–17 hours. After resting and refuelling there for about a month they fly another 14–17 hours, including crossing the Greenland icecap, to their breeding grounds. Neck collars – each with a unique three-digit alphanumeric code – have been fitted to some 2,800 birds for scientific research. Much of our detailed knowledge of wildfowl comes from intensive studies using such devices, and more recently satellite tracking. (Alyn Walsh)

structure, habitat and behaviour. They are all adapted for an aquatic or semi-aquatic life. The front three toes are connected by webbing – only the Hawaiian and magpie geese have partially webbed feet – and the smaller hind toe, sometimes lobed, is positioned higher. The legs of wildfowl are set far apart, and located not in the centre of the body but towards the tail end of the bird to facilitate more effective swimming and diving. When walking on dry land wildfowl appear to waddle, a necessary movement to prevent the bird from toppling over, as its centre of gravity must be shifted backwards over each leg, thus producing a mild rotating effect as the bird moves forward. In flight wildfowl have characteristically long necks and short tails, creating the

FIG 4. Black scoter: upper and lower mandibles open, revealing the lamellae that are used to sieve or strain solid food items from water by many duck and swan species. (Joe Blossom/NHPA)

impression that the wings, often sharply pointed, are set well back on the body. Most wildfowl are fast and strong flyers (Fig. 3), with a well-developed keel protruding from the sternum to accommodate the bulky flight muscles.

The diagnostic feature that separates wildfowl from all other birds is the bill, generally flattened, broad and blunt, which is covered by a thin skin and tipped by a horny plate in the shape of a fingernail known as the 'nail', which in some species is bent over in the form of a hook. The edges of the mandibles are set with rows of horny lamellae (Fig. 4), and the tongue is thick and fleshy, covered with horny spines and papillae. The range of size, shape and nature of the bill of each species is witness to adaptive variation, a response to the great diversity of food eaten by wildfowl, ranging from grass to molluscs. Geese are essentially pluckers of vegetation, and have conical and often short stubby bills with serrated cutting edges to assist in the cutting of grasses; the shoveler, a dabbling duck, has a relatively enormous spatulate bill with well-developed lamellae along its edges for sifting, straining and extracting food from mud and ooze;

the mergansers sport long and narrow bills with saw-tooth-like lamellae, which help to grip small fish underwater.

Wildfowl plumage is thick, with the feathers underlain by a dense coat of downy feathers that are loose, soft and fluffy. The mallard has approximately 12,000 feathers, including downy feathers, while the tundra swan has some 25,000, representing about 10 per cent of the swan's body weight.[5] Underneath is an additional insulation layer of subcutaneous fat, a feature generally lacking in other birds. Anyone who has roasted a goose will have been rapidly brought to an appreciation of the extent of the oil stored in this fatty coating. Wildfowl, unlike most other birds, shed their flight feathers simultaneously at the end of the summer and are generally flightless for up to four weeks. During this relatively short period they take refuge on lakes, generally safe from predators and close to their food. Many of the brightly coloured male ducks moult their body feathers twice: in late summer they moult into an 'eclipse' plumage that renders them less conspicuous while they regrow their flight feathers, and then later in the autumn a second body-feather moult restores their splendid plumage, readying them for the business of courtship. Most other non-wildfowl species undergo a progressive moult of their feathers, allowing them to retain their power of flight. A large proportion of the time budget of wildfowl is spent on preening and feather maintenance. To assist with the waterproofing of the feathers a large and well-developed sebaceous gland, located just above the tail, is a continual source of oil for smearing, by both bill and head, on the feathers of the preening bird.

Geese and swans share a high level of social and family organisation, generally remaining paired for life over a relatively long life. The young remain with their parents after the breeding season, migrating together to the wintering grounds, where the family generally remains intact, and returning together to the spring staging grounds and often the summer breeding grounds. If the adults fail to breed during that summer, more often than not the family will stay together for the second winter, and possibly further winters. While much bird behaviour is instinctive, geese and swans are unusual in that their young must 'learn' the migration routes by travelling with their parents southwards from the Arctic during the autumn and returning in the spring.

Wildfowl, ratites – the ostrich, rhea, emu, cassowary and kiwi – and a few other birds are unusual in possessing an erectable intromittent phallus, an adaptation to facilitate fertilisation in the aquatic environment. It is considered a primitive feature amongst birds.

According to Livezey's classification, the family Anatidae consists of five subfamilies, of which only three are relevant to Britain and Ireland. The swans and geese comprise the subfamily Anserinae, characterised by large size, long necks, relatively long legs and a body adapted for walking. They have a single annual moult rendering them both flightless (for up to four weeks) and vulnerable to predators, display little plumage, structural and voice differences between the sexes, and exhibit relatively simple courtship displays. The three swans of Britain and Ireland belong to the genus *Cygnus*. They are all-white in adult plumage with longer necks (either as long as or longer than body length), shorter legs and larger feet than geese. There are eleven species of geese on the British and Irish lists, several of which are further divided into subspecies or races. The 'grey geese' belong to the genus *Anser* and display generally uniform plumage coloration, while the 'black geese' belong to the genus *Branta* and exhibit a more elaborate plumage with contrasting whites, blacks, greys and, in the case of the red-breasted goose, an additional colour, red.

The subfamily Tadorninae includes the shelducks and sheldgeese, with three species recorded in Britain and Ireland. The true ducks belong to the other subfamily, Anatinae. They are generally smaller than geese and swans, have shorter necks, and are better adapted for swimming and diving. Unlike the geese and swans, they have a double body-feather moult as well as the single flight-feather moult, the sexes have different plumages, and their courtship behaviour is complicated, with males indulging in elaborate displays in contrast with the low-key behaviour of the drabber-plumaged females. The ducks are further subdivided into five tribes, of which four have been recorded in Britain or Ireland. The two largest tribes are the sea ducks or Mergini, with 16 species recorded from these islands, and the Anatini or dabbling ducks, of which there are 13 species on the British and Irish lists (all in the genus Anas apart from the muscovy and mandarin ducks).

A complete classified list of all wildfowl species that have occurred in Britain and Ireland – either in a wild state or in self-sustaining populations following deliberate introduction or escapes – is contained in Appendix 1. The Livezey classification is followed in Appendix 1, although Chapter 3 retains the more familiar BOU/Johnsgard sequence, placing the swans before the geese. Appendix 2 contains a list of all other wildfowl that have occurred in Britain and Ireland as recorded in recent years by the Wetland Bird Survey (WeBS), either as escapes from wildfowl collections or as non-self-sustaining introductions.

CHAPTER 2

Wildfowl and People

E VER SINCE THEIR EARLIEST DAYS, humans have been preoccupied with animals as the source of much of their food. But early people also held magico-religious beliefs about the beasts and birds, as revealed by the extraordinary cave paintings at different sites throughout Europe dating from the upper Palaeolithic period, 50,000–10,000 years ago. These depict an obsession with the chase and the reproduction of animals, a theme that links the killing to a desire to see the prey flourish and multiply and, *inter alia*, facilitate human survival – an early example of ecological thinking.

One of the most famous cave-painting sites is at Lascaux, set in a limestone hill in the Périgord landscape of France. Here, some 17,000 years ago, Cro-Magnon artists perfected their skills, drawing, scratching and colouring magnificent images of the larger animals – bulls, aurochs, reindeer, bison, horses, cows with the odd musk ox, ibex, lions, brown bear and a woolly rhinoceros – that appear to float in a kaleidoscopic, mystical way across the cave's calcite walls. These caves were not used as dwelling places but as art galleries, where the paintings held some kind of ritual or magical significance, to be visited occasionally. Hidden amongst these, on a surface in the deepest recess of the cave, is an astonishing scene of a four-fingered man with a distinctive bird-like head, lying on the ground with a large erect penis while being charged down by a bison that has just been speared by the man, with entrails spilling from its belly (Fig. 5). Near the man is a bird, set on the top of a pole.

This is a rare image among the Lascaux paintings, as neither human nor bird figures are to be found elsewhere in the cave. The bird set on the pole may represent the external soul of the prostrate bird-man, suggesting a mythological connection between humans and birds concerning death and life thereafter.

FIG 5. Lascaux cave painting depicting a prostrate man, having been charged down by a bison. Note the highly symbolic bird at the end of the pole. (Norbert Aujoult, National Centre of Prehistory, France)

The sudden appearance and disappearance of birds must have baffled early people. There was always the possibility that the birds had some form of contact with higher spirits or gods – made plausible by their powers of flight, up and away into the skies above, later to descend after communicating with the deities.

WILDFOWL IN MYTH AND LEGEND

Myths and legends concerning birds and other animals arose to explain the unexplainable in the natural world at a time when the understanding of nature and natural cycles was primordial. Wildfowl, because of their large size, powerfulness and migratory habits, feature disproportionately among the myths and legends concerning birds. Among these myths are two particularly intriguing stories, one about geese and the other concerning swans. Each is a tale that persisted for an exceptionally long time, and both of them had important social and conservation consequences.

The first is the bird–fish myth that was in vogue for over a thousand years in Europe and the Middle East, and whose roots may be even older. In its simplest form, shellfish turn into birds. The myth apparently started life as an oral tradition, and scholars then transmogrified it into literature, thus providing interesting

insights into pre-scientific thought. The myth was repeatedly copied by many
writers over the centuries. As Edward Armstrong wrote in his New Naturalist
The Folklore of Birds,[1] the frequent copying of the myth in many texts throws light
on the credulity or mendacity of scholars, which is also well exposed in Edward
Heron-Allen's marvellous and scholarly book *Barnacles in Nature and Myth*.[2]

The first authoritative statement of the myth was by Giraldus Cambrensis, a
Welshman whose real name was Gerald de Barri, who became chaplain to King
Henry II in 1184. He had first visited Ireland in 1183, and was chosen to
accompany one of the King's sons, John, as a tutor on another Irish tour the
following year. Based on his observations in Ireland he wrote his famous
Topographia Hibernica, which was read – the form of publishing at that time –
before the masters and scholars of Oxford in 1186. In the first section of the
book, in Chapter XI, *De bernacis ex abiete nascentibus earumque natura* – barnacles
that are born of the fir-tree and their nature – he wrote

> *There are many birds here that are called barnacles, which nature, acting against
> her own laws, produces in a wonderful way. They are like marsh geese, but smaller.
> At first they appear as excrescences on fir-logs carried down upon the waters.
> Then they hang by their beaks from what seems like sea-weed clinging to the log,
> while their bodies, to allow for their more unimpeded development, are enclosed
> in shells. And so in the course of time, having put on a stout covering of feathers,
> they either slip into the water, or take themselves in flight to the freedom of the
> air. They take their food and nourishment from the juice of wood and water during
> their mysterious and remarkable generation. I myself have seen many times and
> with my own eyes more than a thousand of these small bird-like creatures hanging
> from a single log upon the sea-shore. They were in their shells and already formed.
> No eggs are laid as is usual as a result of mating. No bird ever sits upon eggs to
> hatch and in no corner of the land will you see them breeding or building nests.
> Accordingly in some parts of Ireland bishops and religious men eat them without
> sin during a fasting time, regarding them as not being flesh, since they were not
> born of flesh.*[3]

Edward Armstrong argues that the bird–fish myth can be traced back to
about the tenth century, when references in an early Jewish Rabbinic text speak
about black birds, 'similar to the bird called the Diver', developing from white
jelly in the shape of an egg when it fell into the water from trees growing on the
seashore. The location of the myth was most probably Ireland. When Allah wills
it, the egg, which has changed into the form of a bird with its feet and bill
attached to the wood, develops feathers and drops to the water. The birds then

FIG 6. Tree geese. (British Library, Harley MS 4751 Folio 36r)

scuttle on the water surface, but they are never found alive, only dead, washed up on the shore. Geese are not mentioned in the account. The 'black diving birds' washed up dead on the shores of Ireland were most likely to have been little auks, which often occur in large numbers or 'wrecks', especially after severe winter storms. If barnacle geese were observed along the shoreline among flotsam and jetsam where dead little auks were also found, it would have been an easy leap of the imagination to assume that the little auks, like the shellfish, were the early stages of the geese.

As barnacle geese were found on floating timber (produced ex lignis abiegnis), it was assumed that they were generated from trees overhanging the sea – and thus they became 'tree geese'. The illustration shown in Figure 6 dates from about 1230–40, and the text that accompanied it states that

> Barnacle geese come from trees that grow over water. The trees produce birds that look like small geese; the young birds hang from their beaks from the trees. When the birds are mature enough, they fall from the trees; any that fall into the water float and are safe, but those that fall on land die.

Thus were explained the mysterious comings and goings of barnacle geese, which arrived on the west coasts of Scotland and Ireland each October, as if created spontaneously, and then suddenly disappeared at the end of winter in April. Anyone who has encountered goose barnacles, attached by their fleshy-looking stalks on floating or washed-up wood along the shoreline, would forgive the credulity of the early naturalists. With some imagination one can see how the

FIG 7. Goose barnacle, *Lepas* spp. The feather-like appendages are cirri, used for sifting out and capturing the plankton on which the barnacle feeds. (Anthony Bannister/ NHPA)

grey-shelled, generally tulip-shaped goose barnacles, with protruding plumose appendages superficially resembling feathers, might have been the origin of the barnacle geese (Fig. 7).

As the barnacle goose arose from a shellfish (the goose barnacle is a crustacean) it was classified as fish, not fowl, and thus could be eaten during Lent and on Fridays. Brant geese, not that dissimilar to barnacles and easily confused with the barnacle goose, were also eaten as 'fish'. Giraldus Cambrensis, in a moralistic rant, condemned Irish Bishops and clergy for regarding geese as 'fish'. His ire eventually reached Rome, and Pope Innocent III, as reported by Vincent of Beauvais, at the Fourth General Lateran Council in 1215 issued a Papal Bull that forbade the eating of barnacle geese during Lent and on Fridays.[4] Perhaps some barnacle and brant geese derived some protection from this Bull, but even as late as 1914 in certain parts of Ireland – County Donegal and elsewhere in Ulster – barnacle geese were being killed and eaten during Lent, as they were still regarded as 'more fish than fowl'.[5]

At the end of the sixteenth century, John Gerard, the great British herbalist, straying somewhat outside his brief, went further than most in propagating the bird–fish myth. In his *Herbal* (1597) the last entry in the book concerns the 'Goose tree, Barnacle tree, or the tree bearing Geese'. He wrote that

FIG 8. The barnacle tree, from Gerard's *Herbal*.

There are found in the North parts of Scotland and islands adjacent, called the Orkneys, certain trees whereon do grow certain shells of a white colour tending to russet, wherein are contained little living creatures: which shells in time of maturity do open, and out of them grow those little living things, which falling into the water do become fowles, which we call Barnakles; in the North of England, brent geese; and in Lancashire, tree geese: but the other that do fall upon the land perish and come to nothing.[6]

Spinning the myth further, and after declaring that 'what our eyes have seen and our hands have touched', he collected some shells found growing on the trunk of an old rotten tree on the shore between Dover and Romney. He took them to London and when he opened them he found 'living things without form or shape and in others'... and 'birds covered with soft down, the shell half open and the birds ready to fall out, which no doubt were the fowles called Barnakles'.... 'They spawn as it were in March and April; the geese are formed in May and June, and come to the fullness of feathers the month after.' He 'borrowed' an illustration from Mathias de Lobel's *Stirpium Historia* (1570) and added in geese, nestling within the shells, ready to tumble out (Fig. 8).

The outline of the bird–fish myth is probably known to most naturalists today. But the pervasiveness and longevity of the myth may not be so well appreciated, nor the fact that the barnacle goose and the brant goose received early protection and conservation status through the issuing of a Papal Bull of 1215.

Swans are spectacular wildfowl, large, conspicuously white and noisy. Moreover, the two wild species occurring as winter visitors to Britain and Ireland – whooper and Bewick's – undertook mysterious migrations, not understood until very recently. The trumpeting calls of the wild swans, and the waxy-swishing sound of the mute swan's wings while in flight overhead, added to the mystery of these birds and made them prime candidates for mythology – and that in turn led to their elevation to the status of special species that were not to be hunted or shot. It was believed that the souls of the dead were embodied in swans, and to kill a swan would bring bad luck to the hunter, even leading to death within the year. Nowhere is the association of the human soul and spirit with those of birds better exemplified than in the Irish legend of the Children of Lir.

The Children of Lir is one of the Three Sorrows or Pieties of Story-telling that form part of the Irish mythological cycle. They are founded on love, jealousy and murder and set in the mists of time of magic, when belief in druids and other supernatural phenomena was the culture. It was the time when the ancient tribes of Tuatha Dé Danaan occupied Ireland. The theme of the Children of Lir was jealousy. The mythical King Lir, lord of the sea, had been defeated by the Gaelic people. He and his wife Aoibh had four beautiful children, Fionnuala, Aodh (both of whom had gills and webbed feet), Fiachra and Conn. Their mother Aoibh died and Lir married her sister, Aoife, who possessed magical powers. Aoife at first loved her stepchildren, but because of Lir's affection for them she became jealous and plotted their death. One day, on a visit to the new King Bodhbh, she flunked killing them but instead encouraged the children to swim in a lake that they were passing. Out came her magic wand and the children were turned into four beautiful swans (Figs 9 and 10), condemned to spend 300 years on Lough Derravaragh (Loch Dairbhreach), County Westmeath, 300 on the stormy sea of the Moyle between Ireland and Scotland (Sruth na Maoile), and 300 off the west coast of County Mayo (Iorras Domhnann), where they found a home on the island of Inishglora (Inis Gluaire). They spent much of their time on Loch na-nEan or Lake of the Birds, where they sang so sweetly that all the sea-fowl came to hear them, crowding onto the shore. Each day the swans set off from Inishglora to feed along the nearby coast and islands:

> But the swans,
> During the day would take their flight to seek
> For food along the coasts, or wing their way
> To Iniskea, where stands upon one leg
> The lonely crane that never had a mate
> But lives companionless, who never left.[7]

Their wicked stepmother had told them that the spell that had transformed them into swans would not be broken until they heard the bell of the new God (the conversion of Ireland to Christianity by St Patrick). Whilst based on Inishglora

FIG 9. Children of Lir, by Maud Gonne.
From Ella Young, *Celtic Wonder Tales* (Dublin, 1910).

FIG 10. King Lir and
the swans, by
J. H. Bacon, ARA.
From Charles Squire,
Celtic Myths
(London, 1912).

they met St Mochaomhóg, a local ecclesiastic from the mainland who provided
shelter for the swans in a small chapel that he had built, possibly the church at
Cross Lough on the mainland opposite the island, and the swans attended his
religious services. During the sixth century St Brendan the Navigator (d. 577) also
established an ecclesiastical settlement on the island, consisting of a monastic
cashel with a chapel, nunnery, monastery and other structures.

I know Inishglora well, having visited it many times. The monastic settlement remains, although in a dilapidated state, and there is indeed a small lake there that could have been the Lake of the Birds. Another candidate is Cross Lough on the mainland, which today is an important wildfowl wetland with many wintering whooper swans. On the island itself there are barnacle and greylag geese, but wild swans are unusual. However, I have seen whooper swans during spring migration in April flying low over the sea northwards, close to the island.

One day Lairgren, King of Connacht, arrived to gather up the swans and present them to his wife, who had heard that they sang beautifully and had expressed a wish to have them. As they were being loaded up into a cart the bell rang and a great mist descended, as it had done 900 years earlier when the children were transformed into swans. The mist then turned into the colours of the rainbow before being blown away. The swans had been magically transformed back into humans, but they were old and withered. Lairgren fled when he saw the human bodies, but Saint Mochaomhóg baptised the ageing children just before they died, and buried them on the island. The christening suggests some sort of Church approval of the myth.

The story of the Children of Lir is thought to have been based on a migratory legend known as 'the Knight of the Swan', which may have reached Ireland from Britain at the end of the Middle Ages,[8] though Edward Armstrong is more specific, believing that it reached Ireland earlier, from the British Kingdom of Strathclyde in the eighth century. Whatever its origin, the belief that our souls reposed in wild swans was so strong that for many centuries wild swans were afforded special conservation status among hunters.

In the mid-1960s, just after the Irish Wildfowl Conservancy was established in Galway, Ireland, it was common for foreign shooters to visit Ireland, especially from Italy and France. On one occasion a car-boot-full of wild swans was found, shot by unknown perpetrators. The eminent Bill Finlay, Chairman of the IWC at the time and later Governor of the Bank of Ireland, stated that no Irishman could have been responsible because of their deep belief that human souls resided within swans. It was later discovered that it was indeed heathen hunters from the Continent who had done the massacre!

WILDFOWL AS A SOURCE OF FOOD

For centuries geese and swans have provided essential food (meat and eggs) for people living in the Arctic – the Inuit of Canada and Greenland, the Samoyedic people of western Siberia, and some Icelandic farmers. The easiest way to capture the birds was during the annual moult, when they shed their flight feathers and become flightless for a few weeks in late summer and early autumn. The moulting birds could then be rounded up and driven like sheep into holding pens with funnel entrances, constructed with stones or any other suitable materials that were available. The pens were placed on elevated sites on flat plains, where moulting birds misguidedly sought refuge.

Other pens were constructed on natural breakout points on the edges of lakes. Moulting geese seek immediate refuge in any lake or water body when disturbed by people, either on foot or on horseback. They could then be driven out of the often-shallow lake into the previously constructed pen, which would normally have a large-mouthed funnel opening to stream the geese into the catching pen. Once secure in the pens they were slaughtered in their thousands. Most of the geese were 'cached' – first plucked and cleaned, then placed in 'pit fridges' hacked out of the permafrost. The frozen geese thus provided a supply of food throughout the year. Some geese would be cut up into strips and air-dried or salted before storing. Thousands of Arctic-nesting geese were caught and killed this way each year. Whenever nests were found, eggs would also be taken. The mortality may have had a significant historical impact on the breeding populations, but today very few geese and swans are trapped for food.

Moulting geese and swans are still caught today on their Arctic breeding grounds, but almost solely for the purposes of scientific research, which involves marking the birds with large plastic leg-rings that can be read in the field when the birds are in their European or American wintering quarters. In addition, some are fitted with engraved neck-bands (Fig. 3), while others have lightweight satellite transmitters strapped onto them that allow satellite tracking. Visual monitoring of the birds carrying their engraved plastic rings or 'licence plates' over a period of years provides invaluable information about migration routes, longevity, mortality and the breeding performance of individual birds.

Shooting during the spring and autumn migration periods is today the main cause of mortality of Arctic breeding geese, followed by losses during migration. Much of the shooting occurs in Arctic areas, but significant numbers are shot, both legally and illegally, in Iceland during both spring and autumn. When the birds arrive in their wintering areas in Ireland and Britain they are subject to further shooting mortality, but on an increasingly controlled basis.

Moulting ducks and their flightless young were once caught in large numbers further south, particularly in northwest Europe and especially in the Netherlands and in Britain, by driving them into traps set on the margins of wetlands. The success of such trapping depended upon large wild breeding populations and extensive wetlands. When both declined as a result of drainage operations during the seventeenth and eighteenth centuries, duck trapping became an unprofitable activity, but an ingenious Dutch invention, the duck decoy, then came into its own. Duck decoys (from the Dutch eende-kooi, duck trap) were capable of catching considerable numbers of migrating and wintering birds during the autumn, winter and spring. Taking wildfowl in these decoys was one of the most sophisticated and effective ways of trapping and killing wildfowl.

The basic duck decoy consisted of a pond or shallow lake of about one hectare, often set in woodland that provided a degree of security and cover for the visiting wildfowl. Radiating from the lake was a series of usually up to eight curved and covered tunnels, or pipes, up which the wildfowl were enticed until they reached the narrow tapering end, which terminated in a catching bag. The large number of pipes was necessary so that the decoy could operate in all different wind directions – wildfowl prefer to fly into the wind and often will move on the water surface facing into the wind. The netting- or wire-covered pipes could be up to 80 m long, 8 m wide at the entrance, with a height of 5 m above the water surface. Food was sometimes used to encourage the ducks into the mouth of a pipe. The sides of the pipes were blanked off, up to a height of about 2 m, or slightly higher than a person, with rush or reed screens that were set in such a way that they allowed the ducks to observe a specially trained dog that moved ahead of them. Ducks, like many other animals, have an innate mobbing behaviour and will follow and mob a predator. This alerts and secures the safety of the bird group by keeping a collective eye on the predator and making it harder for the predator to attack an individual in the group than if it were isolated. The dog – simulating a fox – ran ahead of the ducks, drawing them further and further up the pipe while the decoy man followed behind, initially keeping out of sight and then revealing himself to 'push' them on (Fig. 11). The ducks, when cut off from the pond by the decoy man, flew into the wind and up the pipe to be bagged at the end of the pipe. Successful decoying was a highly skilled art, requiring a special relationship between dog and decoy man. Call ducks, a type of miniature mallard with a distinctive call, were also used to decoy the wild birds into and up the pipes (see p. 32).

The Dutch, past masters in the art of trapping waterfowl, built hundreds of decoys during the sixteenth century. Many were highly profitable, often run by farmers in conjunction with other farming activities. But the English already had duck decoys in operation in the reign of King John (1199–1216). The earliest English decoy for which there are records was built at Waxham, Norfolk, in about 1620. By 1790 duck decoys were apparently supplying over 200,000 ducks for eating in London. However, many of the British – there were none in Scotland – and Irish decoys were non-commercial, existing to supply the 'big house' with an additional stream of fresh food. In 1886 Sir Ralph Payne-Gallwey was able to list some 200 British and Irish decoys in his magnificent *Book of Duck Decoys* (Fig. 12).[9] Some 32 years later the number in use had declined to 19, according to the next major work on the subject.[10] Running and maintenance expenses continued to spiral upwards, with declining numbers of ducks being caught. By 1936 only four British decoys remained open on a commercial basis.[11] It was calculated then that a decoy needed to catch about 3,500 ducks per annum – mallard were the most frequently caught, followed by Eurasian wigeon and Eurasian teal – to remain economically viable, and the few remaining decoys could not produce those numbers. In their hey or duck days some Dutch decoys caught prodigious numbers – the decoy at Kampen, for example, caught more than 25,000 ducks in the year 1841. During the hundred years from 1809 over 650,000 were trapped and killed for eating at Kampen. During the late 1930s the annual catch from approximately 150 Dutch decoys was a million wildfowl. In contrast, some 11,500 wildfowl were caught per annum in the ten working British decoys between 1924 and 1935. Due to high maintenance and running costs most decoys have long since fallen into disuse, melting back into the landscape.

FIG 11. 'Entrance to a decoy pipe with dog at work and wild fowl following him up the pipe.' From Payne-Gallwey, *The Book of Duck Decoys* (Van Voorst, 1886).

FIG 12. 'View of a decoy pipe as seen from the head shew place.' From Payne-Gallwey, *The Book of Duck Decoys* (Van Voorst, 1886).

Some time before most duck decoys ceased commercial operations a pioneering Danish schoolmaster by the name of Christian Mortensen (also known as 'Fugle-Mortensen') was using decoys in Denmark to catch ducks for ringing, He was the first person to ring large numbers of birds. Working with the decoy on the island of Fanø he ringed large numbers of Eurasian teal and 320 northern pintail between 1908 and 1910. He was encouraged by the high rates of recovery, 20 per cent for northern pintail.

Today four British duck decoys remain open to the public, and they are certainly worth visiting. **Borough Fen Decoy** (1776), near Peakirk, Cambridgeshire, is the only remaining example of an old-style commercial decoy with eight pipes. Designated an Ancient Monument by the Department of the Environment in 1976, it has been managed under lease by the Wildfowl & Wetlands Trust since 1951 and it still operates to catch ducks for ringing. Over 41,000 ducks have been ringed there since 1947. **Boarstall Decoy** (existing before 1697), near Aylesbury, is owned by the National Trust and managed by the Berkshire, Buckinghamshire and Oxfordshire Wildlife Trust as a ringing demonstration station and museum. Today about 300 ducks, mostly Eurasian teal, are caught each winter. **Abbotsbury Duck Decoy** (built around 1655 – one of the oldest in Britain) is located within the Swannery at Abbotsbury in Dorset. Since 1976 it has caught over 1,400 duck for ringing, mostly Eurasian teal, with much smaller numbers of northern pintail. The **Berkeley New Decoy** was built in 1834 and renovated by the late Peter Scott when he established the Wildfowl Trust in 1946. It has four pipes, two at each end of the pool, and is set within the Wildfowl & Wetlands Trust grounds at Slimbridge. The decoy has caught over 27,000 duck, mostly mallard with some Eurasian teal, and a few northern shoveler and northern pintail.

Orielton Decoy (1868), near Pembroke, was the first British decoy employed for ringing ducks. Over 12,000 birds were ringed there between the decoy's refurbishment in 1934 (at the instigation of Peter Scott) and when it ceased operations in 1960. The Wildfowl Trust formerly operated the Nacton Decoy (built 1830), Suffolk, from 1968 to 1982. During this period 15,631 birds were ringed, including large numbers of Eurasian wigeon, Eurasian teal and northern pintail. More than 50 per cent of all northern pintail ringed in Britain were caught at Nacton during its 14 years of operation. A few other decoys have been used for duck ringing, including Dersingham Decoy (built 1818 – now disused), Norfolk.

Payne-Gallwey, writing in *The Fowler in Ireland* (1882), could not understand why there were not more duck decoys in Ireland, especially as they were 'a lucrative amusement' in a country that was 'so admirably adapted by nature where there is an abundance of wildfowl'. Only 22 Irish decoys were listed by Payne-Gallwey, all of which have now fallen into decay or totally disappeared.

The Fowler in Ireland listed only three decoys still in operation. The first was at Longueville, County Cork, originally constructed in 1750 with four pipes, later reduced to two, which were fed to attract the ducks. About 300 birds were caught annually, and the biggest catch was 730 – mostly mallard, Eurasian teal and Eurasian wigeon – during the winter 1845/46. The decoy ceased working when the estate was sold in the 1920s. It was the last decoy to operate in Ireland, and probably the longest in operation on a continuous basis, but with a break during World War I. The second was the decoy at Desart, County Kilkenny, which had been near to failure during the 1880s. The third was at Kellyville (now Kellavil), County Kildare, constructed around 1848 but not worked regularly until 1873. It had a total of nine pipes. Between 1,000 and 3,000 ducks – mostly Eurasian wigeon and Eurasian teal – were taken each year on this 5-hectare water. During 24 seasons from 1880 a total of 25,919 ducks were caught – nearly two-thirds Eurasian teal and one-third mallard, with Eurasian wigeon, northern shoveler and northern pintail making up most of the balance. When the estate was sold to the Irish Land Commission during the 1920s the decoy ceased. Following the fate of many another 'big house', Kellyville was demolished about 1950 and the lake drained.[12]

Abandoned decoys mentioned by Payne-Gallwey in *The Fowler in Ireland* and the *Book of Duck Decoys* were at Caledon, Co. Tyrone, where 200–400 wildfowl were taken each week; Coy Meadows, on the edge of Lough Beg, Co. Down; Eyre Court, Co. Galway, discontinued in 1860, which took similar numbers of wildfowl to Caledon; Clonfert, Co. Galway, discontinued from 1820; Markree Castle, Co. Sligo; Donerail Court, Co. Cork; Parteen, Co. Limerick; Mount Louise, Co. Monaghan; Mountainstown, Co. Meath; Lismullen, Co. Meath, discontinued about 1840; Lyons, Co. Kildare; Ballynakill, Co. Kildare; Kilcooley Abbey, Co. Tipperary; Anamoe, Co. Wicklow; Kellyville, Co. Kildare, discontinued in the 1920s; and long discontinued decoys at Glyde, Lisrenny, Beaulieu, Rathescar and Oriel, Co. Louth.

DOMESTICATED WILDFOWL

As soon as our ancestors had escaped from the hardships of a hunting and food-gathering culture and moved into an easier way of life as Neolithic farmers, they gathered animals around them and grew crops in nearby fields. The animals required a degree of domestication, a process that started some 10,000–12,000 years ago. While food production was the first priority, there were other benefits of the domestication process – production of hides, wool and other animal products, animals for protection and the management of farm stock, and the development of pets. The larger beasts such as sheep and goats were first favoured because of their obvious benefits (copious products in the form of meat, milk, wool, hides and fleeces), and they generally ate what people did not want. Dogs were among the earliest domesticated animals, bred to defend people and safeguard property and domestic animals. Most of our animal stock originated in the Middle East, with most domestication occurring in Asia. In contrast our crops arose generally from tropical America, China and southwest Asia.[13]

Wildfowl were lower down the scale of animal domestication priorities, but despite their smaller size they possessed many prized qualities – easy to manage, fast growers, tasty flesh, good egg production, abundant grease and oil (for lamps, preserving meat and ointment) as well as down feathers for bedding. They also provided quills for arrows and writing pens. Moreover, they were easy to subdue, required little or no maintenance and, like goats and sheep, did not compete for human food. Thus they converted unwanted vegetation into valuable protein, fat and feathers.

The general effects of domestication on wildfowl have been birds that mature more quickly, increased levels of polygamy, prolongation of the breeding season with production of more eggs, larger clutches, and larger bodies that in many cases are obese. Many domesticated breeds have lost the power of flight, and some have been developed for exhibition features such as crests and other feather patterns, body shapes, sizes and colouring. Some have knobs and wattles near their bills as well as dewlaps or gullets. Most of these structures are featherless, probably functioning as heat exchangers on the larger, heavier birds.

There are four wildfowl species that have lent themselves to successful domestication. Two are geese (the greylag *Anser anser* and the swan goose *Anser cygnoides*), and two are ducks (the mallard *Anas platyrhynchos* and the muscovy duck *Cairina moschata*). The Egyptian goose *Alopochen aegyptiacus* was once domesticated, in Egypt only, but ceased to be a farm animal when the Persians invaded the country in 525 BC.[14] The mute swan and the greater Canada goose are often found in semi-domesticated situations.

The semi-domesticated mute swan was farmed for its meat and feathers. It was the cygnets, not the adults, that were eaten, as they were apparently much tastier than the adults. They were taken from their parents and kept in special enclosures, where they were fattened up on barley. They were then roasted for special occasions, such as at medieval feasts – often several hundred were consumed at such events.

The Canada goose was originally imported to Britain from North America for ornamental purposes, and to aggrandise country estates. They were valued for their visual impact rather than as a source of meat, eggs or feathers. However, as they multiplied and spread out over the wider countryside, they became the quarry of many wildfowlers.

Another species that is used for the benefit of humans, the common eider, is not exactly domesticated, but it is certainly farmed in a structured way for its down feathers. The effectiveness of down as insulation is legendary, but for incubating wildfowl in the Arctic and sub-Arctic it is an essential defence against the cold. The female plucks down from her own breast and uses it both to line the nest and to cover the eggs and retain the heat of the clutch while she is off feeding. The down also helps to retain the moisture of the eggs.

In Iceland, for more than a thousand years, eiders have been farmed for their down (Fig. 13). They nest in colonies, and the colony is protected by the farmer on whose land they happen to be. Flat stone 'nesting boxes' are provided, and the birds nest under the slabs, which offer some protection from the two most dangerous predators, the Arctic Fox and the introduced American mink. Sometimes small, brightly coloured flags are erected in the colony: these not only mark the location of the birds but may also give comfort to the eiders.

FIG 13. Collecting down from an eider nest. The normal clutch size of the eider is between four and six eggs but nests may contain as many as eight eggs, probably laid by two females. Duvets with eider down are superior to those filled with goose down because eider down interlocks with itself and does not move around, creating bare patches. Goose-down duvets have to be divided into compartments to prevent bare patches. (Bryan and Cherry Alexander/NHPA)

Common eiders often nest in gull colonies, deriving extra protection from the gulls – mammalian predators would seldom penetrate such tightly packed colonies. The flapping flags resemble the wings of the ever-active gulls, and perhaps reassure the eiders that they are 'protected', as well as fooling potential predators.

The farmer twice collects the down from the nests, first when the clutch is completed, whereupon the bird replaces the down immediately, and then again after the ducklings have left the nest. Some 350 Icelandic farms produce about 3,000 kg of down annually, which at 2001 prices was worth approximately €1.5 million, or €4,285 per farm.[15]

GEESE

The greylag goose is one of the longest-domesticated birds, with a known history going back 5,000 years. Today almost all Irish and British farmyard geese are imports of foreign-bred varieties of the greylag, with a few from the swan goose. Our domestic greylag goose and all its varieties were bred from the eastern *Anser a. rubrirostris* rather than the western race *Anser a. anser*, as they have the eastern-race characteristics of a grey cast to the feathers and a pinkish bill and eye-ring.[16]

In the process of domestication greylag geese have become tame, accepting human company (aided by the imprinting process), are sexually mature earlier (also polygamous), produce more eggs (up to 300 per year, compared with a clutch of five to six eggs for wild birds), have became fatter and heavier (up to three times the weight of wild birds), often flightless, and certainly more sedentary. White plumage is a feature of domesticated geese, the whiteness probably genetically linked to the bird's ability to put on weight faster than the normal grey-coloured form – it needs more food but converts it into meat faster. White forms do not start laying eggs as early as dark birds, and their breeding season is shorter. So breeders of domesticated geese (and indeed ducks, chickens and turkeys) have the choice of developing either birds that put on weight fast or birds that produce more eggs. To complicate matters further, the flavour of goose meat is affected by the speed of the bird's growth. The grey varieties are slower-growing, but have the tastiest meat, and larger and fatter livers than the white varieties.

The British Waterfowl Association has produced standards for 16 different types of geese derived from the eastern greylag, and five from the swan goose.[17] For the purposes of illustrating the range of domesticated geese, eight types bred from the eastern graylag,[18] and two bred from the swan goose, are briefly described.

The **Pilgrim** is a small to medium-sized goose, weighing up to 8.2 kg (gander), sometimes called the West of England goose. Ganders are pure or creamy white with blue eyes; the goose is soft grey with a white head and neck, or grey speckled with white, with dark brown eyes. This is the only domestic breed of goose that is sexually dimorphic both as goslings and as adults. It originated in Britain but was first standardised in America. It is thought to have been taken by the Pilgrim Fathers to Massachusetts in the *Mayflower* in 1620, but was probably sourced in the Netherlands, where the pilgrims had fled from British persecution. The American Declaration of Independence was signed with a goose quill pen reputed to have come from a Pilgrim goose.[19] The breed has become rare in Britain and scarce elsewhere in Europe.

The **Roman** is another smallish variety, 4.5–6.3 kg in weight, fitting well into the modern oven. It is the preferred goose for meat production under intensive conditions. Imported to Britain from Italy around 1903, it probably originated in Romania, though it is often believed to be a descendant of the white geese (kept in the Temple of Juno) that saved Rome from the Gauls in 390 BC when their cackling calls awakened the sleeping Roman garrison. In thanksgiving a golden goose was carried in procession to Rome each year while the local dogs were whipped for their silence. In North America there are crested forms known as the **Crested** goose.

The **Buff** is a heavier North American breed, greyish buff with the same pattern as the greylag but paler. **Brecon Buffs** were bred from pale-coloured greylags collected from Breconshire hill farms, and were recognised by the Poultry Club of Great Britain in 1934. They are the only domestic breed with pink feet, suggesting out-breeding with wild greylags or even pink-footed geese. This is one of the few breeds to have originated in Britain.

Embden geese are enormous and glossy white, the ganders weighing 12.7–15.4 kg and the geese 10.9–12.7 kg. The American Embden is claimed to be the fastest-growing domestic bird, putting on 24 times its hatching weight (113 g) by the end of its fourth week, a faster weight increase than that shown by the domestic chicken. Popular and extensively reared for its meat, it originated in Prussia and was first brought to Britain early in the nineteenth century.

The **Toulouse** (Fig. 14) is another large goose, with large dewlaps and folds, kept both for its flesh and for egg production. It weighs 9.1–13.6 kg, and the adults are grey and brown. Originating in southwest France, it was first introduced into Britain about 1840, when it also travelled under the name of the **Mediterranean** or **Marseilles** goose. Their livers were formerly the source of *pâté de foie gras* in the Dordogne region, a task discharged today by the smaller pale brown **Landes** goose from Alsace.

FIG 14. Toulouse goose. From Ashton & Ashton, *British Wildfowl Standards* (Senecio Press, 1999).

Bantams are very small white geese, well sized for roasting in an ordinary-sized oven. The breed was first developed in the Netherlands before 1940 and later improved by further breeding in Britain.

The **Sebastopol** (Fig. 15) is one of the strangest of domestic geese. It is small, weighing 4.5–7.3 kg, and either white with bright blue eyes or buff with brown eyes, with orange bill and feet. Both sexes have long curling feathers on the back or wings, or all over the body, due to a genetic condition in which the feather shafts have split open and curled apart. Because of its weird, almost poodle-like appearance it is sometimes known as the **Pantomime** goose. Developed for its long feathers, used in quilts and pillows, it originated in the Lower Danube and Black Sea region and is found in Hungary and the Balkans. It was imported into Britain as an ornamental goose after 1856.

FIG 15. Sebastopol goose. From Ashton & Ashton, *British Wildfowl Standards* (Senecio Press, 1999).

The **Russian** goose is represented by several different breeds characterised by short necks, thick bills and aggressive behaviour. They were bred in Russia for fighting, especially in the goose pits of St Petersburg, where ganders were set upon each other until they beat their opponent to death or drew blood.[20] Goose fighting was banned in the nineteenth century, and pure breeds such as the **Tula** (a cross between the European western greylags and eastern geese developed from the swan goose) and the **Arsamas** have since more or less disappeared.

The wild swan goose of Asia has given rise to two domestic breeds, the Chinese goose and the African goose. The domestication process started in China some 3,000 years ago and spread to India, Africa and Europe. Both forms are more tolerant of warm climates than the greylag – they are traditionally the farmyard geese of tropical countries. They are also present in Britain and

FIG 16. Chinese goose. From Ashton & Ashton, *British Wildfowl Standards* (Senecio Press, 1999).

Ireland, often crossed with greylag breeds to produce fertile hybrids. They will also cross with *Branta* geese, but the offspring are infertile. The domestic breeds are very different from the swan goose, with much elongated necks, and shorter and thicker bills with a large frontal lobe unknown in the wild form.

The **Chinese** goose (Fig. 16) comes in two colour forms, brown/grey (with black head knob) and a less common white (with yellow head knob). Their necks are long, held almost vertically. They are prized for their meat and eggs (approximately 80 per year) and they make good watchdogs – they are the noisiest of all geese. They were first brought to Europe from China in the eighteenth century.

The **African** goose (Fig. 17) is much heavier (8.2–12.7 kg) with a large dewlap on the throat and a sagging abdomen, somewhat resembling the Toulouse goose. There are three colour forms – brown/grey, buff and white. Their origin is uncertain, but they arrived in Europe at least 200 years before the Chinese goose.[21]

FIG 17. African goose. From Ashton
& Ashton, *British Wildfowl Standards*
(Senecio Press, 1999).

DUCKS

Ducks have been domesticated for only about half as long as geese. The mallard was probably first domesticated by the Romans some 2,500 years ago, but it had been kept in captivity without full domestication for several centuries in Egypt, Greece, China and Southeast Asia. The mallard has given rise to more domesticated forms or mutant strains than any other duck or goose, with some 22 different breeds listed by the British Waterfowl Association. The drakes of all domestic ducks descended from the mallard have curly tails. There have been three lines of domestication – meat producers, egg layers and ornamental birds. Unlike our domesticated geese, many breeds have been 'developed' in Britain. Only a few examples of the better-known breeds of the three lines are mentioned below.

Meat producers

The **Rouen** (Fig. 18) is large and heavy (drakes up to 5.4 kg), developed in Normandy. The French Rouen resembles a larger and slightly lighter-coloured wild mallard but standing more erect. The English or dark Rouen has a more horizontal stance, with the females darker and redder. In common with other brown domesticated wildfowl they take much longer to mature for eating (about 5–6 months). The excellent flavour of its meat has made the Rouen one of the most prized and favoured ducks with chefs.

The **Aylesbury** is another large duck (drakes 4.5–5.4 kg), white, with a pink-white bill and bright orange feet. It was developed in Britain in the early eighteenth century. Most white ducks seen on farms are either Aylesburys or white Campbells – traditionally kept by the wife and kids for pin money. Described as 'lazy eating machines that enjoy their pond', they have a broad breast and are ideal for eating. It is increasingly uncommon to find pure stock, because of interbreeding with the Pekin duck (originally from China, imported to Britain around 1874), which is creamy white, but smaller, with an almost upright stance.

FIG 18. Rouen duck. From Ashton & Ashton, *British Wildfowl Standards* (Senecio Press, 1999).

Egg layers

The **Khaki Campbell** was first developed as a variety of the **Campbell** duck in Gloucestershire in 1901 by crossing an Indian Runner female, a wild mallard and a Rouen. The breed was formerly very popular as a farmyard duck, but is now less common. It is a great egg producer, some birds producing an egg a day for the entire year. There are also white Campbells, a sport from the khaki, but these lay fewer eggs (about 200 a year). Being white, it grows more quickly as a meat producer and its white flesh is popular.

The **Indian Runner** (Fig. 19) has also been known as the **Penguin** duck, because of its very slim, almost upright, penguin-like stance. As the great French

FIG 19. Indian Runner duck. From Ashton & Ashton, *British Wildfowl Standards* (Senecio Press, 1999).

wildfowl expert Jean Delacour observed, its vertical posture is exaggerated to the point of ridicule. When standing bolt upright its length, from the tip of the bill to the tip of the middle toe, is 65–80 cm (drakes) and 60–70 cm (ducks). Selectively bred some 2,000 years ago in Asia – the Malayan archipelago, according to Charles Darwin – it was designed to forage for snails, insects and seeds in rice paddies, and it was daily walked in flocks to and from the fields, trained to follow coloured rags tied to poles. It was introduced to the Solway region, Scotland, from Indonesia around 1835. Its weird physique caught the eye of Charles Darwin, who pondered its origin. He concluded that its four curled central tail feathers showed that it was a mallard, selectively bred. Of all the ducks, only the mallard has these four feathers curled upwards.[22] The Indian Runner is good for the table, although very slim, and a great egg layer, with some ducks laying upwards of 300 eggs a year. It comes in a variety of colours, including pure white, black, chocolate, blue, green, fawn, and fawn and white.

Ornamental ducks

Call ducks are like miniature mallard, dwarf or bantam forms, and they come in many different plumages. It was originally called the coy or decoy duck, referring to its former use in duck decoys, where the wild duck were enticed to travel up the narrowing pipes by the high-pitched calls of call ducks placed close to the catching pens. Some call ducks have a plumage similar to mallard, while others are totally white or buff. They were probably imported from Asia, and were present in the Netherlands from the seventeenth century.

Muscovy duck

The final duck that succumbed to domestication was the muscovy duck, a perching species related to the mandarin. When the Spanish Conquistadors arrived in Peru and on the north coast of Colombia in the early sixteenth century they found muscovy ducks already domesticated by the native Americans. Muscovies also live in the Amazonian rainforests. The species was probably originally domesticated as a pet, but it also had value for eating the insects that abounded in houses. It was also eaten (the drakes reach up to 7 kg) and it was a good egg layer. They were brought back to Europe in the early 1550s and by 1670 had reached England,[23] where, despite their tropical origin, they happily settled down in a colder climate The old drakes look ugly and unpleasant with large red facial warts (caruncles) and large wattles, together with a scruffy-looking plumage. After two or three generations of domestication they become heavier with even larger caruncles. They cross well with mallard, producing a sterile hybrid that grows fast and has good eating flesh. When crossed with a Rouen the result is a mule known as a mulard in France, where they are force-fed for their *foie gras*. Their breasts or *magret* (up to 400 g each) are also delicacies, smoked or dried.

There are many other varieties of domesticated geese and ducks in these islands, and there is a wide range of specialist organisations catering for these and other wildfowl interests. The principal organisations, listed below alphabetically, should be consulted for further information on the range of domesticated wildfowl:

British Call Duck Club (**www.britishcallduckclub.org.uk**)
British Waterfowl Association (**www.waterfowl.org.uk**)
Call Duck Association (UK) (**www.callducks.net**)
Domestic Waterfowl Club of Great Britain
(**www.domesticwaterfowl.co.uk**)
Goose Club (**www.gooseclub.org.uk**)
Indian Runner Duck Association (**www.runnerduck.net**)
Poultry Club of Great Britain (**www.poultryclub.org**)
Scottish Waterfowl Club (**www.scottishwaterfowlclub.co.uk**)

CHAPTER 3

Status and Distribution of 56 Species in Britain and Ireland

INTRODUCTION

THIS CHAPTER DISCUSSES THE 56 SPECIES OF WILDFOWL that have been recorded either in a *natural* state, or that have been *introduced* and now maintain *self-sustaining* populations in Britain and Ireland. I have used the British Ornithologists' Union (BOU) British List and the Irish Rare Birds Committee (IRBC) Irish List, but I have taken the liberty of adding the lesser Canada goose and the muscovy duck.[1] The status of these two species is currently under review by the BOU's Records Committee (BOURC) and the IRBC, and there is a possibility that both may be upgraded, to Categories A and C1 respectively. The 56 species, apart from the two above at the time of writing, fall into one or more of the following three BOU/IRBC categories:

A: Species that have been recorded in an apparently natural state at least once since 1 January 1950.

B: Species that were recorded in an apparently natural state at least once between 1 January 1800 and 31 December 1949, but have not been recorded subsequently.

C: Species that, although introduced, now derive from the resulting self-sustaining populations. There are six subcategories of C, indicating different types of naturalisation.

Many other wildfowl species are present in Britain and Ireland but are outside Categories A, B and C. These are mainly escapes from wildfowl collections, and they are excluded from this chapter. Appendices 1 and 2 provide further details of the BOU categories, including the subdivisions of Category C, and a listing of wildfowl species in Categories D and E.

In this chapter a brief account is provided of each of the 56 species, with information on identification, when relevant; locations and size of the world and European breeding population; size, trends and origin of British and Irish wintering populations; fossil history in Britain and Ireland; breeding distribution and habitat preferences; breeding biology and mortality/survival. Lack of space necessitated difficult choices on what to include or exclude, but I have incorporated what I believe are the more interesting aspects of each species while trying to maintain a consistency of approach. More extended accounts of the mute swan, barnacle goose and mallard are provided, to support the discussion of their population dynamics presented in Chapter 6.

Tabular information on the numbers of wildfowl and their distribution in the UK has been extracted from the most recent available Wetland Bird Survey (WeBS) report, *Waterbirds in the UK 2006/07*.[2] The WeBS is a joint scheme of the British Trust for Ornithology (BTO), the Wildfowl & Wetlands Trust (WWT), the Royal Society for the Protection of Birds (RSPB) and the Joint Nature Conservation Committee (JNCC) to monitor non-breeding waterbirds including escapes and naturalised species in the UK. The principal aims of the scheme are to identify population sizes, to determine trends in numbers and distribution, and to identify important sites for waterbirds. WeBS is a continuation of two wildfowl count schemes that commenced in 1947. Monthly coordinated counts are made at approximately 2,100 count sites (covering the majority of the UK's important wetland sites) each year, mostly by several thousands of volunteers, principally from September to March. Data are also incorporated into WeBS from other sources such as aerial surveys and surveys conducted by researchers investigating a single species. A complementary scheme (I-WeBS) operates in the Republic of Ireland, with identical aims. I-WeBS was launched in 1994 and is a partnership between BirdWatch Ireland (BWI), the National Parks & Wildlife Service (NP&WS), the Heritage Service of the Department of the Environment, Heritage and Local Government (DoE), and the WWT with support from the Irish Heritage Council and the World Wide Fund for Nature (WWF). In the Republic of Ireland there are several hundreds of volunteer counters and most of the principal wetland sites are counted. A certain amount of caution is necessary in the interpretation and application of wildfowl counts, given the limitations of these data. Poor weather conditions and incomplete counts, especially at complex sites (e.g. large estuaries), can result in missing a significant proportion of one or more of a species.

Wildfowl enthusiasts owe a great debt of gratitude to the organisations responsible for overseeing the efficient planning and execution of WeBS and I-WeBS. But the real heroes are the many keen wildfowl counters – several thousand in the UK and several hundred in Ireland. Most of these are amateurs, carrying out surveys for pleasure and enjoyment. Without them we would not have the raw data that provide the basis for a better understanding of wildfowl numbers and their distribution throughout these islands. Moreover, without this knowledge we would be unable to prepare effective conservation and management programmes for wildfowl.

In the tabular presentation of data additional information sources have been incorporated from non-WeBS sources and these (total 55) are listed in the WeBS report. Where data are presented in brackets, this indicates incomplete counts. Data for the Republic of Ireland have been extracted from the I-WeBS report *Ireland's Wetlands and their Waterbirds* (2005).[3] The tables contain more up-to-date data from WeBS than from I-WeBS because of different publication dates of national reports. The WeBS data generally refer to the period 2003/04–2006/07, while the I-WeBS data are from 1996/97–2000/01. Where WeBS data (from Northern Ireland) appear in the tables relating to Ireland, this is marked with an asterisk (*). In the table captions, *International threshold* means more than 1 per cent of the individuals in a population of one species or subspecies of wildfowl, while *National threshold* means more than 1 per cent of the estimated British or Irish numbers. In the case of Ireland, this refers to all-Ireland data (Northern Ireland and the Republic combined). A dash in the tables indicates no data available.

For ease of reading, I have truncated spans of winters in the text to give only the second calendar year of each winter. So the five winters from 1996/97 to 2000/01 inclusive appear as 1997–2001. This applies only to the text; in the tables, the full date span (1996/97–2000/01) is used. Single winters are referred to in the form 1996/97.

Where appropriate, I have used data from earlier WeBS and I-WeBS reports. Information on estimates of wintering wildfowl in the UK has also been extracted from a review paper covering the period 1995–99, and figures for Ireland come from a recent review that includes estimates for 2000–04.[4] For international population data I have drawn upon the *Atlas of Anatidae Populations in Africa and Western Eurasia* (1996), the *EBCC Atlas of European Breeding Birds* (1997), *Goose Populations of the Western Palearctic* (1999), *Birds in Europe: Population Estimates, Trends and Conservation Status* (2004) and the fourth edition of *Waterbird Population Estimates* (2006).[5] The numbers of duck breeding in North America are sourced from the US Fish and Wildlife Service *Waterfowl Population Statistics* (2008).[6]

Most information concerning the recovery of ringed birds and migration patterns has been taken from *The Migration Atlas* (2002).[7] Data on the history of birds in Britain and Ireland have come from Fisher's *Shell Bird Book* (1966) and Holloway's *Historical Atlas of Breeding Birds* (1996), while more recent breeding information has been extracted from the *New Atlas of Breeding Birds in Britain and Ireland* (1993).[8] Irish historical records are from *The Birds of Ireland* (1900).[9] Fossil records not explicitly referenced have been extracted from Tyrberg (1998), while records of bones from Lagore, Co. Meath, have been taken from Stelfox (1938).[10] Unreferenced biological and ecological data are from *Birds of the Western Palearctic* (BWP) and its updates, and figures for mortality/survival rates for ducks have been taken from Boyd (1962);[11] all other mortality/survival data are referenced.

In the case of rare and vagrant wildfowl, records for Great Britain (including the sea area within the 320 km economic exclusion zone) for the period 1950–2006 as well as pre-1949 records have been taken from the British Birds Rarities Committee's (BBRC) website at www.bbrc.org.uk as of the end of November 2008. Other records have been extracted from the most recent available Irish Bird Reports from BirdWatch Ireland (BWI) and the reports of the Northern Ireland Birdwatchers' Association (NIBA), as well as from a number of reviews of rare breeding birds in Ireland.[12] In all cases the statistics on occurrences refer to the number of new *individuals*, and do not include subsequent records of the same bird or birds.

The ordering of the species and the scientific names are those recommended by the BOU in the British List as of 30 July 2008. The letters and numbers following the scientific names refer to the BOU categories accorded to the species. These are explained in Appendix 1.

In 2006 the International Ornithological Congress (IOC) published a definitive list of standardised international English names for each species, and in April 2007 the BOU adopted these international names (the Gill & Wright names), with the proviso of using the familiar English vernacular name alongside the new international name.[13] Throughout this book, however, I have used the new international name alone to save space (except when referring to a specific subspecies such as Bewick's swan or Greenland white-fronted goose). Table 1 lists the 16 wildfowl species for which the international English name differs from the familiar English vernacular name.

TABLE 1. International English names (Gill & Wright names) of wildfowl, as used in this book.

ENGLISH VERNACULAR NAME	INTERNATIONAL ENGLISH NAME	SCIENTIFIC NAME
Bewick's swan	Tundra swan	*Cygnus columbianus*
White-fronted goose	Greater white-fronted goose	*Anser albifrons*
Brent goose	Brant goose	*Branta bernicla*
Shelduck	Common shelduck	*Tadorna tadorna*
Wigeon	Eurasian wigeon	*Anas penelope*
Teal	Eurasian teal	*Anas crecca*
Black duck	American black duck	*Anas rubripes*
Pintail	Northern pintail	*Anas acuta*
Shoveler	Northern shoveler	*Anas clypeata*
Pochard	Common pochard	*Aythya ferina*
Scaup	Greater scaup	*Aythya marila*
Eider	Common eider	*Somateria mollissima*
Common scoter	Black scoter	*Melanitta nigra*
Black scoter	American scoter	*Melanitta americana*
Goldeneye	Common goldeneye	*Bucephala clangula*
Goosander	Common merganser	*Mergus merganser*

I have treated Ireland (Northern Ireland and the Republic of Ireland) and Britain (England, Scotland and Wales) as separate biological entities for estimated wintering and breeding populations, but this has sometimes been difficult because of variations in the way data are presented. I have used the following geographic terminology: *Great Britain* (England, Scotland, Wales); *United Kingdom* (UK) (England, Scotland, Wales, Northern Ireland, Isle of Man, the Channel Islands); *Ireland* (Northern Ireland and the Republic of Ireland).

When dealing with wildfowl fossil history I have used 'ky' for thousands of years, 'my' for millions of years, and 'BP' for before the present.

1. MUTE SWAN *CYGNUS OLOR* (**AC2**)

The mute swan (Fig. 20) is the largest and heaviest flying wildfowl in the world, with some wild males in Poland weighing up to 22.5 kg. It is best known for its beauty, elegance and ornamental presence, and is also famous for its unique position as a 'royal' bird – because the sovereign once owned most mute swans in Britain. The brilliant whiteness of the mute swan requires an explanation: why has it not, like most birds, and especially other wildfowl, evolved a less conspicuous coloration? The mute swan, together with the whooper and tundra swans, is so large and powerful that it has no need to conceal itself. In fact, the white plumage confers an advantage in advertising the birds' presence during the breeding season, thus warning off other swans from their territory.

Juvenile and immature mute swans are brown-plumaged (except for the morph, or variety, known as the Polish swan, whose cygnets are white),

FIG 20. Mute swans and cygnets. Both parents guard and protect their cygnets. When the cygnets are small the female protects them from aquatic predators such as pike by carrying them on her back. (Mike Lane/NHPA)

affording greater concealment during their most vulnerable stage of life. Throughout the first winter and subsequent spring their plumage becomes increasingly white, until full adult plumage is attained by the second summer.

While not so vocal as the whooper and tundra swans, the mute swan is not entirely without oral repertoire, albeit one that sounds more mechanical than that of the other two species. It contains a range of noises, from hissing, grunting and barking to explosive snorts when the birds are vexed by human intrusion, especially during the breeding season, or when defending their territory against other swans.

When in flight its wings generate a remarkable rhythmic throb that can be heard at distances of up to 1–2 km, a feature not found in its wild cousins. Lacking the bugle-like and honking calls of the latter, the mute swan probably relies on its singing wings to make contact with other birds in flight, especially at night or in fog.

The mute swan is considered by many ornithologists to be semi-domesticated, at worst a tame bird, descended from swans kept in ornamental waterfowl collections. Our mute swans are not truly 'wild', as they are in many parts of continental Europe, where several of the populations are migratory. Indeed, British and Irish mute swans have assumed an almost pet-like status, many existing on a diet of bread and other scraps proffered at ornamental lakes in public parks, and on ponds, rivers, canals, harbours and estuaries. Our mute swans are among the most mollycoddled of birds, and have adroitly exploited their symbiotic relationship. In exchange for plentiful supplies of food, especially during winter, and generally predator-free nesting sites, they grace our public waterways with their elegance and majesty to provide endless hours of aesthetic enjoyment. Less comfortable are those breeding in the northern parts of Europe, where they are, by and large, migratory – southern and central Sweden, southern Norway, south and west Finland, the Baltic States, Denmark and Poland – especially under harsh winter conditions. They also breed in the Netherlands, Belgium and France, with smaller numbers, mostly derived from introduced birds, in several other European countries. They breed in parts of the former USSR (Ukraine to Kazakhstan), Turkey, Persia, Turkestan and east to Mongolia and eastern Siberia. There have been multiple introductions to establish feral populations in North America (first to British Columbia in 1889, then Massachusetts in 1909), South Africa, Australia (several introductions from 1866 to 1871) and New Zealand (1866–71).

Was the mute swan an indigenous wild species in Britain and Ireland, or was it introduced to these islands in an already domesticated state? The apocryphal legend that British mute swans are descended from birds brought back by

Richard I from Cyprus, on his return from the Crusades, is not supported by evidence. In his monograph *The Mute Swan in England*, Norman Ticehurst, basing his arguments on historical documentation, concluded that it was indeed an indigenous British species and bred in a truly wild state within and around East Anglia until at least the tenth century.[14] The water-world of fen, rivers, lakes and marshland habitats of this area was ideal for the swan. Moreover, the region was physically linked to the European mainland before sea levels rose during the Holocene to isolate Britain from what is now the Netherlands. The southern North Sea evolved from dry land around 10 ky BP into two separate basins (the Southern Bight and the German Bight). The basins were separated by a land bridge between Britain and northern Holland. Around 8 ky BP, the land bridge was flooded and the basins merged. The flooding of the southern North Sea continued until the coastlines were close to their present location around 7 ky BP.[15] The mute swan is known to be indigenous in the Netherlands, based on archaeological evidence of swan hunting some 2 ky BP.[16]

Fossils have been found in Britain and Ireland indicating its presence from the late Pleistocene or Holocene (10–0 ky BP) in Somerset (Aveline's Hole); probable fossils from the Late Glacial period (13–10 ky BP) in Sutherland (Creag nan Uamh Cave) and probable fossils from the Holocene in Co. Cork (Castlepook Cave). Bones have been found in postglacial peat beds (6 ky BP) in East Anglia,[17] and at Glastonbury, Somerset, close to the Avalon Marshes, dating from the late Iron Age (about 250 BC) to the time of the Romans, as well as from the Romano-British site at Colchester. Thus the mute swan was clearly an indigenous and a wild species of Britain, and almost certainly of Ireland as well. However, no mute swan bones were found at Lagore, Co. Meath (AD 750–950), despite the discovery there of whooper and Bewick's swan bones.

The first proof of the domestication of wild mute swans in Britain dates from AD 966, when the Abbots of Croyland were granted the right by King Edgar to take possession of stray swans.[18] From about the middle of the twelfth century the swan was gradually coerced into domestication through the capture and confinement of wild breeding adults and their cygnets. Pinioned in custody over a period of at least three or four centuries, the subsequent generations lost their instinct for the wild. The swans were initially subjected to management because of their considerable value as food. In 1274 the price of a swan was fixed by the *Statuta de Poletria* of the City of London at 3 shillings (about 19 euro cent) compared with a mere 5 pence (6 cent) for a goose, 4 pence (5 cent) for a pheasant and 2.5 pence (3 cent) for the best capon (a castrated rooster).[19] Swans also conferred prestige and status as creatures of grace and beauty – every true gentleman had to have at least one pair adorning his estate.

With so many beneficial attributes it was inevitable that the monarch would appropriate the mute swan. King Edgar's grant to the Abbots of Croyland indicates that the Royals had already assumed ownership of the mute swan, while Giraldus Cambrensis, in an undated manuscript (*Lincoln Treatises*) written some time before his death in c.1220, describes the mute swan as already regarded as a royal bird. An *Act for Swans* (22 Ed. IV, c.6) in 1482 laid down that all mute swans in 'divers parts of the Realm of England' not owned by persons with freehold land, as well as stray swans, became the property of the Crown. Private persons, communities and corporations were allowed to keep swans but only under a system of strict Crown licences, managed by the King's Swan-Master and agents, which obliged owners to mark their swans with a complicated system of notches and designs – *cygninotae* – cut onto the swans' bills, or by special foot markings. Upwards of 630 different insignia were employed between 1450 and 1600.[20] During the eighteenth century swan keeping declined, coinciding with the increasing popularity of the turkey (introduced into Britain around 1525) and the domestic hen, and the rise of the domestic goose. The system of markings had greatly diminished everywhere except for a few locations such as the River Thames and east Norfolk. Licensed royal swans still exist at Abbotsbury, on the Fleet lagoon in Dorset, where Benedictine monks, during the reign of King Canute in the early eleventh century, established a unique breeding colony as a source of income; in 1541 the swans passed into the ownership of Henry VIII, who then dissolved the monastery. The swans endured at Abbotsbury, and today there are approximately 700–800, still marked but virtually wild. The only other royal licences granted today for swan ownership are to the Worshipful Dyers' and the Worshipful Vintners' Livery Companies in the City of London, conveying the right to own swans on the River Thames between London Bridge and Henley-on-Thames (Fig. 21).

The mute swan was never a royal bird in Scotland, Wales or Ireland, and there is no evidence of swan keeping in these countries. Its history in Ireland is vague. William Thompson wrote, in his monumental *Natural History of Ireland*, that they were not known to occur in Ireland in a wild state and that the date of its introduction to Ireland was unknown to him.[21] Two fossils of a swan, probably a mute, dating from the late Pleistocene – Holocene were found in Castlepook Cave, Co. Cork, suggesting that they may have been once native, but whether their occupation was continuous is not known.[22] No other mute swan fossils have been unearthed in Irish caves. By the early eighteenth century mute swans had found their way, almost certainly from Britain, to gentrify the ponds and lakes of country estates in Co. Cork. Thompson reports encountering them on the ponds around Belfast when he was a child (c.1810).[23] Recent examination of

FIG 21. Swan upping: annual ceremonial activity on the River Thames when swans are rounded up, caught and marked and then released. Chris Perrins is shown weighing a swan. (David Higgs/NHPA)

mute swan genetics by protein electrophoresis has shown no significant genetic difference between flocks within Ireland, or between those in Britain and Ireland, thus supporting the hypothesis that the mute swan was either introduced to Ireland from Britain or arrived naturally from Britain.[24] Domesticated mute swans were probably introduced into Scotland and Wales to satisfy the whims of gentleman landowners.

Many individual mute swans, especially the two- and three-year-olds, together with non-breeders and unsuccessful breeders, form substantial moulting flocks in the security of shallow waters, particularly in coastal regions, where they become flightless while shedding and replacing their wing feathers. The inland Loch Leven, Perth & Kinross, used to be an important moulting area for upwards of 500 birds. Numbers declined to approximately 50–100 when pollution reduced the aquatic plants on which the swans fed, but have recently recovered to a peak of 542 in August 2006. There is some evidence, from the recovery of ringed birds, of a northerly moult migration to the Loch from Northumberland and Durham, a distance of c.200 km[25]. When numbers declined at Loch Leven, the Montrose Basin, Angus (some 80 km to the northeast), was used as an alternative site. In August 2000 the Montrose Basin hosted an annual summer gathering of several hundred swans, with 327 noted. There is also evidence of another northerly moult migration from the Thames Valley and West Midlands to a site near Barrow-in-Furness, Lancashire, some 185–193 km to the northwest.[26] The estuary at Berwick-upon-Tweed, Northumberland, has a resident flock of mute swans (c.140–300) that is augmented by moult migrants (c.250–300) from the surrounding area, arriving during May and June. A total of 583 were recorded there in August 2006. Abundant supplies of algal food, especially sea lettuce (*Ulva*) and *Enteromorpha*, are a principal attraction for the moult migrants. Most of the moulting swans originate from less than 50 km away, with about a fifth from 51–100 km and the remainder travelling more than 100 km, the maximum distance being 167 km.[27] Lough Bee, South Uist, and Christchurch Harbour, Hampshire, are also well-known moulting areas.

The largest moulting flock in Britain, where birds congregate from May onwards, is the tidal lagoon of Fleet/Wey, Dorset. Total breeding and wintering numbers have averaged 1,148 birds for the five years 2003–07. Each year about 300–400 immigrants arrive to moult, joining the Abbotsbury breeding birds. The Stour Estuary, Essex, used to support one of the largest congregations of mute swans in England, with up to 1,000 occurring for the summer moult and 200–400 remaining throughout the winter, attracted by waste grain tipped into the river from maltings. That no longer occurs, and fewer than 200 swans are found there today.

A comprehensive survey of breeding mute swans in Great Britain in spring 2002 estimated 31,700 birds (c.6,150 breeding pairs and a further 19,400 non-breeding individuals),[28] while analysis of WeBS data from the late 1990s suggested a larger population of 37,500. Mute swans in Ireland are now considered to form a separate 'biogeographic population' because of their generally sedentary nature. Numbers have never been satisfactorily counted, but an estimate of 5,000–6,000 birds was produced for the early 1970s, later updated to 7,000.[29] In the late 1980s there were an estimated 10,000 birds, based on data collected by Ralph Sheppard during winter counts 1985–87 covering the major wetland sites in Ireland.[30] However, it is known that mute swans are widely distributed and use a variety of wetland types. To incorporate these dispersed and uncounted swans on small wetlands, canals and other water bodies an extrapolation multiplier of 1.65, derived from a study in Britain,[31] was applied. Therefore it is possible that the estimate of 19,000–20,000 breeding birds obtained from extrapolation of data from the *New Atlas* is a more accurate reflection of the true numbers of mute swans present in Ireland. The UK extrapolation factor was applied to the total estimated from I-WeBS/WeBS for 1995–99 to produce the figure of 21,100 birds quoted in *Ireland's Wetlands and Their Waterbirds*. However, a more recent estimate, based on I-WeBS and WeBS counts from 2000 to 2004 and employing the extrapolation factor, produced a population of 11,440 birds. See Chapter 6 for further discussion on trends and numbers.

TABLE 2. Mute swan: sites in Britain where the mean five-year peak exceeded 320 birds (International threshold).

LOCATION COUNT 2006/07	MEAN 5-YEAR PEAK 2002/03–2006/07	PEAK COUNT 2006/07
Fleet and Wey, Dorset	1,148	1,013 (Aug)
Somerset Levels, Somerset	1,091	1,164 (Jan)
Ouse Washes, Cambridgeshire/ Norfolk	626	770 (Sep)
Rutland Water, Leicestershire	565	508 (Nov)
Tweed Estuary, Northumberland	531	588 (Jul)
Hornsea Mere, E Yorkshire	474	583 (Aug)
Loch of Harray, Orkney	435	375 (Jul)
Loch Leven, Perth & Kinross	428	263 (Dec)
Lough Bee, South Uist, Western Isles	400	542 (Aug)
Severn Estuary, Gloucestershire/ Somerset/etc	371	401 (Dec)
Abberton Reservoir, Essex	371	421 (Feb)
Tring Reservoirs, Hertfordshire	363	(339) (Aug)

Figures in parentheses represent incomplete counts.

TABLE 3. Mute swan: sites in Ireland where the mean five-year peak exceeded 110 birds (National threshold).

LOCATION	MEAN 5-YEAR PEAK 1996/97–2000/01	PEAK COUNT 2000/01
Loughs Neagh & Beg, Co. Armagh/Down/etc	1,035*	770 (Sep)*
Lough Ennell, Co. Westmeath	375	—
River Shannon Callows, Co. Offaly	367	—
Upper Lough Erne, Co. Fermanagh	360*	457 (Jan)*
River Slaney, Co. Wexford	281	—
Lower Lough Erne, Co. Fermanagh	272*	266 (Mar)*
Wexford Harbour and Slobs, Co. Wexford	268	303
Lough Swilly, Co. Donegal	267	—
Lough Derg, R. Shannon, Co. Tipperary	237	—
Corofin Wetlands, Co. Clare	225	—
Tacumshin Lake, Co. Wexford	217	—
Corofin Lakes, Co. Clare	215	232
Lough Ree (Aerial), Co. Westmeath	193	—
Ballyhaunis Lakes, Co. Mayo	190	225
Lough Corrib, Co. Galway	186	108
Tralee Bay, L. Gill & Akeragh Lough, Co. Kerry	173	146
Lough Derravaragh, Co. Westmeath	167	—
Inner Galway Bay, Co. Galway	151	—
Strangford Lough, Co. Down	150*	59 (Mar)*
Lough Oughter Complex, Co. Cavan	136	102
Inishcarra Reservoirs, Co. Cork	131	111
Shannon & Fergus estuaries, Co. Limerick/Kerry/Clare	129	20
Lough Ree, Co. Westmeath	118	305
Upper Quoile River, Co. Down	108*	121 (Jan)*
Castlecaldwell Refuge Area, Cos. Fermanagh & Derry	116	—
Lough Foyle, Co. Derry	114	98 (Nov)
Lough Kinale & Derragh Lough, Co. Longford	112	—

Figures marked with an asterisk (*) are from UK WeBS data: five-year counts for the period 2002/03–2006/07 and peak counts for 2006/07.

2. TUNDRA SWAN *CYGNUS COLUMBIANUS* (A)

The Taxonomic Advisory Committee (TAC) of the Association of European Records and Rarities Committees (AERC) recommended in 2003 the maintenance of the single-species status of the tundra swan, *Cygnus columbianus*, with two subspecies: whistling swan, *C. c. columbianus*, and Bewick's swan, *C. c. bewickii*. It had been suggested that the tundra swan be treated as two species: whistling swan, *C. columbianus* (monotypic) and Bewick's swan, *C. bewickii* (monotypic).[32]

They are the most closely related of all swans based on DNA affinities, but one diagnostic morphological difference (bill colour) provides a basis for some distinction. The bill of the whistling swan is mostly black, the yellow either absent or restricted to a small spot before the eye. A survey found that the extent of yellow on the bill was an average of 3.1 per cent in the whistling swan, compared to 31.5 per cent in the Bewick's swan (Fig. 22).[33] However, individual variation may have been underestimated, because the samples examined were not large enough. The whistling swan is restricted to North America, where more than 185,900 birds bred across the northern tundra in 2008. Some whistling swans nest in the easternmost parts of Siberia, overlapping and hybridising with Bewick's swans to an unknown extent, adding to the taxonomic jungle of these two races.

Although there are records of the Bewick's swan in Britain from 1824, it was only officially distinguished from the larger and similar whooper swan in 1830 by the ornithologist William Yarrell, who named it in honour of the engraver Thomas Bewick, who had died two years previously. About one-third smaller than the whooper, the Bewick's swan has a much more musical repertoire of higher-pitched call notes. It is one of the wildest and most elegant of our wildfowl, undertaking prodigious annual migrations between its tundra nesting grounds in Arctic Russia and the wintering grounds in northwest Europe.

Earliest fossil records in Britain date from the Middle Pleistocene at West Runton, Suffolk (Cromerian period, c.500–450 ky BP) and East Runton, Norfolk (Forest-bed Pastonian period, c.500–400 ky BP); and from the Late Pleistocene at Cathole, Glamorgan, at Pin Hole Cave, Derbyshire, in levels 4 (c.20 ky BP) and 5 (35–20 ky BP), at Ossiferous Fissure, Derbyshire, and at Shandon Cave, Co. Waterford (Late Pleistocene–Holocene). Fossils were recorded from an offshore site in the North Sea dating from the Late Pleistocene–Holocene. Tundra swans are likely to have bred in Britain during the colder periods of tundra vegetation. Fossil remains have also been found in the Fens, from the Neolithic/Bronze Age periods (4,500–700 BC) and more recently at Lagore, Co. Meath (AD c.750–950).

FIG 22. Bewick's swan (the Palaearctic race of the tundra swan), showing the diagnostic black and yellow bill pattern. (Bill Coster/NHPA)

FIG 23. Bewick's swans are prone to move considerable distances in response to cold weather. In flight they are very vocal, their calls less trumpeting and more excited and highly pitched than whooper swans. (Bill Coster/NHPA)

The breeding territory of the Bewick's swan extends across a vast swath of Arctic Russia from 48° to 180° E. The population appears to be divided into two parts. The northwest European wintering swans originate from the 29,000-strong population that breeds west of the Ural Mountains (68° E).[34] Here they nest in scattered pairs throughout the tundra, the density varying with the quality of the feeding and the number of swans attempting to breed in any one year. Nest densities range from 35–40 per 10 km² on the Russkiy Zavorot Peninsula to 1 per 10 km² on Vaigach Island. Another population of some 86,500 birds breeds further east in the Russian Arctic tundra, the dividing line between the two parts of the population appearing to be the Lena Delta (125° E). These swans travel south to spend their winter months in Japan, China and Korea.

Migration from the breeding grounds commences in September, the birds moving along the Russian Arctic coast to the White Sea, southwest to the southern shores of the Baltic Sea and onwards to spend the winter (mid-October to mid-March) in the Netherlands and Britain, with small numbers in Ireland. Fewer birds winter in Denmark, northern Germany, Belgium and in northern and southern France. Of our three swans, Bewick's are the most sensitive to cold weather, which can trigger extensive movements from continental Europe west to Britain and Ireland, leading to wide fluctuations in numbers (Fig. 23).

Numbers wintering in northwest Europe were stable during the mid-1980s, around 6,000–17,000 birds. A European census in January 1987 revealed 8,000 in Britain and a further 1,150 in Ireland. The Netherlands held some 5,200–6,560, while the remainder were in Denmark (22), Belgium (120), France (77) and Sweden (1).[35] By 1994 the population had more or less doubled to an estimated 29,000 birds, boosted by three years of exceptional breeding success.[36] The size of the population is subject to considerable divergence from year to year, influenced by good or bad breeding seasons, with the percentage of young birds in the winter flocks ranging from 4 to 18 per cent as monitored between 1982 and 1996 and based on large sample sizes in the Netherlands. Even larger variations, between 7 and 44 per cent, were reported in British and Irish wintering flocks during the period 1956–69.[37] The proportion of young birds in the winter flocks during the international census of Britain and Ireland in 2005 was low, at 10.9 per cent, well under the five-year mean of 14.7 per cent.[38]

In Ireland, during the mid-1980s, there were an estimated 2,300 birds.[39] Numbers have since declined: by the mid-1990s only about 1,000 birds were wintering, and subsequently numbers began to decrease again. Annual indices derived from I-WeBS show a decline of over 50 per cent in the five-year period 1995–99. Only 382 birds were found during the international swan census in January 2000, and by the next international census (January 2005) numbers had further declined to 224. It is probable that a series of mild winters, coupled with the availability of good feeding on the Continent and in Britain, held back swans travelling on to Ireland.

The maximum number counted during WeBS in Britain in 2006/07 was 3,775 in December 2006, half that of the previous year and the lowest for over 30 years. The annual WeBS index fell by about 45 per cent. Fewer birds were recorded from the East Anglian Fens. Despite this decline, the Ouse Washes are the most important wintering site in northwest Europe, holding nearly 90 per cent of the total national population during the winter 2006/07. Birds are remaining further east on the Continent, probably in response to milder winters. However, there may also be a decline in the overall population level, as numbers wintering in the Netherlands have also been decreasing for the past two winters. The 2007 breeding season was exceptionally poor, with only 5 per cent young birds in the Ouse Washes wintering flocks – the lowest recorded there since 1996/97.[40]

The birds' habitat preferences have also gradually changed, with birds moving from shallow lakes, flooded fields, turloughs, marshes and brackish coastal lakes to arable land and improved pastureland. The shift reflects a switching of food preferences from aquatic macrophytes to arable crops.

The main habitats occupied during the survey of Ireland in January 2000 were: (1) improved and rough pastures – 89 per cent of the birds; (2) permanent lakes – 6 per cent; and (3) arable land – 5 per cent.[41] In Denmark, where the wintering population of Bewick's swans was 1,279 in January 1994, about 40 per cent of the birds shifted from feeding in stubble fields, on artificial grassland, on pasture and in water onto arable lands to feed on winter wheat and winter oilseed rape from late December until their departure in March or April. Some 40 per cent of the balance of the swans fed on flooded grasslands and cultivated grasslands, while the remainder fed on aquatic vegetation.[42]

One of the most unusual sights of these swans to be had is at the Slimbridge headquarters of the Wildfowl & Wetlands Trust (Fig. 24). When the Trust was founded by Peter Scott in 1946 only small numbers of these swans, fewer than 30, visited the salt marsh between the estuary and the sea wall. In February 1964 a flock of 24 flew in to the Rushy Pen, overlooked by Peter Scott's large picture window, to join seven captive Bewick's swans. Scott quickly saw that the swans could be individually identified by variations in their black and yellow bill markings. This was the start of a remarkable long-term scientific study.

FIG 24. Adult Bewick's swans with some cygnets at the Wildfowl & Wetlands Trust headquarters, Slimbridge. (David Tipling/NHPA)

The protection offered by the pond, plus the twice-daily provision of wheat grain on cold and frosty winter days, shovelled into the lake from a wheelbarrow pushed by a man named Shakespeare attired in wellingtons and shorts down to his knees, encouraged numbers to increase annually. By 1970/71 some 627 swans were individually identified by bill pattern, and there were up to 411 different swans present on one day. The rise in visiting swan numbers coincided with the expansion of the northwest European population. Adults showed strong winter site fidelity, returning year after year to the pond, and remained paired for life.

The swans' return to their Arctic breeding grounds, already paired, starts a race against time. They must complete their breeding cycle and depart within fewer than three months before the ice and cold return. The complete breeding season – nest building to fledged young – is finished generally within 100 days. After pairing at age 2–4 years, first breeding takes place at age 4–7 years. Breeding success improves with pair duration, even up to age 16 years. Unlike ducks, the male plays an active role during nest construction, passing grasses and other materials to the female, who makes the nest. During egg laying and incubation he will sit on the eggs during the female's absence. Whistling swan females incubated, on average, 71 per cent and males 27 per cent of total time of five continuously monitored nests.[43] The male Bewick's swan assists with the care of the cygnets, often driving off mammalian predators such as the Arctic Fox.

Despite being the smallest of the northern swans, the tundra swan lays the largest egg in proportion to its body size – each being 4.6 per cent of the female's body weight – but has the smallest clutch size, ranging from 2.8 to 3.6 eggs. Incubation lasts 29–30 days, the shortest of all swans. The fledging period is 60–70 days, by which time the adults have completed their moult. The birds are then ready for their 4,000–4,600 km flight southwest to Britain and Ireland as well as to other northwest European countries.

On Vaygach Island (70° 15′ N 58° 46′ E) nesting density of 127 pairs varied greatly over six study years from 0.12 to 0.36 nests per km² with a mean clutch size varying from 2.4 to 3.0. Hatching success was high at 89.8 per cent of 137 eggs monitored in 45 nests. Overall nesting success was 73.5 per cent of 68 nests, with an average number of 2.7 young cygnets per successful pair. It was concluded that spring weather was the most important factor determining breeding success.[44] On the North Slope of Alaska 77 per cent of adult whistling swans (Fig. 25) held territories, 34 per cent nested successfully and the average number of cygnets per successful pair was 2.46.[45] Observations at Slimbridge have shown high mortality of juveniles during their first autumn, the survival rate of first-winter birds to their second winter being 0.66. Thereafter the annual adult survival rate of wintering birds is 0.87, possibly higher, as some wintering birds shift their wintering sites.[46] Mean annual adult survival rates (1966–90) for whistling swans, based on resightings and recaptures of 5,963 birds neck-banded in Maryland and North Carolina, USA, was estimated to be 0.92; for juvenile males it was 0.81 and for juvenile females 0.52.[47]

In a poor breeding year, determined by bad weather on the breeding grounds, up to 70 per cent of the adult Bewick's swans will not breed, remaining in summer non-breeding flocks. During these 'off' years only 2,000–3,000 pairs provide the productivity for the whole population. Research carried out on wintering birds in the Netherlands shows an even bleaker situation: in bad years only 500–2,500 pairs, or 5–25 per cent of the adult birds, successfully breed. Another study, over 15 years and based on Slimbridge wintering swans found that successful adults comprised 28 per cent of total pairs.[48]

FIG 25. A whistling swan (the Nearctic race of the tundra swan) defends its nest. Larger than Bewick's swans, they are quite effective in chasing off predators – foxes, brown bears, eagles, skuas and ravens – if they come within 1 km of the breeding territory. (Stephen Krasemann/NHPA)

The first record of a whistling swan from Britain and Ireland was a single adult at Lough Gill, Co. Kerry, between 31 December 1978 and 1 February 1979. Subsequent sightings of four other individuals from Counties Cork and Wexford were accepted by the IRBC to the end of 2007.

In Britain the BBRC has accepted two records (with multiple sightings) for 1950–2006. One adult was seen at Hay Moor and Curry Moor, Somerset, in January 1986, and the same bird was present at Ibsley, Hampshire, from December 1986 to January 1987, returning to Somerset each winter until 1990. The other record, first reported 22 January 1998, was in Lincolnshire. There are no BBRC accepted records prior to 1950.

TABLE 4. Bewick's swan: sites in Britain where the mean five-year peak exceeded 200 birds (International threshold).

LOCATION	MEAN 5-YEAR PEAK 2002/03– 2006/07	PEAK COUNT 2006/07
Ouse Washes, Cambridgeshire	5,571	3,407 (Dec)
Nene Washes, Cambridgeshire	894	703 (Jan)
St Benet's Levels, Norfolk	284	—
Hickling Broad, Norfolk	282	—
Severn Estuary, Gloucestershire/ Somerset/etc	244	196 (Feb)
Breydon Water & Berney Marshes, Norfolk	215	147 (Feb)

TABLE 5. Bewick's swan: sites in Ireland where the mean five-year peak exceeded 20 birds (National threshold).

LOCATION	MEAN 5-YEAR PEAK 1996/97–	PEAK COUNT 2000/01 2000/01
Tacumshin Lake, Co. Wexford	200	—
Wexford Harbour & Slobs, Co. Wexford	196	164 (Jan)
Boghill Fields, Coleraine, Co. Derry	48	—
Ballycotton/Shanagarry, Co. Cork	47	—
River Lagan, Flatfield, Co. Down	44	—
Upper Lough Erne, Co. Fermanagh	32	—
Canary Road, Moy, Co. Armagh	26	—
Lough Foyle, Co. Derry	26	—

3. WHOOPER SWAN *CYGNUS CYGNUS* (AE*)

The whooper swan (Fig. 26), the most goose-like of our swans, is big, powerful and highly vocal. Their magnificent and magical behaviour, one of autumn's defining points, can be witnessed with the arrival of the first migrants from Iceland in early October. When a fresh party of swans arrives on a lake already occupied by other whoopers there follows a most boisterous and frenzied display of wing flapping and head pumping, accompanied by a cacophony of wild callings, while the swans face each other as if in combat. However, this behaviour is less threatening and sinister than it appears – just a ritualised greeting or triumph ceremony. After several minutes of drama the swans settle down to proceed with the essential business of feeding and preening.

British and Irish wintering whooper swans originate almost exclusively from Iceland, where the population increased by 57 per cent over the period 1986–2005 (Table 6). Over the past four decades the population has almost quadrupled from an estimated 5,000–6,000 birds in 1961, the rate of growth accelerating in recent years.[49] The average annual rate of increase between 1995 and 2000 was 6.3 per cent. The average annual productivity over this period was 18.1 per cent, suggesting an average annual adult mortality of 11.8 per cent.[50]

FIG 26. Whooper Swan. The whooper has a mostly yellow bill with a black tip, while the Bewick's has a black bill with yellow base. The differential amount of yellow is one of several field characteristics separating these two species. (Ken Kinsella)

TABLE 6. Whooper swan: numbers counted and estimated in Britain, Ireland and Iceland 1986–2005, together with the proportion of first-winter birds in the flocks and mean brood size.

REGION	1986	1991	1995	2000	2005
Britain	5,136	5,225	5,016	6,926	10,731
Northern Ireland	2,363	3,484	2,783	3,663	4,331
Republic of Ireland	7,943	8,490	7,072	9,067	9,748
Iceland	1,300	831	971	1,200	1,556
Total	16,742	18,030	15,842	20,856	26,366
% first-winter birds	not available	9.8	17.9	16.8	12.1
Mean brood size	not available	1.9	2.3	2.3	2.5

Of the whooper swans wintering in these islands a majority (53 per cent) are in Ireland, the residue in Britain (Fig. 27), mostly in Scotland. With increasingly mild Icelandic winters, about 1,500 have remained at home in recent years. Other Icelandic whoopers travel to winter on the European continent. Observations of birds marked with neck-bands (197 in 1984 and 1985) suggested that up to 600 birds, principally from east Iceland, wintered in Norway, Denmark and the Netherlands during that period, intermixing with the c.45,000-strong (January 1995) Scandinavian/Russian population that normally winters in Sweden, northern Germany and Denmark. Most of these Icelandic birds return 'home', but there is at least one case of an Icelandic whooper switching populations and breeding in Finland. Many of the whoopers wintering in eastern Britain may in fact come from the Scandinavian/Russian population. Observations of colour-ringed birds have suggested that at least 200 Finnish-breeding birds spend each winter in southern Britain, and there are noted upsurges in numbers in eastern Britain following cold weather on the Continent, in which upwards of 3,000 birds may be involved. Whoopers also regularly move, within the same winter and in both directions, between Ireland and Britain. There has been one record of a Fennoscandian bird detected in Ireland.[51]

During their migrations whoopers traverse some 800–1,200 km over sea to and from Britain/Ireland and Iceland each trip – the longest non-stop migration of any swan. It was once thought that the swans flew entirely non-stop, but satellite tracking has shown that during difficult weather conditions they may land and sit on the sea for many hours: the flight time between Iceland and Scotland can be as short as 13 hours, or it may extend up to four days.[52]

FIG 27. Wintering whooper swans at the Wildfowl & Wetlands Trust reserve at Martin Mere, Lancashire. (Alan Williams/NHPA)

TABLE 7. Whooper swan: sites in Britain where the mean five-year peak exceeded 210 birds (International threshold).

LOCATION	MEAN 5-YEAR PEAK 2002/03–2006/07	PEAK COUNT 2006/07
Ouse Washes, Cambridgeshire	3,614	3,756 (Jan)
Martin Mere and Ribble Estuary, Lancashire	1,713	1,713 (Dec)
Loch of Strathbeg, Aberdeenshire	529	285 (Dec)
Solway Firth, Cumbria/ Dumfries & Galloway	424	(194) (Feb)
Dalreoch, Perthshire	264	264 (Dec)
Lough Eye and Cromarty Firth, Highland	263	518 (Oct)
Loans of Tullich, Highland	253	—
Wigtown Bay, Dumfries & Galloway	230	(164) (Jan)
Bridge of Crathies, Perth & Kinross	(220)	—

TABLE 8. Whooper swan: sites in Ireland where the mean five-year peak of whooper swans exceeded 130 birds (National threshold).

LOCATION	MEAN 5-YEAR PEAK 1996/97–2000/01	PEAK COUNT 2000/01
Lough Swilly, Co. Donegal	1,866	1,622 (Oct)
Loughs Neagh & Beg, Co. Armagh/Down/etc	1,514*	1,731* (Mar)
Lough Foyle, Co. Derry	1,397*	956* (Jan)
Upper Lough Erne, Co. Fermanagh	883*	822 (Feb)
R. Foyle, Cos. Donegal & Derry	571	556 (Nov)
Lough Gara, Co. Sligo	495	336 (Jan)
Lough Oughter Complex, Co. Cavan	422	296 (Jan)
Coole/Garryland complex, Co. Clare	327	386 (Jan)
Shannon Callows	321	—
Glen Lough, Co. Westmeath	305	—
Tacumshin Lake, Co. Wexford	243	—
Lough Iron, Co. Westmeath	227	—
River Blackwater Callows, Co. Cork	214	—
L. Coy–Ballylee Complex, Co. Galway	206	185 (Dec)
Strangford Lough, Co. Down	205*	199 (Nov)*
R. Blackwater, Co. Meath	182	—
North Central Galway Lakes, Co. Galway	179	300 (Jan)
Castleplunket Turloughs, Co. Roscommon	152	110 (Jan)
Lough Ree, Co. Westmeath	144	274 (Jan)
Cashen River & Estuary, Co. Kerry	141	133 (Jan)
Donegal Bay, Co. Donegal	140	—
Rahasane Turlough, Co. Galway	140	121 (Feb)
Boghill Fields, Coleraine, Co. Derry	137	—
Cloghanhill, Co. Offaly	130	—

The whooper swan has a long history in these islands, with fossils dating from the Middle Pleistocene (Cromerian interglacial, c.600–500 ky BP – a relatively warm period) from Boxgrove, Sussex; more recent Late Pleistocene (Ipswichian, c.127–117 ky BP) deposits with fossils found in two separate caves in Essex; and fossils from the Late Glacial (13–12 ky BP) cave deposits at Gough's Cave, Somerset. Whoopers were plentiful in Britain during the Roman period (AD 43–400), judging by the number of bones recovered from ancient dwellings at Colchester, and there are later fossil records at the lake dwelling at Lagore, Co. Meath, dating from AD 750–950. There are also records in Anglo-Saxon literature, from *The Seafarer* (mid seventh century) and *Beowulf* (eighth century).

A small, well-established breeding colony of 'several pairs' of wild whoopers on Orkney became extinct by the 1880s. Spasmodic breeding, mostly of feral or injured birds, also occurred, mainly in Scotland, during the twentieth century. In recent years between two and five pairs have bred each year in Great Britain (Table 9), although their provenance is unclear. At least five pairs bred in 1990, and in 1998 two apparently wild pairs bred in Scotland. In the Shetlands whoopers bred in three consecutive years, 1994–96. Mark Brazil has chronicled their recent British breeding and summering history.[53]

TABLE 9. Whooper swan: history of summering and breeding in Great Britain, 1990–98.

YEAR	SUMMERING LOCATIONS	PAIRS PRESENT	PAIRS BRED	CYGNETS PRODUCED
1990	15	5–32	5+	11
1991	18	4–21	4+	7
1992	11	7+	7	1
1993	20	4+	4	1
1994	14	5+	5	11
1995	0	1	1	0
1996	5	4	4	6
1997	9+	9	4	3
1998	3	2+	2	1+

The overall breeding success in Great Britain between 1990 and 1998 was poor, with a mean of 1.1 young produced per breeding pair, compared with 2.7 per breeding pair in Ireland more recently (p 60).

Prior to the first recorded breeding of wild whoopers in Ireland there had been at least one successful cross between a male whooper and a female mute swan in 1973 at Lough Corrib, Co. Galway. Five of the seven eggs hatched but the young did not survive beyond about one month. Breeding may have occurred for several years previously. Another whooper was observed mated to a mute swan on Inishmore, Aran Islands, Co. Galway.[54] Elsewhere whoopers have been known to hybridise with black, mute, trumpeter and whistling swans, and even with greylag and Canada geese in captive collections.[55]

The first recorded breeding of whoopers in Ireland occurred in 1992. Since then one or two pairs have bred more or less every year (Table 10).

TABLE 10. Whooper swan: history of breeding in Ireland, 1992–2008.

YEAR	LOCATION	NOTES
1992	Co. Donegal	1 pair bred Lough Swilly, with 1 cygnet observed in July, August and September; another pair was present but did not breed
	Co. Sligo	1 pair bred with 5 cygnets
1993	Co. Donegal	1 pair bred successfully Lough Swilly with 4 cygnets
1994	Co. Donegal	1 pair bred with 2 cygnets at the same site as in 1992 and 1993; 5 summering adults at same site on 14 August
1995		No breeding records
1996	Co. Donegal	2 pairs Lough Swilly with a brood/crèche of 4 well-grown cygnets 10 August
	Co. Derry	1 pair bred Lough Beg for the first time with 5 cygnets in August
	Co. Fermanagh	1–2 pairs bred
1997	Co. Derry	1 pair bred Lough Beg with 2 cygnets seen in June
	Co. Fermanagh	1–2 pairs bred
1998	Co. Derry	1 pair bred Lough Derg with 6 cygnets in August
	Co. Fermanagh	1–2 pairs bred
1999	Co. Derry	2 pairs bred successfully, Lough Beg
	Co. Fermanagh	1–2 pairs bred
2000	Co. Derry	1 pair bred at the site used in previous years with 3 cygnets
	Co. Fermanagh	1–2 pairs bred
2001	Co. Donegal	1 pair bred Tory Island, 1 cygnet, not fledged, observed September

TABLE 10. – *Cont.*

2002		No information
2003	Co. Fermanagh	1 pair bred with 2 downy cygnets (30 June); 2 out of 4 cygnets fledged
	Co. Donegal	1 pair bred Tory Island
2004	Co. Fermanagh	1 pair bred: 1 out of 4 cygnets fledged; 3 other adults present
	Co. Derry	1 pair with 2 cygnets; on 11 July these plus 5 other adults present
2005	Co. Fermanagh	1 adult with 2 cygnets, May, June and July
	Co. Derry	1 pair with 5 cygnets and 3 other adults, Lough Neagh area, 12 July
2006	Co. Fermanagh	1 pair with 1 cygnet, Lower Lough Erne
	Co. Derry	1 adult with 2 cygnets, Lough Neagh area, 7 June
2007	Co. Fermanagh	1 pair probably bred
	Co. Derry	1 adult with 7 cygnets
2008	Co. Fermanagh	1 pair probably bred
	Co. Donegal	1 breeding pair

Data from Hillis, 2005, 2006, 2007; Irish Bird Network website; Irish Bird Reports; Northern Ireland Bird Reports; W. McDowell, personal communication; R. Sheppard, personal communication.

The average production of cygnets – mainly determined in August – from 18 successful breeding pairs up to and including 2008 was 3.3, compared with 3.2 in Finland for the years 1964–70 and 3.1 in Iceland for 1968.[56] It is expected that the number of breeding whoopers in Ireland may increase over the next decade, in view of the numbers of summering birds, between 8 and 19 in recent years (2005–08).

The whooper is less in a hurry to complete its breeding cycle than the Bewick's swan, as it nests at lower latitudes with longer summers. The incubation period is some four days longer and the fledging period a leisurely 105–115 days, 45 days longer than that of Bewick's. Long-term monogamy is normal (Fig. 28) and age of first breeding is variable – most probably commencing at 4 years, but sometimes delayed up to age 6, if sites are unavailable. As with the Bewick's swan, the male participates in nest building, passing material over his shoulder to his mate. Contrary to some statements, the male does not normally incubate during the female's absence – amounting to about 25 per cent of total incubation time – but usually remains close to the nest as a guard.[57] Both parents tend the cygnets, directing them to food. The family remains together throughout the winter and

FIG 28. Pair of whooper swans. The orange head and upper-neck stains of this pair are due to ferrous oxides that have adhered to the feathers. The swans have picked these up when dipping their heads down into the water in search of weeds and other vegetable foods. One would normally see these stains during spring. (Ken Kinsella)

during the spring migration until their return to the breeding grounds. The benefits to the offspring are numerous – knowledge of the migration routes, how to recognise dangers and hazards, location of good feeding areas, optimisation of feeding opportunities and general social behaviour. The enormous amount of time, effort and training invested in the offspring is a behavioural characteristic, shared with the geese but not with ducks, of the long-lived and monogamous swans.

As with other long-lived wildfowl, the proportion of successful breeding birds is relatively small. Only 29 and 27 per cent of whoopers studied in Finland in 1968–70 and 1973–76 respectively bred successfully. In the more northern and harsher Finnish sub-Arctic vegetation zone the proportion fell to 5 per cent. A study in Iceland in 1988 showed that an estimated 30–40 per cent of all adults contributed to annual recruitment. Finnish studies found that of 86 eggs in 18 clutches some 74 per cent hatched. Other studies showed that of 110 cygnets hatched in 29 broods some 90 per cent fledged. The average clutch size was 4.4, with an average brood size of 3.8 at hatching and 3.3 at fledging. Mortality of young was stable at about 10 per cent per month from hatching to autumn migration, and was significantly higher (10–14 per cent) in northern Finland than in southern Finland (3–6 per cent). Only 60 per cent of summers in northern Finland were long enough for cygnets to reach fledging stage before waters froze. The structure of a theoretical autumn population of whoopers in Finland, based on productivity data 1964–1970, consisted of 19.8 per cent successful breeders; 2.3 per cent unsuccessful breeders; 51.8 per cent non-breeders and 25.9 per cent fledged cygnets.[58]

Estimated mortality of Finnish birds was 30 per cent in the first year, 25 per cent in the second year, and thereafter an annual rate of 12 per cent, assuming that the birds first bred in their sixth year.[59] Estimated figures based on studies in Iceland showed mortality rates of 17 per cent for birds from their first to second winters, 20 per cent for birds 2–6 years old and 22 per cent for birds of unknown ages 8 years after ringing.[60] Counts of Icelandic birds wintering in Britain show annual variations in the proportion of young birds, from under 10 per cent to over 40 per cent, and a mean brood size from about 1 to 3–4.[61]

4. BEAN GOOSE *ANSER FABALIS* (AE)

The bean goose, a taxonomic nightmare with disagreement among experts on the number of its subspecies/species, is closely related to the similar-looking pink-footed goose – which itself has been classified by some ornithologists as a subspecies of the bean goose. The TAC of the AERC recommended in 2003 that the status quo of a single-species bean goose with five forms or subspecies be maintained pending further research.[62] The accepted five subspecies are three that winter in western Europe (*Anser fabalis fabalis*, *A. f. rossicus* and *A. f. johanseni* (often included with *A. f. fabalis*)) and two that winter in China, Japan and Korea (*A. f. middendorfii* and *A. f. serrirostris*). The breeding range of the bean goose spans the entire Eurasian continent from northern Norway, Sweden and Finland east across Russia to the Bering Sea, in both the tundra and boreal zones, even stretching south into the mountainous regions of central Asia.[63]

The bean geese that winter in Britain and spasmodically visit Ireland mostly belong to the taiga subspecies, *Anser fabalis fabalis* (Fig. 29), which have relatively long orange-yellow bills, and whose total population size has been estimated at 70,000–90,000 birds (2005). They breed in the marshy pine-forested or taiga zone, lying between the tundra and the steppe, from northern Norway (principally Finnmark), Sweden, Finland and east through western Russia to the Kola Peninsula. After breeding, most taiga bean geese move to Scania,

FIG 29. Bean goose, taiga race (*fabalis*). Bean geese are the second-largest of the grey geese, with only two well-established wintering haunts in Britain. Could be confused with pink-footed goose, but has dull orange, not pink, legs. (Jari Peltomaki/NHPA)

the southernmost province in Sweden, while others travel to northern Poland and the northern part of eastern Germany. Numbers in Poland and Germany may reach 20,000–30,000 at the same time that there are 60,000–80,000 individuals in Sweden. Many, but not all, Swedish birds move south with the advent of cold weather and end up principally in southeast Denmark (normally 8,000–10,000, but peaking at 35,000 when it is cold), while some move on to the Netherlands (normally 1,000–1,500 but up to 2,000 in cold weather).

The taiga geese that winter in Britain arrive late, usually in November, and are assumed to have travelled on from Continental wintering flocks. During the nineteenth century the species was considered quite numerous in Scotland and northern England – it is possible that there may have been some confusion with the pink-footed goose at the time – but today it is relatively rare, with only some 400 birds wintering (1995–99) in Great Britain. There are only two areas where flocks of any size occur (Table 11). The largest haunt today is at the Slamannan Plateau, Falkirk, where birds arrive from late September to early October, remain in stable numbers between October and February, and depart often sooner than mid-February. Numbers increased from a mean annual peak of 165 in 1996/97 to 300 during winter 2005/06 (but down again to 255 the next winter), and then some 300 were present during February 2008.[64] Observations of colour-ringed birds show that some of the geese originate from a Swedish reintroduction scheme. Cold weather on the Continent brings in more geese, such as in February 1982, when 329 were counted. The geese feed on wet grassland. The major Scottish haunt, at least from 1950 onwards, used to be at Threave, Kirkcudbright. As the numbers there dwindled those at Slamannan increased, and Threave is now deserted. The other important wintering site is in the Middle Yare Marshes of the River Yare, Norfolk, where the geese arrive in mid-November and depart in late February. Some, if not all, come from the wintering flocks in north Jutland, Denmark, as shown by the observation of neck-banded birds that had originally been trapped in southern Lapland but were wintering in Denmark.[65] The Yare geese feed on marshes, taking the poorer grasses in the sward. Numbers in the Yare valley have fluctuated since 1941, becoming more robust following the introduction of a voluntary protection scheme in the 1970s. However, they have been declining, reaching their lowest peak levels since 1980/81 during the winter 2003/04. During 2006/07 the peak count was only 111, the lowest number there since 1977/78, but the peak count during 2007/08 was 135 in November 2007.[66]

TABLE 11. Taiga bean goose: sites in Britain where the mean peak numbers exceeded 50 birds (National threshold).

LOCATION	MEAN 5-YEAR PEAK 2002/03–2006/07	PEAK COUNT 2006/07
Slamannan area, Falkirk	257	255 (Nov)
Middle Yare Marshes, Norfolk	152	111 (Feb)

There are fossil records of bean goose from the last Late Pleistocene interglacial period, the Ipswichian (127–117 ky BP), from Bacon Hole cave, Glamorgan, and from the more recent Holocene period (10–0 ky BP) from Shandon Cave, Co. Waterford.

Little is known about the breeding biology of the taiga bean goose. In southern Swedish Lapland breeding density is one pair per 1,165 ha in suitable wetland habitat.[67] Mortality has been estimated, by resightings of northern Finnish neck-banded geese, at 43 per cent for first-year birds and 20–25 per cent for adults.[68] An adult mortality rate of 23 per cent was based on captured moulting subadults in Finnmark, north Norway.[69]

Ireland is the only European country without regular visits. When they do appear they are rare, occurring mainly between September and April. During the period 1950–2006 a total of 131 individuals was recorded, including two – possibly a pair – on the North Slob, Co. Wexford, in March 2004. Both were caught and ringed on 10 March, and the female was subsequently controlled at Lappi, Finland, on 25 May 2004. It was later seen at Vaasa, Finland on 22 March 2006. It had not been seen in Ireland during the intervening winters.

The other form that occurs in Britain is the tundra bean goose, *Anser fabalis rossicus* (Fig. 30). It breeds in low Arctic northern Russia and western Siberia as far

FIG 30. Bean Goose, tundra race (*rossicus*). This race is difficult to distinguish from the closely related *fabalis* race. *Rossicus* is slightly smaller, with a shorter neck and shorter bill, and with a darker head and neck contrasting with the paler brown breast. Of the two races fewer *rossicus* visit Britain and Ireland each winter. (Roger Tidman/NHPA)

west as the Kola Peninsula, on Novaya Zemlya, and east to the Taymyr Peninsula. It is smaller than the taiga subspecies, with a shorter bill, the orange-yellow being confined to a small area on the upper mandible just behind the nail. The dividing line between the breeding ranges of the taiga and tundra varieties lies somewhere on the Kola Peninsula. The size of the wintering population is uncertain, but it is thought to be approximately 600,000 individuals. It is the most widespread winter goose visitor to Europe, found chiefly in Germany and the Netherlands, with smaller numbers in central Europe, especially Hungary. Its breeding success is highly variable, the proportion of young birds in winter flocks in the Netherlands and Germany over 15 years averaging 21.7 per cent. Many thousands are shot each year, accounting for about 10 per cent of the total population annually. The annual mortality of adults, 25–30 per cent, is similar to that of the European white-fronted goose.[70]

An estimated 100 tundra bean geese winter in Britain (Table 12), with very great variation between years, and they are often associated with taigas on the southeast coast. On occasions they arrive with European white-fronted geese. The Ouse Washes, Cambridgeshire, is a winter haunt to a small flock of tundra geese. They are scarce visitors to Ireland, with a total of nine individuals recorded between 1950 and 2007. The first record was of two birds at Braganstown, Co. Louth, in November 1993 remaining to 28 January 1994. Four birds seen at Braganstown on 27 December 1997 remained until 22 February 1998, while there were another two in Co. Derry from 5 to 25 January 2004.

TABLE 12. Presumed or known tundra bean goose: sites in Britain where the mean peak numbers exceeded 4 birds (National threshold).

LOCATION	MEAN 5-YEAR PEAK 2002/03–2006/07	PEAK COUNT 2006/07
Ouse Washes, Cambridgeshire	23	6 (Feb)
Walland Marsh, Kent	17	0
N Warren & Thorpeness Mere, Suffolk	11	2 (Dec)
Somerset Levels, Somerset	5	0
Balnakeil Bay, Highland	5	—
Dungeness Gravel Pits, Kent	4	0

5. PINK-FOOTED GOOSE
ANSER BRACHYRHYNCHUS (AE*)

The world population of the pink-footed goose (Fig. 31) consists of some 312,000 birds separated into two populations – one breeding in east Greenland and Iceland and the other breeding in Svalbard.

The British and Irish wintering birds come exclusively from the population breeding in Iceland and scattered along the coastal strip of east Greenland from 250 km south of Ammassalik (62° N) to Nordmarken (78° N).[71] Another population, numbering some 42,000 birds, breeds in Svalbard and spends the winter in continental Europe – principally in Denmark, Germany and Belgium, remaining separate from the Greenland/Iceland birds – though, as with other 'discrete' populations of wintering geese, a little intermixing takes place: some Svalbard birds wintering and ringed in Denmark have been observed in the wintering range of the Icelandic birds in Britain.[72]

The pink-footed goose has the distinction of being the most numerous wintering goose in Britain, having increased from c.20,000–30,000 in the 1930s–1950s to c.200,000–250,000 in the mid-1990s. Since the early 1980s numbers almost trebled to the year 2003, with the last available population estimate (November 2007) yielding an estimated 287,563 geese – including estimates for key sites not covered – an increase of 25.5 per cent on the previous year.[73] Their principal wintering areas are in eastern and southern Scotland, with more birds in northwest and east England. The pink-foot was a winter visitor to Ireland in small numbers until recently, when some large flocks have been recorded: the annual number recorded for the period 1996–2003 was approximately 120 individuals, most of them in the northern and northeastern counties. A flock of 140, the largest number ever seen in Ireland at the time, was observed flying over Lough Beg, Co. Down, in September 2007. A migrating flock of some 200 was reported in Donegal in the autumn of 2008.

Fossil records in Britain date from the Middle Pleistocene period (710–127 ky BP) and have been found in Derbyshire and Jersey. Most records were in association with barnacle, brant and greylag geese, and in two instances with Bewick's swan.

More than 50 years ago the Wildfowl Trust embarked on pioneering studies on the biology of the pink-footed goose in Iceland, not only stirring public imagination through the publication of Peter Scott and James Fisher's book *A Thousand Geese* and their television programmes but also setting the foundations for future research on goose population dynamics.[74] The first

FIG 31. Pink-footed goose. Its dark head, shortish pink bill with black base, and pink legs are key identification features. However, at a distance, under poor light conditions, the pink legs can look orange – leading to confusion with the bean goose. (William Paton/NHPA)

expedition, in 1951, discovered the principal breeding colony in the central oasis of Thjórsárver, central Iceland, where 1,151 goslings and adult geese were ringed. In 1953 the goose men returned to the area, banding a further 8,745 birds as well as recapturing 260 previously marked geese – a remarkable achievement. This pioneering work was matched in Britain by the development of rocket-propelled nets, which made it possible to catch and ring 11,800 pink-feet between 1950 and 1959. The recaptures and recoveries of these geese allowed the calculation of estimates of population size, mortality rates, migration and distribution of birds in a way that had not been previously possible for any geese. Scientific investigation of the population dynamics of wild geese had been born.

The numbers wintering in Britain started to increase dramatically from the mid-1980s onwards, due probably to reduced adult mortality as more winter roosts became protected. Better winter feeding conditions also became available.[75] Historically the pink-feet fed on salt marsh, but they switched onto farmland around 1900. Today the geese feed on spilt grain in stubble fields during the autumn after their arrival any time from early to mid September. Soon afterwards they move to root crops, such as waste potatoes, left behind after the harvest. Later, sprouting winter wheat is devoured, followed in the spring by grass – principally perennial ryegrass, the main species of managed grassland – capitalising on the high protein content found in the initial stages of its growth.

Despite the substantial increase in the population, there was no significant trend in breeding success over a 26-year period (1970–95), measured by the proportion of young birds in the autumn flocks (average 17.9 per cent). If density-dependent factors were at work then breeding success would have declined. The mean brood size was 2.1 for 1970–95, also showing no significant trend. Extension of the Icelandic breeding range is thought to have been an important factor in the population's continued breeding success. Adult annual mortality, estimated by capture–recapture models based on resightings of leg-banded birds, gave a 21 per cent rate (or survival of 0.79) for adults and 46 per cent (or survival of 0.54) for first-winter birds, both perhaps slight underestimates.[76] There are no trends of estimated annual survival probability when plotted against lagged population size using both old and new data. However, it has been concluded that, although density dependence in productivity is the most important *regulating* factor for populations, the size of the population is largely *determined* by adult survival rates.[77]

From late June to early July there is a huge northerly moult migration of birds from the Icelandic population into northeast Greenland, involving at least 30,000 non-breeding birds. These join up with the local breeding population.[78] When I was in northeast Greenland at Nordmarken (77° 39' N) from the end of May to mid August 1987, I counted a total of 354 flying north in 16 small flocks, the first appearing on 21 June. While carrying out helicopter surveys later that summer we recorded at least 1,000 moulting birds in Nordmarken and discovered new moulting grounds, the most northerly and previously unrecorded site being the lake at 77° 56' N.[79] Since then, moulting geese have been pushing further north, with several thousand birds to be found today along the most northerly coast of Greenland at 83° N.[80] The remaining non-breeding Icelandic birds moult at home, often in large congregations.

It might appear extraordinary that so many geese would invest such large amounts of the precious energy required for the flight, and expose themselves to the risks of unknown hazards, on their 2,400 km round trip from Iceland. Moreover, after their return to Iceland the geese then embark on another journey of about the same distance to their Scottish wintering grounds. Thus within a typical year these moulting birds would have flown a minimum of 4,800 km. The biological advantages of the northerly moult migration are principally to escape from the crowded Icelandic moulting areas and consequent food shortages, and to capitalise on the onset of vegetation growth and peak nutrient levels in the vegetation further north. However, the trend of increasing numbers travelling north to moult cannot continue for ever with the existing benefits, because with the increase in the goose numbers several Greenland pink-foot moulting grounds, especially in Jameson Land, appear to have reached their carrying capacity. There, the moulting birds feed for 43 per cent of a 24-hour period. Barnacle geese share the moulting ponds and lakes but are less successful in competing with their more robust, aggressive relatives for the limited food resources around the lake margins. Studies in 1983 and 1984 showed that pink-feet grazed further out from the water's edge, up to 200–250 m, and removed between 60 and 100 per cent of the above-ground primary production in a Hoppner's sedge marsh.[81] The northerly moult migration, so dramatically exemplified by the pink-footed goose, is also a feature of many other Anatidae.

TABLE 13. Pink-footed goose: roost sites in Britain where the mean five-year peak exceeded 14,000 birds. A further 28 roosts exceeded the National threshold of 2,400.

LOCATION	MEAN 5-YEAR PEAK 2002/03–2006/07	PEAK COUNT 2006/07
Scolt Head, Norfolk	56,140	17,200 (Dec)
Holkham Marshes, Norfolk	55,730	69,100 (Dec)
Loch of Strathbeg, Aberdeenshire	55,259	37,396 (Oct)

TABLE 13. – *Cont.*

West Water Reservoir, Borders	44,948	43,252 (Oct)
Snettisham, Norfolk	36.571	33,485 (Nov)
SW Lancashire	34,702	39,030 (Nov)
Montrose Basin, Tayside	21,745	25,000 (Oct)
Morecambe Bay, Lancashire	19,885	(7,145) (Dec)
Loch of Skene, Aberdeenshire	17,553	22,930 (Nov)
Aberlady Bay, Lothian	17,480	—
Loch Leven, Perth & Kinross	16,661	14,600 (Oct)
Loch Spynie, Moray	16,360	9,000 (Oct)
Ythan Estuary/Slains Lochs, Aberdeenshire	16,340	10,360 (Oct)
Findhorn Bay, Moray	14,050	3,800 (Oct)

TABLE 14. Pink-footed goose: sites in Ireland that have supported geese during I-WeBS counts 1996/7–2000/01 (National threshold 5 birds).

LOCATION	PEAK COUNT	NUMBER OF RECORDS
Stabannan/Braganstown, Co. Louth	33	8
Lough Swilly, Co. Donegal	27	15
Dundalk Bay, Co. Louth	27	2
Wexford Harbour & Slobs, Co. Wexford	16	36
Lough Foyle, Co. Derry	6	2
Rahasane Turlough, Co. Galway	3	6
North Wicklow Coastal Marshes, Co. Wicklow	2	5
Turrane Nature Reserve, Co. Offaly	2	5
Tralee Bay, L. Gill & Akeragh Lough, Co. Kerry	3	4
Dunfanaghy New Lake, Co. Donegal	2	3
Lough Gur, Co. Limerick	2	2

6. GREATER WHITE-FRONTED GOOSE
ANSER ALBIFRONS (AE*)

The greater white-fronted goose is the most numerous of all geese wintering in Europe. There are five races recognised, of which two winter in Britain and Ireland. These are (1) the European white-fronted goose, *A. a. albifrons* (Fig. 32), which breeds in the Russian tundra zone from the Kanin Peninsula (44° E) east to the Chatanga River on the Taymyr Peninsula, and (2) the Greenland white-fronted goose, *A. a. flavirostris*, which breeds in west Greenland and winters almost exclusively in Ireland and Britain, with a few outlying birds in Norway. The other three races are (3) *A. a. frontalis*, which breeds in east Siberia, the Yukon–Kuskokwim Delta in Alaska, central and northwest Alaska, and across Arctic Canada to Foxe Basin; (4) *A. a. gambeli*, which breeds in the Alaskan taiga, and (5) *A. a. elgasi*, which breeds in southwest Alaska. The taxonomic status of *elgasi* has been uncertain, but the subspecies was recognised by the American Ornithological Union in 1998.

The western Palaearctic population, numbering some 1 million birds (1999), migrates west and south to spend the winter months in three separate groups extending from the Baltic–North Sea to the Caspian Sea (Fig. 33). The Baltic–North Sea group, including Britain and Ireland, has an estimated 450,000–600,000 birds. The numbers wintering in Britain are small – approximately 8,000 birds from the early 1950s increasing to some 12,000 between 1967 and 1970. Since then they have been in decline, not only nationally – the average national count for the period 1990–94 was 4,600 – but also at their two key wintering sites at Slimbridge, Gloucestershire, and the Swale Estuary, Kent. Numbers during winter 2006/07 fell by about 70 per cent to their lowest level so far, with a WeBS maximum count of 1,341 in February 2007. Their decline in Britain is a classic case of 'short stopping', geese wintering closer to their breeding grounds in response to better feeding conditions on the Continent.[82]

The species may have bred in Britain during the colder phases of the Pleistocene period. The oldest fossils, with a question mark over their identification, are from Swanscombe, Kent, and date from 420–360 ky BP. Other fossils, clearly identified as greater white-front, date from the Ipswichian period (127–117 ky BP) at an Essex site, while records from five other British caves are more recent, dating from 50–22 ky BP. Four Irish caves have produced fossils: three of these were uncertainly identified, while a definite greater white-front was found in Plunkett Cave, Co. Sligo. All Irish fossils date from the Holocene (10–0 ky BP). Associated goose fossils were greylag (most frequent) and barnacle geese.

FIG 32. European white-fronted goose. The European race of the greater white-fronted goose (*albifrons*) is distinguished from its Greenland cousin by its pink, not orange-yellow, bill. Its overall plumage is lighter than that of *flavirostris*. (Joe Blossom/NHPA)

FIG 33. A winter flock of European white-fronted geese at Dobruja, Romania. (Woodfall Wild Images/Photoshot; Martin Zwick/NHPA)

In Britain these geese were traditionally found on coastal grasslands and in flooded river valleys, but today they occur mainly on arable land, with all key sites within a kilometre or two of the coast, with the exception of the Mid Yare Marshes. They feed almost exclusively on pastureland where the grasses perennial ryegrass, rough meadow-grass and Yorkshire fog are most frequently taken.[83]

TABLE 15. European white-fronted goose: sites in Britain where the mean five-year peak exceeded 58 birds (National threshold).

LOCATION	MEAN 5-YEAR PEAK 2002/03–2006/07	PEAK COUNT 2006/07
Severn Estuary, Gloucestershire/ Somerset/etc	761	542 (Jan)
Swale Estuary, Kent	442	355 (Feb)
N Norfolk Coast, Norfolk	366	200 (Jan)
N Warren & Thorpeness Mere, Suffolk	262	180 (Feb)
Breydon Water & Berney Marshes, Norfolk	239	0
Dungeness Gravel Pits, Kent	205	1 (Jan)
Walland Marsh, Kent	203	127 (Feb)
Alde Complex, Suffolk	95	0 (Feb)
Middle Yare Marshes, Norfolk	92	66 (Jan)

In Ireland the European white-front is a rare winter visitor. Only 134 individuals were recorded between 1880 and 2007, mainly in small groups of up to five birds on the east and southeast coasts.

The Greenland race of the white-fronted goose (Fig. 34) is the most celebrated of all wintering geese of Britain and Ireland on two accounts: first because of their remarkably concentrated winter distribution and their recent recognition as a separate subspecies, and second because of their involvement in a landmark conservation battle.

The entire population – 24,804 birds counted during the national census in the spring of 2006 – winters almost exclusively in these islands, with fewer than 10 birds overwintering in Rogaland, southwest Norway.[84] In addition, a few birds

FIG 34. Greenland white-fronted goose family. Two parents, at either end of the juveniles, the male on the right. The adults have well-developed black patches on their bellies. (Alyn Walsh)

occur annually on the Atlantic seaboard of North America, where three Greenland-ringed birds have been recovered – a much closer destination and less hazardous migration than to Ireland or Britain. Their scarcity in North America, where very large numbers of white-fronted geese breed in Alaska and the central Canadian Arctic, supports the thesis that these Greenland geese, together with the light-bellied brant goose, spread historically to their Arctic breeding grounds from northwest Europe, rather than originating in North America. During the autumn the migrants return to their ancestral wintering grounds.

The Greenland race was not officially recognised until 1948, when C. T. Dalgety and Peter Scott shot some darker-plumaged white-fronts on the Wexford Slobs in the southeast of Ireland. The geese had longer and heavier orange-yellow, rather than pink, bills. Dalgety and Scott showed that they differed significantly from other forms of the greater white-fronted goose.[85] Recent research has reinforced their distinctive nature, and the race may eventually be elevated to full species rank. It is the most morphologically distinct of the five races of greater white-front.

The Greenland white-fronts' more recent claim to fame was their embroilment in a contentious conservation battle when their most important single roost site in Britain – Eilean na Muic Dubh/Duich Moss – on Islay,

Strathclyde, was threatened by peat extraction in the 1980s. An Islay distillery required the peat to manufacture one of the island's famous and smoky-tasting whiskies. The confrontations involving ornithologists and environmentalists, the distillery, islanders, the British Government, the Commission of the European Union, and the Nature Conservancy Council were often acrimonious. Many lessons were learnt. The EU Commission insisted that the Government should implement the legal requirements of the EU Wild Birds and Habitats Directives to safeguard the location for the geese. The site was eventually purchased by the Government and an alternative source of peat for the distillery found. The controversy was a turning point both for conservationists and for the British authorities, marking a heightened appreciation of the need to respect EU Directives and the legal obligations they place on member states. The incident also sent out a strong message to other member states about the protection of important habitats and species.

The Greenland white-fronted goose breeds along the low Arctic west coast of Greenland, where there is a relatively mild, oceanic climate. Most of the population is found between Nuuk (64° N) and Upernavik (73° N), with the greatest densities – it does not nest colonially – close to the icecap in fertile flat areas with numerous lakes and wetlands. Snow-melt in these areas generally occurs a month earlier than closer to the coast. Compared with other races of the greater white-fronted goose, Greenland birds have a low productivity of young, averaging 14.7 per cent young birds in autumn flocks observed on Islay (1962–99) and 15.8 per cent on the Wexford Slobs (1968–99).[86] Because of its small population and the international responsibilities of Ireland and Britain to protect it during its winter stay it has become one of the most intensely studied of all our wintering geese.

After breeding, the geese migrate south from late August onwards, crossing the 2,410 m high Greenland icecap and spending a short time staging in western and southern Iceland before arriving in their Irish and British wintering haunts from early to mid October. During spring migration north from Ireland and Britain one goose tagged with a satellite transmitter made the c.1,600 km journey to southwest Iceland in just 13 hours, with an average ground speed of 124 km/hour. Other geese were recorded at 11 different spring staging areas, spending an average of 11 days at each site, some of which were 600 km south of their breeding area in Greenland.

Unravelling the history of wintering numbers in Britain and Ireland has not been without controversy, because population estimates made in Ireland during 1946–56 by the late Major R. F. Ruttledge were retrospectively increased by 50 per cent some 21 years after their original publication. Some wildfowlers believed the figures had been 'cooked' or inflated to show that there had been a population crash between 1946–56 and the early 1980s, in order to justify a shooting ban that was subsequently introduced. Be that as it may, a genuine decline in numbers, accompanied by a contraction of range and the loss of many former wintering sites, was sufficiently worrying, especially in the case of a bird with such a small world population, for the respective wildlife authorities to initiate a shooting moratorium from the winter of 1982/83 – and it remains in place today. The first comprehensive winter census took place that winter. Numbers of the geese improved, rising from 16,000–17,000 to 30,000–35,000 birds in the late 1990s. The absence of hunting in Britain and Ireland, together with a series of mild springs and warm summers on the breeding grounds, was responsible for the 6 per cent annual increase. Numbers peaked at 35,573 during the spring 1999 national census, but thereafter the geese have experienced a widespread decline throughout Ireland and Scotland, to fewer than 26,454 birds in the spring of 2002. The population appears to have since stabilised at 24,000–25,000 birds. Breeding success has been well below average for the last 15 years, at 9.9 per cent young in winter flocks.[87]

TABLE 16. Greenland white-fronted geese: results from national counts, spring 1997 to spring 2007.

LOCATION	Wexford	Rest of Ireland	Islay	Rest of Britain	**Total**
Spring 1997	8,751	4,788	11,210	8,357	**34,442**
Spring 1998	8,306	4,899	12,224	7,396	**32,835**
Spring 1999	8,958	4,617	13,560	8,438	**35,573**
Spring 2000	8,330	(4,617)	11,201	8,056	**32,204**
Spring 2001	—	—	13,281	7,787	—
Spring 2002	7,133	3,158	9,161	7,002	**26,454**
Spring 2003	7,915	—	10,677	7,595	**c.30,000**
Spring 2004	8,424	—	9,653	6,734	—
Spring 2005	7,707	—	7,152	6,876	**c.24,000**
Spring 2006	7,892	2,716	7,111	7,085	**24,804**
Spring 2007	9,713	—	6,025	6,428	—

Data from Fox & Francis, 2004, 2007; A. D. Fox, personal communication, A. Walsh, personal communication.

The trend for poor reproductive performance in recent years continued in 2007, and after little change in annual numbers wintering in Britain in the previous two years, there was a 13 per cent decline over the previous season, with a 15 per cent fall in numbers on Islay compared to spring 2006 (Table 16). The spring counts from Ireland are not available at the present time, so we do not yet know the global population in spring 2007. The encouraging number at Wexford in spring 2007 (9,713, a remarkable 19 per cent increase over the previous spring count there) suggests that the overall decline may be less than was first feared, though this cannot be confirmed until full details are available from Ireland. However, with continuing low reproductive output in the population, there was certainly another serious decline in the British numbers in 2006/07 compared to the previous winter.

Adult mortality rates have remained constant, but fewer young birds are being produced in Greenland and of these the proportion that survive to breed has declined from 15 per cent in the 1980s to less than 5 per cent today. The productivity of geese breeding in the northern part of the breeding grounds (most of these birds winter in Ireland) is being affected by poor summer weather. More importantly, the intrusion of the more aggressive greater Canada goose from northern Canada into western Greenland has displaced many white-fronts from their traditional breeding grounds. Interspecific competition is contributing to declining breeding success, as the Canada geese have driven the white-fronted geese from the best brood-rearing and adult moulting areas.

The vast majority of the Canada geese that have been encountered in the southern part of the Greenland white-fronted goose breeding range are the subspecies *interior* of the greater Canada goose, originating from northern Quebec, as shown from genetic and telemetry studies. It has also been reported from Newfoundland and Labrador that there are more and more moult migrants from feral and other populations coming in to the area, and it is suspected that they are continuing further into west Greenland.

In addition, the legal shooting of some 3,000 birds in Iceland and 2,000 in Greenland annually has had an adverse impact on the declining population.[88] But the good news is that following representations to the Icelandic government by the Greenland White-fronted Goose Study, hunting of the species has been banned in Iceland from autumn 2006.

The most recent published (2002) annual adult mortality rate, calculated from the recovery of ringed birds and the resightings of neck-banded birds marked at Wexford, was a weighted mean of 21.5 per cent – mean survival rate 0.78 – taking into account a constant annual emigration rate of 7 per cent. For juveniles the mortality rate was higher at 32.2 per cent.[89]

TABLE 17. Greenland white-fronted goose: sites in Britain where the mean five-year peak exceeded 270 (International threshold) and 209 birds (National threshold).

LOCATION	MEAN 5-YEAR PEAK 2002/03–2006/07	PEAK COUNT 2006/07
Island of Islay, Argyll & Bute	9,447	7,902 (Mar)
Machrihanish, Argyll & Bute	1,487	1,716 (Mar)
Tiree, Argyll & Bute	1,081	974 (Feb)
Rhunahaorine, Argyll & Bute	1,097	940 (Mar)
Isle of Coll, Argyll & Bute	677	687 (Dec)
Isle of Colonsay, Argyll & Bute	414	76 (Dec)
Keills Peninsula & Isle of Danna, Argyll & Bute	364	350 (Nov)
Stranraer Lochs, Dumfries & Galloway	309	360 (Dec)
Isle of Lismore, Argyll & Bute	301	273 (Mar)
Loch Lomond, Stirling/W Dumbarton/ Argyll & Bute	274	210 (Mar)

TABLE 18. Greenland white-fronted goose: sites in Ireland where the mean five-year peak exceeded 110 birds (National threshold).

LOCATION	MEAN 5-YEAR PEAK 1996/97–2000/01	PEAK COUNT 2000/01
Wexford Harbour, Slobs, Tacumshin & Cahore, Co. Wexford	9,613	10,194 (Jan)
Lough Swilly and Foyle, Co. Donegal	970	1,164 (Feb)
Lough Gara, Co. Roscommon	493	580

TABLE 18. – *Cont.*

Loughs Iron, Derravaragh, Owel & Ennell, Co. Westmeath	492	679
Little Brosna Callows, Co. Offaly	477	562
River Suck/ Shannonbridge, Co. Roscommon	301	842
Dunfanaghy, Co. Donegal	231	334
Rostaff and Killower, Co. Galway	166	213
Rahasane Turlough, Co. Galway	166	181
Bog of Erris, Co. Mayo	155	166
Loughs Kilglass and Castleforbes, Co. Longford	142	240
Errif and Derrycraft, Co. Mayo	141	171

Greenland white-fronted geese traditionally fed on the rhizomes of the common cotton grass and deer sedge found in peatlands, especially raised and blanket boglands, but today most feed on reseeded grassland, especially in the spring. In the autumn they will often feed on waste root crops and spilt grain.

7. LESSER WHITE-FRONTED GOOSE
ANSER ERYTHROPUS (AE*)

The lesser white-fronted goose is not only a smaller version of the greater white-fronted goose, weighing on average 500 g or 21 per cent less, but its white front is much more extensive, often extending to the crown of the head (Fig. 35). Its bill is smaller, and there is a conspicuous swollen yellow eye-ring. They are the smallest of all the grey geese. They are now considered endangered due to their tiny and declining world population. In addition, their breeding and wintering ranges are contracting. The species breeds in areas of wooded tundra or forest edges up to 700 m above sea level from northern Scandinavia to northeast Siberia, with their main breeding grounds between the Kola Peninsula in the west and the Anadyr River in the east. The preferred habitats range from mountain willow and birch

FIG 35. Lesser white-fronted goose. The smallest grey goose, with characteristic stubby yellow bill, white forehead and conspicuous yellow eye-ring. When the bird is standing, the wing tips usually extend beyond the tail. (Bill Coster/NHPA)

woods to low-lying bogs and areas with lakes, extending northwards from the northern edge of the taiga.

One fossil record has been reported from the late glacial period at Soldiers Hole, Cheddar Gorge, Somerset.(Yalden and Albarella). There are records from France, Italy, Romania and the Czech Republic.

The Fennoscandian breeding population has declined from more than 10,000 birds in the early twentieth century to no more than 30–50 pairs during the period 1986–96. The Swedish breeding population stood at about ten pairs in 1988, and was close to extinction by 1994. The former Finnish breeding population is now extinct. The Russian population was estimated at 30,000–50,000 birds in 1995, but these figures were not supported by winter counts. Its breeding range in the Taymyr area has contracted by about 92 per cent during the past 50 years. The estimated population for northern Scandinavia and Arctic west Russia was 8,000–13,000 birds in 1999. It is classified by the IUCN as a globally threatened species, and as endangered in Europe.

There have been several reintroduction programmes. One project in Sweden commenced in 1981. Barnacle geese were used as foster parents for the lesser white-fronts. Up to 348 young geese were introduced into former breeding grounds in Swedish Lapland, and between 1995 and 2004 there were at least 40 successful broods and 111 fledged young recorded. The total breeding population today is about five pairs, and it is reported to be gradually building up. The annual mortality is about 20–40 per cent for geese in their first year.

Another programme commenced in Finland in 1989. Artificially reared lesser white-fronts were released onto the breeding grounds of the small remaining native breeding population. Some 143 geese – 123 young, 5 second-year birds and 15 adults – were released. Less than 10 per cent returned to the breeding colony. An 80 per cent mortality was recorded for first-year geese, and no breeding has been reported. No birds now breed in Finland. It is thought that this programme failed because no foster parents were used.

In another attempt to assist the species, 'Operation Lesser Whitefront' proposed to lead 25 young geese, imprinted on a microlight aircraft, from Swedish Lapland to wintering grounds in the Lower Rhine region during 2007/08. By introducing the geese to a westerly autumn migration route, it is hoped that they will avoid the shooting mortality along the traditional eastern route that has been responsible for reducing the numbers of wintering lesser white-fronts in western Europe.

The first lesser white-front recorded in Britain or Ireland was an immature shot at Fenham Flats near Holy Island, Northumberland, on 16 September 1886. On their rare visits to Britain – generally one or two birds each winter – they are usually in the company of European white-fronts, though occasionally with bean geese in Scotland. Most sightings have been at Slimbridge, where the largest wintering flock in Britain of European white-fronts occurs. An increasing number of records are likely to be escapes from wildfowl collections, and it has become more and more difficult to assess which records relate to truly wild birds. There are 122 accepted occurrences in the BBRC database for Britain from 1950–2006. Prior to 1950 there were nine occurrences. Four birds recorded during WeBS 2005/06 were thought to be escapes. During WeBS 2006/07 birds were present at four sites, at Testbourne Estate, Hampshire (September to May), Tundry Pond, Hampshire (October), Middle Yare Marshes, Norfolk (December) and Llyn Traffwll, Gwynedd (April to June).

There has only been one record in Ireland to the end of 2006, an adult on the North Slob, Co. Wexford, 23–30 March 1969. Several European white-fronts were also present at the same time. It is likely that the lesser white-front arrived from Slimbridge, where one had been reported three weeks earlier.

8. GREYLAG GOOSE *ANSER ANSER* (AC2C4E*)

The greylag goose (Fig. 36) is the sole native breeding wild goose in these islands. It was also one of the first birds to be domesticated, with records dating back some 5,000 years, although the domestic geese originated in west Asia from the eastern race, not from the European stocks (see Chapter 2).

There are two recognised races: the western form, *Anser. a. anser*, and the eastern form, *A. a. rubrirostris*. The former numbers some 516,800 birds, breeding in northwest Europe, while *rubrirostris* has some 385,000–335,000 birds. *Rubrirostris* differs from the western form by having a slightly longer wholly raspberry-pink bill. *Rubrirostris* has several populations stretching from west of the Urals eastwards to China. There is also, however, a central European population (*c*.28,000 birds), often with intermediate types between *anser* and *rubrirostris*, that breeds mainly in Hungary, the Czech and Slovak Republics and Austria. Others breed in the Baltic states, including Finland. Some of the non-

FIG 36. Greylag goose in flight, showing the striking and diagnostic pale forewing. This is the largest of our grey geese, with a large and heavy body. The bill is also big and (in the western race) pale orange. (Alan Williams/NHPA)

breeding Baltic birds move south to moult in Denmark, the Netherlands and Poland. Birds resembling *rubrirostris* have been recorded in Britain, but their status is unclear and this race is not on the BBRC British List. Introduced population of *rubrirostris* on the Continent have apparently been 'genetically swamped' by local *anser* populations, with the resultant offspring not displaying *rubrirostris* characteristics.[90] Several feral populations of greylags in Britain contain birds with pink bills. A bird from Co. Limerick in November 1901 answered the description of a *rubrirostris*, with a wing length of c.490 mm, outside the range of *anser*.[91] There is one accepted record from northeast Iceland, July 1999.[92]

The population breeding in lowland Iceland migrates to winter more or less exclusively in Britain and Ireland. However, it has recently been discovered that a few winter in southern Norway.[93] Small numbers also winter on the Faeroe Islands, while increasing numbers winter on Orkney. Birds arrive in Scotland from mid October onwards and return to Iceland in early April.

Coordinated counts of the wintering population in the UK commenced in 1960. Since then the population increased from about 30,000 birds to 110,000 in the early 1990s. They subsequently declined to around 80,000 but have increased since then to peak at 107,137 in November 2007 (Table 19). One outstanding feature of the recent increase has been the rapid rise in numbers wintering in Orkney, where almost half the wintering UK population now occurs. These numbers represent a significant shift northwards within Scotland. Far fewer greylags winter in Ireland, where there were an estimated 3,800 during the 1980s. By November 2007 numbers had increased to 5,989 birds, the majority of which were considered Icelandic migrants.[94]

TABLE 19. Greylag goose: estimated size of Icelandic population.

DATE	ESTIMATED NUMBER OF BIRDS
1950s	20,000–30,000
Early 1990s	c.110,000
1999	75,866
2000	80,324
2005*	95,938
2006*	82,339
2007*	107,137

* UK, Iceland, southwest Norway, Faeroes and Ireland.

Data from *Goose News* **5**, 10 (2006); **6**, 12 (2007).

Breeding success was relatively steady between 1960 and 1999, with the mean number of first-winter birds in the flocks at 19.9 per cent (range 5.9–45.5 per cent). The decrease in population size during the 1990s was very probably due to a great increase in goose shooting in Iceland, with an estimated 30,000–40,000 shot each year. A total of 30,471 were reported shot in Iceland during 2002, less than the annual mean of 35,720 since 1995.[95] Icelandic goose hunters are now legally obliged, as they are in Denmark, to report what they killed the previous year when renewing their hunting permits. A further estimated 15,000–25,000 are shot annually in the UK. With such apparent shooting pressure, it is hard to understand the overall resilience of the population.

The greylag has probably been a long-time resident, on and off, in Britain and Ireland. There are fossil records at Boxgrove, Sussex, from the warm Cromerian interglacial period (600–500 ky BP) as well as in Suffolk from 500–450 ky BP. Fossils from the Holocene period (10–0 ky BP) have also been found in Irish caves. It was a well-known breeding species up until the last quarter of the eighteenth century in the East Anglian fenlands, but soon afterwards became extinct due to drainage and land reclamation. It also died out at its other English breeding sites in Norfolk, Cambridgeshire, Lincolnshire, East Yorkshire and the Lake District, with the last known wild breeding record in 1831.

An indigenous population endures in the Outer Hebrides, at several sites on the northwest Scottish mainland and in the Highlands. Numbers in this population declined close to extinction in the late 1930s, but were up to about 200 pairs in the 1950s and 1960s and have been increasing since. During the summer of 1997 the population estimate on the Uists (where most of the indigenous population is found, chiefly at Loch Druidibeg on South Uist), Coll–Tiree, Harris–Lewis and other Hebridean islands, and across Caithness and Sutherland, was 10,000 birds, representing a 12 per cent annual increase since the mid-1980s, when there had been an estimated 3,800 geese. The populations breeding on the Inner Hebridean islands of Coll and Tiree have continued to increase during the past ten years. During surveys in August 2007 some 3,694 geese (including goslings) were found on Tiree, and a further 6,440 geese on the Uists (Outer Hebrides).[96] Breeding success of the indigenous population is less variable than that of the Icelandic population. The mean proportion of young birds in the autumn flocks of the Uist breeders is 26.8 per cent, and the mean brood size is 3.7. There has been no significant trend in these figures since 1986. Rough annual adult mortality rates have been calculated, from the proportion of young birds in the flocks together with the total population size of the Uist birds, at approximately 21 per cent. There are also growing breeding populations – more than likely derived from overwintering Icelandic birds and added to by

FIG 37. Greylag goose family. Feral populations of greylag geese are now widespread across Britain and are increasing in number. Clutch size is normally 4–6 eggs. Incubation, by the female only, commences when the last egg is laid to ensure synchronous hatching. The young fledge 50–60 days after hatching and families stay intact until the following winter. (Manfred Danegger/NHPA)

released feral birds – on Orkney (580 breeding pairs plus a further 2,070 non-breeders in 2007) and on Shetland (about 200 birds in total).[97]

Greylags used to breed on the Faeroes until 1830. They re-established themselves around 1940, and in 2005 there were an estimated 250 pairs. Moult migrants, probably from Iceland and exhibiting a curious southward migration, have increased greatly from the first flock of five in 1988 to over 1,200 in 2005. Two of the 111 geese ringed in the semi-tame population in Tórshavn have been recovered in Scotland and Denmark.[98]

There have been numerous translocations and reintroduction programmes, the first during the 1930s, when birds were established in southwest Scotland and East Anglia. Later, more widespread introductions led to large concentrations in gravel pits, lowland river systems, reservoirs and lake complexes (Fig. 37). During these introductions 'indigenous' and 'feral' birds more or less merged into one population. Moreover, many of the feral birds have interbred with white farmyard geese, yielding some bizarrely plumaged offspring. The estimated re-established greylag population in Britain was 22,000 birds in 1989. Surveys conducted during the breeding season in 1999 showed that the geese in southern Britain, on land with a minimum of 5 per cent water cover, had increased at 12 per cent annually since 1989 to reach 30,000 birds. The geese had been increasing even more rapidly than previously estimated, and in many areas they have become a threat to native waterfowl, water quality, agriculture and aviation.[99]

In Ireland the greylag was almost certainly the goose breeding in the Bog of Allen, and in the great red bog in the Ards, near Kirkistown, Co. Down, prior to the mid eighteenth century. The Irish naturalist William Thompson reported that eggs were robbed from the nests of the Co. Down birds prior to 1775. A semi-domesticated population was established at Castle Coole, Co. Fermanagh, around 1700, but it was not until 1960, when other birds were added, that many of the estate birds became feral, spreading out into the surrounding countryside. A feral population was established in Strangford Lough, Co. Down, in 1967 and some 50 birds were reared in 1971. By March 1986 there were an estimated 527 feral birds in the Lough and in nearby lakes.[100] There are also other feral populations in Ireland – at Drumgay Lough and Lower Lough Erne, Co. Fermanagh; Doneraile, Kilcolman and the Gearagh in Co. Cork – that are increasing and expanding their range throughout the country. Some 977 adults were counted at 30 sites throughout the country during July 1994. All breeding greylags in Ireland are thought to be of naturalised origin.

Over 500 adult greylags breeding on the Uists have been ringed during the moulting season. Recoveries of these birds show local movements of up to 30 km between breeding and wintering areas, with only five birds reported travelling away from the Uists – one to Iceland, three to Coll and one to Lewis. Other summering birds ringed at Loch Loyal, Sutherland, showed similar local movements, most within 50 km, with the exception of two birds ringed later in the summer and recovered in the Netherlands during the winter. Reintroduced populations are even more sedentary, with an average recovery distance of 20 km for birds breeding in southwest Scotland. For birds breeding in southeast Britain the median dispersal was 11 km, and only 7 km for birds breeding in southwest Britain. However, it has recently been discovered that some birds ringed on Speech House ponds in the Forest of Dean, Gloucestershire, perform a northerly moult migration to Hogganfield Loch, in the Glasgow suburbs, a round trip of approximately 1,200 km, somewhat akin to the northerly moult migration of Canada geese from Yorkshire and the West Midlands to Beauly Firth, Moray. Geese ringed at Hogganfield have been subsequently observed at the Wildfowl & Wetlands Trust, Slimbridge, Gloucestershire.[101] No ringed Scottish birds have yet been recovered in Ireland, but one Irish-ringed bird from Strangford Lough has travelled across the North Channel to Galloway.

TABLE 20. Greylag goose, Icelandic population: sites in Britain where the mean five-year peak exceeded 2,000 birds. A further 13 sites exceeded the National threshold of 870 birds.

LOCATION	MEAN 5-YEAR PEAK 2002/03–2006/07	PEAK COUNT 2006/07
Orkney	41,645	55,521 (Dec)
Loch Eye/Cromarty Firth, Highland	7,642	2,463 (Nov)
Caithness Lochs, Highland	5,796	2,734 (Mar)
Easterton – Fort George, Highland	3,500	—
Loch of Skene, Aberdeenshire	2,664	500 (Nov)
Dornoch Firth, Highland	2,277	2,858 (Dec)

TABLE 21. Greylag goose, northwest Scottish population: sites in Britain where the mean five-year peak exceeded 90 birds (National threshold).

LOCATION	MEAN 5-YEAR PEAK 2002/03–2006/07	PEAK COUNT 2006/07
Tiree, Argyll & Bute	3,796	4,005 (Aug)
North Uist, Western Isles	2,572	2,318 (Sep)
South Uist, Western Isles	2,029	1,719 (Feb)
Coll, Argyll & Bute	842	856 (Mar)
Benbecula, Western Isles	384	224 (Jan)
Machrihanish, Argyll	272	—
Moine Mhor and Add Estuary, Highland	254	—
Isle of Islay	183	166 (Mar)
Tayinloan, Argyll	141	—
Kentra Moss/ Lower Loch Shiel, Highland	106	90 (Jan)

TABLE 22. Greylag goose, re-established population. Sites in Britain where the mean five-year peak exceeded 800 birds. A further 27 sites exceeded the mean five-year peak of 500 birds (National threshold not yet set).

LOCATION	MEAN 5-YEAR PEAK 2002/03–2006/07	PEAK COUNT 2006/07
Nosterfield Gravel Pits, N Yorkshire	1,875	—
North Norfolk Coast, Norfolk	1,716	(1,725) (Aug)
Lower Derwent Ings, N/E Yorkshire	1,149	—
The Wash, Lincolnshire/Norfolk	1,057	1,337 (Oct)
Tophill Low Reservoirs, E Yorkshire	994	1,190 (Sep)
Livermere and Ampton Water, Suffolk	851	—
Eccup Reservoir, W Yorkshire	841	825 (Oct)
Kikby-on-Bain Gravel Pits, Lincolnshire	802	724 (Nov)

TABLE 23. Greylag goose, Icelandic and re-established populations: sites in Ireland where the mean five-year peak exceeded 100 birds (National threshold 50) or the peak count for 2007/08 exceeded 100. Sites marked # are known mixed flocks of Icelandic and re-established populations.

LOCATION	MEAN 5-YEAR PEAK 1996/97–2000/01	PEAK COUNT 2003/04	PEAK COUNT 2007/08
Lough Swilly, Co. Donegal #	2,388	—	3,413 (Nov)
Stabannan/ Braganstown, Co. Louth + Fane River Plain	1,294	—	650 (Nov)
Loughs Neagh & Beg, Co. Armagh/Down/etc	1,029*	(662) (Feb)*	501 (Jan)
Lough Foyle, Co. Derry	1,024*	974 (Mar)*	218 (Jan)
River Foyle, Co. Donegal	—	—	501 (Dec)

TABLE 23. – *Cont.*

Poulaphouca Reservoir, Co. Wicklow	760	950 (Jan 01)	144 (Jan)
Mountseskin/ Gortlum, Co. Dublin	750	—	—
River Suir Lower, Co. Tipperary	743	1,068 (Jan 00)	201 (Nov)
River Glyde, Co. Louth	509	—	122 (Jan)
Dundalk Bay, Co. Louth	451	—	854 (Dec)
Lambay Island, Co. Dublin	400	—	—
Strangford Lough, Co. Down #	378*	277 (Dec)*	455 (Jan)
N Wicklow coastal marshes, Co. Wicklow	314	501 (Feb 00)	315 (Dec)
Skerries grasslands, Co. Dublin	216	—	—
Belfast Lough, Co. Down.	147*	196 (Nov)*	131 (Nov)
Lower Lough Erne, Co. Fermanagh	139*	(140) (Mar)*	119 (Jan)
Rogerstown Estuary, Co. Dublin	87	—	120 (Nov)
Tacumshin Lake, Co. Wexford #	62	—	121 (Nov)
Shannon & Fergus estuaries, Co. Limerick/ Kerry/Clare	52	—	160 (Jan)
Kilcolman Marsh, Co. Cork	47	—	148 (Dec)
Lough Fern, Co. Donegal	—	—	162 (Nov)
Mullet, Broadhaven & Blacksod Bays, Co. Mayo	—	—	139 (Nov)
Lady's Island Lake, Co. Wexford	—	—	149 (Dec)
Barrow Estuary, Co. Wexford	—	—	156 (Nov)

9. SNOW GOOSE *ANSER CAERULESCENS* (AC2E*)

The snow goose breeds in Arctic North America, northwest Greenland, Alaska and on Wrangel Island off the Siberian coast. There are two races, differing both in body size and in breeding distribution. Both are white-plumaged with black primaries so that in flight the birds look white with black wing tips (Fig. 38). Their bills and feet are deep pink.

The lesser snow goose, *Anser caerulescens caerulescens*, is the smaller of the two races, and the most numerous goose in the world with 7.56 million birds and breeding colonies of upwards 150,000 pairs. Its breeding range extends from Wrangel Island along the west and north coasts of Alaska and through the Canadian Arctic tundra east to Baffin Island. The dark phase of this race – the lesser blue goose, with white only on the head and upper neck and dusky blue-grey elsewhere – was once thought to be an immature snow goose, or even a separate species, but in 1961 it was shown to be only a colour phase of the lesser snow goose. The two phases (also known as morphs) interbreed, giving rise to a bewildering mixture of different-plumaged birds. As the blue phase is genetically dominant it is gradually spreading throughout the breeding range. The American Ornithologists' Union (AOU) has placed the snow geese in the genus *Chen*.

The greater snow goose, *A. c. atlanticus*, breeds further north on Baffin Island, on Bylot Island (off the north coast of Baffin Island) and in the Queen Elizabeth Islands. The total population increased from about 3,000 some hundred years ago to 50,000 in the 1960s, and then to nearly a million in the mid-1990s – but it has been reduced to about 800,000 by deliberately increasing the hunting kill, including the resumption of spring hunting, which had been banned since 1916. This onslaught was justified by complaints about crop damage in Quebec in spring and along the US Atlantic coast in winter. Small numbers breed in northwest Greenland, where some 1,000 adults, not all necessarily breeding, were counted by aerial census in 1970. A few pairs also occur in northeast Greenland. There is no colour phase of this subspecies. Its breeding range now overlaps with that of the lesser snow goose on the west coast of Baffin Island, and they will interbreed.

Serious ecological damage has occurred on the breeding grounds from the sheer density of birds – once valuable feeding areas have been overgrazed and overeaten to such an extent that they are no longer any use to the geese. Similarly, vast flocks of migrating birds can cause considerable damage to agricultural crops while en route to their southern wintering grounds (Fig. 39).

FIG 38. Snow geese in flight. Unlikely to be confused with any other geese apart from Ross's goose, which has similar plumage but is smaller. The average wing length of the male greater and lesser snow geese are 450 mm and 430 mm respectively, while Ross's goose is 385 mm. (Andy Rouse/NHPA)

FIG 39. Snow geese on their wintering grounds at Bosque del Apache, Mexico. (Rich Kirchner/ NHPA)

Their migrations are spectacular, with up to 500,000 birds congregating at one spring staging area between Montreal and Trois-Rivières. During October 2007 I visited their largest stopover in New England, at the Dead Creek Waterfowl refuge near Addison, Vermont (Fig. 40). Here 2,000–3,000 greater snow geese, along with lesser snow geese, including the blue morph, plus a few Ross's geese, were eating corn on the cob, walking around with the cobs hanging from their massive bills and tossing them around as if they were toys. The geese had become so accustomed to the security of the refuge that they allowed me to approach within 10 m.

There are no published fossil records of snow geese from Britain and Ireland, as might be expected from a Nearctic species. There is, however, a doubtful Late Pleistocene record from Italy.

Snow geese, in their various forms, are winter vagrants to Britain and Ireland, occurring almost annually – but more frequently in Ireland and Scotland than further south in Britain. These are genuine transatlantic birds, with records for most years, often in the company of other wild geese, especially Greenland

FIG 40. Greater snow geese at Otter Creek, Vermont – a favourite halting place during the autumn migration when the geese are on their way to their wintering grounds on the Atlantic coastline, mainly around Chesapeake Bay but also south to North Carolina. (David Cabot)

white-fronts. In Ireland a total of 58 wild snow geese were recorded between 1800 and 1949, with a further 44 (including some returning birds) during 1950–2006. Most records were of indeterminate snow geese, with four certain lesser and two greater snow geese. The blue morph (Fig. 41) is by far the rarer of the two forms in Ireland, outnumbered by pale birds by about 9 to 1. It has been recorded about 12 times to the end of 2006. As the species is a scarce but no longer rare winter visitor to Great Britain, statistics are not published by the BBRC.

For several years between 1937 and 1946 various white-headed geese were reported from the Wexford Slobs that were almost certainly blue geese. In January and April 1946 three were positively identified as blue geese – two possibly immatures, the other an adult – the first ever recorded in these islands. They were the forerunners of more to come. Some have been paired to Greenland white-fronts with hybrid young, the first recorded during the winter 1953/54, followed by more in subsequent winters. The first record of a blue goose in Ireland outside the Wexford Slobs was a single adult I saw on the Inishkea Islands, Co. Mayo, in early January 1973, and again it was closely associated with Greenland white-fronts.

A total of 16 snow geese, almost all considered feral or escaped birds, were noted in Britain during WeBS 2006/07, the lowest ever recorded by WeBS and some 25 per cent fewer than in the previous winter. Most were single birds, but a few sites held more than eight birds. Blenheim Park, Oxfordshire, had 14 in

FIG 41. Lesser snow goose, blue morph. The proportion of blue geese breeding with lesser snow geese in eastern Canadian colonies has increased in recent years, and the proportion declines from east to west. (Bill Coster/NHPA)

FIG 42. Lesser snow goose adult with five goslings. The average clutch size is
3–4 eggs, and during incubation by the female the male remains close to the nest.
The female and male lose 35–40 and 15–20 per cent of their body weight respectively
during incubation. The goslings leave the nest within 24 hours of hatching and
fledge at 6–8 weeks old, just as the adults regain their flight after the moult. Of all
eggs laid, only some 30–60 per cent result in fledged goslings. (Brian Hawkes/NHPA)

September, with lower numbers at Lower Windrush Gravel Pits, Oxfordshire.
There were four possible genuine vagrants. In Northern Ireland there is at least
one feral flock established around Larne and Strangford Loughs. It is highly
doubtful if the occasionally reported blue geese in Northern Ireland (four in 2001
and six in 2002) were wild birds.

Some of the escaped snow geese seen in Britain and Ireland have bred as
singles, while others have formed self-sustaining populations. In western
Scotland there is a self-sustaining free-winged population of approximately
40–50 birds breeding on the islands of Mull and Coll, Argyll. Coll, now the main
breeding location, had nine pairs that raised at least 28 goslings in 2000. Twenty-
four adults raised ten young in 2002 (Fig. 42). The total population on Coll has
not increased despite good productivity. Many of the birds were colour-ringed in
2002 but none has been reported from the immediate vicinity of Coll,

suggesting that birds seen elsewhere in Britain have not originated from here. In Hampshire declining numbers – 13 in 2003, no successful breeding – occur at Eversley, while one or two pairs breed annually at Stratfield Saye. In Oxfordshire small numbers have bred in the Lower Windrush area and small numbers have fledged near Stanton Harcourt and Lynch Hill, the birds spending the non-breeding season at Blenheim. Birds in this population peaked at 33 in 1991 but declined to 17 by 2002. None of these southern English populations is considered self-sustaining.[102]

In Ireland it is unusual to find escapes nesting in the wild. However, in May 1973 I found a pair with a clutch of six eggs on Little Saltee Island, Co. Wexford – but breeding was unsuccessful.

10. GREATER CANADA GOOSE
BRANTA CANADENSIS (**AC2E***; **A** Ireland only)

The Canada goose is a native to North America, where until recently, depending upon one's taxonomic stance, there were 10–12 subspecies. However, in 2005 the American Ornithologists' Union (AOU) split the Canada goose into two species,[103] a decision accepted by Taxonomic Sub-Committee (TSC) of the BOURC. The decision was based on mitochondrial DNA differences and supported by the absence of interbreeding and differences in arrival dates, nesting habits and nest structure. The two species are:

1 The greater Canada goose, *Branta canadensis*. Polytypic, with seven subspecies: *canadensis* (Atlantic), *fulva* (Vancouver), *interior* (interior), *maxima* (giant), *moffitti* (Moffit's), *occidentalis* (dusky) and *parvipes*. This species has a mainly continental distribution within North America.
2 The lesser Canada goose, or cackling goose, *Branta hutchinsii*. Polytypic, with five subspecies: *hutchinsii* (Richardson's), *leucopareia* (Aleutian), *minima* (cackling), *taverneri* and *asiatica* (probably extinct). This species breeds in coastal Alaska and Arctic Canada.

The two species look similar, although the greater Canada goose is considerably larger than the lesser, and there are also differences in the proportion of the neck, the darkness and barring of the plumage, the amount of white on the lower neck and the pattern of the cheek patch. However, a study of mitochondrial DNA sequences has indicated that the two groups are not each other's closest relatives. The lesser Canada goose clade/group is more closely

FIG 43. Greater Canada goose in flight over southern England. This is the largest and longest-necked goose in Europe. Easily distinguished from other black geese by dark brown plumage, black bill and white facial patch on black head. Often heard flying at night, uttering their characteristic honking call, 'ah hank'. (Bill Coster/NHPA)

related to the barnacle goose, while the greater Canada goose forms a sister-group relationship with a group of geese endemic to Hawaii, of which the Hawaiian goose is the sole extant species.[104] The Canada goose (greater and lesser) is the second most numerous goose in the world, numbering 6.23 million birds.

King Charles II can be held responsible for its introduction to Britain in 1665 when birds were imported to enhance his waterfowl collection in St James's Park, London (Fig. 43). Elsewhere in Europe captive Canada geese were also breeding in large numbers in the park at Versailles during the reign (1643–1715) of Louis XIV.[105] They were much later introduced to Sweden (1929), Norway (1936) and Finland (early 1960s), subsequently spreading to other European countries. Their large size, and the tendency of British-resident Canada geese to have a backwards-pointing hook at the top of the white cheek, strongly suggests that British birds originated principally from the nominate race of the greater Canada goose (*B. c. canadensis*), with some contribution from the giant Canada goose (*B. c. maxima*).[106] These races are highly migratory in America, in contrast with the sedentary nature of British and Irish resident birds. However, some British populations, mostly from the Midlands, have a pronounced northerly moult migration. There are no published fossil records of Canada geese from Britain or Ireland.

Those introduced into Britain remained relatively scarce until the second half of the twentieth century. They then adapted so successfully to the new environment created by changes in agriculture that within 50 years they have reached pest proportions in many locations, causing agricultural damage, enhancing water eutrophication, interfering with public amenities, disrupting the ecology of other water birds, causing genetic pollution through hybridising with other geese, as well as posing collision hazards to air traffic. Their introduction and subsequent expansion – aided by hunters – provides a classic example of human folly in tinkering around with nature. Or is it more simply a case, albeit artificially speeded up, of the natural expansion and spread of this species? On the positive side, introduced Canada geese have brought much pleasure to people visiting urban and rural parks, gravel pits and other areas frequented by the geese. They are spectacular birds, often allowing close approach and thus offering the general public their best opportunity of encountering a goose.

Despite being widespread throughout Britain by the 1950s, there were only an estimated 2,200–4,000 birds in 1953. By 1991 they had risen to 64,000. More recently, during the breeding season 1999, a minimum of 82,000 geese was estimated to be in Britain (based on a sample of 246 tetrads from the 1988–91 *New Atlas*). The average rate of increase of greater Canada geese in lowland areas with at least 5 per cent water cover was 9.9 per cent a year over the previous ten years, and numbers were still rising very rapidly.[107] Indices of wintering numbers monitored by WeBS show an increase of 24 per cent during the period 1991–2001 and a remarkable fivefold increase from 1971 to 2001. The long-term increase looks set to continue, with the WeBS index at its highest level during 2006/07. If the population resumes its previous high rates of growth, population control measures – seldom popular with the public – may have to be intensified. Each year between 1991 and 1995 some 2,000 adults and 4,000–10,000 eggs were destroyed, under licence, mainly in England. The estimated annual adult mortality, based on ringing recoveries, is 10–20 per cent. There is little regional variation in mortality, suggesting the absence of density-dependent regulation of survival and hence more room for expansion of the population (Fig. 44).

Far fewer breed in Ireland. There are feral populations on Strangford Lough, Co. Down, on Upper and Lower Lough Erne, Co. Fermanagh, and elsewhere in Northern Ireland. There is also a feral population breeding at The Lough, Cork. Despite the attractiveness of Loughs Neagh and Beg, none have been recorded there by WeBS. Overall numbers in Ireland are increasing. WeBS recorded a 50 per cent increase in Northern Ireland between 2004/05 and 2005/06, and while there is no I-WeBS figure for the total Irish population, I would estimate total numbers in 2008 to be somewhere between 1,800 and 2,400 birds.

FIG 44. Greater Canada goose. The British population is booming, kept in check to some extent by population control measures. (Ken Kinsella)

Some British-breeding Canada geese have a pronounced northerly moult migration, a genetic echo of their North American ancestors. The geese involved are non-breeders, failed breeders and immature birds. They originate principally from Yorkshire and the Midlands, with smaller numbers coming from further south. Most of the moulters set off on their journey north in May and June to the Beauly Firth, a shallow estuary in northern Scotland. Several hundreds spend the summer months there, benefiting from the rich food supplies. The advantages of the moult migration – safe and secure areas and abundant food supplies – must outweigh the disadvantages of the round trip of at least 1,200 km. In the 1970s, Yorkshire-ringed birds undertaking the journey were found to have a 16 per cent lower survival rate compared with geese that remained at home to moult locally.[108]

Successful breeders moult locally, moving to large water bodies – flooded gravel pits, lakes and reservoirs – for safety and security. Recoveries from over 56,000 British-ringed birds show that most geese are sedentary, with a median recovery distance of 11 km (range 4–29 km). During severe weather birds may move further, as shown by the four geese that travelled to France during the intense cold of January/February 1963. Other records of long-distance movements have been two from the Faeroes, one from the USA, seven from France (including the three mentioned above) and one from the River Ob in western Siberia. Birds ringed abroad and recovered in Britain have been one from the USA (probably a genuine transatlantic migrant), four from Norway (one of which was a captive bird) and one from Sweden.

In Ireland 60 sightings of Canada geese between 1950 and 2006, mainly between October and April, were of genuine vagrants and accepted by the IRBC. These Canada geese, assumed to belong to the greater Canada goose group, are now almost annual winter visitors with Greenland barnacle geese to west Mayo. During early April of 2008 Larry Griffin of the WWT and I identified two separate birds feeding among the barnacle goose flocks on the Inishkea Islands. These Canada geese were about the same size as the barnacle geese. Some of these have been observed in previous years paired to barnacle geese with hybrid offspring.

TABLE 24. Greater Canada goose: sites in Britain where the mean five-year peak exceeded 800 birds (no National threshold). Another 21 sites exceeded 600 birds.

LOCATION	MEAN 5-YEAR PEAK 2002/03–2006/07	PEAK COUNT 2006/07
Dyfi Estuary, Dyfed	2,643	2,420 (Nov)
Dee Estuary (England and Wales)	2,097	2,087 (Jun)
Mersey Estuary, Cheshire	1,763	1,923 (Nov)
Colliford Reservoir, Cornwall	1,585	2,439 (Jun)
Rutland Water, Leicestershire	1,215	1,118 (Jun)
Fairburn Ings, W Yorkshire	1,209	609 (Jul)
Arun Valley, W Sussex	1,135	1,076 (Dec)
Taw-Torridge Estuary, Devon	924	986 (Jan)
Alde Complex, Suffolk	903	684 (Dec)
Ellesmere Lakes, Shropshire	890	873 (Sep)
Doxey Marshes, Staffordshire	859	802 (Jan)
Stour Estuary, Essex	857	569 (Jan)
Bewl Water, Sussex	856	518 (Jan)
Osberton, Nottinghamshire	820	1,212 (Nov)

TABLE 25. Greater Canada goose: sites in Ireland where the mean five-year peak exceeded 20 birds (no National threshold).

LOCATION	MEAN 5-YEAR PEAK FROM 1996/97	PEAK COUNT 2000/01
Upper Lough Erne, Co. Fermanagh	418*	665 (Jan)*
Lower Lough Erne, Co. Fermanagh	313*	365 (Jan)*
Strangford Lough, Co. Down	273*	247 (Oct)*
Lough Oughter Complex, Co. Cavan	86	83 (Jan)
Lough McNean Lower, Cos. Leitrim, Cavan & Fermanagh	77*	44 (Mar)*
Woodford River Lakes, Co. Cavan	70	—
River Erne N of Belturbet, Co. Cavan	63	93 (Jan)
East Ballinamore Lakes, Co. Cavan	57	110 (Sep)
Lough Swilly, Co. Donegal	50	60 (Sep)
Ballycotton, Shanagarry, Co. Cork	28	15 (Sep)

11. LESSER CANADA GOOSE *BRANTA HUTCHINSII* (C2E*; currently under review by BOURC and IRBC)

Virtually every winter there are records of almost certain genuine vagrant lesser Canada geese (Fig. 45) that have crossed the Atlantic, often in the company of Greenland white-fronts. They also sometimes arrive with Greenland barnacle geese. Most records have come from Ireland, especially the northwest coast, with fewer from Scotland. However, neither the BOURC nor the IRBC has yet been able to accept any records of lesser Canada geese. The issue is under active review.[109] When the matter of its status on the British and Irish Lists has been resolved it is possible that the lesser Canada goose may be renamed the cackling goose. For the moment the status of the lesser Canada goose is a vexing situation for the many ornithologists who have observed these supposed transatlantic vagrants.

FIG 45. Lesser Canada goose, probable race *hutchinsii*, with barnacle geese in Co. Sligo. About the same size as a barnacle goose, possibly smaller, with pale chest and very small bill. This bird arrived with barnacle geese from the breeding grounds in northeast Greenland. Adult *hutchinsii* has mean wing length and weight 371 mm and 1.95 kg; barnacle goose 412 mm and 2.10 kg. (Mícheál Casey)

At the end of November 1992, a neck-banded Canada goose was seen in the company of an unringed bird close to Alford, near Aberdeen. Both remained in the area until they were shot in January 1993. The banded bird had been ringed as a second-year male in Maryland, USA, in February 1992, and it was the first transatlantic recovery of a ringed Canada goose. The marked Alford bird was described as being about the size of a pink-footed goose, and was therefore considered to belong to the lesser Canada goose group.

During WeBS 2006/07 lesser Canada geese were noted at Bothal Pond, Northumberland (January/February) and at Pennington Flash, Wigan (September to March). The Bothal Pond bird arrived with wild barnacle geese and was suspected of being a genuine vagrant.

Some lesser Canada geese are found in the naturalised British population of the greater Canada goose, but they do not occur in significant or self-sustaining numbers.[110]

There are no published records of fossils of this goose from Britain or Ireland.

12. BARNACLE GOOSE *BRANTA LEUCOPSIS* (AC2E*)

Barnacle geese are the most visually striking of all our wintering wild geese – boldly contrasted black, white and grey with a prominent white face and forehead. Their calls are less musical than those of the grey geese, consisting of a series of rapidly repeated monosyllabic barks that, when made by a flock in flight, have been likened to the yelping of a pack of small terriers. They are highly gregarious, feeding in tightly packed winter flocks. British and Irish wintering barnacle geese nest in the Arctic and are visitors here from October to the end of April, frequenting remote coastal regions of the west and north of Ireland as well as the west and north coasts of Scotland. There is also a feral breeding population in Britain and Ireland, thought to have been derived from Greenland breeding stock.

There are three separate Arctic breeding populations located in: (1) northeast Greenland (70° to 79° N), wintering on the west and north coasts of Ireland and Scotland (Fig. 46); (2) the Svalbard archipelago (76° 30′ to 80° N), wintering on the north and south sides of the Solway Firth, principally at Caerlaverock and Southerness in Scotland and at Rockcliffe Marsh, Burgh Marsh and Moricambe Bay (not to be confused with Morecambe Bay further south) in England; (3) the Russian Arctic, along the coast of the Barents Sea and the western Kara Sea (67° to 73° N). There are two other breeding populations: (4) a Baltic breeding population, probably derived from Russian birds, which became established in the early 1970s on the islands off Sweden, Estonia and Finland; and (5) a North Sea population breeding along the North Sea coast of Denmark. The Russian, Baltic and North Sea breeding birds winter together in northern Germany and the Netherlands, and their combined population size is 420,000 birds. Most of the Russian breeders travel some 3,000 km from their Arctic staging grounds near the breeding grounds, departing just before the onset of frost and snowfall. They arrive directly on the wintering grounds in the Wadden Sea some one to three days after departing Arctic Russia. Only the Greenland and Svalbard breeding populations that winter in Britain and Ireland will be considered in this chapter.

Despite the close proximity of the Solway Firth (principal wintering site of Svalbard birds) and Islay (principal wintering site of Greenland birds) – a distance of some 190 km – the Svalbard and Greenland birds retain their discreteness, demonstrating little interchange between the wintering populations. Up to the end of December 1992 some 14 individuals from the Svalbard population, marked either in Svalbard or on the Solway Firth, had been observed on Islay,[111] and six Svalbard birds had been recorded among the

FIG 46. Barnacle geese on Islay. The geese that winter on Islay are part of the Greenland breeding population. (Andy Rouse/NHPA)

Greenland population wintering in the west of Ireland, while two birds ringed on the Inishkea Islands, Co. Mayo, travelled to the Solway Firth. Some Svalbard geese have also joined the Russian population wintering in the Netherlands, and to the end of 1990 eight Svalbard birds had been recorded wintering with Russian birds. Three subsequently returned to winter on the Solway Firth, and at least four became permanent members of the Russian population. It was estimated by extrapolation that at least 40 Svalbard geese had visited the winter grounds of the Russian population.[112] Despite these meanderings, over 8,000 Svalbard geese have been colour-ringed, and subsequent observations of these have confirmed the separateness of the population – no recorded immigration and only a 0.1 per cent annual emigration rate.[113]

While the interchange of geese between the three populations is infrequent, to what degree are the populations genetically isolated? Unlike some other geese – white-fronted, bean and brant – that winter in Britain and Ireland, barnacle geese have yet to be shown to have developed significant DNA, morphological or plumage differences that would merit the designation of races, or subspecies. It may be that despite the apparent low frequency of population interchange there is sufficient gene flow to work against the evolution of subspecies. It has been suggested that as few as 5–16 immigrants per generation inhibit the formation of a new species,[114] but in the case of the Svalbard barnacle goose population there are 17 effective immigrants per generation – and this may account for the fact that there has been no subspeciation in the barnacle goose.[115] In addition, it is thought that the populations have only been geographically separated for a relatively short historic period.

Unlike other wildfowl populations such as the mallard, whose breeding population has increased steadily since the 1960s, probably enhanced by large-scale releases of hand-reared birds, but whose wintering population has declined since the late 1980s and has probably been held in check by density-dependent factors, the Greenland and Svalbard barnacle goose populations have increased dramatically during the past 40 years. The Greenland population expanded from 8,300 individuals in 1959 to 56,386 in March/April 2003, and then to 70,501 in March 2008, an approximate 847 per cent increase.[116]

The Svalbard population grew from 3,000–4,000 birds in the 1960s to a peak of 29,815 counted in the Solway Firth in November 2007, a gain of approximately 840 per cent, remarkably similar to the performance of the Greenland population over the same period. The wintering Solway Firth population has remained more or less stable over the past ten years, increasing only by about 5 per cent since 1997/98. In recent years productivity has been exceptionally low, with less than 4 per cent young in the winter flocks in four of the past five years.

However, in the winter 2007/08 there were 12.8 per cent young birds, well above the current ten-year mean of 8.5 per cent. Mean brood size was 2.4 per successful pair, well up on the ten-year mean of 1.9.[117] Historically, mortality from shooting held down both populations to the point where they were considered to be at dangerously low levels in the late 1950s.[118] When shooting was banned in Britain and Ireland, in association with the creation of nature reserves, numbers took off without any density-dependent factors to restrain the increases. Shooting had been responsible for most of the adult mortality, and when it ceased adult survival rates increased dramatically. Abundant food resources on the wintering grounds and in the spring and autumn staging areas, together with the availability of unlimited safe breeding sites, aided the population increases.

TABLE 26. Barnacle goose, Svalbard population: sites in Britain where the mean five-year peak exceeded 270 birds (International threshold; National threshold 220).

LOCATION	MEAN 5-YEAR PEAK 2002/03–2006/07	PEAK COUNT 2006/07
Solway Firth, Cumbria/ Dumfries & Galloway	28,409	29,370 (Dec)
Loch of Strathbeg, Aberdeenshire	736	181 (Oct)
Lindisfarne, Northumberland	612	1,202 (Oct)

After breeding, Greenland barnacle geese travel to southern Iceland at the end of August, remaining there until departing, at the end of September or early October, to winter in Scotland and Ireland. In late August many of the Svalbard birds move some 250 km south to the southernmost of the Svalbard islands, Bjørnøya (Bear Island), where they spend three weeks before travelling on to the Solway Firth – while others probably travel directly from Svalbard to Solway.

Islay is the favoured wintering haunt of the Greenland population (Fig. 47), holding nearly 64 per cent of the total British and Irish population in 2007/08. That winter, numbers peaked on Islay at 51,485, underpinning the increase of approximately 23 per cent over the past five years. The food resources on the island are particularly attractive, and the geese preferentially select reseeded Italian ryegrass pastures. They also feed on spilt and sprouting grain in barley and oat stubble fields during the autumn. At another important winter haunt, on the Inishkea Islands, Co. Mayo, the geese feed mainly on white clover stolons

during the autumn, switching to red fescue and smooth meadow-grass as the
stolons become depleted. The mainland population at Lissadell–Ballintemple,
Co. Sligo, feeds on improved grassland. On the Solway Firth the barnacle geese
feed on the salt marsh, where the stolons of white clover comprise the bulk of
the autumn food, and later turn to grasses and herbs, red fescue, common
saltmarsh-grass and sea arrowgrass. On the improved pastures at Caerlaverock
NNR the geese feed principally on perennial ryegrass.[119]

The large numbers on Islay have created agricultural conflicts. Shooting the
geese was permitted until a total ban in 1981, but thereafter licences for killing
were issued by the Scottish Office Agriculture, Environment and Fisheries
Department to protect crops from 'serious agricultural damage', an option
available under the EU Wild Birds Directive. However, rather than shooting the
geese, about 100 of the affected farmers have found it more convenient to receive
about £400,000 (about €450,000) per annum for the past seven years from
Scottish National Heritage in compensation for goose damage. Damage is
assessed on the average goose use per affected holding of land. The geese are also
'encouraged' off farmland into three island sanctuaries, including the RSPB's
Lough Gruinart reserve, as alternative feeding locations. Barnacle goose breeding
biology is discussed in Chapter 6.

FIG 47. Barnacle geese on Islay. All these are adult geese, as indicated by the white tips
to their wing coverts. Juvenile and first-winter birds are identified by brown tips on the
wing coverts. (Laurie Campbell/NHPA)

TABLE 27. Barnacle goose, Greenland population: sites in Britain where the mean five-year peak exceeded 560 birds (International threshold).

LOCATION	MEAN 5-YEAR PEAK 2002/03–2006/07	MARCH 2008
Isle of Islay, Argyll & Bute	44,139	44,961
Tiree, Argyll & Bute	3,330	3,393
North Uist, Western Isles	2,579	4,005*
South Walls (Hoy), Orkney	1,858	1,612
Isle of Coll, Argyll & Bute	1,559	167
Colonsay/Oronsay, Argyll & Bute	870	1,200
Sound of Harris (NW) (Harris) Western Isles	706	—
North Sutherland, Highland	669	—
Balnakeil Bay, Highland	642	—

* Outer Hebrides. Data from Mitchell *et al.*, 2008.

TABLE 28. Barnacle goose, Greenland population: sites in Ireland where counts exceeded 300 birds during the 2008 census (National threshold 90). Results from the 2003 census are included for comparison purposes.

LOCATION	MARCH 2003 AERIAL/GROUND SURVEY RESULTS	MARCH 2008 AERIAL/GROUND SURVEY RESULTS
Lissadell/Ballintemple, Co. Sligo	2,300	3,930
Inishkea Islands, Co. Mayo	2,052	2,525
Termoncarragh, Co. Mayo	210	850
Inishark, Co. Galway	470	444
Rathlin O'Birne, Co. Donegal	475	370
Croaghnkeela, Co. Galway	4	330
Duvillaun, Co. Galway	161	320
Dunfanaghy, Co. Donegal	—	320
Trawbreaga Bay, Co. Donegal	254	317

Data from Worden *et al.*, 2004a; A. Walsh, personal communication.

It is probable that barnacles once bred much further south than at present, possibly in Scotland and Ireland, moving their breeding and wintering grounds according to the extent of ice during the last 150,000 years. During the Weichselian glacial period the present-day northeast Greenland and Russian breeding grounds were covered by up to 500 m and 2,000 m of ice respectively. During the glacial retreat, breeding grounds became available in Svalbard about 10,000 years ago, followed by present breeding areas in northeast Greenland and Russia about 2,000 years ago.[120] When the breeding populations were pushed south by the glaciers (115–35 ky BP) the geese migrated, during the winter period, to north and south Spain (four fossil remains), southern Italy (four sites), Malta (four sites) as well to Jersey.

The earliest known probable fossils from the UK, dating from the Middle Pleistocene period (c.420–360 ky BP), come from Swanscombe, Kent. More remains, dating from the Late Pleistocene, have been recorded at four other UK sites: Sutherland (13–10 ky BP); Little Hoyle, Pembrokeshire (bone dated 22,800 ± 300 BP); Somerset (10 ky BP); and Derbyshire (c.20 ky BP). More recent fossils, dating from the Late Pleistocene–Holocene (10–0 ky BP), have been found in Co. Waterford, and bones have been recorded from the Lagore crannog site, Co. Meath, (AD 750–950).

Escaped birds from captive collections breed widely in Britain and on Strangford Lough, Co. Down, where a feral population was established in the 1940s. The Strangford population appears to be self-sustaining; a total of 279 were counted there in October 2006, representing almost all the naturalised barnacle geese in Northern Ireland.

After the first British breeding was recorded at London Zoo in 1848, the species became well established at Woburn and other locations before 1914. During the 1968–72 *Atlas* survey breeding or suspected breeding birds were recorded in two 10 km squares. The *New Atlas* survey in 1988–91 revealed that they were breeding in 45 squares in widely scattered locations, but not thought to be self-sustaining. However, those breeding in Bedfordshire and Norfolk/Suffolk were considered self-sustaining in 2005. During 2002 there were probably between 20 and 30 breeding pairs in nine localities in eight British counties, rearing a minimum of 65 young.[121] After a notable increase during the 20 years to 2000/01, the WeBS index of the naturalised population has remained relatively stable (Table 29). Counts of 'naturalised' barnacle geese are based on geographic location, however, and it is possible that some extralimital birds from the Svalbard, Greenland and Russian populations may have been included amongst these birds. In Table 29 the winter numbers are swollen by non-breeding birds and possible immigrants.

TABLE 29. Barnacle goose, naturalised population: sites in Britain where the mean five-year peak exceeded 50 birds (no National threshold).

LOCATION	MEAN 5-YEAR PEAK 2002/03–2006/07	PEAK COUNT 2006/07
Lound Waterworks, Suffolk	249	104 (Feb)
Willington, Bedfordshire	191	—
Benacre Broad, Suffolk	182	359 (Sep)
Humber Estuary, E Yorkshire	172	318 (Feb)
Roxton Gravel Pits, Bedfordshire	162	128 (Apr)
Eversley Cross & Yateley GPs, Hampshire	119	49 (Oct)
Ullswater, Cumbria	115	186 (Mar)
Severn Estuary, Gloucestershire/Somerset/etc	109	126 (Jan)
Derwent Water, Cumbria	102	137 (Jun)
Frampton Pools, Gloucestershire	91	114 (Mar)
Hornsea Mere, E Yorkshire	89	72 (Feb)
Duddon Estuary, Cumbria	(88)	(10) (Dec)
Minsmere, Suffolk	81	17 (May)
Middle Yare Marsh, Norfolk	80	70 (Oct)
The Hen Reedbeds, Suffolk	(68)	(0)
Barcombe Mills Reservoir, E Sussex	58	53 (Nov)

13. BRANT GOOSE *BRANTA BERNICLA* (AE)

There are, at present, three recognised subspecies of this goose, two of which winter in Britain and Ireland – the dark-bellied nominate race, *Branta bernicla bernicla*, and the light-bellied form, *B. b. bernicla hrota*. Both are small, mostly black above and either light (*hrota*) or dark (*bernicla*) on the belly, with a small whitish patch on either side of the neck. They are, like the barnacle goose,

FIG 48. Dark-bellied brant geese in flight, Kent. Both are adults, as indicated by their conspicuous white necklaces. First-winter brant have no or much less conspicuous necklaces. Their dark bellies, almost uniform with the black chest, distinguish them from light-bellied brant. (Bill Coster/NHPA)

gregarious and often noisy – fast and acrobatic flyers with a characteristic call, 'rott-rott', the r rolled. When feeding on mudflats they exhibit a small, muscular-like demeanour, heads down, walking fast and purposefully over the ooze and mud. But today many have developed the habit of feeding on improved grassland, on football pitches, in public parks, on golf courses and even on busy roadside grass verges adjacent to petrol stations in Dublin city.

Because of the taxonomic complexity of *Branta bernicla* the AERC's TAC carried out a review in 2003 as to whether to upgrade the three subspecies to full species, namely the dark-bellied brant goose, *Branta bernicla*, the light-bellied brant goose, *B. hrota*, and the black brant, *B. nigricans*. This proposal was not supported, and so, for the moment, a single species with three subspecies is recognised. The issue of the possibility of another form, the grey-bellied brant, is discussed later.

The dark-bellied form (Fig. 48) breeds principally along the Russian Arctic coastline of the Taymyr Peninsula from 73° to 79° N and from 75° to 122° E.[122] They are famous for their population crash in the early 1930s, when their principal coastal and estuarine food, the eelgrass, was decimated by a 'wasting disease' associated with a slime-mould that wiped out much of the eelgrass in western Europe. Numbers plummeted from several hundred thousands to fewer than 20,000, declining even further to 12,000–15,000 in the 1950s due to excessive shooting. Since then, encouraged by protection from hunting, especially in Denmark from 1972 onwards, numbers have recovered and appear to have stabilised at approximately 300,000 in the early 1990s. In recent years the rate of population growth has slowed, with reduced breeding success suggesting the onset of density-dependent control factors. The population was estimated at 200,000 in 1992.

Fossil remains have been found in five British locations dating from the Middle Pleistocene to recent times.

Approximately 98,100 dark-bellied brant geese winter in Britain, distributed along the south and east coasts from the Bury Inlet in south Wales around to the Humber Estuary in Yorkshire/Lincolnshire. Poor breeding success since the early 1990s was responsible for a 29 per cent decline in numbers wintering in the UK, as determined by WeBS, between 1994 and 2004. However, wintering numbers now show a clear sign of recovering following the ten-year decline. The WeBS national index rose for the third consecutive year in 2006/07. Those that winter on the Maplin Sands off Foulness, attracted there by vast beds of eelgrass, are well known for the star roles they played in discouraging the development of London's proposed third airport during the early 1970s. The balance of the population winters along the Atlantic coast of France (including the Channel Islands) and in the Wadden Sea (Denmark, Germany and the Netherlands).

There is some evidence to suggest a correlation between the abundance of lemmings at the brant's breeding grounds and the breeding success of the geese. When lemmings are abundant there is little need for Arctic Foxes to prey on the geese, whereas during lemming scarcity foxes and other predators turn to brant goslings as an important source of food. Breeding success of the geese, judged by the proportion of young birds in the winter flocks, has recently followed the three-year cycle of lemming abundance and scarcity.

Small numbers of dark-bellied brant are recorded each winter in Ireland. Between 1950 and the end of 2006 there were approximately 225 individuals recorded, mostly singles or pairs. Their frequency of occurrence has been increasing in recent years.

TABLE 30. Dark-bellied brant goose: sites in Britain where the mean five-year peak exceeded 2,000 birds (International threshold; National threshold 981). A further 13 sites exceeded the National threshold.

LOCATION	MEAN 5-YEAR PEAK 2002/03–2006/07	PEAK COUNT 2006/07
The Wash, Lincolnshire/Norfolk	21,276	20,870 (Feb)
Thames Estuary, Kent/Essex/Greater London	10,041	8,100 (Nov)
Chichester Harbour, West Sussex	8,341	9,605 (Dec)
North Norfolk Coast, Norfolk	7,486	7,091 (Nov)
Blackwater Estuary, Essex	6,029	(2,217) (Feb)
Hamford Water, Essex	4,567	4,089 (Jan)
Langstone Harbour, Hampshire	4,333	4,650 (Feb)
Crouch-Roach Estuary, Essex	3,693	(4,312) (Feb)
Humber Estuary, E Yorkshire/Lincolnshire	3,352	4,586 (Feb)
Portsmouth Harbour, Hampshire	3,604	3,162 (Feb)
Pagham Harbour, W Sussex	2,336	2,744 (Dec)
Colne Estuary, Essex	2,331	(1,296) (Feb)
Dengie Flats, Essex	2,003	2,901 (Dec)

Light-bellied brant geese (Fig. 49) wintering in Britain and Ireland arise from two separate breeding populations. The first is the smallest discrete population of geese in the world, breeding on Svalbard (4,000–5,800 individuals), on Franz Josef Land (c.1,000 individuals) and also in a remote valley at Kilen in northeastern Greenland (c.1,000 individuals).[123] The Kilen breeding population had formerly been thought to be part of the Canadian high Arctic population, but in 1997 Preben Clausen and Jan Bustnes, using satellite telemetry, showed that some of the birds wintering in Denmark migrated a further 700 km north of Svalbard to Kilen, flying further than aerodynamic models predicted without the geese stopping to feed.[124] Either the models were wrong or the geese exploited favourable wind conditions.

FIG 49. Light-bellied brant goose. The light, almost whitish underbody distinguishes this subspecies from the dark-bellied brant. Otherwise there are virtually no other plumage or behavioural differences. (Joe Blossom/NHPA)

These goose populations belong to the so-called 'East Atlantic population'. They winter in Denmark and at Lindisfarne, Northumberland. Each September about 3,000 (mean five-year peak from 2003–07 was 3,315 birds) arrive at Lindisfarne NNR, departing for Denmark in February–March. Numbers fluctuate from year to year, depending upon the severity of Continental winters and how many birds are driven west from Denmark. Smaller numbers are recorded annually in the Inner Moray Firth, Highland, and in a few other British localities. The remaining geese from this population winter in Denmark, especially in north and west Jutland. Small numbers also find their way to the Netherlands each winter, rising to 100–200 when severe weather pushes birds out of Denmark. Breeding success is highly variable – a mean 15 per cent young birds in winter flocks between 1980 and 1996, with no apparent trend. Annual survival rates, based on ring recoveries from Svalbard in 1954 and on population counts 1981–95, are 0.83 and 0.87 respectively.[125]

TABLE 31. Light-bellied brant goose, East Atlantic population: sites in Britain where the mean five-year peak exceeded 35 birds (National threshold). No other recorded sites.

LOCATION	MEAN 5-YEAR PEAK 2002/03–2006/07	PEAK COUNT 2006/07
Lindisfarne, Northumberland	3,315	3,350 (Oct)
Inner Moray and Inverness Firth, Highland	59	43 (Jan)

The other population of light-bellied brant geese wintering in Ireland and Britain is of transatlantic origin, from the high Arctic of eastern Canada, hence their alternative name of 'East Canadian High Arctic population'. Breeding on the eastern Queen Elizabeth Islands from Melville Island (c.108° W) to northern Ellesmere Island (c.80° N), they spend their winter almost exclusively in Ireland, with some outliers in Wales, upwards of 100 in the Channel Islands, several hundred in western France and a few in Galicia in northwest Spain. During the 2007 (October) international census, the highest ever total of c.39,000 birds was found, mostly in Ireland, while 4,241 were still in western Iceland. Strangford Lough, Co. Down, held 75 per cent of the population, while the other two major sites, Lough Foyle, Co. Derry, and Tralee Bay and Castlemaine Bay, Co. Kerry, each held approximately 5 per cent of the total.

During their migration to Ireland upwards of 1,000 birds have been recorded during late September/early October at Lough Gruinart, Islay. By mid October most of the birds have moved on, presumably to Strangford Lough in Northern Ireland. Smaller passage numbers have been noted on Skye and Tiree, and along the Ayrshire coast. Increasing wintering numbers have been noted at the Dee Estuary, on Loch Ryan, and in Jersey and Guernsey.

Later in the winter, when much of their food has been eaten out of the principal staging sites, the geese spread out around the coastline in search of new feeding grounds. Breeding success is highly irregular, reflecting the harshness of the high Arctic. The proportion of first-winter birds seen in Ireland ranges from 0 to 47 per cent with a mean of 16.6 per cent between 1960 and 1990.[127] No long-term change in productivity has been evident. Strange as it may seem for such a small and potentially vulnerable population of geese, neither adult nor juvenile mortality rates have yet been calculated. Mortality rates have obviously been lower than recruitment rates otherwise the population would not have expanded during the past few decades. Several banded birds from this population have been observed with Svalbard birds at Lindisfarne.

The East Canadian High Arctic and East Atlantic populations retain a certain degree of discreteness during the winter period but, as with the Greenland and Svalbard barnacle geese, there is some interchange between the populations, evidenced by sightings of two Icelandic-ringed birds in Denmark, two Lindisfarne birds in Ireland and one in Iceland, three Danish birds in Ireland, and two Canadian birds observed at Lindisfarne. Other unmarked birds have without doubt also moved from one population to another, and each ringed bird could represent a movement of 25–75 unmarked birds. Will this limited gene flow slow down any tendency towards subspeciation between the two populations?[128]

TABLE 32. Light-bellied brant goose, East Canadian High Arctic population: sites in Britain where the mean five-year peak exceeded 25 birds (no National threshold).

LOCATION	MEAN 5-YEAR PEAK 2002/03–2006/07	PEAK COUNT 2006/07
Traeth Melynog, Anglesey	175	
Dee Estuary (England & Wales)	91	104 (Jan)
Inland Sea, Beddmanarch & Alaw Estuary, Anglesey	83	79 (Nov)
Loch Gruinart, Islay	73	1 (Oct)
Foryd Bay, Caernarfon, Gwynedd	64	47 (Nov)
Loch Ryan, Dumfries & Galloway	53	37 (Nov)
Morecambe Bay, Lancashire, Cumbria	47	65 (Nov)

The third subspecies of the brant goose, the black brant, breeds in eastern Siberia from the Anadyr River to the Bering Strait (c.5,000 birds), with the bulk of the population (c.136,200 birds) breeding from western Alaska to central northern Canada, where they overlap with light-bellied brant in the Perry River region. Most black brant winter along the Pacific coast of North America, but each year a few become caught up with light-bellied brant travelling to winter in Britain and Ireland.

The black brant has a dark-black belly sharply contrasting with whitish flanks; its back is also much blacker than that of other brant geese. Prior to the 1980s they were extremely rare vagrants to Britain and Ireland, but with increasing records they became just 'rare' – and they are now regarded as regular

TABLE 33. Light-bellied brant goose, East Canadian High Arctic population: sites in Ireland where the mean five-year peak exceeded 220 birds (National threshold).

LOCATION	MEAN 5-YEAR PEAK 1996/97–2000/01	PEAK COUNT 2003/04
Strangford Lough, Co. Down	22,363*	24,658 (Oct)*
Dublin Bay, Co. Dublin	2,310	
Lough Foyle, Co. Derry	2,452*	1,850 (Oct)*
Tralee Bay, Lough Gill & Akeragh Lough, Co. Kerry	1,999	
Rogerstown Estuary, Co. Dublin	1,194	
Wexford Harbour & Slobs, Co. Wexford	1,148	
Malahide Estuary, Co. Dublin	940	
North Wicklow Coastal Marshes, Co. Wicklow	904	
Inner Galway Bay, Co. Galway	746	
Baldoyle Bay, Co. Dublin	675	
Outer Ards Shoreline, Co. Down	660*	577 (Mar)*
Seagrange Park, beside Baldoyle Bay, Co. Dublin	554	
Castlemaine Harbour & Rossbehy, Co. Kerry	539	
Dungarvan Harbour, Co. Waterford	521	
Shannon & Fergus estuaries, Co. Limerick/Kerry/Clare	509	
Carlingford Lough, Co. Down	495*	542 (Feb)*
Killough Harbour, Co. Down	417*	282 (Mar)*
Dundrum Bay Inner, Co. Down	389*	575 (Feb)*
Larne Lough, Co. Antrim	226*	254 (Jan)*

visitors. As from 1 July 2005 the BBRC no longer considers records of black brant, as they are now 'a regular but scarce to rare winter visitor.'

A total of 171 occurrences have been accepted by the BBRC in Britain for 1950–2004, with more than 78 per cent of all records occurring from 1994 onwards. As of 1 July 2005 the BBRC no longer considers the black brant a rare bird. Most records are from the east and south coasts of Britain. During WeBS 2006/07 black brant were recorded in every month from November to April, at a total of ten sites in Britain and a further two in Northern Ireland.

In Ireland there were 69 records, involving probably only 15–20 individuals, between 1978 and 2005, mostly on the east coast between Strangford Lough and Wexford Harbour. Among the seven recorded during 2001 was one in Co. Kerry, and two were seen during 2002, both on the west coast (Kerry and Mayo).

A possible fourth form or subspecies, known as the grey-bellied brant goose, may exist, based on field records of wintering birds observed in the UK, Ireland and the USA.[129] These putative grey-bellied brant appear to be an intermediate form between the light-bellied and black brant, and are thought to come from a small population of some 4,000–8,000 birds mainly breeding on Melville Island, Northwest Territories, Canada. They are intermediate in appearance between black brant and light-bellied brant, having brown upperparts and grey underparts which give less of a contrast with the white flank patch. Given that this population exhibits mixed characters, it has also been proposed that, rather than being a separate subspecies, it is actually a result of interbreeding between these two forms. Another possibility is that they are variants of the light-bellied brant. Grey-bellied brant have been recognised in the field since 1975.[130] Research by Shields on mitochondrial DNA suggests that the grey-bellied brant nesting on Melville Island are genetically distinct from the black brant and that there is extensive divergence between black brant and light-bellied brant.[131] We must await further results from DNA examination to resolve the position of the grey-bellied brant. Meanwhile the BBRC is reviewing the diagnosability of this difficult form in a British context.

Geese answering the description of grey-bellied brant have been recorded in Ireland since 1992 at Newcastle, Co. Down, and later in the 1990s also at Tyrella and Strangford Lough, Co. Down. At Dundrum Inner Bay, Co. Down, two adults with five young were observed.[132] More recently there have been records from Co. Mayo and Co. Donegal in Ireland, and from Norfolk, Hampshire (late 1990 and early 2000) and East Yorkshire (2000 and 2008) in Britain.[133]

14. RED-BREASTED GOOSE *BRANTA RUFICOLLIS* (AE*)

The unmistakable plumage of this small black, red and white goose – the world's smallest true goose – marks it out as one the most unusual of European wintering geese (Fig. 50). How and why it developed its remarkable colourings remains a mystery: no other goose displays such an extent of red, or such complex head patterning. Despite its bizarre markings, it blends in well with other geese at a distance, especially the white-fronts with which it often consorts. The world population is estimated at 38,500 individuals – the mean of winter counts between 2003 and 2005 – most of which nest in the sub-Arctic tundra of the Taymyr, Gydan and Yamal peninsulas in northern Russia, between 70° E and 110° E. About 70 per cent of the population breeds on the Taymyr Peninsula, especially in the Pura–Pyasina river catchment in west Taymyr, where they nest in small colonies on steep river-banks and cliffs. The combination of exotic plumage, rarity as winter visitors to Britain and Ireland, uncertainty about their true population size, and interesting breeding biology in inaccessible areas, makes the red-breasted goose the most intriguing of all the geese that visit us.

FIG 50. Red-breasted goose in snow, Bulgaria. Their bright and gaudy plumage makes them the most striking of all geese that visit Britain. But at a distance they appear black and white, often associated with European white-fronted geese. In flight they are undisciplined, not remaining in traditional goose formation, more resembling a loose, ever-twisting small flock of starlings. (Roger Tidman/NHPA)

Much remains to be learnt about the population dynamics of this most intriguing goose.

Being a small goose, they are unable by themselves to successfully defend their nests from Arctic Foxes. The other two small geese have their own strategies: barnacles nest on fox-free cliffs, often close to a gyrfalcon nest, or on small offshore islands, while brant ideally select fox-free islands, or place their nests close to a nesting snowy owl. The red-breasted goose is the most vulnerable of the three, as their nests, despite being almost always located on river-valley cliffs, are not well protected from fox intrusion. They secure their protection by almost invariably nesting close to birds of prey. Nearly half of all red-breast colonies studied by Kostin on the Taymyr Peninsula were situated near the nest of a peregrine falcon, with 14 per cent close to the nest of rough-legged buzzards, 14 per cent near both species, and 14 per cent without any apparent bird of prey – although in most cases remnants of a nest were found. The birds of prey protect the geese and the geese, in return, alert the birds of prey – also victims of foxes – to the presence of foxes.[134]

Nesting colonies in the Taymyr study were small, with a mean of 5–6 pairs, and an average of 24.4 per cent of all birds present breeding in any one year. Breeding success was highly variable, influenced by body condition of arriving females, temperature on the breeding grounds, and population levels of predators and of the birds of prey that provide some protection to the nesting geese. Nest predation by foxes reached 59 per cent in some years, but averaged 14.6 per cent for 343 nests studied between 1977 and 1983. Predation rates were largely determined by the abundance of the Siberian lemming and the Arctic lemming, and were highest the year following a peak lemming season because, with fewer lemmings and more foxes, alternative food sources had to be found. The average clutch was 5.3 eggs and both incubation and fledging periods were relatively short for Arctic-nesting geese – the breeding cycle was completed in just over 100 days, similar to that of Bewick's swan. The mean brood size per pair after leaving the breeding colony was 4.5. Adult annual mortality rates are unknown. The proportion of young birds in Bulgarian and Romanian wintering flocks during 1990–95 indicated annual recruitment rates ranging from 0 to 6 per cent, a remarkably low figure that would appear barely able to sustain the population.[135] During 2002–04 breeding success improved, with juveniles comprising 10 per cent of the birds. Surveys of wintering geese in Bulgaria in late February 2005 found a much higher proportion of juveniles in the flocks, 23 per cent, indicating much better breeding success.[136]

After moulting close to the breeding grounds the geese travel south, then west, along a fairly restricted flyway to winter on the north and west coasts of the

Black Sea, in Ukraine, Romania and Bulgaria. Today the Shabla and Durankulak lakes in Bulgaria hold up to 70 per cent of the wintering population. On the wintering grounds they appear to be dependent upon the green parts of winter wheat, barley and maize and some pasture grasses.[137] I have watched them at dusk, flying from their inland feeding sites on the Dobruja Plain to roost on the coastal lagoons south of the Danube Delta in Romania – their flight is swift and fast, small flocks moving with an agility not unlike that of a flock of large starlings. There is much agricultural restructuring in their feeding areas close to the Black Sea as the former Communist states move towards market economies. Agricultural land use is changing and possibly affecting the geese. Their small population qualifies them as a globally threatened species.

Red-breasted geese were present in England during the Late Pleistocene, in the Ipswichian period (c.127–117 ky BP). Fossils have been found at Grays Thurrock Cave, Essex, along with fossils of the whooper swan, greylag goose and cormorant. There are no fossil records from Ireland.

The geese are very rare vagrants to Britain, with 64 BBRC accepted records of genuine wild birds between 1950 and 2006. Prior to 1950 there were nine occurrences. The first record, a goose, was shot near London in early 1776, probably in the north Kent marshes. Since 1993 the species has become an annual vagrant to Britain, with up to six occurrences in both 2000 and 2001. Records after 1993 became more regular, when wintering numbers began to increase in northwest Europe. Red-breasted geese generally occur among flocks of dark-bellied brant geese, but have also been noted with European white-fronted and barnacle geese (Fig. 33).

There are many instances of escapes from wildfowl collections, and some birds seen in the wild are undoubtedly from these sources. WeBS 2005/06 reported two singles and two together from three sites, all probably escapes.

Ireland is very much outside their wintering range. One possible wild adult was seen by Alyn Walsh on the North Slob, Co. Wexford, on 26 October 1997. It came during the main period of arrival of the Greenland white-fronted geese, when some 4,500 were already on the Slob. It remained throughout the winter and departed with a group of Greenland white-fronts on 16 March 1998. The record was rejected by the IRBC on the basis that the goose was not accompanied by any Siberian congeners such as the European white-front, bean or dark-bellied brant geese, that it was too early in the autumn, and that there was a high probability of it being an escaped collection bird. If accepted, it would have been the first record for Ireland.

15. EGYPTIAN GOOSE
ALOPOCHEN AEGYPTIACA (C1E*)

'Egyptian goose' is a misnomer, as the bird is not a true goose. Because it possesses characteristics of both the true geese and the ducks it is classified in a halfway house, in the tribe Tadornini along with other sheldgeese and the closely related shelducks. Thus the Egyptian goose is half a goose, half a duck, as well as a naturalised introduction from sub-Saharan Africa, where it occurs throughout most of west, east and south Africa. There are some 205,000–510,000 individuals in Africa.

The Egyptian goose (Fig. 51) was first brought to Britain during the seventeenth century, or possibly earlier. In their *Ornithologia* (1676–78) Willoughby and Ray record that some were added to King Charles II's ornamental wildfowl collection in St James's Park, London.[138] Some of the geese escaped from the collection – the first free-flying bird being shot at Thatcham, west of Newbury, Berkshire, in 1795. By the nineteenth century many more were free-flying, and the species had become semi-domesticated and widespread. Today the headquarters of the feral population, with some 380–400 breeding pairs, is north Norfolk, mainly in the Holkham–Beeston area and in the valley of the River Bure, where it benefits from protection.[139] It breeds commonly throughout most of Norfolk and Suffolk and is increasing rapidly in the Midlands (especially at Rutland Water) and in the home counties. In recent years it has been spreading both west and south, with first breeding records in Essex (1979), Somerset (1982) and Cambridgeshire (1988). It has been a much less successful colonist in terms of expanding its numbers and range than two other introduced wildfowl – the Canada goose and mandarin duck – and is probably held in check by cold summers and winters that reduce breeding success and increase adult mortality. The estimated British population in 1991 was 750–800 pairs.[140] It is also well established in the Netherlands (1,300 pairs in 1994 and 4,500–5,000 pairs in 2000, having grown from a few escapes in 1967), in Belgium (50–100 pairs), Germany (tenfold increase during past decade) and more recently in northwest France. It is likely to extend its range elsewhere in lowland Europe in years to come.

Since they were first regularly recorded by WeBS in 1993/94, numbers have shown a striking increase. For the period 1991–99, the wintering population in Great Britain was estimated at 1,000 birds, while a more recent (2007) estimate put the population between 2,520 and 3,160.[141] They have not yet been recorded from Northern Ireland during WeBS.

FIG 51. Egyptian goose in flight. Classified as a member of the tribe *Tadornini* – the sheldgeese and shelducks – Egyptian geese appear like weirdly plumaged, large and bulky, long-legged shelducks. Their posture is more goose-like, standing upright, and often perching on trees. Their plumage is greyish brown with green-black wings and a prominent white forewing. The dark brown eye patch is distinctive, as are their pinkish legs and small bill. (Roger Tidman/NHPA)

There is no recorded fossil history of the Egyptian goose in Britain or Ireland, or elsewhere in Europe.

Its favoured breeding habitats in Britain shadow those of the Canada goose: gravel pits, small lakes, wooded parkland and ponds in the rural environment. It has adapted well to the British environment and continues to extend its range, albeit slowly. Parkland is favoured where there are suitable large trees for nesting. They nest in tree cavities and in holes, sometimes taking over abandoned nests of other large birds. The trees are also important for roosting and perching.

The average clutch size is 8–9 eggs, and incubation is by the female only. The young fledge within 70–75 days and remain with their parents for several weeks or some months. The age of first breeding is probably 1 year. In Norfolk, a population of about 25 pairs reared on average only two young per pair to fledging. This low productivity was thought to be due largely to predation (mainly by carrion crows) combined with competition from Canada and greylag geese. The few ringing recoveries available – five from 80 ringed birds – show only local movements of less than 5 km. No published data on adult survival rates are available.

In Ireland the history of the Egyptian goose is not fully known, but by 1815 they were kept in numbers on lakes in Hillsborough Park, Co. Down, where they were noted as surviving up to 1890.[142] The first record of a free-flying bird being shot was at Moira, Co. Down, in January 1833, originating probably from the Hillsborough collection. Two were subsequently shot from a flock of fifteen on the River Lagan, near Belfast, in October 1834.[143] A large flock was seen at North Bull Island, Dublin Bay, in January 1863; around this time small parties were seen in Belfast Lough and on the Boyne Estuary, and a pair was shot on the Shannon Estuary. A flock of 13 was seen at Magilligan Point, Co. Derry, in July 1888 and four birds were shot in January 1889.[144] Other occurrences were in Cork, Limerick, Laois, Monaghan, Dublin (2), Louth (2) and Down (4). The last bird recorded in the wild in Ireland was shot on Lough Neagh on 3 January 1892. Their frequency of occurrence suggests escapes from collections rather than any seasonal migrations. They were also kept and bred (prior to 1900) in the waterfowl collection of Sir A. Bellingham in Co. Louth, 'of which a good many flew away'. It would appear that no feral birds survived into the twentieth century. A single bird, probably a collection escape, was seen during spring 2005 at the RSPB reserve on Lough Erne, Co. Fermanagh. A single was also seen at Portmore Lough, Co. Antrim, and the next day one was seen, possibly the same bird, at Belfast Duck Pond.

TABLE 34. Egyptian goose: sites in Britain where the mean five-year peak exceeded 25 birds (no National threshold). At a further nine sites the mean five-year peak exceeded 10 birds.

LOCATION	MEAN 5-YEAR PEAK 2002/03–2006/07	PEAK COUNT 2006/07
N Norfolk Coast, Norfolk	222	211 (Oct)
Sennowe Park Lake, Guist, Norfolk	92	—
Breydon Water & Berney Marshes, Norfolk	70	55 (Jul)
Rutland Water, Leicestershire	58	64 (Jul)
St Benet's Levels, Norfolk	56	—
Yare Valley: Marlingford–Bawburgh, Norfolk	52	52 (Jun)
Middle Yare Marshes, Norfolk	47	(65) (Sep)
Nunnery Lakes, Norfolk	35	36 (Jun)
Cranwich Gravel Pits, Norfolk	34	—
Weybread Pits, Suffolk	34	—
Spade Oak Gravel Pit (Little Marlow), Bucks	27	11 (Sep)
Whitlingham Country Park, Norfolk	26	24 (Jul)

16. RUDDY SHELDUCK *TADORNA FERRUGINEA* (BDE*)

The ruddy shelduck (Fig. 52) is a widespread breeding species over much of southeastern Europe. Its European headquarters are in the Black Sea area, especially where there are freshwater and brackish lakes. Turkey holds probably the largest breeding population (c.4,000–8,000 pairs), with smaller numbers in northern Greece, Romania, Bulgaria, Moldova and Ukraine. A discrete population of about 2,500 birds breeds in northwest Africa, with up to 200 individuals formerly wintering in southern Spain, the only example of an African nesting species migrating to Europe. Introduced birds have also bred in the Netherlands (about 7 pairs in 1992), Germany, Switzerland (over 300 were recorded during waterbird counts in November 2005, a dramatic increase over

FIG 52. Ruddy shelduck. Goose-like, the ruddy shelduck is a uniform orange-brown with a paler head, palest in the female. The bill, legs and tail are black. In flight the white forewing contrasts with the other green-black wing feathers. The male has a narrow black neck ring. (Anne & Steve Toon/NHPA)

the previous ten years) and Ireland.[145] These feral populations, together with escapes from wildfowl collections, are almost certainly the source of all birds seen in Britain and Ireland today.

There are fossil records from five British sites – four in Derbyshire and one in Devonshire dating from the Late Pleistocene Mousterian period (115-35 ky BP) and from the Later Upper Palaeolithic (< 20 ky BP).

There have been some notable historical invasions of genuine wild ruddy shelducks, at a time when they were rarely kept in collections. These occurred in Britain in 1892 and Ireland in 1886 (parties of up to six birds) and 1892 (parties of up to 20 birds and individuals). It is on this basis that the BOURC decided to retain the species in Category B, species that have been recorded in an apparently natural state at least once up to 31 December 1949. It was also agreed by the BOURC that no post-1950 records could be confirmed as referring to definitely wild birds, and that some of these were best placed in Category D.

The last record of a bird in an apparently wild state was in 1946. Thus the ruddy shelduck seen today in the wild are treated as escapes from waterfowl collections, such as those recorded during WeBS 2005/06, when a maximum of 22 birds were seen at 13 sites throughout the year in Britain. All records of more than two birds were from the north Norfolk coast. Some escaped British birds have occasionally been recorded breeding, but they are not considered an established species.[146] After the exceptionally high numbers recorded during WeBS 2005/06, the 2006/07 totals were similar to recent years.

In Ireland approximately 73 records of wild birds in the period 1800–1949 have been accepted by the IRBC. All more recent records have involved birds of doubtful origin. There was a large invasion of apparently wild birds from central Asia into Fennoscandia in 1994; several flocks turned up at about the same time in Britain too, but the evidence that these were genuine immigrants was not considered compelling enough for them to make it into the BOU's Category A.

A flock of five (three females and two males) appeared on the North Slob, Co. Wexford, in July 2006. It is unlikely that these were wildfowl collection escapes, and they may have originated from the feral populations in Germany, the Netherlands or Switzerland. Three were cannon-netted and ringed. The recovery of these birds is awaited with interest.

17. COMMON SHELDUCK *TADORNA TADORNA* (A)

This large, brightly coloured duck (Fig. 53) is easily mistaken for an exotic goose, bewildering the observer on first encounter. I remember well, at the somewhat tender age of 16, my first sighting of one on the River Dart, Devon – I was initially dumbfounded and thought it was a rare, exotic goose. Essentially a bird of the estuary and muddy shores, it is relatively common around the British and Irish coastlines in suitable habitats. Once popular as an item in waterfowl collections, it was also regularly shot during the nineteenth and early twentieth centuries – they were attractive items, stuffed, behind glass, adorning many a country-house entrance hall. Increased protection from shooting throughout Europe permitted expansion of the northwest European population from some 125,000 birds in the 1970s to about 250,000 in 1980/81, and to 300,000 in 1995/96.[147]

Today there are about 11,000 breeding pairs of common shelduck in Britain and a further 1,100 pairs in Ireland. It is rarely seen on the sea further than 2 km from the coast, and traditionally it has seldom been observed on fresh water, or inland more than 4 km from the sea. However, it is now common well inland in parts of East Anglia, notably Livermore, south of Thetford, where double-figure

FIG 53. Common shelduck. Distinctive black, white and chestnut plumage resembling an exotic goose. There is little plumage difference between male and female, but males have a conspicuous fleshy knob at the base of the bill, largest in spring and virtually absent by late summer. It varies in size according to testis size. (Ken Kinsella)

FIG 54. Male common shelduck in flight. With relatively slower wing beats and slower speed than most ducks, the flight of shelducks is more reminiscent of geese. When travelling long distances, such as to and from moulting grounds, they fly in long strings or in V-formation. (Alan Williams/NHPA)

counts are normal and three-figure counts are regular.[148] As the population grows and competition for favoured coastal nesting sites increases, more birds are driven to breeding on large inland freshwater lakes. In Ireland there are now some 30 pairs on Lough Neagh, while in Scotland Lough Leven hosts 40–55 pairs and there are a further 25–35 pairs on Loch Lomond.

The estimated wintering population in Great Britain is 78,200 birds (five-year mean 1995–99), whilst in Ireland the estimated wintering population is 14,610 (five-year mean 2000–04).

There is one fossil record from an interglacial period of the Late Pleistocene (127–10 ky BP) in Devon. All other fossil records are more recent, mainly from the Holocene (10–0 ky BP), from Devon (three sites), Glamorgan (probable record) and Kent. There is one record from the Holocene in Ireland at Barntick Cave, Co. Clare.

The shelduck is famous for its remarkable moult migration, when virtually the entire northwest European population, including birds from the western Mediterranean, travels to the mudflats in the Heligoland Bight, off the northwest coast of Germany. Upwards of 100,000 birds congregate there each June–October, to spend several weeks on the vast mudflats, extending some 20 km offshore, while they grow their new feathers.[149] There are some less extensive but equally important moulting areas for other British and Irish birds in Bridgwater Bay, the Firth of Forth and the Wash. The Mersey Estuary is now the key site in Britain in late summer, with over 10,000 shelduck every summer from 1997 onwards, with a peak of 19,810 in August 2002.[150] Other moulting birds gather in the west Dutch Wadden Sea (over 30,000 birds) and in the southwestern Netherlands Delta (over 2,000 birds). Young birds do not moult their flight feathers during their first autumn, and do not join the large moulting flocks but move south, many to France, sometimes accompanied by their parents. Some adults wander south after the moult, but the vast majority are back in their home territories by late November or early December, and all have returned to their breeding grounds from March onwards. Young birds do not breed until their third summer. Adults are monogamous and maintain some of the most enduring of all pair bonds among ducks.

The female selects the nest site, the male in attendance, usually close to water in a coastal location and in a hole in the ground – rabbit burrows are favourite sites, but hollow trees and thick vegetation are also used. Occasionally, and probably due to nest-site shortages, another female will lay in an already occupied nest site, resulting in up to 32 eggs (average clutch size 8.8 eggs) which, in many cases, are incubated successfully. Common shelducks are monogamous, the pair bond usually persisting from year to year, as with swans and geese. Male shelducks (Fig. 54), unlike other male ducks, generally remain with the female during incubation and help with rearing the young. Some parents stay with the brood until they are fledged (45–50 days), while others may leave the ducklings when they are 10–15 days old, to migrate to the moulting grounds. The young will then join a crèche supervised by either failed breeding birds or adults remaining longer at the breeding grounds before departing to moult.

In coastal habitats, shelduck feed on the small saltwater snail *Hydrobia ulvae*, which occurs there in vast numbers, with densities of upwards of 60,000 snails per square metre in some estuaries. Shelduck feed on the *Hydrobia* by sifting them out of the mud and ooze, using the lamellae on their bills as sieves as they waddle through the soft mud. Other foods – crustaceans, shelled molluscs and polychaete worms – are also eaten, and these may in fact provide the major source of energy required by the shelduck. A recent study of shelduck feeding in Traeth Melynog and Bangor Harbour, north Wales, found that shelduck were less dependent than formerly thought on *Hydrobia* as a food source, and that predation upon the snail was not important in the population dynamics of *Hydrobia*. Moreover, the consumption of *Hydrobia* contributed only a very small percentage (0.03 per cent) of the energy requirements of the shelduck.[151]

A study in the Ythan Estuary, Aberdeenshire, between 1962 and 1964, found that breeding success was low, with 24 per cent of clutches lost. Seventy-six per cent of 458 young, in 67 carefully monitored broods, were lost between hatching and fledging. The productivity of fledged young per territorial pair averaged only 1.5 (range 1.2–1.9), considered inadequate to replace the calculated annual adult mortality of 20–34 per cent. However, the study period was short, possibly not capturing the complete picture. Productivity was inversely related to population size in the same year and would have been higher in years when there were fewer adults present in May.[152] Using ring recoveries of German-marked shelduck, Hugh Boyd calculated the mean adult mortality of adults to be 20 per cent, in agreement with the Ythan estimate.

TABLE 35. Common shelduck: sites in Britain where the mean five-year peak exceeded 3,000 birds (International threshold). Sixteen additional sites qualified as of National importance (National threshold 782).

LOCATION	MEAN 5-YEAR PEAK 2002/03–2006/07	PEAK COUNT 2006/07
Mersey Estuary, Cheshire	16,676	(16,676) (Jul)
Dee Estuary (England & Wales)	11,842	10,869 (Oct)

TABLE 35. – *Cont.*

Morecambe Bay, Lancashire/Cumbria	8,000	8,880 (Oct)
The Wash, Lincolnshire/Norfolk	7,277	6,855 (Dec)
Humber Estuary, E Yorkshire/Lincolnshire	5,825	(4,576) (Sep)
Solway Firth, Cumbria/Dumfries & Galloway	4,271	(874) (Oct)
Severn Estuary, Gloucestershire/Somerset/etc	3,492	3,711 (Nov)
Firth of Forth, Lothian/Fife/etc	3,350	(3,538) (Aug)
Ribble Estuary, Lancashire	3,251	2,577 (Nov)

TABLE 36. Common shelduck: sites in Ireland where the mean five-year peak has exceeded more than 400 (National threshold 150).

LOCATION	MEAN 5-YEAR PEAK 1996/97–2000/01	PEAK COUNT 2000/01
Strangford Lough, Co. Down	4,068*	3,413 (Dec)*
Cork Harbour, Co. Cork	1,979	722 (Feb)
Shannon & Fergus estuaries, Co. Limerick/Kerry/Clare	1,243	697 (Jan)
Dublin Bay, Co. Dublin	1,210	953 (Jan)
Wexford Harbour & Slobs, Co. Wexford	852	125 (Jan)
Lough Swilly, Co. Donegal	781	884 (Feb)
Rogerstown Estuary, Co. Dublin	781	865 (Dec)
Larne Lough, Co. Antrim.	758*	832 (Jan)*
Carlingford Louth, Co. Down	482*	(349) (Feb)*
Dundalk Bay, Co. Louth	526	408 (Feb)
Bannow Bay, Co. Waterford	502	—
Dungarvan Harbour, Co. Waterford	497	—
Malahide Estuary, Co. Dublin	423	456 (Jan)

18. MUSCOVY DUCK *CAIRINA MOSCHATA*
(**E***; currently under review by BOURC for possible inclusion in Category C1)

The muscovy duck (Fig. 55) is a native of Central and South America, inhabiting rivers, lagoons and marshes associated with tropical rainforests. They are hole-nesting, perch in trees at night and, when domesticated by the native people, were sources of feathers and valued for their ability to rid houses of ants and other unpleasant invertebrates. As the males are great food converters (weighing up to 7 kg under domestication) they have considerable value as a source of meat, and their eggs are also eaten. Their name may be connected with the Muisca Indians of Colombia, or with the Mosquito Coast of Nicaragua.[153]

FIG 55. Muscovy duck. The domesticated forms, such as this bird, come in a bewildering range of plumages – white, black and piebald. The wild ancestor is much sleeker, and black with conspicuous white wing coverts. Most domesticated birds have naked warty faces, red bills and legs. As in the common shelduck, males have an enlarged knob at the base of the bill, much smaller in the female. They are large, ungainly-looking and bulky ducks, hardly likely to win any avian beauty contest. (Joe Blossom/NHPA)

There are no reported fossil records from Britain or Ireland, nor indeed from Europe, which is as one would expect for a New World species. The birds were unknown to Europeans before the sixteenth century. It is thought that they were first imported to England in 1550 and then spread to France. Since then they have been kept in many wildfowl and ornamental collections as well as on farms throughout Britain and to a lesser extent in Ireland. Drake muscovies will breed with mallard. Their offspring – *mules* or *mulard* ducks – are sterile and increase in weight at a great rate. The *mules* are commercially bred and reared in France, where the males are force-fed to produce *pâté de fois gras* while the females are farmed for their *magrets* or breast fillets. Many are imported into Britain from France and sold as Barbary duck.

In the wild the female lays a clutch of 8–15 eggs in a hole in a tree, the male deserting her soon after laying. After hatching, the young climb, aided by their sharp claws and hooked bill, to the nest entrance and jump down to the ground below. Fledging is a long process – up to three and a half months – making them vulnerable to predation, especially by caimans. They will breed in nest boxes when these are provided. Pair and brood bonds are not well developed, and they show little evidence of migration patterns.

There is now a well-established breeding population at Ely, Cambridgeshire, where 59–69+ young were reared during 2004, the highest annual total at this site. This population benefits from supplementary feeding, principally during summer, by the public. Despite periodic culling by the local authority the population appears to be spreading along the banks of the River Great Ouse, and they appear to be resident on several areas of the nearby Ouse Washes. It is considered that this population is now a naturalised feral establishment that is self-sustaining.

The BOURC is continuing to assess the Ely breeding population as to its sustainability and possible admission to Category C of the British List. There are some questions about their dependence on supplementary feeding and their likely longevity due to the limited gene pool. For the time being it remains only a Category E* species. If accepted to the British List then it will be Category C1.[154]

Hybrid muscovy mallard offspring have been reported in the Ely population. Breeding also occurred or is thought to have taken place in Devon (2001, not 2002), Dorset (2001), Derbyshire (2002), Cheshire (2001, not 2002) and Norfolk (2002).[155] The number of birds (annual maximum) and sites recorded with birds during WeBS has increased from 72 birds at five sites in 1993 to 86 birds at 33 sites in 2003.

During WeBS 2006/07 a maximum of 91 (October and November) muscovy ducks were recorded at 27 sites in the UK – 23 sites in England, three in Wales and one in Scotland. The key site remains Fort Henry Ponds and Exton Park

Lakes, Leicestershire, where 22 were present throughout the winter. None have been recorded in Ireland by I-WeBS or WeBS. The data in Table 37 are from the 2005/06 WeBS report, as there is no tabular information in the 2006/07 report.

TABLE 37. Muscovy duck: sites in Britain where the mean five-year peak exceeded 5 birds.

LOCATION	MEAN 5-YEAR PEAK 2002/03–2006/07	PEAK COUNT 2006/07
Fort Henry Ponds/ Exton Park Lakes, Leicestershire	16	43 (Oct)
Brayford Pool, Lincoln	13	26 (Oct)
Wilderness Pond, Glamorgan	10	—
High Batts recording, N Yorkshire	8	—
Derwent Water, Cumbria	7	5 (Dec)

19. MANDARIN DUCK *AIX GALERICULATA* (C1E*)

Probably the most brilliantly and decoratively coloured of all British and Irish breeding ducks, albeit a relatively recent addition to our native avifauna, the mandarin (Fig. 56) is a native of the Far East – Japan, China, Korea and Russia. It was accepted onto the British and Irish lists in 1971 as a resident, self-sustaining species.

The species was possibly breeding in Britain during the Middle Pleistocene period during one of the warmer periods when much of the country was covered with temperate oak woodland. Fossils have been found in the Upper Freshwater Bed of the Middle Pleistocene Cromerian interglacial (c.475 ky BP) at West Runton, Suffolk. Its fossils were associated with many other Anatidae. West Runton is the only site in the Palaearctic where mandarin duck fossils have been found so far.

It was not until shortly before 1745 that they were first brought to Britain to embellish waterfowl collections. The first recorded breeding success was at

FIG 56. Mandarin duck, male. Perhaps one of our most elegant and beautiful ducks. The males are unmistakable – red bill, wide whitish band from bill to behind eye and feathered, brown crest. Large orange 'sails' at rear. Female is a drab olive grey without sails. (Ken Kinsella)

London Zoo in Regent's Park in 1834. Today's self-sustaining population appears to stem from Alfred Ezra, the illustrious benefactor of Whipsnade Zoo, who was keen to introduce exotics into London's parks. He was given a number of birds in the 1920s, and eventually released a large number of the offspring in London. Many perished, but a feral population was established, boosted by birds released by Lord Grey, another keen ornithologist. Sufficient numbers were subsequently released, or escaped from waterfowl collections, to lay the foundations of a flourishing breeding population.

During the early 1950s their main stronghold was in Surrey and Kent, where they numbered not less than 400 birds.[156] Today there are at least 3,500 breeding pairs in Britain, having expanded from some 250 pairs in the early 1950s, and the British wintering population is estimated, with poor reliability, at 7,000 birds (1970–87). The breeding population is focused in Surrey, east Berkshire (especially in Windsor Great Park and Virginia Water, where about half the population resides) and in south Buckinghamshire. Others occur in East Anglia, in the Tay Valley near Perth and a few other locations in Wales and Devon and Cornwall. In general there has been little expansion of the breeding population outside their traditional areas in south and central England. As so many now nest in Britain (11 per cent of the estimated world population of 72,350–72,500 birds, including British breeders), the British population has become of world conservation importance. It is possible that, in years to come, mandarin ducks may be exported back to China, to boost the declining population there.

There are several recoveries in Britain of birds ringed abroad, suggesting that the self-sustaining populations are being added to by these immigrants. Single birds have been recovered from the Netherlands and France, while two have originated in Norway and two from Guernsey.

The first mandarin duck to appear in the wild in Ireland, probably a wanderer from Wales, was shot on the North Slob, Co. Wexford, in December 1971. Today it is a rare local resident, with one well-established self-sustaining population since 1978 in the vicinity of the Shimna River, Co. Down, probably originating from a pair that had escaped from an ornamental waterfowl collection within Tollymore Forest Park. The population was estimated at 20–30 pairs in 2002. Free-flying birds were first observed in 1985 in the Shimna River valley. They have spread along the river, and in the winter 1995/96 the population was estimated at 25 individuals. Productivity is low, reflecting reduced invertebrate food availability for the ducklings (the river is very acidic: pH 4.3), with an estimated mortality rate of 82 per cent over a two- to eight-week period.[157] They are frequently seen on the boating lake, 100 m from the sea, at Newcastle, Co. Down, where the Shimna River meets the sea. Fourteen juveniles were seen there in July 2004, indicating a good breeding season. As they are resident, rarely venturing more than 8 km from their nesting area, and in the absence of more suitable breeding habitat (Castlewellan Forest Park, 6 km away, holds the only suitable local habitat), it is unlikely that they will spread far.

There would appear to be a small population at the Lough, Cork, where there were two pairs in 1987 and one or two pairs today. The birds there are not self-sustaining. Elsewhere in Co. Cork, there were two pairs in Farran Woods in 1987, probably escapes from a waterfowl collection, and no breeding has been recorded. A single bird was seen near Fota Wildlife Park in March 1995, while a pair were displaying near Kealkill, Bantry, in March 1987.[158]

Mandarin ducks are generally monogamous, pairs remaining together for many years (a rare characteristic among the ducks), and they have been symbols of connubial bliss, fidelity and mutual affection for Chinese and Japanese Buddhists for nearly 2,000 years.[159]

Bizarre in habits, as in plumage, these perching ducks breed in holes up to 3 m deep – as high as 15 m above the ground – in old trees near water. Nesting boxes are also used. Eggs are laid from late March until the end of April and clutch size is normally 9–12, but egg 'dumping' occurs – more frequently in natural rather than in artificial nest sites. Incubation is undertaken by the female alone, and lasts 28–33 days. Some 25 per cent of all completed clutches are not incubated.[160] Within 24 hours of hatching the ducklings drop to the ground, encouraged by the female's 'melodious exodus call', and make their way to water. The survival rate of ducklings is in the range of 30–40 per cent.[161] There are no available published data either on breeding success or on adult survival rates.

The adults feed principally by night, manifesting a predilection for acorns, walnuts, chestnuts and beech mast during the autumn and winter. They will also feed on spilt grain in stubble fields during the autumn, and later in the winter they feed on vegetation. Their success as neo-colonists has been due mainly to exploitation of a vacant ecological niche – a hole in a tree – not the domain of other wildfowl but increasingly sought after by jackdaws and grey squirrels. They also nest in nest boxes. Like the Canada goose, they have lost their urge for migration, possibly because, in a temperate environment, there is no longer any biological imperative for it. Thus the ducks are freed from the stresses and strains of long-distance travel. Despite the attenuated migratory urge – recoveries of British-ringed mandarins showing few long-distance movements – there have been some remarkable recoveries of birds possibly caught up with flocks of other migratory wildfowl. Or perhaps these travellers have been driven by a migratory gene that has not been completely repressed. One free-flying ringed bird introduced to St James's Park in London ended up on a poulterer's slab in Hungary – possibly on its way back home! There have also been recoveries of single birds from the former USSR and the Netherlands, but most of the recoveries of British-ringed birds have been less than 50 km from the site of ringing, mostly in the Home Counties.

It is likely that the population will continue to grow in Britain and Ireland, although the expansion in Ireland has been sluggish to date, as well as in other European countries – Germany, the Netherlands, Belgium and France – where there are small breeding populations. A hard cold winter is the mandarin's greatest enemy for survival, so it is likely that the species will be one of the beneficiaries of global warming.

TABLE 38. Mandarin duck: sites in Britain where the mean five-year peak exceeded 39 birds (no National threshold). A further 17 sites had a mean five-year peak of 10 or more.

LOCATION	MEAN 5-YEAR PEAK 2002/03–2006/07	PEAK COUNT 2006/07
Forest of Dean Ponds, Gloucestershire	142	—
Bradley Pools, Derbyshire	113	—
Headley Mill Pond, Hampshire	64	15 (Feb)
Stockgrove County Park, Bedfordshire	57	—
Wraysbury Pond, Berkshire	55	51 (Dec)
Busbridge Lakes, Surrey	53	41 (Mar)
Cuttmill Ponds, Surrey	53	27 (Oct)
Bough Beech Reservoir, Kent	51	60 (Jan)
Dee Flood Meadows, Cheshire	48	83 (Oct)
Darwell Reservoir, E Sussex	45	74 (Sep)
Passfield Pond, Hampshire	49	30 (Sep)

20. EURASIAN WIGEON *ANAS PENELOPE* (AE*)

The Eurasian wigeon (Fig. 57) is one of Europe's best-known and most successful ducks with regard to the extent of its breeding range, stretching from Iceland across Scandinavia and Russia as far as 70° E, and from the arctic tundra at 70° N southwards through the sub-Arctic and boreal regions into the temperate steppe zones to 50° N. Russia hosts the bulk of the breeding population, approximately 200,000 breeding pairs. Finland has some 60,000–80,000 pairs, while Sweden, with 20,000–30,000 pairs, takes third place.

Eurasian wigeon are highly migratory, undertaking extensive movements during the autumn, travelling from Siberia, Russia, Scandinavia and Iceland to winter in northwest Europe. Of the 1.5 million birds that comprise the northwest European wintering population, about a third make their way to Britain and

FIG 57. Eurasian wigeon, male. Wigeon are small, compact ducks – not much larger than a teal – with a short neck and bill and a black pointed tail. Males have a bright creamy-yellow crown on a chestnut head. Females are subdued in colour with a rufous grey-brown body that appears mottled, especially in the tail area and upper parts of the folded wings. Within the populations there are some female variants, or morphs, and these appear greyish in overall colour. Both male and female bills are pale blue with a black tip. (Guy Edwardes/NHPA)

Ireland. Numbers in Britain peaked at some 382,000 in January 2001, close to the previous high of 400,000 birds in the winter of 1996/97. The estimated annual wintering population in Great Britain for the period 1995–99 was 406,000 birds. The highest monthly WeBS count was 462,632 in January 2004. Data from I-WeBS for 2000–04 put the wintering population in Ireland at 82,370 birds, down from an estimated 105,000 in the mid-1980s. Migrants arrive in Britain and Ireland from late September onwards (some as early as August), but the main influxes occur in October and early November. Numbers peak in January, with departure from mid March to early April onwards, and most of the birds are back on their Russian breeding grounds around the second half of May. Wigeon are sensitive to cold weather, which can drive many birds from Britain into Ireland and south to the Iberian peninsula.

FIG 58. A large flock of Eurasian wigeon. Not so difficult to identify in flight – males have striking white wing coverts (wing panels), grey body, white belly, chestnut head and long narrow tail. The females lack the striking white wing coverts. Their flight is rapid, but not so fast as teal, and they can take off almost vertically from the water. Their wings are long and narrow, and they fly in close formation, often wheeling and gyrating over a wetland, then suddenly dashing down to the water and sweeping up again. Quite noisy in flight, the males uttering a loud and whistling 'whee-oo'. (Roger Tidman/NHPA)

Wigeon wintering in Britain and Ireland declined, along with brant geese, during the 1930s, with the demise of their principal estuarine food, eelgrass. However, demonstrating their versatility, wigeon switched to feed on inland grassland, especially in flooded marshy areas. Many spend their day sleeping, often in large rafts in estuaries or offshore, to feed later under cover of darkness. Apart from the green seaweeds *Enteromorpha* and eelgrass, their main coastal food is principally marshland grasses – common saltmarsh-grass and red fescue. They will also eat roots and stolons, especially those of white clover.

When large flocks are wheeling over estuaries and coastal loughs with their distinctive whistling 'whee-oo' – from male birds only – and the rasping and growling 'churr' of females, they epitomise the magic of wildfowl. Sometimes flocks are so large – upwards of 25,000 birds – that they seem to darken the sky

(Fig. 58). Despite being one of the favourite targets of wildfowlers – it is the third most shot bird in Britain, with an annual 'bag' estimated at 60,000,[162] and was one of the principal species caught in duck decoys from the sixteenth century onwards – numbers have remained remarkably robust over the years, especially since the 1970s. Indeed, several British estuaries and coastal sites hold between 10,000 and 50,000 birds during winter, with over 100,000 counted on the Ribble Estuary, Lancashire, in the winter of 1994/95.[163] In Ireland a high percentage of the wintering birds occur, unusually, at inland sites – such as on the callows of the rivers Shannon and Little Brosna, on Lough Neagh and Lough Beg, and at Rahasane Turlough, Co. Galway.

Fossil records show that the Eurasian wigeon was in Britain from the Middle Pleistocene period – the Cromerian interglacial (c.475 ky BP) – at many locations to the late Dark Ages (AD 1066). Fossils have also been found at five Irish cave sites, dating probably from the Holocene interglacial period (10–0 ky BP), and bones have been found at Lagore, Co. Meath (AD 750–950). The first historical record of wigeon in Britain dates from 1508.

In addition to their importance for wintering flocks, Britain and Ireland are at the southern limit of the Eurasian wigeon's breeding range. The first breeding – in Scotland – took place in 1834. Since then, it has spread through central and southern Scotland, and further south to the Tweed (1890s), Cumberland (1903) and Northumberland (1913). Today the breeding population is estimated at 300–500 pairs, mainly focused in the Pennines and the uplands of east and northeast Scotland, where moorland lakes are favoured habitats. Only small numbers – fewer than 30 pairs – breed in Ireland, with nesting suspected long before the first confirmed breeding record, in 1933 at Lough Neagh, Co. Armagh, and later in 1953 on Rathlin Island, Co. Antrim. Studies in Caithness and Sutherland have shown that wigeon select neutral or alkaline waters as breeding habitat and avoid lakes with a pH less than 5.5. The female incubates a clutch of 8–9 eggs, in a nest hollow in thick cover on the ground. A high proportion of nests are predated – 44 per cent of 148 nests studied in Scotland and 32 per cent of 551 nests in Iceland. Birds will re-lay if the clutch is lost. Productivity in a Finnish study over three years was 4.3, 1.1 and 3.3 fledged young per pair.[164]
The estimated mean annual adult survival rate is 0.53, based on the recovery of British and Icelandic ringed birds, and for British birds, including more recent recoveries, it is 0.64.[165]

TABLE 39. Eurasian wigeon: sites in Britain where the mean five-year peak exceeded 15,000 birds (International threshold). A further 18 sites exceeded the National threshold of 4,060 birds.

LOCATION	MEAN 5-YEAR PEAK 2002/03–2006/07	PEAK COUNT 2006/07
Ribble Estuary, Lancashire	81,915	(57,385) (Dec)
Ouse Washes, Cambridgeshire	35,636	26,984 (Jan)
Somerset Levels, Somerset	25,964	27,391 (Jan)
Swale Estuary, Kent	18,521	(4,180) (Feb)
Breydon Water & Berney Marshes, Norfolk	17,974	15,905 (Feb)
North Norfolk Coast, Norfolk	17,874	16,750 (Nov)
Lindisfarne, Northumberland	15,108	10,840 (Sep)

TABLE 40. Eurasian wigeon: sites in Ireland where the mean five-year peak exceeded 2,000 birds. A further 14 sites exceeded the National threshold of 820 birds.

LOCATION	MEAN 5-YEAR PEAK 1996/97–2000/01	PEAK COUNT 2000/01
Little Brosna Callows, Co. Offaly	8,696	10,350 (Jan)
Castlemaine Harbour & Rossbehy, Co. Kerry	6,811	4,053 (Dec)
Shannon & Fergus estuaries, Co. Limerick/Kerry/Clare	5,799	—
Tacumshin Lake, Co Wexford	4,661	—
Lough Foyle, Co. Derry	4,628*	5,406 (Oct)*
Strangford Lough, Co. Down	3,418*	3,476 (Oct)*
Shannon Callows	2,907	—
Wexford Harbour & Slobs, Co. Wexford	2,891	1,103 (Dec)
Rahasane Turlough, Co. Galway	2,886	3,500 (Nov)
Corofin Wetlands, Co. Clare	2,835	888 (Dec)
Shannon Callows	2,800	—
Loughs Neagh & Beg, Co. Armagh/Down/etc	2.632*	1,878 (Mar)*
Lough Ree, Co. Westmeath	2,422	5,179 (Jan)

21. AMERICAN WIGEON *ANAS AMERICANA* (AE)

The male American wigeon (Fig. 59) is best distinguished from its Eurasian cousin by its *white*, not golden, crown and forehead, its dark green ear patch and eye-stripe and a generally pinkish-brown rather than a grey body. The females and juveniles are more difficult, but not impossible, to separate from the Eurasian species.

The breeding grounds are in north and northwest North America, from the Yukon and Mackenzie valleys east to Hudson Bay and south to Oregon. The population was estimated at 2.5 ± 0.2 million breeding birds during 2008, similar to the long-term average. The species occurs on the Atlantic coast during autumn migration, and the genuine vagrants that have made it to Europe have almost certainly come from these Eastern-seaboard migrants.

Transatlantic movements are supported by the recovery of five Canadian-ringed birds and one bird about which little is known, other than that it was ringed in North America (Table 41).

FIG 59. American wigeon. Separating American from Eurasian wigeon can be difficult, especially in poor light. Diagnostic features of American wigeon are the creamy-white crown stripe and the broad dark green stripe over the eye, extending to the nape, some-times appearing as a dark eye patch. The female is similar to the female Eurasian wigeon but with a dark eye patch. (John Shaw/NHPA)

TABLE 41. American wigeon: transatlantic ringing recoveries.

RINGING LOCATION	RINGING DATE	AGE/SEX	RECOVERY LOCATION	RECOVERY DATE
New Brunswick, Canada	6 August 1966	Duckling	Shot, Shetland	7 October 1966
New Brunswick, Canada	13 August 1968	Juvenile male	Fair Isle, Shetland	21 September to 3 October 1968
New Brunswick, Canada	29 August 1968	Juvenile	Shot, Akeragh Lough, Co. Kerry *	12 October 1968
North America **	Not known	First-winter Female	Shot, Wexford	30 November 1968
Prince Edward Island, Canada	30 August 1977	Female	Shot, near Tuam, Co. Galway	8/9 October 1977
Prince Edward Island, Canada	29 July 1994	Juvenile male	Shot, Newtown-cunningham, Co. Donegal	15 October 2003

* Thirteen American wigeon had been seen at Akeragh Lough on 10 October 1968.
** Probably shot on the North Slob by Lord Dunamore. No further details available (*Irish Birds* 2006, **8**, 129).

Most European records have been in the period November to February. Between 1958 and the end of 2001 there were 336 BBRC-accepted occurrences of genuine vagrants in Britain, averaging 16 per year since 1990. They were removed from the BBRC list of rare birds as of 1 January 2002 because they had become so frequent and were no longer regarded as a rare vagrant.

All WeBS 2004/05 records came from Scotland, apart from one bird at the Ouse Washes, with records at the Loch of Hillwell, Shetland (November/December); Loch Bee, South Uist, Western Isles (November); Inner Moray Firth and Inverness Firth, Highland (December); Lossie Estuary and Moray coast, Moray (January); and Kinnordy Loch, Angus (June). All these birds were considered vagrants.[166] There were five records of single birds during WeBS

2005/06, and records from seven sites throughout Britain during Webs 2006/07.

There were no records of American wigeon in Ireland between 1800 and 1949, but a total of 114 records have been accepted by the IRBC between 1950 and the end of 2006, including six records in June.

As with other Nearctic species, no fossils of American wigeon have been reported from Europe.

22. GADWALL *ANAS STREPERA* (AC2)

The white speculum, on the hind edge of the wing, is the diagnostic feature separating gadwall from all other ducks that occur in these islands. Although difficult to see when the birds sit on water, it is immediately noticeable in flight (Fig. 60). The male is greyish with chestnut wing coverts, and the white belly contrasts with black tail coverts – at a distance the males on water look like grey duck with black ends. The female resembles the female mallard. Although closely related to mallard, they are more reserved and much less raucous. Thus it is easy to overlook them as they sit quietly on the water in small or larger flocks.

The gadwall is a widespread breeder throughout both the Palaearctic and the Nearctic, with significant breeding population increases in recent decades, reflected in rising numbers of wintering birds in northwest Europe. Between a third and a half of all our wintering birds originate in eastern Europe (including the Czech Republic and the Baltic states). Those breeding in Iceland (200–300 pairs)[167] winter mostly in Ireland, as do the Scottish breeding birds. Within Britain most wintering birds congregate in southeast England, East Anglia and the Midlands at their favourite habitats – gravel pits, the larger reservoirs and some flooded or marshy grasslands.

The most recent estimate of the number wintering in northwest Europe (1997–99) is 60,000 birds,[168] and of these some 17,100 and 630 winter in Great Britain and Ireland (for the periods 1995–99 and 2000–04, respectively). These numbers underline the importance of Britain and Ireland as winter locations for 30 per cent of the northwest Europe population. The numbers wintering in Britain over the past 30 years have steadily increased, with a ninefold increase since the mid-1970s reflecting the expansion of the gadwall's breeding range and general prospering of the European population. However, WeBS 2006/07 recorded a 20 per cent drop in Britain, with the index falling to levels equivalent to those of ten years ago. Numbers in Northern Ireland reached an all-time low since 1988/89, reflecting the population fall elsewhere in the UK.

FIG 60. Male gadwall in flight, clearly showing the diagnostic white speculum, a feature shared by the female. Orange edges to the upper mandible distinguish females from female mallard. (Alan Williams/NHPA)

High water levels in the key UK site, the Ouse Washes, and disturbance at other important sites, may have been responsible.

Gadwall fossils have been found in deposits from the Ipswichian interglacial period (127–117 ky BP) in southeast England, and from the Iron Age (700 BC – AD 43) in Somerset.[169] Probable fossils at Cathole, Glamorgan, date from the Late Glacial period (13–10 ky BP), and more recent fossils have been recorded from six other UK sites. Fossils have been found in six Irish caves from the Holocene period. The Little Ice Age (1550–1850) may have prevented the gadwall from breeding until 1850, when a pair of birds that had been caught in the Dersingham decoy, Norfolk, in 1849 were wing-clipped prior to their release on a nearby lake at Narborough – where they bred the following year, and ever since. Twenty-five years later a healthy population had developed in Norfolk, from where they spread over the Breckland border into Suffolk (1895), on into east Suffolk (1930s) and then to the Norfolk Broads (1950s).

Such introductions may in fact have played a substantial role in establishing the gadwall as a breeding species in Britain, and it comes somewhat as a shock to discover that this inconspicuous, easy-going and endearing dabbling duck may be another example of a non-indigenous species establishing a self-sustaining population in Britain and Ireland, largely derived from birds that were deliberately released into the wild, or escaped from waterfowl collections.

During the 1960s about 1,000 feral birds were liberated in Britain to augment the breeding stock, and more populations became established in Leicestershire, in Cumbria, and at Sevenoaks, Kent.[170] A breeding colony was also founded at Chew Valley Lake, Somerset, by birds that escaped from the Wildfowl Trust, Slimbridge. In recent years the feral birds have been augmented by immigrants from the expanding European population, raising the question – to what extent are British and Irish breeding birds derived solely from introduced stock? Feral populations are generally sedentary, demonstrating little eagerness for migration, but recoveries of summer-ringed birds show that only 13 per cent of gadwall remained in Britain and Ireland until late February, while the others migrated to France, Italy, Spain, the Netherlands and Denmark, suggesting that the breeding population is not solely derived from introduced stock. There is also evidence of an autumn moult migration of post-breeding adults to the Netherlands, where the birds congregate on the Ijsselmeer. This site is also an important staging location for immatures, prior to winter dispersal.

Thus until the 1970s the gadwall was a relatively scarce breeding duck in these islands. In 1990 there were at least 770 breeding pairs in Britain, and 30 in Ireland, and since then the population has expanded at about 5 per cent per annum. Within Britain the birds favour nutrient-rich wetlands in south and southeast Britain. East Anglia is one of their strongholds. Gadwall also breed sparingly in Scotland and Wales. There is no evidence that escapes from wildfowl collections are being incorporated into the present population.[171]

In Ireland the first breeding was recorded in 1933, and it is now a rare local resident with an estimated 50 pairs, with two small populations centred on the Lough Neagh area, Co. Down (at least 14 families in 2007, plus another six families nearby). They also breed on Strangford Lough (five pairs in 2005), possibly augmented by the release of feral birds.[172] County Wexford is the other stronghold: Lady's Island Lake (16 breeding pairs in 2007) and Tacumshin (eight families, 2006). Small numbers breed in counties Roscommon, Galway and Kerry. The wintering population of 630 birds represents almost a doubling of numbers since the 1970s.

There is nothing startling about the breeding biology of the gadwall. Females spend much of the year feeding on nutrient-poor vegetation but switch, prior to and during laying, to protein-rich macroinvertebrate food (mostly cladocerans – water fleas), which then comprises 72 per cent of their diet.[173] Clutch size is 8–11. Females lose up to 16 per cent of their body weight during incubation.[174] Of 168 Scottish nests studied, 43 per cent hatched, 55 per cent were predated and 2 per cent deserted. Losses of young up to 2 weeks old were 53 per cent, and up to pre-fledging 73 per cent in Alberta, Canada.[175] Annual adult survival for males was 0.75 and females 0.69 in a North American study.[176] No published survival rates for British and Irish adults are available.

Outside the breeding season, gadwall are generally vegetarian, eating leaves, shoots, roots, seeds, tubers, buds, and seeds of pondweeds, sedges, hornwort, wigeon-grass, grasses (including *Glyceria*) and stoneworts.

TABLE 42. Gadwall: sites in Britain where the mean five-year peak exceeded 500 birds (International threshold 600; National threshold 171). A further 34 sites exceeded the National threshold.

LOCATION	MEAN 5-YEAR PEAK 2002/03–2006/07	PEAK COUNT 2006/07
Ouse Washes, Cambridgeshire	1,196	200 (Nov)
Rutland Water, Leicestershire	806	904 (Aug)
River Avon, Fordingbridge–Ringwood, Hampshire	716	(113) (Feb)

TABLE 42. – *Cont.*

Lee Valley Gravel Pits, Hertfordshire	677	518 (Nov)
Abberton Reservoir, Essex	675	(535) (Aug)
Somerset Levels, Somerset	673	424 (Jan)
Thames Estuary, Kent/Essex/Greater London	526	414 (Feb)
Loch Leven, Perth & Kinross	507	309 (Sep)

TABLE 43. Gadwall: sites in Ireland where the mean five-year peak exceeded 20 birds (National threshold).

LOCATION	MEAN 5-YEAR PEAK 1996/97–2000/01	PEAK COUNT 2000/01
Loughs Neagh & Beg, Co. Armagh/Down/etc	153*	143 (Sep)*
Tacumshin Lake, Co. Wexford	127	–
Lady's Island Lake, Co. Wexford	93	–
Strangford Lough, Co. Down	72*	68 (Dec)*
Corofin Wetlands, Co. Clare	71	6 (Nov)
Ballyallia Lake, Co. Clare	52	12 (Sep)
Lough Corrib, Co. Galway	50	45 (Dec)
Tralee Bay, Lough Gill & Akeragh Lough, Co. Kerry	40	48 (Dec)
Lough Aderry, Co. Cork	40	68 (Nov)
Lough Carra, Co. Mayo	39	78 (Feb)
South East Clare Lakes, Co. Clare	37	–
Shannon & Fergus estuaries, Co. Limerick/Kerry/Clare	32	
Pat Reddan's Lake, Co. Tipperary	31	44 (Jan)
Rahasane Turlough, Co. Galway	29	
Lough Gur, Co. Limerick	28	67 (Jan)
Wexford Harbour & Slobs, Co. Wexford	27	12 (Oct)
Hillsborough Main Lake, Co. Down	17*	6 (Jan)*

23. EURASIAN TEAL *ANAS CRECCA* (AC2)

As the smallest European dabbling duck, the Eurasian teal cannot be easily confused with any other species apart from the garganey – a summer visitor/breeder in small numbers – and the closely related green-winged teal, a scarce vagrant from North America. Their small size adds to their abilities as extraordinarily versatile flyers, able to take off almost vertically, fly extremely fast and often erratically, in close, tight flocks, and suddenly plunging down like falling stones, into a watery reed bed or marsh. As such they are a favourite of the hunter, reflected by the high proportion of birds shot, totalling 97 per cent of all reported ring recoveries. The males have a distinctive call, a short, sharp 'krit-krit'.

The teal is an abundant and widespread breeder throughout the west European Palaearctic as well as in northern Asia, occupying areas from the sub-Arctic to the temperate zones. Numbers breeding in northwest Europe, including western Russia, are vast and uncertain. Recent information suggests some 2.5–3.5 million birds in western Russia alone, with a further 600,000–750,000 breeding in Finland. Another 100,000–150,000 birds occur further west, including Britain and Ireland. The numbers estimated in Britain in the *New Atlas* seem low at 1,500–2,600 pairs. Recent declines in Ireland have brought the population down to an estimated 350–550 pairs.[177] The teal's geographical and biological success is due, in part, to their catholic taste when it comes to breeding habitat – they will breed in virtually any kind of shallow water with dense marginal vegetation, such as tundra, forest ponds, bogland and farmland. About 500,000 birds, originating from a vast breeding range, spend the winter months in northwest Europe.

They undertake great migrations over long distances, and are one of the best-studied ducks with regard to their movements. The large numbers ringed in Britain and Ireland (more than any other duck except the mallard – 85,654 up to the end of 1997) have generated some 13,505 recoveries for migration studies. In addition, 3,045 foreign-ringed birds have been recovered in Britain and Ireland. The large number ringed is a tribute to the dedicated efforts of the Wildfowl & Wetlands Trust, whose various duck decoys, especially at Abberton, Essex, and Borough Fen, Northamptonshire, have accounted for nearly 50,000 of all teal ringed.

Most British and Irish breeding birds remain at home, with some moving south to France and Spain, especially during cold weather when their shallow-water habitats freeze up. Our large wintering population – 192,000 birds in Great Britain and some 45,010 in Ireland – is drawn from almost the complete breeding range – Iceland, northern Europe, the Baltic states, and a large area of the Russian Federation north of about 55° N and extending east to 60° E.

FIG 61. Male Eurasian teal on ice. Teal rely on shallow-water habitats, and may make substantial hard-weather movements in response to frozen conditions. (Paal Hermansen/NHPA)

They have a well-developed rapid-response capacity to local conditions affecting their winter feeding habitats – drought, excessive rain or freezing weather – and under such circumstances they will move quickly and restlessly in search of new feeding areas (Fig. 61).[178] They are especially prone to hard-weather movements, and extreme cold conditions push birds out of Britain and Ireland south into France and further into the Iberian peninsula.

The fossil history of the teal in Britain and Ireland dates back to the Middle Pleistocene (600–500 ky BP) at Boxgrove, Sussex. Fossils were also found in Late Glacial deposits in a Sutherland cave and in Ireland at Newhall Cave, Co. Clare (probably late Holocene).

Teal nest much closer to the water than most other ducks. Their nests are usually in dense vegetation on the edges of lakes, ponds in peatland, farmland, and other inland and coastal habitats. Pairing takes place generally in October/November, the monogamous pair bond lasting until the female starts her incubation, when the male departs. Eggs, 8–11, are laid from mid April onwards, the female incubating for 21–23 days. A replacement clutch is laid if the first is lost. The young, like other ducks, are nidifugous but usually return to the nest for the first few nights. Fledging takes place after 25–30 days. The average size of 15 well-grown broods was 4.8 in a Finnish study.[179] The mean annual survival of adults is 0.49 for British wintering birds, one of the lowest rates for dabbling ducks, reflecting not only their popularity as a quarry species but also their small body size – the smaller the duck the lower its survival rate.

Teal are omnivorous and catholic in their food requirements, feeding mainly on seeds during the winter and autumn, ideally in shallow waters, less than 25 cm deep. They dabble while walking, picking up plant seeds, especially knotweed, spike-rushes, buttercups, spearworts and water-crowfeet, oraches and glasswort. During winter small invertebrates such as chironomid midge larvae and small molluscs – freshwater snails of the families Hydrobiidae, Physidae and Lymnaeidae – contribute up to 25 per cent of their diet. Competition with the mallard, usually sharing the same habitat, is avoided by concentrating on the smaller seeds and invertebrates. Daily food requirements for birds wintering in the Camargue, France, have been estimated at 20–30 g fresh weight, i.e. 7–8 per cent body weight.[180] Teal feed mainly at night, especially where they are much disturbed by day.

Wintering numbers have been generally increasing over the past decades, but WeBS recorded a decline in 2006/07 numbers, falling by about 25 per cent in Britain and by about 50 per cent in Northern Ireland, dropping to levels similar in 1998/99.

TABLE 44. Eurasian teal: sites in Britain where the mean five-year peak exceeded 4,000 birds (International threshold 5,000). A further 25 sites exceeded the National threshold of 1,920 birds.

LOCATION	MEAN 5-YEAR PEAK 2002/03–2006/07	PEAK COUNT 2006/07
Somerset Levels, Somerset	17,615	21,581 (Jan)
Ribble Estuary, Lancashire	7,588	(6,959) (Dec)
Mersey Estuary, Cheshire	6,738	2,249 (Nov)
Thames Estuary, Essex	6,253	3,940 (Dec)
Ouse Washes, Cambridgeshire	6,131	4,333 (Nov)
Swale Estuary, Kent	5,288	(2,582) (Oct)
Loch Leven, Perth & Kinross	4,967	2,527 (Oct)

TABLE 44. – *Cont.*

WWT Martin Mere, Lancashire	4,276	1,430 (Nov)
N Norfolk Coast, Norfolk	4,216	3,638 (Sep)
Lower Derwent Ings, N/E Yorkshire	4,203	—

TABLE 45. Eurasian teal: sites in Ireland where the mean five-year peak exceeded 1,000 birds (National threshold 450).

LOCATION	MEAN 5-YEAR PEAK 1996/97–2000/01	PEAK COUNT 2000/01
Shannon & Fergus estuaries, Co. Limerick/Kerry/Clare	2,610	2,016 (Dec)
Strangford Lough, Co. Down	2,144*	1,724 (Oct)*
Little Brosna Callows, Co Offaly	1,966	1,130 (Feb)
Lough Ree, Co. Westmeath	1,943	3,348 (Jan)
Loughs Neagh & Beg, Co. Armagh/Down/etc	1,823*	1,049 (Mar)*
Lough Swilly, Co. Donegal	1,448	1,000 (Feb)
South Roscommon Lakes, Co. Roscommon	1,302	—
Lough Foyle, Co. Derry	1,243*	915 (Nov)*
Wexford Harbour & Slobs, Co. Wexford	1,227	784 (Nov)
Blackwater Railway Lake, Co. Offaly	1,135	740 (Feb)
Ballyallia Lake, Co. Clare	1,080	1,040 (Feb)
Inishcarra Reservoirs, Co. Cork	1,048	1,423 (Jan)

24. GREEN-WINGED TEAL *ANAS CAROLINENSIS* (**A**)

Until recently the green-winged teal was regarded as a subspecies of the Eurasian teal, *Anas crecca*, and travelled under the scientific name of *Anas crecca carolinensis*. It has now been elevated to full species status by the TSC of the BOURC. The females and juveniles of the green-winged and Eurasian teal are almost impossible to distinguish in the field. But the adult male green-winged teal can be differentiated from the Eurasian by the vertical white mark in front of the wing, rather than a horizontal white bar above the wing (Fig. 62).

The green-winged teal is a widespread breeder on the North American Continent, ranging from Alaska through Canada and across the northern USA, south to about 45° N. The population size was some 3.0 ± 0.2 million birds in 2008, more than 50 per cent above the long-term average and the second-highest

FIG 62. Male green-winged teal, sleeping. Note the vertical white mark in front of the wing, and the absence of a horizontal white bar. (Lee Dalton/NHPA)

total ever. During autumn migration birds travel south down the east coast of America, and it is from these movements that individuals are blown, or drift, off course, ending up in Europe as scarce vagrants. There is at least one transatlantic ringing recovery, of a juvenile ringed in New Brunswick, Canada, in August 1970, and shot on the Scilly Isles in January 1971.

A total of 509 occurrences have been accepted as wild vagrants in Britain by the BBRC for the period 1958 to 2001. As they had become too numerous, and were no longer regarded as rare, they were removed from the BBRC list of rare birds as of 1 January 2002. There are now about 30 recorded occurrences each year, and during WeBS 2006/07 there were records from 15 sites in Britain, all involving single birds. They were also recorded at two sites in Northern Ireland.

In Ireland there were accepted records of 127 individuals from 1950 to the end of 2006, occurring mainly between October and April, with a notable increase in records since the mid-1990s. Approximately 21 birds were recorded each year in 2005 and 2006. There are no records prior to 1950. For the same reasons as in Britain they have been removed from the IRBC's rare list. As green-winged teal are kept in waterfowl collections the possibility that some of the birds seen in the wild may have been escapes cannot be totally ruled out.

25. MALLARD ANAS PLATYRHYNCHOS (AC2C4E*)

The mallard (Fig. 63) is the commonest and most widely distributed duck in Britain and Ireland, with estimated breeding populations of 100,000 pairs[181] and 23,000 pairs respectively. The UK wintering population is estimated at 352,000 birds, a five-year mean from WeBS counts 1995–99. The approximate wintering total for Ireland is 38,250, derived from recent I-WeBS counts for the period 2000–04. The annual index of mallard wintering in Britain, derived from WeBS data, reveals a continuing long-term decline that commenced in the early 1980s. The British maximum fell by about 10 per cent in 2006/07 to its lowest level since 1977/78. A sharper decline was noted in Northern Ireland. The reasons are complex and could involve any of the following factors: a reduction of winter immigrants, poor breeding success, fewer birds being released by gun clubs, and possibly a scattering of the wintering population into smaller uncounted wetland due to milder weather.[182]

The species' adaptability and ubiquity are reflected in the wide distribution of fossils. In Britain these date back to the Middle Pleistocene (780–128 ky BP), but most are found in Holocene deposits (10–0 ky BP). Mallard fossils have been

FIG 63. Mallard, male. Mallard are our most familiar duck, ancestor of several of our domestic breeds as well as the inspiration for Donald Duck. The male's characteristic plumage, and the colours of the bill are feet, are fully revealed here. The bright iridescent blue speculum, bordered on either side by white, is a feature shared with the female. (Bill Coster/NHPA)

recorded in 31 per cent of the 75 British sites examined, and in a much higher proportion of the 11 Irish sites examined, 64 per cent. All the Irish mallard sites are relatively recent, dating from the Holocene.

Like the mute swan, mallard have evolved a cosy relationship with humans, especially in the urban environment, where they are found on most park ponds and other public-amenity water bodies, where the coarse 'quack' of the duck, the decrescendo call, resonates loudly across the waters. While this quack functions as a contact call, it might sometimes be interpreted as a begging call on urban leisure waters to encourage the release of more bread scraps from well-intentioned visitors. Their persistent quacking is more seriously associated with the process of nest-site selection, as a predator-lure to draw out any foxes – if they don't emerge then the duck knows the locality is safe for nesting.[187] The drake's call is more subdued.

Mallard are ideal shooting quarry, and are the most widely and commonly hunted duck in Great Britain with some 600,000–700,000 shot annually, representing 63 per cent of the total duck kill.[184] Many of the birds shot will have been hand-reared and released by gun clubs, but others are wild indigenous birds and continental immigrants. They are the shooter's favourites because they are plump and their meat tasty. Moreover, they provide attractive sport as they 'flight' into wetlands to feed at dusk. Every year upwards of 400,000 birds are hand-reared and released onto ponds by shooting syndicates and gun clubs in Britain, augmenting the wild breeding populations. In Ireland approximately 10,000 hand-reared birds were released annually during the 1970s, but today very few are released.[185]

Some of the rearing and release programmes have been responsible for the introduction of aberrant genes that have infiltrated, often unwittingly, from farmyard and domesticated stock or other dodgy genetic provenance into the wild mallard population. The result is that, in most localities, it is not unusual to encounter mallard that display weird plumages of white, black and brown. Some domestic breeds will also mix with wild birds, interbreeding with them and jumbling up wild mallard genes even further. The drakes of these genetically modified birds and genuine hybrids retain the characteristic green metallic head, as well as the curled tail of their ancestors. Drake mallards are also well known for their amorous conduct, and they have bred in captivity with almost any other duck, some of them from different genera or tribes – up to 45 different hybrids have been documented.[186] Some of the resulting hybrids have bred successfully with hybrids of a different species cross to produce 'multiple hybrids'. The prevention of such hybridisation in wildfowl collections is a daunting task.

Although showing a preference for low farmland and river-valley habitats, their adaptability and opportunism has allowed them to exploit virtually all habitats from 2000 m high mountains to coastal islands. Mallard usually nest in thick cover, under bushes, in undergrowth or protected by other tall vegetation, at the ideal height of up to 1 m, and nests are invariably close to water. Some birds also nest in hollows in trees, up to 15 m off the ground, presenting challenging prospects for the ducklings when leaving the nest. One clutch of 15 eggs was recorded in an abandoned magpie's nest at the top of a silver fir 12 m above the ground, in Hillsborough Park, Co. Down. All the ducklings hatched, and apparently survived the jump.[187]

Lake islands are particularly favoured breeding locations because of the extra protection afforded by their isolation. Nests are generally widely scattered throughout suitable habitat but in remarkably high densities on islands such as

St Serf's island (14 ha) in Loch Leven, Perth & Kinross. This shallow eutrophic loch – 13.3 km² in extent, half of it less than 3 m deep – holds the largest concentration of breeding duck in Britain. Some 400–450 pairs of mallard nest on the island, with an average of 7 m between each nest, one of the highest densities known in Britain. For comparison, the islands of Lough Neagh, Co. Antrim (combined area 43.75 ha) supported approximately 700 breeding pairs of mallard in 1987, at half the breeding density reported for St Serf's island.[188] Mallards nesting in tall vegetation are more successful than those breeding in short vegetation, and those on islands are more successful than those on the mainland.[189] But nest density can also affect predation rates, principally by carrion/hooded crows and magpies, which increase as the density of nests increases.[190] However, the selective advantages of nesting at high densities must outweigh the disadvantage of the increased mortality from predation.

The mallard breeding season spans from February to October – one of the longest seasons of any European duck – and like other dabbling ducks they commence breeding at the age of 1 year, although Hugh Boyd noted some precocious mallards breeding at age 6–7 months.[191] After hatching, the downy ducklings feed on protein-rich emerging aquatic insects, plucked from the water surface, often after a mad skittering chase, somewhat reminiscent of Donald Duck speeding along, legs spinning like wheels. Hatching midge larvae and midge pupae, stoneflies and mayflies are eaten by the ducklings. If the supplies of insects are inadequate, the ducklings have to search, and as they spread out over a larger area they suffer higher rates of mortality as they become more vulnerable to predators such as pike, American mink, red foxes, herons and carrion/hooded crows. The abundance of aquatic insects in 'immature' water bodies such as flooded gravel pits is considerably less than in longer-established wetlands. The presence of high densities of coarse fish – common bream, tench and roach – in the youthful waters can significantly reduce the number of aquatic insects. Removal of fish from these wetlands resulted in a significant increase in invertebrate density and biomass, and consequently more food for the ducklings. In one study, in the years following fish removal, mallard brood density increased from 0.22 to 0.81 per hectare.[192]

Drakes do not participate in brooding, although they attend in a waiting area not far from the nest. They abandon the duck as soon as the clutch is complete and play no role in duckling care. Some indulge in forced copulations – sometimes leading to the death of the duck – with other females once their primary mate commences incubation. One study found that up to 60 per cent of ducklings came from broods that were multi-fathered.[193] Males then gather together in food-rich lakes or large ponds. By the beginning of July they will have completed the first part of their moult, producing a plumage resembling that of the female (Fig. 64). While in this 'eclipsed' state and conveniently camouflaged from land-based predators such as the red fox and man, their flight feathers are then moulted in rapid succession, rendering them flightless for about four weeks, mainly between early July and mid August (peak mid July). The female moults about four weeks after the drake while still looking after the ducklings. When the ducklings fly, at about six or seven weeks, the family ceases to operate as a unit, unlike the geese and swans. By October the drakes have regained full plumage and, resplendent in their new outfits, set off to court a new duck. Re-pairing with old mates occurs only occasionally. Many pairs are formed by the end of October, and the break-up of winter flocks occurs in February when pairs go off to search for a nesting site.

Mallard breeding biology is discussed in more detail in Chapter 6.

FIG 64. Mallard, female. The camouflaged brown plumage provides great concealment for incubating females, which often stay on the nest to the very last moment before a predator reaches it. (Ken Kinsella)

TABLE 46. Mallard: sites in Britain where the mean five-year peak exceeded 2,000 birds (National threshold 3,520).

LOCATION	MEAN 5-YEAR PEAK 2002/03–2006/07	PEAK COUNT 2006/07
Severn Estuary, Gloucestershire/Somerset/etc	3,396	3,661 (Sep)
Ouse Washes, Cambridgeshire	3,245	2,606 (Nov)
WWT Martin Mere, Lancashire	2,984	2,221 (Oct)
Livermere and Ampton Water, Suffolk	2,678	—
Humber Estuary, E Yorkshire/Lincolnshire	2,522	(1,752) (Dec)
The Wash, Lincolnshire/Norfolk	2,482	2,417 (Oct)
Tring Reservoirs, Hertfordshire	2,169	1,988 (Oct)
Lower Derwent Ings, Yorkshire/Lincolnshire	2,139	—
Morecambe Bay, Lancashire & Cumbria	2,036	1,837 (Oct)

TABLE 47. Mallard: sites in Ireland where the mean five-year peak exceeded 500 birds (National threshold 380).

LOCATION	MEAN 5-YEAR PEAK 1996/97–2000/01	PEAK COUNT 2000/01
Loughs Neagh & Beg, Co. Armagh/Down/etc	4,505*	4,351 (Sep)*
Wexford Harbour & Slobs, Co. Wexford	3,321	—
Strangford Lough, Co. Down	1,657*	(1,010) (Dec)*
Lough Swilly, Co. Donegal	1,271	1,724 (Sep)
Lough Ree, Co. Longford	1,020	817 (Jan)

TABLE 47. – *Cont.*

Lough Foyle, Co. Derry	938*	1,036 (Oct)*
Dundalk Bay, Co. Louth	853	611 (Nov)
Tralee Bay, Lough Gill & Akeragh Lough, Co. Kerry	680	570 (Nov)
Cork Harbour, Co. Cork	620	—
Lower Lough Erne, Co. Fermanagh	599*	551 (Jan)*
Shannon & Fergus estuaries, Co. Limerick/Kerry/Clare	568	—
Ballyallia Lake, Co. Clare	522	682 (Nov)

26. AMERICAN BLACK DUCK *ANAS RUBRIPES* (A)

Similar in size and shape to the mallard, the American black duck has a blackish-brown plumage and a yellow bill, while the female has a dark olive bill. The face and fore-neck are greyish. Because some of our mallard ducks are darker than normal they can be confused with the American black duck. The black duck also hybridises with the mallard in North America to produce even more confusing hybrids. Thus it is important to observe, in flight, the black-bordered purple speculum of the male (Fig. 65). During 2008 there were an estimated 568,700 individual breeding black duck in North America.

The black duck is a scarce vagrant to Britain and Ireland, with only a few records in recent years. The first European record came from Ireland – a female shot near Mullinavat, Co. Kilkenny, in February 1954. It was submitted to Sir Peter Scott, who confirmed its identity. It had been found in a poulterer's shop – after which it was discovered that another had been shot and winged but escaped. The next one was seen on the North Slob, Co. Wexford, in February 1961, followed by another, shot, in Co. Wexford, in November 1966. A total of 12 birds – all singles – have been accepted by the IRBC in Ireland from 1950 to the end of 2006. One bird has returned to the same wintering haunt for several winters, a behaviour shared by several other vagrant ducks.

The first British record was of a probable male at Yantlett Creek, Stoke, Kent, on 18 and 25 March 1967. A total of 31 occurrences between 1950 and 2006 have been accepted by the BBRC, with nearly 57 per cent of the records since 1997. During WeBS 2000/01 long-staying birds were noted as still present (from 1999/2000) in Cornwall in Stithian's Reservoir (November) and at Loch Fleet, Highland. Another was seen at Colliford Reservoir, Cornwall, in October 2000.

Several have remained for extended periods, creating the impression that it is a commoner species than is in fact the case. In Britain sporadic hybridisation takes place with mallards. This has occurred for long-staying birds in Scilly, Gwynedd and Highland – good numbers of hybrid offspring were produced, some of which were very difficult to distinguish from the adults.

There are no fossil remains recorded so far from Europe, as with other Nearctic species. The separation of their fossils from those of the mallard could present considerable difficulties.

FIG 65. American black duck in flight, showing the diagnostic black-bordered bluish-purple speculum. Both male and female resemble a dark female mallard with pale brown head and upper neck. Bill of male is yellow-green. Conspicuous white under-wings. Beware of melanistic female mallards. (T. Kitchin & V. Hurst/NHPA)

27. NORTHERN PINTAIL *ANAS ACUTA* (A)

The northern pintail is one of the most elegant dabbling ducks in Britain and Ireland (Fig. 66). The male's white chest, extending upwards through the long chocolate-coloured neck to the chocolate head, and two long central tail feathers (lost in the eclipse plumage) are distinctive features. It is a scarce breeder in central Europe, most occupying the northern tundra, forest–tundra and forest–steppe zones between 60° and 70° N in northern and central Russia (150,000–300,000 pairs), with fewer in Finland (20,000–30,000 pairs), Sweden (700–2,000 pairs), Norway (100–500 pairs) and Estonia (200–400 pairs).

Pintail are essentially winter visitors to Britain and Ireland. Of the estimated 60,000 birds that winter in northwest Europe, almost half occur in Great Britain, the highest proportion of the European population of any duck species. Some 1,235 are estimated to winter in Ireland, most of which are in the Republic. Within Britain, the Dee and Solway estuaries and Morecambe Bay, together with the Bury Inlet, hold about 32 per cent of the population. Favoured wintering habitats are sheltered and shallow estuaries, fringed with marshes and close to agricultural land. Flooded grass fields, turloughs and callow lands, together with stubble fields, are also visited. In recent years there has been a drift out of estuaries onto fresh water such as reservoirs. Estuarine wintering pintail feed mostly on small snails (the mud snail or laver spire shell, *Hydrobia ulvae*) and on seeds. In marshland seeds can form 80 per cent of the diet, the most frequently taken being common spike-rush.

Looking at the WeBS and I-WeBS figures, January totals of pintail in Britain and Ireland increased remarkably in the early 1970s, probably due to a series of successful breeding seasons rather than reduced adult mortality from shooting. A decline followed from the early 1980s until the early 1990s, to a low point in 2000/01. Since then, the annual index of wintering birds has increased each winter to reach a peak in 2005/06, with numbers during 2006/07 falling off slightly. Numbers in Ireland similarly declined from the 1970s (3,000–7,000) to an estimated 1,235 wintering birds for the period 2000–04. Loss of wetlands throughout the pintail's geographic range and excessive hunting at the local level are thought to be the principal reasons for the decline in wintering numbers to 2000/01. These pressures led to the designation of 'unfavourable conservation status' for the pintail within Europe. The decline has not been limited to Europe. In North America breeding numbers fell from 6 million to 3 million birds from the early 1970s to the late 1980s. There were 2.6 ± 0.1 million breeding birds in 2008, some 36 per cent below the long-term average. The decrease has been

FIG 66. Northern pintail are elegant and graceful dabbling ducks with elongated necks that allow them to feed deeper under water than other shorter-necked species. During spring courtship males chase females for many hours, often high in the sky, sometimes exhausting the females – which may then be gang-raped and die. (Ken Kinsella)

ascribed to farming operations – drainage, intensification, and periods of intense drought on the prairie breeding grounds,[194] but numbers have decreased more in the far north of the breeding range, where there is no farming and where droughts are unknown.

The first pintail arrive from September onwards and are thought to be from Iceland, followed by more birds from Fennoscandia, the Baltic states and the Russian Federation. Most reach their favoured wetlands between mid September and mid November. Males predominate among the first arrivals: having completed their moult some time before the females, they are able to travel first. Virtually the entire Icelandic breeding population (c.500 pairs)[195] winters in Ireland and Britain, while other wintering birds originate from Finland, Sweden and Norway. But it appears that the vast majority of British wintering birds are from the Russian breeding population. The majority of pintail recovered in Britain were ringed in Russia, north of 60° N and east to about 80° E.

Pintails are weather-sensitive, like teal, many pushing on southwards from Britain into France and Spain during cold conditions. Some birds ringed in Britain while on passage end up even further south, with one recovery from west Africa. Remarkably, some of our winter visitors are of transatlantic origin – one duckling ringed in 1969 on Prince Edward Island, Canada, was shot in Co. Sligo in January 1974. Two other transatlantic ringed birds were both recovered in Britain during September.

Only three caves in Britain and Ireland have so far revealed fossil remains, indicating a historical scarceness of pintail. At Clevedon Cave, Somerset, the pintail dates from the Late Pleistocene (127–10 ky BP), while the fossils in Coffey's Cave, Co. Sligo, are more recent, from the Holocene (10–0 ky BP). Those in Newhall Cave, Co. Clare, are also probably from the Holocene. At the crannog site at Lagore, Co Meath (AD 750–950), an exceptional number of pintail bones – the most numerous of nine duck species recorded there – were recovered.

Pintail are scare and rare breeders in Britain and Ireland, with a minimum of 11–51 and 30–40 pairs respectively.[196] The first proven breeding records in Britain were in 1869 at widely separated sites in Inverness-shire and Kent. Ireland had to wait until 1917, when a pair was discovered breeding in Co. Roscommon. It was subsequently recorded nesting, with eight ducklings, in Co. Armagh in 1927, and later in other areas in and around Lough Neagh. Breeding was proven at Lough Beg, Co. Derry, from 1959 until the mid-1970s. It also bred in Strangford Lough, Co. Down, in 1938.[197] Breeding records exist for at least six counties throughout Ireland, but numbers remain extremely small.

They are ground-nesters, the female making the nest, lined with down, frequently under cover of vegetation and often far (up to 2 km) from water. The female diet during the laying period is mostly (up to 99 per cent) protein-rich invertebrates, similar to that of the gadwall. The European clutch size is normally 7–9, and the clutch will be replaced if lost. The female incubates for 22–23 days. The ducklings hatch synchronously and are taken to water by the female after a day in the nest. Both the adults – the male is often present during the first stages of duckling development – and the ducklings mostly consume high-protein aquatic insects – mosquitoes, gnats and midges, especially chironomid midges, snails and shrimps. In a Finnish study of 33 nests 76 per cent of eggs hatched, with a mean brood size of 7.1 on hatching, reduced to 4.7 at about halfway to fledging.[198] In a study in Alberta, Canada, there was a 53 per cent mortality of ducklings by the end of the first two weeks and a 73 per cent loss to fledging.[199] The mean annual survival rate for adults is 0.52, calculated from recoveries of Russian-ringed birds. In North America, first-year survival rates were calculated at 0.56 for males and 0.51 for females, while the figure for adult males was 0.63–0.81, and for adult females 0.42–0.77.[200]

TABLE 48. Northern pintail: sites in Britain where the mean five-year peak exceeded 600 birds (International threshold). A further 20 sites exceeded the National threshold of 279 birds.

LOCATION	MEAN 5-YEAR PEAK 2002/03–2006/07	PEAK COUNT 2006/07
Dee Estuary, England/Wales	5,825	6,172 (Oct)
Burry Inlet, Dyfed	4,491	4,692 (Feb)
Solway Firth, Cumbria	4,268	(2,329) (Nov)
Morecambe Bay, Lancashire	3,369	2,609 (Oct)
Ouse Washes, Cambridgeshire	2,769	1,823 (Feb)
Ribble Estuary, Lancashire	2,651	(1,094) (Jan)
Duddon Estuary, Cumbria	2,051	2,317 (Jan)
Nene Washes, Cambridgeshire	1,559	1,931 (Feb)
Severn Estuary, Gloucestershire/Somerset/etc	1,033	(1,161) (Jan)
The Wash, Lincolnshire	1,007	1,215 (Feb)
Mersehead RSPB Reserve, Dumfries & Galloway	900	1,010 (Dec)
Medway Estuary, Kent	812	(582) (Feb)
Swale Estuary, Kent	790	(231) (Feb)
N Norfolk Coast, Norfolk.	673	753 (Feb)
Pagham Harbour, W Sussex	615	566 (Feb)
Dee Flood Meadows, Cheshire	615	916 (Jan)

TABLE 49. Northern pintail: sites in Ireland where the mean five-year peak exceeded 50 birds (National threshold 20). A further eight sites exceeded the National threshold.

LOCATION	MEAN 5-YEAR PEAK 1996/97–2000/01	PEAK COUNT 2000/01
Strangford Lough, Co. Down	490*	496 (Dec)*
Tacumshin Lake, Co. Wexford	293	—
Dublin Bay, Co. Dublin	219	151 (Dec)
Little Brosna Callows, Co. Offaly	140	288 (Jan)

TABLE 49. – *Cont.*

Dundalk Bay, Co. Louth	122	135 (Feb)
Castlemaine Harbour & Rossbehy, Co. Kerry	117	12 (Jan)
Wexford Harbour & Slobs, Co. Wexford	82	10 (Sep)
Shannon & Fergus estuaries, Co. Limerick/Kerry/Clare	69	—
Lough Foyle, Co. Derry	58	—
Lough Ree, Co. Westmeath	57	112 (Jan)
Malahide Estuary, Co. Dublin	55	70 (Jan)

28. GARGANEY *ANAS QUERQUEDULA* (A)

Garganey are unique among British and Irish wildfowl as our only summer visitor, coming to breed here from their subtropical African wintering grounds. They are small dabbling ducks, noticeably larger than teal. The male is instantly distinguished by the conspicuous broad white stripe on the head, extending from the eye to the lower nape (Fig. 67). His remarkable appearance is lost during the eclipse plumage – which can last for 5–6 months – when he resembles the female. In flight the pale blue-grey forewing is a diagnostic feature of both sexes. In contrast, the female is a drab brown thing, similar to the female teal but slightly larger with a more striped head and a not very noticeable pale white crescent over the eye. There is also a pale loral patch at the base of the all-grey bill. They are often considered the Palaearctic ecological equivalent of the blue-winged teal, though there is no close genetic relationship. The male utters an extraordinary rapid and wooden-sounding rattling call, somewhat akin to a chopstick being rapidly run over a series of small, thin wooden strips. He uses this call both on the water and in the air, mainly during courtship and communal displays. In flight their rapid wing beats create a characteristic hiss, which experienced wildfowlers can identify at night.[201]

The name garganey is from the Italian *garganello*, in turn from the onomatopoeic *garg*, from the male's rattling/raucous call.[202] They are an important game bird for hunters – comprising up to 17 per cent of the total number of duck shot in the central region of the European part of the former USSR.[203]

Their breeding range extends throughout the Palaearctic, from Britain and France to southern Sweden, Finland, east to northern Russia and across Asia between 65° and 42° N as far as Kamchatka. The vast majority of the west

FIG 67. The male garganey, slightly larger than a teal, is unmistakable with a broad white band along the side of the head, extending from the eye to nape. Found in pairs or small parties, from the end of March onwards, in shallow freshwater lakes and marshes with good vegetation cover on the water margins. (Manfred Danegger/NHPA)

Palaearctic population, 2–3.3 million birds,[204] including our few breeders, migrate, crossing the Mediterranean to Algeria and Morocco to winter in the northern tropics just to the south of the Sahara. It is the most common Palaearctic duck in Senegal and the Gambia, where upwards of 93,000 birds are recorded in some years, but where most spend the winter remains a mystery.

Fossil remains show the garganey to have been present in Sussex at Boxgrove during the Middle Pleistocene, Cromerian era (600–500 ky BP). It was also present in Derbyshire at Pin Hole Cave during the Mousterian period (115–35 ky BP) of the Late Pleistocene, while the most recent fossils come from Thatcham Cave, Berkshire, during the Holocene, dated at 10,400–9,500 years BP. The Thatcham fossil was ascribed to *A. querquedula/crecca*. James Fisher reports it as present in Britain during the Bronze Age as a fossil, and Brian Martin notes its presence in Somerset as a fossil during the Iron Age (700 BC – AD 43).[205] It was also present during the Dark Ages at Lagore, Co. Meath (AD 750–950). The Romans reared them for the table.[206]

Garganey were almost certainly breeding in the Norfolk Broads – their only known British location at the time – during the early nineteenth century, and thereafter in Essex and Suffolk spasmodically, but they may have ceased to breed by the end of the nineteenth century. During the early twentieth century there was a gradual increase in numbers, from a few to c.100 pairs, associated with an expansion of the breeding range into some 10 counties with intermittent breeding in 13 until 1952. Climatic amelioration and the availability of its specialist breeding habitat – shallow standing waters, swampy pools and ponds with associated wet ditches and channels – had provided encouragement. However, breeding numbers in western Europe have declined by some 50 per cent since 1970, probably due to the deterioration and degradation of their wetland breeding habitats.

Numbers breeding in Britain and Ireland in any year are highly variable, dependent upon the number of spring migrants turning up – peaking in March – which is in turn influenced by warm and dry spring weather in Europe. They are elusive and difficult to track down, but normally some 15–125 pairs breed, mostly in central and southeastern Britain – particularly in East Anglia, Essex and Lincolnshire. Most breeders are located in nature reserves, where critical water levels are carefully monitored and controlled.[207] The Ouse Washes is the most important breeding area, holding 25–35 pairs in 1962 but only 4–15 during the 1980s. The males are extremely territorial, and thus small water bodies can only accommodate one pair.

They were first recorded nesting in Scotland in 1928, followed by Wales in 1936. Breeding in both these countries is intermittent, related to the number of immigrants during spring.

Fewer than ten pairs bred in Ireland in 2004.[208] The most likely breeding locations today are in the Lough Neagh/Beg complex and in south Wexford. It is not an unusual spring migrant in many Irish counties and it is likely that further breeding records will occur. The first breeding occurred at Lough Neagh in 1956, but no details were provided,[209] and it has bred on at least three, possibly more, subsequent occasions, in Northern Ireland – one pair at Strangford Lough, Co. Down, in 1993 (five young) and 1994 (eight juveniles) and another in the Lough Neagh Basin in 1999 (five young).[210] Breeding took place in Co. Kerry in 1959, and possibly at Lady's Island Lake, Co. Wexford, in 1978. One pair at least bred there between 1988 and 1991, seen with 4–5 young, and a female was seen there in July 1994 with 13 young. Juveniles or young were recorded at Lady's Island Lake in 1995 and 1998–2000; a female with three or four very recently fledged juveniles was noted at Tacumshin, Co. Wexford, in late July 2003, and one juvenile in 2004. Juveniles were seen at the same location in 2005, 2006 and 2007.

Garganey arrive in Britain and Ireland generally already paired, an advantage allowing rapid commencement of breeding, from late March through to July. The female makes the nest on the ground, usually in tall grass or thick vegetation, normally within 20 m of water in shallow freshwater marshes, ponds and small lakes with emergent vegetation habitat. They are omnivorous. As the breeding season approaches their diet changes from vegetarian to animal – snails, chironomid and other insect larvae and more aquatic invertebrates, including molluscs. In the former USSR garganey often breed in tern or gull colonies, thus securing predator defence. Clutch size is normally 8–11; incubation averages 23 days, with the male generally in attendance. The average loss of clutches – from mammalian and avian predators, human activity and flooding – has been recorded at 33–42 per cent in Ukraine, but up to 84 per cent in reservoirs, due to elevated water levels. Overall nest loss throughout the former USSR is at least 20–30 per cent. Predation by black kites, hooded crows and common gulls can account for the loss of 10 per cent of all broods. The average loss of hatched ducklings is in the range of 30–35 per cent, with rates as high as 45 per cent in some instances. The female cares for the young apparently without assistance from the male. Drake garganey commence their moult in early June; the birds are flightless for 3–4 weeks and are in eclipse plumage during July. The most important moulting location for Russian drakes is the Volga Delta, where many tens of thousands congregate.[211]

Autumn migration commences in July, peaking in August. Some continental birds, mainly ringed in the Netherlands, have been recovered in Britain during the late autumn. WeBS 2000/01 recorded wintering birds – four present in November, with singles remaining to December and January. Wintering birds have also occurred in Ireland: one in 2000, three in 2004 and two in 2006. These could have been either immigrants from the Continent or birds remaining after the breeding season. WeBS 2006/07 recorded peak numbers in September, but the British maximum (82) was the second lowest since 1992. Birds, mostly in ones or twos, were present at 91 sites across Britain.

TABLE 50. Garganey: sites in Britain where the mean five-year peak exceeded 4 birds (no National threshold).

LOCATION	MEAN 5-YEAR PEAK 2002/03–2006/07	PEAK COUNT 2006/07
Wraysbury Gravel Pits, Berkshire	12	6 (Sep)
Middle Yare Marshes, Norfolk	(7)	(0)
Ouse Washes, Cambridgeshire	5	0
Rye Harbour and Pett Level, E Sussex	5	3 (Apr)
Thames Estuary, Essex	(5)	(1) (Aug)

29. BLUE-WINGED TEAL *ANAS DISCORS* (AE)

These teal are garganey-sized. The males have a striking white crescent on the head in front of the eye and a sharply contrasting black and white rear. The female is drab but slightly darker than the female garganey. When in flight the pale blue forewings of both sexes are conspicuous (Fig. 68). It is a native of North America, where there were some 6.6 ± 0.3 million breeding individuals during 2008, 45 per cent above the long-term average. The birds of the east-coast breeding population migrate south in the autumn towards northern South America, and these are probably the source of our transatlantic visitors. Transatlantic crossings are supported by a number of ring recoveries (Table 51). The blue-winged teal that turn up in Europe appear to come from the Canadian Maritime Provinces, as is the case with two other transatlantic vagrants, the green-winged teal and the American wigeon.

TABLE 51. Blue-winged teal: transatlantic ringing recoveries.

RINGING LOCATION	RINGING DATE	AGE/SEX	RECOVERY LOCATION	RECOVERY DATE
New Brunswick, Canada	June 1971	Male	Shot, Suffolk	9 October 1971
Newfoundland, Canada	September 1983	Juvenile	Shot, Co. Offaly	January 1984
Prince Edward Island, Canada	No details available	No details available	Tetuan, Morocco	October 1970
Prince Edward Island, Canada	No details available	No details available	Ebro Delta, Spain	January 1974

The blue-winged teal's habitat preferences are similar to those of the garganey, and they are likely to be seen on sluggish fresh waters, pools and floodlands. Occasionally they occur on brackish waters.

There were 223 occurrences of genuine wild birds accepted by the BBRC in Britain between 1950 and 2006. Prior to 1950 there were 10 occurrences. Before 1970 the species was rare in captivity, and the likelihood of escaped birds was low, but that is not the case now. During WeBS 2000/01 there were three records

FIG 68. Male blue-winged teal, showing off the characteristic pale blue forewing. Males have a striking white crescent on the face from lower crown to chin. They also have a distinct white patch before a black stern. The female is brownish with a faint white spot near the base of the bill. (Melvin Grey/NHPA)

of single birds, at Stodmarsh National Nature Reserve and Collards Lagoon, Kent (first recorded in 1998–99), at Blithfield Reservoir, Staffordshire, and at Cley on the north Norfolk coast. Only one was recorded during WeBS 2003/04, at Chew Valley Lake, Somerset, in August 2003. During WeBS 2004/05 one was recorded at Norton Marsh, north Norfolk, during May. Only one was reported from the Avon Estuary, Devon, during WeBS 2005/06.

It is rare in Ireland, recorded mainly between September and October, with four records accepted by the IRBC as genuine vagrants 1880–1949 and a further 57 between 1950 and the end of 2006. Care should be taken with observations of apparently wild birds, as many are undoubtedly escapes from waterfowl collections.

As discussed earlier, there is always the danger of hybridisation between non-indigenous escaped wildfowl and other closely related species. In the case of the blue-winged teal, a female, presumed an escape, successfully mated with a male northern shoveler in Cambridgeshire in 1988, with the production of three young.[212] There have been other cases of mixed pairs – at Blagdon Lake, Somerset, in 1993 a female blue-winged teal was paired with a male northern shoveler in one bay, while at the same time a female cinnamon teal was paired to another shoveler in an adjacent bay. No young were seen. However, hybrids do occur from time to time. Andy Musgrove saw one in Norfolk in 2002 that, from the plumage, was surely a male blue-winged teal x northern shoveler hybrid.[213] An alternative view of these types of 'undesirable' hybridisation is that they are examples of evolution in action – the production of variants – the raw material for natural selection that may ultimately lead to the formation of a new subspecies or full species.

30. NORTHERN SHOVELER *ANAS CLYPEATA* (A)

The huge spoon-shaped bill – one-fifth longer than the mallard's – sets the northern shoveler apart from all other ducks (Fig. 69). The male, sitting low and heavy in the water like a small battleship, is a contrast of colours – chestnut flanks and belly, white chest and green head. The female is the usual mottled brown, similar to the female mallard.

The shoveler has a widespread breeding range throughout Eurasia, rarely penetrating the Arctic Circle and tundra zones, occurring between 70° and 45° N from Iceland to eastern Russia as far as 162° E. It also occurs in North America, in both Alaska and Canada. Russia hosts about 75 per cent of the Eurasian population, with an estimated 79,000 breeding pairs. The Netherlands (10,000–14,000 pairs) is its west European stronghold, followed closely by Finland (10,000–12,000 pairs).

Fossil records date back to the Middle Pleistocene Hoxnian interglacial period (350–300 ky BP) at Swanscombe, Kent, the only Pleistocene record in these islands. It was also present during the Iron Age (700 BC – AD 43) in Somerset,[214] but the combination of the Little Ice Age (1550–1850) and extensive drainage and reclamation of the Fens led to a reduction of the shoveler population to the point where it became extremely rare as a breeding species during the early 1800s. But it continued to breed regularly in the Norfolk marshes as well as in the Romney Marsh, Kent. By 1850 Norfolk was the only English county known where they bred.

FIG 69. Northern shoveler, male. A muscular-looking duck with a large dark spatulate bill, dark green head, white chest and chestnut flanks. The pale blue forewing is similar in colour and pattern to that of the blue-winged teal. Despite their heavy bodies they can spring almost vertically from the water like teal when disturbed. (Alan Williams/NHPA)

Across the water in Ireland it was first proven breeding near Portumna, Co. Galway, in 1863, having been suspected of breeding for several years. By the end of the century it had spread into at least 13 counties. The first nesting in Scotland was much later, in 1943. Since the respective first breeding records the shoveler has made steady if not spectacular progress, extending its range through England, Wales and Ireland. Today Britain holds about 1,000–1,500 breeding pairs, concentrated in the south and east of the country, especially within the Norfolk Broads, the North Kent Marshes and the East Anglian Fens. There are fewer than an estimated 20 pairs in Ireland (2004), where they are focused in the northeast (in and around Lough Neagh) and the Midlands. In 2005/06 birds were seen during the breeding season at Lough Erne, Co. Fermanagh, but without proof of breeding.

During the autumn some 40,000 migrants, originating in Iceland, Scandinavia, and Russia east to 60° E, arrive to winter in northwest Europe.[215]

Many of these birds end up in Britain and Ireland. Recent estimates show 14,800 wintering in Great Britain and a further 2,545 in Ireland. The British annual index of wintering birds derived from WeBS shows a relatively stable population during the 1970s and 1980s, then an increase from the beginning of the 1990s to the present. The small Icelandic population (10–30 pairs)[216] probably winters principally in Ireland. British and Irish breeding birds migrate south to northern and western France, the Iberian peninsula and north Africa, leaving between mid September and November just as the European winter migrants start arriving in Britain and Ireland. However, a small part of our breeding population probably remains at home – there are two recoveries of adults ringed during the breeding season in eastern England and subsequently recovered in Ireland during the winter. The key staging site for immigrants in Ireland appears to be Lough Owel, Co. Westmeath, where I have counted upwards of 2,000 in October–November in the mid-1960s. Thereafter numbers decline to several hundred for the rest of the winter.

FIG 70. Pair of northern shoveler. They regularly return to the same nesting area year after year, and may spend up to eight days finding a suitable site. Most birds breed at one year old. (Ken Kinsella)

Shovelers nest on the ground, in rushes or grass, generally close to water, and they often return to the same nesting area in subsequent years (Fig. 70). The average clutch of 9–11 eggs is incubated by the mother alone, and the young, which hatch synchronously, are nidifugous and looked after and defended by the female. The clutch is replaced if lost. A three-year study in Finland found that of 451 eggs laid some 74 per cent hatched and 17.5 per cent of all eggs gave rise to fledged young. The survival of young per breeding pair each year was 4.7, 0.2 and 2.0, so losses were 49, 97 and 78 per cent.[217] Of 26 Scottish clutches, 54 per cent hatched, 42 per cent were predated, and 4 per cent deserted.[218] The mean annual survival rate of adults ringed in Britain has been calculated by Hugh Boyd at 0.56, and at 0.67 based on birds ringed at Abberton Reservoir, Essex.[219] Studies in North America suggest that density-dependent regulation on the breeding grounds, attributable to the territorial system, is an important control mechanism for the population.[220]

The shoveler's spatulate bill is adapted for surface feeding, confining the bird to highly productive marshy and other shallow wetlands where zooplankton – especially small crustaceans such as ostracods and cladocerans – are copious. The shoveler cruises through the water, bill thrust forwards, often swinging the head from side to side, gulping in the rich bouillabaisse of microorganisms, extracting them as the water is expelled through the curtain of fine lamellae protruding from the edges of both mandibles. Sometimes a single bird will swim around in small circles, creating a vortex or small whirlpool that sucks more zooplankton into the range of the bill. Such is the efficiency of the feeding instrument, and the calorific richness of the prey, that shovelers can increase their body weight by 10 per cent per day, thus capitalising on an often limited and transitory food supply. Quick refuelling empowers the birds to undertake more migrations and movements during the winter period than most other ducks.

There are advantages and disadvantages for such a specialist feeder. The shoveler can exploit almost exclusively a specific feeding habitat. But if these shallow wetland habitats disappear, either through drought or through drainage, the birds are in difficulties and have to turn to feeding areas where the spatulate bill cannot be used to maximum efficiency. Yet research in North America has shown that the shoveler appears to be less affected by food shortages than other dabbling ducks, a factor that may help to explain the long-term stability of the species in that continent.[221]

TABLE 52. Northern shoveler: sites in Britain where the mean five-year peak exceeded 400 birds (International threshold). A further 33 sites exceeded the National threshold of 148 birds.

LOCATION	MEAN 5-YEAR PEAK 2002/03–2006/07	PEAK COUNT 2006/07
Ouse Washes, Cambridgeshire	1,400	696 (Nov)
Somerset Levels, Somerset	1,335	1,520 (Feb)
Rutland Water, Leicestershire	563	495 (Sep)
Chew Valley Lake, Somerset	491	300 (Oct)
Abberton Reservoir, Essex	485	(152) (Aug)
Thames Estuary, Essex	468	(407) (Feb)
Severn Estuary, Gloucestershire/Somerset, etc	432	600 (Jan)
Breydon Water & Berney Marshes, Norfolk	416	540 (Jan)

TABLE 53. Northern shoveler: sites in Ireland where the mean five-year peak exceeded 100 birds (National threshold 25). A further 14 sites exceeded the National threshold.

LOCATION	MEAN 5-YEAR PEAK 1996/97–2000/01	PEAK COUNT 2000/01
Ballyallia Lake, Co. Clare	400	570 (Jan)
Little Brosna Callows, Co. Offaly	274	639 (Feb)
S Roscommon Lakes, Co. Roscommon	244	95 (Dec)
Lough Rea, Co. Galway	201	153 (Nov)
Lough Iron, Co. Westmeath	165	—
Kilcolman Marsh, Co. Cork	165	200 (Mar)
Strangford Lough, Co. Down	161*	139 (Nov)*
Inner Galway Bay, Co. Galway	130	226 (Jan)
Dublin Bay, Co. Dublin	120	75 (Dec)
Lough Owel, Co. Westmeath	111	—
Shannon & Fergus estuaries, Co. Limerick/Kerry/Clare	107	36 (Jan)
Tacumshin Lake, Co. Wexford	107	—
Cork Harbour, Co. Cork	107	74 (Dec)

31. RED-CRESTED POCHARD *NETTA RUFINA* (AC2E*)

This is an exotic and larger version of the common pochard, sporting a striking pink bill and golden head (Fig. 71). The male's red crest is prominent during courtship display only and, unique among wildfowl, he practises a ritual of offering food to the female. Pieces of vegetation are plucked off the lake bottom and are then proffered up to the female, who almost invariably accepts them. They are scarce winter visitors to Britain and Ireland, very rare during the nineteenth century. Today most sightings are believed to relate to escaped or feral birds.

Their main breeding population is around the Black Sea, especially in Romania, Turkey and eastwards into Asia. There is also a curiously detached breeding outpost in southeast Spain, and other small isolated groups in central and northwest Europe. For nearly 160 years these pochards have been gradually

FIG 71. Red-crested pochard, male. The crested orange-red head contrasts with the crimson bill and glossy black neck, breast and underparts. The unseen legs are orange. In flight the broad white wing patch on the flight feathers extends nearly the whole length of the wing and is more conspicuous than in any other duck. (Alan Williams/NHPA)

extending their breeding range, pushing slowly into northwest Europe through central Europe, where colonisation commenced during the late nineteenth century. By 1920 they had reached western Germany, then Denmark (about 1940) and the Netherlands (1943). The small breeding population of northwest Europe, consisting of some 300–375 birds, is thought to have been derived from feral stock.

The British wintering population, immigrants plus residents, approximates 100–250 birds found in at least 79 different places in recent winters. Their most important wintering area is Cotswold Water Park (West), Gloucestershire, where a recent maximum winter count was 207 in December 2006. The estimated maximum number of birds and sites occupied has shown an upward trend in Britain as determined by WeBS. In 1992/93 there were 174 birds at 35 sites, while in 2006/07 there were 297 birds at 55 sites. Most records are of single birds, but 10 places had peaks of over 10 birds.

Their fossil presence in Britain dates from the Cromerian interglacial of the early Middle Pleistocene period (c.470 ky BP) at West Rushton, Suffolk, and Ostend, Norfolk, when they probably thrived in warmer periods. If any were present before the fifteenth century, the cold period of 1550–1850 would almost certainly have eliminated them. The species was first identified in Britain in 1818, and in 1874 London Zoo first acquired some birds.

The feral breeding population in Britain – originating from escapes and releases from wildfowl collections and deliberate introductions from 2005 onwards in north Suffolk for shooting – is augmented each autumn by immigrants, arriving principally in southeastern Britain, from the Continent, thought to emanate from moulting birds gathered in the Netherlands (breeding population 10–25 pairs), western Germany (a few pairs), Poland (30–40 pairs) and France (a few pairs). The favoured habitats of red-crested pochards are freshwater lakes, reservoirs and gravel pits, especially those fringed by common reed.

During the 1930s and 1940s free-flying birds were reared at Woburn, Bedfordshire. Some were released in London parks in 1933, 1936 and 1950. The breeding record in northeast Lincolnshire in 1937 may have been of genuine wild birds, because at this time they had been spreading into northwest Europe and there had been a small influx of birds during the winter 1936/37. The first feral breeding, escapes from a wildfowl collection, took place in Essex in 1958. Subsequently several pairs became established in southern Britain, and today upwards of 50 pairs comprise a small, naturalised and self-sustaining population. Their headquarters are at the Cotswold Water Park on the Gloucestershire/Wiltshire border (first confirmed breeding 1975, probable annual breeding thereafter, with up to 117 birds in 2001). They first bred at Baston and

Langtoft Gravel Pits, Lincolnshire, in 1996, with 2–4 pairs present from 2002, and other breeding records have come from Nottinghamshire (2002), Norfolk (five broods 2002) and Glamorgan and Gower (one pair present).[222] St James's Park, London, also holds a small but thriving free-flying population. No red-crested pochard have yet attempted to breed in Ireland.

There have been nine recoveries of birds ringed in Britain, the greatest distance travelled being 215 km. A juvenile ringed in St James's Park, London, in September 1952 was found dead in Hoogeveen, the Netherlands, in January 1953.

In Ireland they are rare vagrants. Four were recorded in the period 1800 to 1949, with a further 54 to the end of 2006, mainly seen between October and March. Birds observed outside this period are generally regarded as escapes. Most have been reported from eastern Ireland, especially in Co. Wexford. An adult male was seen on the North Slob, Co. Wexford, in November 2002, while another was present during June and July 2003 at Lady's Island Lake, Co. Wexford, possibly a prelude to the first breeding in the country. In Northern Ireland the species had not been recorded until 1965. Since then, there has been a plethora of records, almost annually since 1980, all of which were probably of captive origin.

TABLE 54. Red-crested pochard: sites in Britain where the mean five-year peak exceeded 10 birds (no National threshold). A further 4 sites held a mean more than 4 birds.

LOCATION	MEAN 5-YEAR PEAK 2002/03–2006/07	PEAK COUNT 2006/07
Cotswold Water Park (West), Gloucestershire	130	207 (Dec)
Cotswold Water Park (East), Gloucestershire	59	106 (Oct)
Lower Windrush Gravel Pits, Oxfordshire	19	26 (Jan)
Hanningfield Reservoir, Essex	18	17 (Aug)
Baston & Langtoft Gravel Pits, Lincolnshire	16	—
Arnot Park Lake, Nottinghamshire	13	16 (Jul)
Sutton and Lound Gravel Pits, Nottinghamshire	13	22 (Dec)

32. CANVASBACK *AYTHYA VALISINERIA* (AE)

Canvasbacks breed in North America from central Alaska and western Canada south to northern California, Colorado and Minnesota, with a breeding population of approximately 500,000 ± 50,000 birds in 2008, some 14 per cent below the long-term average. It is difficult to distinguish from the redhead and common pochard, but if eaten it is the tastiest of the three species, especially when feeding on wild celery (*Vallisneria americana*, hence its scientific name). The high sloping forehead and elongated bill of both sexes gives them a distinctive wedge-shaped profile unlike any other duck apart from the common eider. In general they look like an exaggerated pochard with a bigger bill and head (Fig. 72). The male is distinguished by an all-dark bill – the female's is also dark – and a blackish crown and face. The iris is bright red in spring, slightly

FIG 72. Canvasback, male. Distinguished from its near relative the common pochard by slightly larger size and the lack of a subterminal pale band on its blackish bill. Overall its body is paler and duller. (John Shaw/NHPA)

duller in winter. They are large diving ducks and because they strain many seeds out of bottom muds they are inclined to pick up and ingest lead shot and are particularly prone to lead poisoning. They often fly in V formation and are among the fastest-flying ducks, reaching speeds of up to 115 km/hour.

It is an extreme rarity in Britain as a genuine vagrant. The first record, an immature male, was observed at Cliffe, Kent, on 7 December 1996. The second, also an immature male, was seen intermittently at Welney and Wissington, Norfolk, from 18 January to 10 March 1997, possibly the same one as seen in Kent, given the dates and locations. A total of seven occurrences in Britain have been accepted by the BBRC for the period 1950–2006. None has yet been recorded in Ireland.

They were first introduced into waterfowl collections in Europe in 1922, with breeding recorded in Britain in 1925. They had been kept in captivity earlier in North America.[223] Escapes from collections do occur, and such birds can be easily misidentified as genuine wild vagrants.

As might be expected with a Nearctic species, there are no fossil records from Europe.

33. COMMON POCHARD *AYTHYA FERINA* (AE*)

As a breeding bird the common pochard is widespread throughout central Eurasia between 40° and 60° N, from Iceland, Ireland and Spain in the west to the Lake Baikal region at 118° E. The breeding population from which our winter visitors come exceeds 210,000 pairs, with the largest numbers in Russia (> 95,000 pairs) and Finland (15,000–20,000 pairs).

Of the 350,000 birds that winter in northwest Europe about 59,500 visit Great Britain (mean number for 1995–99). Those at Loughs Neagh and Beg comprise about a quarter of the estimated 37,780 wintering population in Ireland (mean number for 2000–04). Pochard often form large flocks on reservoirs, brackish coastal loughs and other lakes, especially where water depth is less than 3 m, allowing the birds to dive and comfortably forage for their food on the lake bottom.

During the period from the early 1960s to the mid-1970s wintering numbers in Great Britain more than doubled as the birds went through a range expansion in Europe coinciding with the creation of new water bodies in worked-out gravel pits, the construction of more reservoirs and the development of new fish ponds. However, there has been an overall steady decline in wintering numbers in Great Britain over the past ten years, with the annual WeBS national index now at its lowest ever level.

FIG 73. Flock of wintering common pochard in Greece. Large flocks such as this are also a common sight on British and Irish waters. (Andrea Bonetti/NHPA)

FIG 74. Common pochard, male. (Ken Kinsella)

Since the late 1970s numbers in the northwest European population have declined by about 30 per cent, but they now show signs of stabilising at levels seen in the late 1960s and early 1970s. Numbers in Ireland fluctuated widely during the 1990s. Following a dramatic decline in numbers at Loughs Neagh and Beg, Northern Ireland, up to 2003/04 numbers showed a tentative recovery. It is thought that increased nutrient inputs to the loughs had affected the availability of the chironomid midge larvae that form the principal food of the pochard.[224]

Recoveries of ringed pochard show that our wintering birds originate mainly from Baltic countries – about 62 per cent of all British and Irish recoveries ringed abroad come from Latvia – and the former USSR east to at least 61° E. Immigrant males begin to arrive at the principal moulting sites at Loch Leven, Perth & Kinross; Abberton Reservoir, Essex; Lough Corrib, Co. Galway; Lough Cullin, Co. Mayo and Lough Derravaragh, Co. Westmeath, at the end of June. British birds ringed during the breeding season – some of those ringed as adults could be moult migrants or early movers into Britain from the Continent – provide recoveries from France, Spain, the Netherlands, Britain and Ireland, the main wintering areas. There is considerable mobility of birds, and low levels of site fidelity within Britain and Ireland during winter, especially during freezing conditions when birds are driven west and south. There are puzzling recoveries of British birds ringed during the breeding season and recovered during subsequent breeding seasons overseas as far as 65° E in the Russian Federation as well as from Belarus, Finland, Estonia, Poland and the Netherlands.

During summer, between early June and late August, large congregations, mainly of males, gather together in favoured locations to moult. Upwards of 5,300 have been seen at Abberton Reservoir, Essex, in July and August, and 850 at Dungeness Gravel Pits, Kent. In Ireland the largest late-summer congregations, dominated by adult males, have been recorded on Lough Corrib, Co. Galway (formerly up to 22,000 birds, now only some 6,000), and Lough Derravaragh, Co. Westmeath (formerly up to 6,000, now fewer than c.3,000).

Male and female pochard perform differential migrations, males migrating before the females due to their earlier moult, the females held back by duckling-rearing activities. Thus the males (Fig. 74) are in the wintering areas first, occupying the choicest habitats. When the females arrive they leapfrog the males, perhaps driven by intersexual aggression, and travel further south, where they occupy possibly inferior-quality feeding habitat. Perhaps for this reason, together with greater migration distances, females have higher mortality rates. However, some investigations of female wintering grounds have shown that females did not suffer reduced feeding rates. The ratio of males to females is strongly correlated with latitude. Within Britain males predominate in the north

at 59° N, with about eight males to one female, but this ratio drops to about
3 : 2 further south at 50° N.

Fossil remains are present in Cromerian interglacial deposits (c.470 ky BP) from
the early stages of the Middle Pleistocene (two UK sites) and at one Irish site
dating from the Holocene (10–0 ky BP). They also appear in the Iron Age (700 BC –
AD 43) deposits in Somerset but are not recorded from Lagore, Co. Meath
(AD 750–950). Apart from these records, little is known about their early history in
Britain and Ireland. The pochard was first identified in Britain in 1544 or possibly 998.
It was not until the early nineteenth century that they were recorded as breeding
in Britain, with the first published record from Scoulton Mere, Norfolk, in 1818, and
thereafter they bred only spasmodically in the county. They bred in Yorkshire in 1844.

Scotland was colonised in 1871 at Lough Awe, Argyll, although they had been
suspected to be breeding at Loch Loy, Moray, in 1848. Sufficient evidence is
presented in Ussher and Warren's *Birds of Ireland* (1900) to show that pochard
bred in at least seven Irish counties from 1847 onwards, with most records from
the period 1880–97, corresponding with the phase of northward expansion in
Scotland. In 1988–91 there were some 400 pairs breeding in Britain, mostly
restricted to eastern England and Scotland. Fewer than 30 pairs were thought to
breed in Ireland in 2004, principally restricted to the Lough Neagh basin, Co.
Antrim. Nesting has also taken place in counties Westmeath (1995), Cork (1998),
Offaly (2001) and Tipperary (2007).

The nest, located on the ground in dense vegetation or sometimes on an island
or clump of vegetation in the water, is seldom further than 10 m from the water's
edge. The usual clutch size is 8–10. Egg dumping by other females is not uncommon,
and occurs when a female fails to make a nest – which might be because she is
inexperienced, or lacks a mate, or is unable to find a nest site, a strategy to avoid total
breeding failure. Most dumped eggs do not hatch because of non-synchronisation
with those of the host. Incubation (24–28 days) is by the female, who also looks after
the young during the longish fledging period of 50–55 days (although they may be
independent before that). Males usually depart two weeks into the incubation period.
In the former Czechoslovakia, 1968–70, of 1,151 eggs some 56 per cent hatched. In
Germany the average number of young reared to fledging was 4.4 per successful pair,
and 1.8 for all pairs. There are no available published data on adult survival.

Pochard are omnivorous. During the winter they eat seeds, rhizomes, buds,
shoots, leaves, tubers and especially the oospores of stoneworts, as well as the
seeds of pondweeds, water-milfoil, hornworts, sedges and club-rushes,
persicarias and grasses. Animal food includes mainly chironomid midge larvae,
small shrimps, molluscs, worms, insects and their larvae. The young feed mostly
on flies and floating seeds.

TABLE 55. Common pochard: sites in Britain where the mean five-year peak exceeded 800 birds (National threshold 595). A further 4 sites exceed the National threshold.

LOCATION	MEAN 5-YEAR PEAK 2002/03–2006/07	PEAK COUNT 2006/07
Abberton Reservoir, Essex	3,764	3,167 (Nov)
Ouse Washes, Cambridgeshire	3,089	4,197 (Feb)
Loch Leven, Perth & Kinross	2,611	3,666 (Oct)
Hornsea Mere, E Yorkshire	1,150	710 (Jan)
Dungeness Gravel Pits, Kent	901	1,045 (Aug)
Chew Valley Lake, Somerset	878	1,220 (Dec)
Fleet/Wey, Dorset	817	879 (Nov)
Lower Derwent Ings, E Yorkshire	818	—

TABLE 56. Common pochard: sites in Ireland where the mean five-year peak exceeded 380 birds (National threshold).

LOCATION	MEAN 5-YEAR PEAK 1996/97–2000/01	PEAK COUNT 2001/02
Lough Corrib, Co. Galway	11,637	15,650 (Nov)
Loughs Neagh & Beg, Co. Armagh/Down/etc	8,164*	8,884 (Jan)*
Lough Derravaragh, Co. Westmeath	2,986	—
Lough Ennell, Co. Westmeath	923	—
Lough Kinale & Derragh Lough, Co. Westmeath	779	—
Upper Lough Erne, Co. Fermanagh	660*	329 (Feb)*

34. REDHEAD *AYTHYA AMERICANA* (**AE**)

Redheads breed in North America, chiefly in the prairie lands of western Canada and the USA, where the estimated breeding population size was 1.1 ± 0.1 million individuals in 2008, more than 50 per cent higher than the long-term average and the highest number ever recorded. They are the New World counterparts of the common pochard, which they closely resemble (Figs 75 and 76).

It is an extremely rare vagrant to Europe, with only three BBRC-accepted occurrences in Britain between 1950 and 2006. The first bird, a male, was recorded at Bleasby, Nottinghamshire, and Leicestershire from March 1996 into 1997. A male bird was later observed at Kenfig Pool, south Wales, in November

FIG 75. Redhead, male. Slightly larger than the closely related canvasback, darker grey and with a rounded, less sloping, more abrupt forehead. The redhead's iris is yellow, in contrast with the red of the common pochard, with which it might also be confused. The redhead's bill is blue/grey rather than the blackish of the pochard. (Rich Kirchner/NHPA)

FIG 76. Redhead, female and male. The female is a more uniform and warmer brown than the female redhead or pochard. (Ken Kinsella)

2001 into 2002. Possibly the same bird returned in September 2002, and was joined by a female. Another bird was seen in 2003. A single drake was present from October to December 2004. The BBRC announced in October 2007 that following an initial revaluation of the Glamorgan record it felt there was a case to review all of the records to date and generate robust evidence-based criteria for future claims. The BBRC added that there was little doubt that many of the existing records are sound but the best way to clarify criteria is to look at them all together. Elsewhere in Europe it has been recorded in Germany, and two were seen in Iceland in June and July 1998. The first Irish record accepted by the IRBC was from Cape Clear Island, Co. Cork, 12–15 July 2003. The redhead is not commonly kept in wildfowl collections, and was late to be included in European collections, the first arriving at London Zoo in 1902. Some were reared in a British private collection in 1924. This seems to be the easiest of all pochards to manage and breed in captivity.[225]

As would be expected for a Nearctic species, there are no fossil records reported to date from Europe.

35. RING-NECKED DUCK *AYTHYA COLLARIS* (AE)

The ring-necked duck (Fig. 77) is widely distributed throughout North America as a breeder, and has recently extended its range into eastern parts of the country. The breeding population was estimated at 651,000 individuals during 2007. It is an annual vagrant to Britain, with 427 occurrences accepted from 1958 to the end of 1993. As it had become such a frequent visitor it ceased to be classified as a 'rare bird' by the BBRC, and therefore statistics on its frequency are no longer published.

During 2005/06 WeBS recorded singles and two birds (Chew Valley Lake, Somerset) at eleven sites in England and one in Northern Ireland (Upper Lough Erne, Co. Fermanagh). During WeBS 2006/07 ring-necked ducks were observed at eleven sites in England and a further five in Scotland, with peak numbers of eight in February 2006. All records were of individuals apart from a record of two.

It was first reported from Ireland in 1959, and to the end of 2006 a total of 168 individual records, including 28 during 2006 alone, had been accepted by the IRBC. Several of the records almost certainly relate to returning birds, which is a

FIG 77. Ring-necked duck, male. Similar to a tufted duck, but with a distinctively shaped head, and a slightly upcurved bill with two white rings. (Mike Lane/NHPA)

characteristic feature of this duck. It occurs mainly between October and April. They have been recorded from twelve sites in Ireland during I-WeBS core counts and have been most regularly seen in Wexford Harbour, on the Slobs, Co. Wexford, and at Lough Oughter, Co. Cavan.

An adult ringed on 7 September 1967 in New Brunswick, Canada, was shot near Brecon, Wales, on 26 December of the same year. An adult male ringed at Slimbridge, Gloucestershire, on 1 March 1977 was shot in southeast Greenland in May of the same year.

As would be expected for a Nearctic species, there are no reported fossil records to date from Europe.

36. FERRUGINOUS DUCK *AYTHYA NYROCA* (AE)

This smallest and daintiest of all the pochards (Fig. 78) is widely distributed as a breeder throughout central Eurasia, with small numbers in southern and eastern Europe. The northern breeding populations are migratory. It breeds in Germany and Poland, and in small numbers in the Netherlands, Belgium and

FIG 78. Ferruginous duck, male. Smaller than tufted duck with a longer bill and less rounded head. Note the white eye and white undertail coverts. (Roger Tidman/NHPA)

France. It is an accidental visitor to Britain, chiefly to the south and east. Many of the birds seen in the wild in Britain have probably been genuine migrants, displaced during migration to the Mediterranean region. However, as it is present in at least 200 British waterfowl collections (and several more in Ireland), some of the reported British and Irish birds could have emanated from these sources. The escapes and feral birds from collections also migrate. The ferruginous duck was removed, as of 1 January 2006, from the BBRC list of rare birds, as it had become no longer a 'rare species'. A total of 300 records were accepted for the periods 1958–1968 and 1998–2004 – no records were collected between 1968 and 1998. They have not been known to breed in Britain or Ireland,[226] and there are no fossil records from these islands.

Single ferruginous ducks were recorded by WeBS at four sites during 2006/07, with one long-staying bird at Chew Valley Lake, Somerset.

They are very rare visitors to Ireland, recorded mainly between October and March. Between 1800 and 1949 they were recorded on 10 occasions, with a further 19 records between 1950 and the end of 2006. Most records have been from Northern Ireland.

37. TUFTED DUCK *AYTHYA FULIGULA* (A)

The tufted duck (Fig. 79) is the commonest and most widespread of all the diving ducks as a breeder and winter visitor in Britain and Ireland. It is a trans-Palaearctic breeding species, nesting throughout Europe from Iceland to the Bering Sea between 45° and 70° N. More than half of the western Palaearctic population of some 600,000–830,000 pairs occurs in Russia, while a further 147,000–220,000 pairs breed in Fennoscandia, mostly in Finland (100,000–150,000 pairs). There is also a large breeding population, about 10,000 pairs, in Iceland.

From this large breeding population some 1.2 million winter in northwest Europe, and numbers are increasing.[227] Great Britain holds an estimated 90,100 wintering birds. In Ireland there were some 36,610 birds wintering in the years 2000–04, including some 7,000–8,000 on Loughs Neagh and Beg in Northern Ireland. Numbers on these two loughs significantly declined from a peak of 26,360 birds in 2000/01 to 7,871 in January 2006. Most of our wintering tufted duck are from Fennoscandia, Iceland and northern Russia, east to about 65° E. The visitors from eastern parts of the European range are concentrated in Britain, while most of the Icelandic birds winter in Ireland.

FIG 79. Tufted Duck, male. The adult male is easily recognised by its sharply contrasting black plumage with pure white flanks. During the breeding season the male displays a long narrow pendant occipital crest that nearly reaches down to the back. The female is a dark brown with few distinguishing marks. (Ken Kinsella)

Numbers wintering in Britain and Ireland during the past 30 years have more or less remained stable, and represent about 8 per cent of the northwest European population. National index values obtained from WeBS indicate a slight but steady increase over the past ten years, but there was a noted decline during WeBS 2006/07. The decline in numbers at Loughs Neagh and Beg, Northern Ireland – over 75 per cent during the ten years to 2005/06 – continued into 2006/07, with peak numbers the lowest for twenty years. The fall in numbers is thought to be associated with nutrient enrichment leading to a change in the invertebrate food supply.[220] In contrast, numbers recorded at Upper and Lower Lough Erne, Co. Fermanagh, during 2006/07 were the highest for the past five years.

British and Irish breeding birds are generally sedentary during normal winters, as shown by the recovery of birds ringed during the breeding season. However, some sectors of the population show movement. Large numbers of Scottish-ringed birds travel southwest into Ireland during the autumn and winter. Females and immatures ringed at Loch Leven, Perth & Kinross, are four times more likely to move to Ireland than to travel south into England. Tufted ducks ringed in southeastern England also exhibit considerable mobility during the autumn, travelling to five principal locations: to southwest England, East Anglia and the Midlands in Britain, to the Ijsselmeer in the Netherlands, and westwards to Ireland.

Fossil remains show that the species was present in Britain at two sites during the warmer periods of the Late Pleistocene from the Late Cromerian interglacial deposits (c.470 ky BP) onwards, and in Ireland probably from the Holocene (10–0 ky BP) to the Dark Ages (c. AD 400–1066). The Little Ice Age (1550–1850) prevented it from breeding in Britain and Ireland during that period. When the weather warmed up again it recolonised Britain, Ireland and northwest Europe. The first historical record in Britain dates from 1662.

During the first half of the nineteenth century the tufted duck was known only as an uncommon winter visitor in Britain, and it was not recorded breeding until 1849, at Malham, Yorkshire, and at Osberton, Nottinghamshire – though there is some evidence of earlier breeding in both counties. The population increased and spread rapidly during the 1880s, following the introduction of Wild Bird Protection Acts that established shooting seasons.

The expansion of the breeding populations was initially rapid, then slowed down but took off again after the 1930s, coinciding with the construction of new reservoirs and the creation of flooded gravel pits. Another upward surge came after the 1950s, prompted by the increase of two key food species, both aliens. The zebra mussel, a freshwater bivalve from the Caspian and Black Sea areas, was first noticed during 1824 in London docks, having probably arrived on boats. It subsequently spread and colonised freshwater systems throughout Britain. It took longer to reach Ireland, being first noticed at Limerick docks on the River Shannon in 1994. Subsequently it proliferated throughout the River Shannon system, including associated lakes and canals. The second alien is Jenkins' spire shell, a native of New Zealand first observed in Britain in 1889. Since then, it has colonised most aquatic habitats, becoming the most common gastropod in Britain. It invaded Ireland around 1900 and is now widespread throughout the country. Densities of up to half a million per square metre have been recorded. These two alien molluscs form up to 81 and 20 per cent by volume respectively of food taken by tufted ducks during winter, and their wide availability may have contributed to the birds' increased winter survival rates. Tufted ducks are very largely carnivorous, with over 80 per cent of their food being animal material.

The breeding population in Britain during 1986 was estimated at 7,000–8,000 pairs, with a further 1,750–2,000 pairs in Ireland. The commencement of breeding and subsequent spread in Ireland, described by Ussher and Warren as 'one of the most interesting ... facts ... of our ornithology', mirrored that in Britain. It was a regular winter visitor by at least the beginning of the nineteenth century, and the date of first breeding is probably earlier than the often-quoted 1877. A pair of adults were on Lower Lough Erne, Co. Fermanagh, in the summer of 'about 1877'. A brood appeared a couple of years later. In 1882 Sir Ralph Payne-Gallwey, quoted in Ussher and Warren, stated that they were breeding in Loughs Neagh and Beg, as well as in Co. Monaghan and on the Shannon Lakes, where he had seen them in spring and summer long before 1882. Ussher and Warren concluded that because of the widespread breeding established by 1882 they must have commenced breeding in Ireland 'a lapse of time that would carry us back further than 1877'. Thus they were almost certainly breeding prior to 1877, possibly as early as 1834, when an adult male was killed, showing no previous wounds, on Lough Neagh on 17 June.

Tufted ducks are essentially a lowland breeding species, seldom found in uplands and none at more than 400 m above sea level. Flooded gravel pits are the favoured breeding habitat, with highest concentrations in the Thames region, Essex and the Severn–Trent area, demonstrating a preference for calcium-rich and generally eutrophic water bodies of over 1 hectare – also good for the growth of bivalve molluscs. They are absent from large parts of Scotland, west Wales and southwest Britain, where the waters are more oligotrophic and thus hold low densities of chironomid larvae, key food for the growth of ducklings. In Ireland they are scarce south of a line from Dundalk, Co. Louth, to Skibbereen, Co. Cork, reflecting the absence of suitable large water bodies. Loughs Neagh and Beg are their Irish breeding headquarters, and held 1,000 pairs in the 1960s, declining to 300 pairs in 1987. That decrease, attributed to increased competition for invertebrate food by an expanding roach population, then halted, and now tufted duck numbers are again increasing – a 1998 breeding survey estimated 433 pairs with 177 broods and 974 young. Although not colonial breeders, high nesting densities can occur on islands such as St Serf's in Loch Leven, Perth & Kinross, where 200 pairs per hectare have been found. They also show a preference for nesting in or near black-headed or common gull colonies, where they gain added protection from predators through the aggressiveness of the gulls. Their two main predators, carrion/hooded crows and magpies, can destroy over 50 per cent of all tufted clutches.

The nest is usually on the ground, in thick vegetation, within 20 m of water. A single clutch of 8–11 eggs is normally laid, although up to 22 eggs have been recorded, probably due to egg dumping – females laying in others' nests. A second clutch will usually be laid, if the first is lost. Breeding success is highly variable according to location and year – approximately 68 per cent of nests produce young with 11–15 per cent of all young fledging.[229] In Scotland some 57 per cent of 1,115 nests studied hatched, 38 per cent were predated and 5 per cent were deserted. In Finland, during a three-year study with 4,342 eggs monitored, 78 per cent hatched and of those only 11.4 per cent fledged. Productivity per nesting pair in each year was 2.2, 1.0 and 0.5 ducklings surviving to fledging, reflecting losses of 76, 89 and 95 per cent of all eggs laid.[230] In comparison, productivity at Loch Leven, Perth & Kinross, was 0.5 young per breeding adult.[231] Hatching of ducklings is synchronous. They spend 45–50 days feeding by themselves – first on pondweed seeds and adult insects then, later on, under the supervision of the female, on chironomid midge larvae and freshwater snails. Hatching coincides with peak emergence of midge larvae, which are snapped up off the water surface. When densities of coarse fish – competitors for the midge larvae – are high then duckling survival is low, as was seen during the decline at Loughs Neagh and Beg. The mean annual survival rate for adults in northwest Europe is 0.54.

There is a moult migration into Britain from June/July onwards, mostly of males from the eastern parts of the European breeding range. The few females that come arrive later, in August. Those wintering in northwest Europe exhibit allohiemy of the sexes, a characteristic shared with other duck species – i.e. the females travel further south than the males, probably for the same reasons as explained for the common pochard. In Britain the ratio of males to females during winter averages 1.4 : 1.0.

TABLE 57. Tufted duck: sites in Britain where the mean five-year peak exceeded 901 birds (National threshold).

LOCATION	MEAN 5-YEAR PEAK 2002/03–2006/07	PEAK COUNT 2006/07
Rutland Water, Leicestershire	7,809	9,758 (Sep)
Loch Leven, Perth & Kinross	3,993	3,553 (Oct)
Abberton Reservoir, Essex	3,142	1,187 (Apr)
Pitsford Reservoir, Northamptonshire	2,123	1,374 (Sep)

TABLE 57. – *Cont.*

Hanningfield Reservoir, Essex	1,783	2,194 (Aug)
Walhamstow Reservoirs, Greater London	1,751	1,516 (Aug)
Staines Reservoirs, Surrey	1,721	1,865 (Aug)
Ouse Washes, Cambridgeshire	1,523	2,057 (Feb)
Chew Valley Lake, Somerset	1,444	1,325 (Nov)
Middle Tame Gravel Pits, Warwickshire	1,243	1,243 (Feb)
Lee Valley Gravel Pits, Hertfordshire	1,215	1,215 (Nov)
Cotswold Water Park (West), Gloucestershire	1,183	1,372 (Dec)
Wraysbury Gravel Pits, Berkshire	1,035	429 (Dec)
Alton Water, Suffolk	994	1,008 (Nov)
Hornsea Mere, Yorkshire	923	600 (Jan)
Theale Gravel Pits, Berkshire	(918)	(918) (Jan)

TABLE 58. Tufted duck: sites in Ireland where the mean five-year peak exceeded 300 birds (National threshold 370).

LOCATION	MEAN 5-YEAR PEAK 1996/97–2000/01	PEAK COUNT 2000/01
Loughs Neagh & Beg, Co. Armagh/Down/etc	8,472*	6,441 (Jan)*
Lough Corrib, Co. Galway	5,453	2,339 (Jan)
Upper Lough Erne, Co. Fermanagh	1,306*	1,457 (Feb)*
Lough Ree, Co. Westmeath	1,060	1,205 (Jan)
Lough Ennell, Co. Westmeath	1,054	—
Lough Derg (Shannon), Co. Tipperary	1,016	258 (Jan)
Lough Derravaragh, Co. Westmeath	892	—
Lough Sheelin, Co. Cavan	679	711 (Feb)

TABLE 58. – *Cont.*

Lower Lough Erne, Co. Fermanagh	634*	705 (Feb)*
Tacumshin Lake, Co. Wexford	428	—
Lough Mask, Co Mayo	375	—
Lough Kinale & Derragh Lough, Co. Westmeath	343	—
Lough Cullin, Co. Mayo	339	—
Lough Arrow, Co. Sligo	301	—

38. GREATER SCAUP *AYTHYA MARILA* (A)

Greater scaup are the most northerly breeding of the pochard tribe of ducks (the Aythyini), and are widely distributed throughout the Holarctic. The species is polytypic, with two subspecies, *Aythya marila marila* and *A. m. nearctica*.

They are big ducks, larger and more robust than the tufted duck. The males have clearly recognisable grey-white backs so at a distance they look black at the front and rear ends with a white middle, and are thus easily differentiated from the male tufted duck (Fig. 80). The female is distinguished from the female tufted duck by a bold white patch around the base of the bill. Their breeding origins, migrations and wintering numbers, distribution and inter-winter movements are not well understood, as they are difficult to catch and ring.

The European breeding range of the nominate race, *A. m. marila*, extends from Iceland through Fennoscandia, Estonia, and east to western Siberia, with the bulk of the population of some 40,000–80,000 pairs breeding in the Russian tundra. Small numbers also nest in Novya Zemlya and Svalbard, and southwards in Europe to Denmark, Germany, Britain and Ireland. The breeding numbers of this population as estimated by Wetlands International – 310,000 birds – may be on the low side.

Some 310,000 birds winter in western Europe, and numbers are considered stable. Of these about 90 per cent are found off the coasts of Germany, Denmark and the Netherlands. Some 7,560 wintered in Great Britain during the period 1995–99, but during WeBS 2006/07 the maximum had fallen to 3,038 birds. The total estimated population for Ireland in 2000–04 was 4,430 birds. The British population has remained fairly stable over the past few decades, and the decline noted in recent years is within the range of fluctuation. At the European level, fluctuations in the numbers of wintering birds from year to year can be considerable, almost certainly related to the irregular production of birds from the Russian tundra breeding grounds, where weather conditions can have

FIG 80. Greater scaup, male (top). Known as the duck with 'black at both ends, white in the middle'. The pale back with black vermiculations immediately separates it from the adult male tufted duck. Greater scaup are essentially a marine species, while tufted duck are found mostly in freshwater habitats. Female greater scaup (bottom) are brown with a very conspicuous white patch at the base of the bill. (Ken Kinsella)

dramatic impacts on productivity. Scaup are also highly susceptible to oil pollution, due to their dense wintering flocks.

There has been a significant drop-off in British wintering birds since the mid-1970s, when there were tens of thousands of birds, many of them attracted to coastal sewage and other outfalls. In the Firth of Forth during the late 1960s and early 1970s upwards of 25,000 (maximum counts of 40,000) fed on blue mussels whose growth was encouraged by sewage discharges that also stimulated population increases of marine annelid worms. Other outfalls from distilleries containing grain provided additional food supplies. When the sewage works were upgraded and other outfalls controlled in the late 1970s the birds moved on, though not to other British or Irish coastal sites. They possibly withdrew to European mainland coastal sites – the Wadden Sea, the western Baltic or the Ijsselmeer – where in fact they may have originally dispersed from, as suggested by the timing of peak numbers in the Firth of Forth. Today scaup still exploit human munificence at Loch Indaal, Islay, where a flock of some 1,000 birds has been recorded in recent years feeding on grain, and presumably blue mussels, encouraged by effluents from a whisky distillery.

In contrast to reductions in Britain, wintering numbers in Ireland increased markedly between 1990 (c.2,600 birds) and 2001/02 (c.7,255 birds). Numbers then slumped in 2002/03, but smartly recovered in 2004/05 to reach perhaps as many as 7,100 birds for the winter 2006/07. Greater scaup are one of the few species that are counted by WeBS in greater numbers in Northern Ireland than in Britain.

Recoveries of ringed birds show that British wintering scaup originate from throughout their entire breeding range from Iceland to western Siberia. The frequency and pattern of recoveries prove that Icelandic birds – breeding population c.3,000–5,000 pairs – winter mainly in Ireland with fewer in northern and northwestern Scotland and very small numbers reported from mainland Europe. Those occurring on the Scottish and British east coasts are more likely to have originated from the Fennoscandian and Russian populations. A small number from this area also reach Ireland, as illustrated by the recovery of a Finnish bird in Co. Tyrone and one ringed in the winter on the Wexford Slobs, Co. Wexford, subsequently recovered in Siberia. Interchange of scaup between the large wintering haunts occurs, as revealed by comparative counts at Loughs Neagh and Beg and the Solway Firth, where reduced numbers at one site are roughly matched with increases at the other. The two areas are only separated by some 200 km, a flight time of 2–3 hours.

Scaup, along with the eiders and scoters, are the most marine of all our diving duck, occurring during the winter months in small compact flocks, scattered in estuaries and bays where they feed in shallow waters (usually < 4 m) on molluscs, especially the blue mussel, the laver spire shell, and to a lesser extent cockles and periwinkles, other invertebrates and plant material. They are also found on brackish water bodies, close to the sea, and sometimes further inland on freshwater lakes such as Loughs Neagh and Beg in Northern Ireland, where the largest concentrations in these islands are found. It had been feared that the scaup would follow the decline of tufted duck and pochard on these loughs, but this has not been the case to date.

There are no published fossil records for Britain, but there is an uncertain record from the Holocene (10–0 ky BP) from Castlepook Cave, Co. Cork, and a positive record from Plunkett Cave, Co. Sligo, also from the Holocene. There are bone records from Lagore, Co. Meath (AD 750–950) and Ballinderry crannog, Co. Westmeath (Bronze age). In Britain bones have been found at Iron age sites at Meare and Glastonbury, Somerset, and at Peel, Isle of Man (post Mediaeval). It is possible that they may have bred in northern Britain during earlier cooler periods than today.[232]

They are our rarest breeding duck, with less than five pairs nesting spasmodically, mainly in northern Scotland (South and North Uist, Orkney and some northern counties). Two pairs bred on South Uist, Outer Hebrides, in 1897 and 1898–89 at the same site. But the first published authenticated breeding record was from Sutherland, 1899, although breeding in the county was suspected as early as 1834. Intermittent breeding continued at several different locations through the twentieth century. Breeding in Ireland first occurred at Portmore Lough, Co. Antrim (1997), followed by one pair in Lough Neagh during 1999, with none reported breeding since – although summering birds have been recorded.

It is not known if the North American subspecies, *A. m. nearctica* (formerly *mariloides*), has occurred in Britain and Ireland as a vagrant, because it is indistinguishable in the field from the European nominate race. There have been no recoveries in Britain or Ireland of scaup ringed in North America.

As with most other duck, the monogamous pair bond is seasonal. The female incubates the clutch of some 8–11 eggs for 26–28 days. The male usually deserts the female halfway through incubation. The fate of 2,802 eggs from three breeding seasons was followed in Finland: 77 per cent hatched, and of these 6.5 per cent were reared to fledging. The survival of young per breeding pair in each of the three years was 0.9, 0.9 and 0.2.[233] The hatching success of 1,323 Icelandic nests, 1961–70, averaged 67.9 per cent (range 47.6–84.3).[234] The mean annual adult survival of Icelandic-ringed birds has been calculated at 0.48, the lowest rate among ducks in the western Palaearctic.

TABLE 59. Greater scaup: sites in Britain where the mean five-year peak exceeded 76 birds (National threshold).

LOCATION	MEAN 5-YEAR PEAK 2002/03–2006/07	PEAK COUNT 2006/07
Solway Firth, Cumbria	2,132	1,060 (Nov)
Loch Ryan, Dumfries & Galloway	1,107	1,047 (Dec)
Inner Moray Firth, Highland	1,070	690 (Feb)
Inner Loch Indaal, Islay	879	—
Loch of Harry, Orkney	394	306 (Dec)
Loch of Strenness, Orkney	325	429 (Nov)
Cromarty Firth, Highland	204	401 (Jan)
Dornoch Firth, Highland	136	222 (Dec)
Ayr to N Troon, Ayrshire	120	—
Auchenharvie Golf Course, N Ayrshire	112	98 (Feb)
Rough Firth, Dumfries & Galloway	104	—

TABLE 60. Greater scaup: sites in Ireland where the mean five-year peak exceeded 45 birds (National threshold).

LOCATION	MEAN 5-YEAR PEAK 1996/97–2000/01	PEAK COUNT 2000/01
Loughs Neagh & Beg, Co. Armagh/Down/etc	8,472*	6,441 (Feb)*
Belfast Lough, Co. Antrim	843*	849 (Feb)*
Carlingford Lough, Co. Down	212*	225 (Jan)*
Tralee Bay, L. Gill & Akeragh Lough, Co. Kerry	902	118 (Dec)
Wexford Harbour & Slobs, Co. Wexford	411	126 (Dec)
Shannon & Fergus estuaries, Co. Limerick/ Kerry/Clare	129	76 (Jan)
Lady's Island Lake, Co. Wexford	90	—
Castlemaine Harbour & Rossbehy, Co. Kerry	79	—

39. LESSER SCAUP *AYTHYA AFFINIS* (A)

This North American species breeds from northwest Canada through much of the USA, with an estimated population of 2.99 million birds. Possibly due to the difficulty of distinguishing it from the greater scaup (Fig. 81), it was not until May 1985 that it was first recorded in the west Palaearctic, in Denmark. Identification is further complicated by the occasional presence of hybrids from pochard x tufted duck and greater scaup x lesser scaup. Since the first BBRC-accepted record, from Chasewater, Staffordshire, in March 1987, there have been a further 100 occurrences in Britain accepted by the BBRC between 1950 and 2006, of which about one-third have been seen in Scotland.

The lesser scaup is very difficult to distinguish from the greater scaup. It is slightly smaller, with a smaller and less broad bill. At close range males are distinguished by a smaller black nail on a grey bill. The purple head gloss is more regular than in the greater scaup. The best distinguishing feature is the bright white wing bar, much shorter than in tufted duck and greater scaup, but only visible in flight or during the wing flap prior to diving.

The first Irish lesser scaup record accepted by the IRBC was a male seen on 13 February 1988 in Co. Down, and what was thought to be the same bird returning in each of the subsequent five winters. A total of 14 individuals have been seen in Ireland to the end of 2006, mostly in Northern Ireland, while other singles have been seen in Counties Kerry (1996–2000, presumably the same bird), Wexford (1998), Waterford (1999), Donegal (2003) and Cork (2004).

During WeBS 2006/07 there were records from three sites in England and eight in Scotland, all involving single birds apart from two at Lough Leven, Perth & Kinross, in February and two at Loch a Chinn Uacraich (Coot Lough) on Benbecula, Western Isles, during February and March.

The first lesser scaup – four hand-reared birds from North America – were brought to Britain in 1923 and successfully bred in 1924. By 1925 more were in several other European waterfowl collections.[235]

There are no published fossil records to date from Europe.

FIG 81. Lesser scaup, male. Very hard to distinguish from the greater scaup, but smaller with a shorter, narrower bill with a tiny black tip. (John Shaw/NHPA)

40. COMMON EIDER *SOMATERIA MOLLISSIMA* (A)

The common eider, one of the largest and hardiest ducks in the northern hemisphere, is the world's most abundant sea duck, more closely associated with the marine environment than any other sea-going duck. They are well adapted for their normal habitat – the Arctic and sub-Arctic marine regions – provided with down feathers that possess the best thermal qualities of any known natural material. No artificial material can match the combined thermal properties and lightness of down feathers. A sleeping bag packed with 1.5 kg of synthetic fibres provides satisfactory insulation at –7 °C. The same weight of eider down provides equivalent insulation at –35 °C.

Their enlarged supraorbital salt glands permit a totally maritime existence without recourse to fresh water. Sexual dimorphism is striking, the males splendidly plumaged with enlarged, sloping heads that are elaborately coloured black, white and light green (Fig. 82). The more cryptically brown-plumaged female, not without her own special elegance, has evolved to be an unseen incubating mother. The males are exceptionally vocal during courtship, with much cooing and crooning like doves.

Their breeding range extends from the high Arctic at 80° N across Eurasia and North America south to 48° N in Europe, in Brittany, France. Their taxonomy is confusing and requires clarification. Some authorities consider that there are six subspecies,[236] while others propose just four subspecies of the eider.[237]

Accepting the classification of six subspecies, the European eider, *Somateria mollissima mollissima*, breeds in Britain, Ireland and elsewhere in northwest Europe, as well as on Novaya Zemlya and west along the Barents Sea and White Sea.

An indigenous race, the Faeroe eider, *S. m. faeroeensis*, is restricted to the Faeroes, Shetland and Orkney. It is the smallest of all the subspecies and is a slightly smaller version of the European race, with a smaller bill and short pointed frontal lobes, while the females are noticeably darker (some approaching blackness). There are some 6,000–12,000 birds of this subspecies breeding on the Faeroe Islands – they are sedentary – and a further 12,000–13,500 birds in Shetland and Orkney. The latter birds are sufficiently distinct from the nominate race of mainland Scotland, and there is no evidence of intermixing with those on the Faeroe Islands.

Further north, *S. m. borealis* (*islandica*) breeds in Iceland (600,000–900,000 birds), Svalbard/Franz Josef Land (40,000–80,000 birds), west Greenland (12,000–15,000 pairs), northeast Greenland and Arctic northeast Canada (600,000 birds). DNA analysis of eiders from several locations around the Baltic and one in

FIG 82. Common eider, male, nominate subspecies. The largest sea duck, with heavy body – mean winter weight 2.3 kg. Their plumage is a wonderful contrast between black cap, flanks and tail, and white back, chest, neck and much of the head. The eye is concealed within the black crown. Normally they fly low, about 50 cm above the water. (Ken Kinsella)

Iceland suggests a postglacial colonisation of Iceland from continental Europe,[238] although fossils have been recovered from Melabakka, southwest Iceland, dating from the Late Pleistocene/Late Glacial, earlier than 12.3 ky BP.

There are then three North American subspecies: the American eider, *S. m. dresseri*, the Hudson's Bay eider, *S. m. sedentaria*, and the Pacific eider, *S. m. v-nigra*.

Somateria m. borealis is of particular interest to British and Irish ornithologists, as it is increasingly being identified wintering off our northwest coasts. In this subspecies the bill is typically coloured a bright banana-yellow to yellow-orange, ranging to a dull olive-grey. However, there is a cline of bill colour from olive-grey among the eastern Arctic populations (Svalbard and Iceland) to bright and yellowy among western birds (west Greenland and northeast Canada).

The frontal lobes are narrow and pointed at the posterior ends, and the green on the head of the male is limited to a patch on the nape. Adult male *borealis* type eiders possess triangular pointed 'white sails' that protrude rather like a dolphin's fin above the contour of the white back. The sails are formed by longer and more strongly decurved tertials or, as claimed by other authors, modified long scapulars. Some ornithologists consider the sails a diagnostic field character of *borealis* eiders, shared by none of the other subspecies.[239]
The presence of bright yellow or orange on the basal half of the bill strengthens the case for a *borealis* eider, but because of the great variation it cannot be considered a diagnostic character. However, the combination of bright orange at the bill base and prominent scapular sails may prove to be diagnostic.

Borealis vagrants to British and Irish waters are most likely to have come from west Greenland or northeast Canada, as these populations are the most migratory – some northeastern Canadian birds have been satellite-tracked on migration to southwest Greenland (though none of the 515 recoveries of birds ringed as adults or ducklings in west Greenland has been away from Greenland). There is one recovery in Iceland of a bird ringed in east Greenland, and despite large numbers of eider ringed in Iceland, there has only been one recovery – of a hand-reared bird found in the Faeroes.

The estimated wintering population in Great Britain was 73,000 birds for the period 1995–99, with major concentrations in Shetland, northeast and southwest Scotland and northeastern England. There were a further estimated 2,890 in Ireland in 2000–04.

Nearly 5,000 common eider wintered in loughs or bays or off the coast of Northern Ireland during 2006/07, far exceeding the estimated regional breeding population of about 100–125 pairs. The most likely source of these immigrants is western Scotland (very few have been ringed there – almost all ringing has taken place on the British northeast coast), but possibly also Iceland (unlikely, given that there have been no ringing recoveries of Icelandic birds), Greenland (birds 'overshooting' their Icelandic wintering grounds) or indeed Canada. The origin of these birds remains a mystery. Possibly some of the birds are arriving from the large Firth of Clyde population, which peaked at 9,590 birds in September 2006. The increase in the Northern Ireland wintering population is remarkable, with a sharp rise in the WeBS index since 1989/99.

The status of *borealis* in Britain is unclear. Only one British record, based on biometric data – a dead adult male from Musselburgh on the Lothian coast on 2 February 1978 – has been accepted by the BBRC for the period 1950–2006. Since then, individuals have been reported off John o' Groats (January 1985) and off Shetland (May 1989, February 1993, December 1999). There have been many more records of *borealis* from Ireland – Wicklow, March 1998 (accepted by IRBC); Antrim, November 1997; while there have been regular sightings of up to seven males between 1997 and 2004 off Tory Island and Fanad Head, Co. Donegal.[240] Another *borealis* was reported off the coast of Co. Louth in October 2003 – an adult male that had been around since the previous summer.[241]

Eider distribution is very much controlled by the availability of their principal food, the blue mussel, for which they dive in shallow waters; the preferred feeding depth is up to 3 m. The mussels taken are generally in the size range of 5–30 mm, swallowed whole and then crushed in the muscular gizzard. Eiders have a daily food requirement of about 300 g – about 15 per cent of their average body weight – and are thus restricted to areas of high productivity of mussels, other molluscs and crustaceans, where the biomass of the benthos in shallow waters exceeds 25 g/m³.

It is highly probable that the common eider was an ancient breeding bird in Britain. James Fisher notes that it has been recorded from the Late Pleistocene to the Dark Ages (c. AD 400–1066) in Scotland and Ireland. Fossil remains have been found at only two Late Pleistocene sites, at Creag nan Uamh cave, Sutherland, from the Late Glacial period (13–10 ky BP), and at Stratheden, Fife, as well as from a Middle Pleistocene Cromerian (500–450 ky BP) interglacial site at West Runton, Suffolk. The eider was almost certainly present on the Farne Islands from the seventh century onwards, and there are records in the literature from the mid twelfth century. During the nineteenth century the eider's breeding range was restricted to northern Scotland. From the 1950s onwards they have been spreading southwards from sub-Arctic regions. Since then, it has been gradually, but with greater urgency in the past 50 years, extending its range to become the second commonest breeding duck, after the mallard, in Britain and Ireland.

They nest on marine islands and, if on the mainland, invariably close to the seashore, although breeding has been recorded up to 3 km inland. There has been a tenfold increase in the Baltic breeding population, with significant increases reported from the Gulf of Finland (10 per cent annual growth), Sweden and Estonia. The British population, at the southern limit of the breeding range, has increased more slowly, about 2–3 per cent per annum since the 1970s. In 1991 there were an estimated 31,000–32,000 breeding females in Britain and a further 600–1,000 in Ireland.[242] Numbers are likely to have increased since then.

They are numerous in Scotland, with the largest numbers in Orkney, Shetland, in southwest and northeast Scotland, extending southwards into England as far as Coquet Island and the Farne Islands, Northumberland. On the west coast they occur south to Walney Island, Cumbria. In Ireland breeding was first recorded in Co. Donegal in 1912 followed by a record from Rathlin Island,

Co. Antrim, in 1913. They now nest around the north coastline, especially on Inishstrahull and other Co. Donegal islands, and south along the west coast to Co. Mayo, which was first recorded as colonised in 2001.[243] Birds have also nested (1981) in Co. Kerry, at a location off the Dingle Peninsula, and breeding probably continued there to at least 1998.[244] They bred on the Maharee Islands, Co. Kerry, in 2001. The Copeland Islands, Co. Down, were first colonised in 1954, and by 1986 there were nine nests on the lighthouse island, with 15 pairs on the two outer islands by 1997.

British and Irish breeding birds are mainly resident, most adult breeding birds travelling less than 10 km, rarely more than 200 km. A few Scottish-ringed birds have been recovered in Scandinavia. Some Dutch birds winter on the British east coast, from Fife to Kent, as shown by seven winter recoveries. Another, recovered off the Co. Cork coast, might indicate some Dutch birds wintering there too. Ringing recoveries also show that nearly three-quarters of all birds ringed at the Sands of Forvie, Aberdeenshire, spend the winter on the Tay and Forth estuaries, some 110 km south. A large proportion of the breeding adult females ringed on the Farne Islands and Coquet Island move north to join these Forvie birds, but with little apparent interchange of the breeding populations, although pairing usually takes place during the winter. If a male pairs with a female from a different region he will follow her back to her natal area, a case of abmigration, as found in some other duck species. Nearly all overseas recoveries of Forvie-ringed eiders, both ducklings and adults, show transfer of birds into the Baltic breeding population, and this is supported by the recovery of Baltic-ringed eiders on the east coast of Britain. Birds from the Faeroese and Icelandic populations are mainly resident, although Icelandic birds may move to the south coast of Iceland for the winter.

Clutch size is 4–6 eggs; the female seldom leaves the nest, much less frequently than other ducks. During egg laying in the high Arctic females lose approximately 33 per cent of their energy reserves, a further 35 per cent during incubation (Fig. 83), with only 32 per cent remaining at hatching.[245] It is not unusual for some to die of starvation while incubating. Hence the importance of building up substantial energy reserves during the spring, prior to breeding.

A female will often sit tight, allowing a human intruder to stroke her, but when surprised or flushed from the nest she defecates an evil-smelling liquid, a fermenting brew that has lain dormant in her gut for possibly several weeks. Frequently described as a predator deterrent, preventing eggs being taken, it is likely to be effective only against mammals such as Arctic Foxes, rats and American mink because birds – glaucous gulls, hooded crows and others, which are equally serious predators – lack a well-developed sense of smell. In Finland,

FIG 83. Common eider: female on nest, Isle of May, Scotland. This is an unusually exposed nesting site. Eiders normally conceal their nests in longer vegetation or in the shelter of rocks. Competition for nest sites can sometimes lead to ferocious fights between females. (Ann & Steve Toon/NHPA)

over a three-year period, the fate of 1,026 eggs was monitored: 75 per cent hatched and 19 per cent of these produced 'reared' young, with a productivity of fledged young per pair of 2.5, 0.5 and 0.1 per year, giving losses of eggs to fledged young of 46, 90 and 97 per cent respectively.[246] A lower hatching success was found in Scotland, with an average of 61.7 per cent from 417 nests over a four-year period. Annual duckling survival was more variable, at 5.8, 1.9, 40.0 and 0.1 per cent. Food shortage was considered the prime mortality factor in years of poor duckling productivity.[247]

Low reproductive rates are balanced by high adult survival. The mean annual survival rate of breeding females in Scotland, based on mark–recapture methods, was 0.90, and males probably have higher survival rates, as they are not subject to the physiological stress associated with breeding and nesting. Adults do not normally commence breeding until they are 2–4 years old, and it is not unusual for some females to 'rest' intermittently – an average of 22.2 per cent (range 0–65.2) of females did not breed each year on the Farne Islands, Northumberland,[248] a feature of other large wildfowl, especially geese and swans. Upwards of 100 ducklings may gather together in a massive crèche supervised not only by some of the parents but also by non-breeding or unsuccessful female 'nurses'.

TABLE 61. Common eider: sites in Britain where the mean five-year peak exceeded 1,500 birds. A further 12 sites exceeded the National threshold of 730 birds.

LOCATION	MEAN 5-YEAR PEAK 2002/03–2006/07	PEAK COUNT 2006/07
Tay Estuary, Fife	7,400	(9,164) (Jan)
Firth of Forth, Lothian	5,901	5,080 (Aug)
Aberdeen Bay offshore, Aberdeenshire	4,833	6,269 (Aug)
Inner Firth of Clyde, Inverclyde/Argyll	4,759	4,881 (Sep)
Morecambe Bay, Lancashire	4,196	3,374 (May)
Killantringan Bay, Dumfries & Galloway	3,600	—
Ythan Estuary, Aberdeenshire	3,121	2,315 (Jul)
Gare Lough, Dunbarton/Argyll	2,792	2,782 (Sep)
Montrose Basin, Tayside	2,757	2,584 (Dec)
Irvine Bay, Ayrshire and Arran	1,547	—

TABLE 62. Common eider: sites in Ireland where the mean five-year peak exceeded 30 birds (National threshold).

LOCATION	MEAN 5-YEAR PEAK 1996/97–2000/01	PEAK COUNT 2000/01
Belfast Lough, Co. Antrim	1,528*	1,482 (Jan)*
Lough Foyle, Co. Derry	464*	528 (Sep)*
Outer Ards Shoreline, Co. Down	453*	976 (Jan)*
Strangford Lough, Co. Down	383*	728 (Feb)*
Larne Lough, Co. Antrim	77*	76 (Sep)
Streedagh Estuary, Co. Sligo	76	—
Portstewart–Portrush, Co. Antrim	34*	—

41. KING EIDER *SOMATERIA SPECTABILIS* (A)

As the name suggests, the king eider is something more majestic than the common eider. Like its cousin, the drake is predominantly black and white, with a white front suffused with pink and a colourful head, but the king eider's back is mostly black, and its head is even more splendid, differently shaped and differently coloured (Fig. 84). The short orange-red bill has an enormous orange shield; the crown and nape are blue-grey, the white cheeks tinged with 'eider' green.

Some 300,000 birds comprise the breeding populations nesting in the high Arctic in western Russia, northern Europe and east Greenland. There are a few isolated breeding records from the north of Norway, while some 300–1,000 pairs breed on Svalbard. Numbers breeding in western Siberia are in the range 35,000–40,000 pairs. The size of the populations breeding in the northern parts of west and east Greenland is uncertain, but it does not exceed a few thousand pairs,[249] with an estimated 2,000–5,000 pairs nesting in east Greenland.[250] Some 50,000–100,000 birds winter off the Norwegian coast, with fewer than 50 in Icelandic waters. Some 300,000–500,000, possibly augmented by Canadian birds, winter in Greenland waters. Winter stragglers penetrate south to Britain and Ireland.[251]

FIG 84. King eider, male. Slightly smaller than the common eider. Striking and prominent orange knob extending up to the top of the crown from the base of the red bill.
The crown and nape are blue. During winter they tend to stay further offshore in deeper
water than the common eider, and they dive for longer periods. (Jari Peltmaki/NHPA)

A relatively small number of vagrants accepted by the BBRC, totalling 130 for
the period 1950–2006, have been seen in British waters. A further 57 occurrences
were recorded up to 1950. Most have been in Scotland, especially around
Shetland, although they are also recorded off the east coast of England and at
other locations. Over the years a number of individuals have returned to the
same sites. In 1979 and 1980 a male mated with a female common eider on the
island of Arran, but the outcome was unknown. However, a likely hybrid was
observed off Loch Fleet, Highland, in 1981.[252]

Only one was recorded by WeBS 2005/06 at Nairn Bar on the Inner Moray
Firth, Highland, in February 2005. WeBS 2006/7 reported no records. There are
very few Irish records. There were only four between 1800 and 1949, but better
observer coverage since then has yielded increased sightings – 14 from 1950 to
the end of 2006, with records mostly from northern counties, although three
have occurred off the east coast.

There are no known fossil records from Britain or Ireland. However, there
are Late Pleistocene records from Romania, Norway (two sites) and Russia.

42. STELLER'S EIDER *POLYSTICTA STELLERI* (A)

The adult male maintains the spectacular colourings of other drake eiders –
in this case a white head, black eye patch, green on the white nape and rufous
underparts with a distinctive black spot on the side of the breast (Fig. 85).
They are taxonomically different from other eiders, justifying a separate genus.
The female is again somewhat drab, uniformly mottled brown. The population
from which we probably receive our vagrants breeds in the coastal tundra zone
of northern Siberia – other birds breed further east, as far as north and southeast
Alaska. About 40,000 birds comprise the western Siberian breeding population,
and their wintering range is northern Norway and the southeastern Baltic.

The Steller's eider is an extremely rare visitor to Britain, with just ten BBRC-
accepted occurrences for 1950–2006, five of which have been in Orkney. There
are also five pre-1950 records. The first, a subadult male, was from Caister,
Norfolk, in February 1830. Two drakes have made extended stays over the period
– one on South Uist that remained from 1972 to 1984 and another on Westray,
Orkney, that stayed from 1974 to 1982. The Steller's eider that was recorded in
2000 was the first since the demise of the male on South Uist in 1984. The species
has not yet been recorded in Irish waters.

There are no known fossil records from Britain or Ireland, or from elsewhere
in Europe.

FIG 85. Steller's eider,
male. The smallest eider,
with a short bill. Neat-
looking in comparison to
the bulky common eider.
Key features are white
head, chestnut underparts
contrasting with black
upperparts, and a curious
black spot on the side of
the breast. Their white
forewing is conspicuous
in flight. (Bill
Coster/NHPA)

43. HARLEQUIN DUCK *HISTRIONICUS HISTRIONICUS* (A)

The harlequin is another sea-going duck able to endure extreme environmental conditions – not so much low temperatures as rough, tumultuous, wild and cascading river torrents, the bases of waterfalls or turbulent conditions at sea. They could be described as 'whitewater ducks'. Why they endure such harsh conditions, replete with many physical hazards and taxing energy demands, seems initially a mystery as the disadvantages would seem to outweigh any apparent advantages. It could be argued that they evolved to occupy this specialist niche because it was available, untenanted by other ducks. On the positive side, there are more than adequate invertebrate food supplies, facilitated by high dissolved oxygen levels. Moreover, predators – avian and mammalian – would have greater difficulties in pursuing and securing the ducks in such turbulent conditions than in calmer environments. Harlequins have certainly not been restrained by their harsh environment from thriving. Their greatest threat is from an entirely different source – maritime oil pollution.

Harlequin ducks are small and compact, with a noticeably small bill, and they ride the water high and buoyantly. The male at a distance appears dark but on closer view reveals a dark blue colour to the head, back and parts of the sides with a bold pattern of white streaks on the head, neck, breast and wings (Fig. 86). There is a white spot near the tail. The flanks are chestnut coloured. Its variegated colouring and bold back patterning are reminiscent of the eighteenth-century clown Harlequin who appears in Italian comic operas. The female is dark brown with three white head spots – the one behind the head being the most obvious (Fig. 87).

There are three population groupings. The Atlantic grouping includes an estimated 10,000–30,000 birds breeding in eastern Canada, west and southeast Greenland, with a further 3,000–4,000 pairs (9,000–12,000 individuals) in Iceland.[253] Another population breeds in Alaska, northwest Canada and northwest USA. A third population breeds in eastern Siberia and northern Japan. Harlequins were considered to be resident until recently when satellite tracking revealed that some Canadian birds migrated to moult in southwest Greenland, while others, breeding in Alberta, move to the Pacific coast of British Columbia.[254]

Birds visiting Britain are likely to be from the Icelandic population, though this assumption is unsupported by evidence other than close geographical proximity. Although most are winter resident in Iceland, a few wander south, as shown by recovery of ringed birds well over 200 km from the point of ringing.[255] The distance from Iceland to the north of Scotland is about 950 km.

FIG 86. Harlequin duck, male. The complex colourful plumage of the male appears dark at distance, but white streaks and a white facial crescent are normally visible. Their flight is rapid, somewhat similar to that of the long-tailed duck. (Ken Kinsella)

FIG 87. Pair of harlequin ducks. The female is dark brown with three light, almost white, face spots. They are sociable breeders, often several pairs together on a rocky island in a turbulent river. (Ken Kinsella)

They are extremely rare winter vagrants to Britain. The first record was an immature drake picked up dead on the shore at Filey, North Yorkshire, in the autumn of 1862. The skin is at Mansfield Museum. There were a further three records up to 1950, and nine more records accepted by the BBRC for the period 1950–2006. Nearly all the records have been from Scotland. Ireland has been less lucky, with none yet recorded.

There are no known fossil records from Europe. Two Late Pleistocene fossils from Sweden were misidentified, according to Tyrberg.

Their nests, seldom located further than 5 m from the river's edge, are concealed in tall vegetation or under rocks. Most clutches, usually of 5–7 eggs in Iceland, are laid at the end of May. The incubation period of 30–32 days is among the longest of any sea duck. Their breeding success is high compared with other sea ducks such as the common eider. During a study in Iceland, 1966–70, the fate of 504 eggs was followed: 81 per cent hatched and of these 50–70 per cent gave rise to fledged young.[256] However, annual production of young is variable. At the main breeding location at Myvatn, in the years 1975–2002 the number of young produced ranged from 3 to 235 and correlated with abundance of blackflies in the river.[257] The fledging period is exceptionally long at 60–70 days. At the end of the breeding season the birds move down river to the sea, seldom straying more than 300 m from the shore, remaining in small compact flocks of usually up to 50 birds. Annual adult female survival has been estimated at 0.71.[258]

Harlequins mostly dive for their food, but they can also walk under water on the bottom of streams, head down and wings closed, and can overturn small stones in search of insects – reminiscent of the behaviour of another bird of fast-flowing water, the dipper. Their diet in Iceland during spring and summer is almost entirely animal, obtained by surface-diving – principally larvae and pupae of caddis fly, mayfly and blackfly – all indicators of highly oxygenated waters. Towards the end of the summer the young and adults feed on salmon eggs on the lower reaches of the rivers. During their maritime winter on the Pacific coast of North America they feed mostly on periwinkles, the commonest dietary item (25 per cent of all food) in Puget Sound, Washington State.[259] Other food taken includes the common limpet, as well as a range of other molluscs and crustaceans. They are specialists, aided by a strong nail on the bill, at prising chitons and limpets from rocks.

44. LONG-TAILED DUCK *CLANGULA HYEMALIS* (**A**)

The long-tailed duck is the only member of its genus and not closely related to any other sea ducks. It is probably the most numerous of all Arctic breeding ducks. They are unique among ducks for their three, instead of the normal two, plumages. The male's sharply contrasting white and black plumage is worn only in the winter, while in spring it acquires a brown back and more black on the neck and head, a plumage that persists through the summer (Fig. 88). They also have the largest relative heart mass of all waterfowl, a presumed adaptation for their deep diving. They are possibly the deepest divers among waterfowl, having been caught in a net 66 m under water. However, more normal dives for food would be in the range of 5–15 m with excursions down to 22 m.

FIG 88. Long-tailed duck flying over the ice. The summer plumage of the male is one of black and white. The wings are dark, and there is conspicuous white on the head and body. The long tail comprises the two central feathers, which exceed the next feathers in length by some 70–130 mm. (Jari Peltomaki/NHPA)

They are small, compact, noisy, fidgety and restless on the water. Indeed, the description of the field characters of this duck has not been bettered since Bernard Tucker described it in the *Handbook of British Birds* as 'a lively, restless, noisy bird, delighting in the open sea'.[260]

Their breeding distribution is Holarctic, like that of the greater scaup, occurring in the tundra and taiga regions, almost entirely restricted to within the Arctic Circle and extending north to 80° N. Most of the northwest European wintering population (excluding Greenland and Iceland), numbering about 4.6 million birds, breeds in western Siberia and northern Europe, while there are smaller populations on Bear Island and Svalbard. The breeding population of Iceland has been estimated at 2,000–5,000 pairs, and that of Greenland at more than 10,000 pairs,[261] but it seems more likely that there are in fact 100,000–150,000 birds between these two populations, with 100,000 birds estimated to winter in coastal west Greenland. Despite its circumpolar distribution and widely scattered breeding regions, there is an interesting lack of subspeciation, probably reflecting high mobility and consequent gene flow throughout the Holarctic. Most long-tailed duck are migratory, wintering south of their breeding range between 75° and 55° N – especially in the Baltic Sea, where 90 per cent of the population resides. Those breeding in Iceland are partial migrants, most remaining in coastal waters with some travelling to Greenland – about ten ringed birds have been recovered in southwest Greenland. Others have travelled to Scotland (see below).[262]

The precise origin of British and Irish wintering birds is uncertain, but there are several recoveries in British waters of birds ringed in northern Fennoscandia and Russia. There have been other recoveries in Scottish waters of Icelandic-ringed birds. Russian-ringed birds have been found in Denmark and in the Baltic. One bird, ringed in October as a winter visitor on Fair Isle, Scotland, was recovered 20 years later in October in Denmark. Birds ringed in west Greenland have travelled to Denmark, and to the MacKenzie River in Canada.[263] Wintering birds arrive in our coastal waters much later than most other duck, from mid October onwards, with peak numbers in late December to early January. The estimated annual number wintering in Britain between 1995 and 1999 was 16,000 birds. The tendency for some birds to remain several kilometres offshore makes it difficult to obtain a complete census of wintering birds. They mostly occur in Scottish waters, especially on the east coast where there are shallow sandy bays such as the Moray Firth – the most important wintering site in Great Britain. Here they have access to abundant food supplies – blue mussels, cockles, periwinkles and other molluscs and crustaceans that constitute the bulk of their diet. Large numbers also occur around Orkney and Shetland.

The maximum count in British waters during WeBS 2006/07 was the second highest on record and 40 per cent higher than the mean for the previous ten years.

The long-tailed duck is an uncommon local visitor in Irish coastal waters – numbers are small as Ireland is at the southwestern limit of the duck's wintering range. A thorough winter census has never been attempted, but it is thought that numbers are perhaps in the range of 200–500 birds, or possibly as low as 100–150.[264] Most are located in small flocks, upwards of 25–30, seldom more than 50, in the north and northwest coastal areas, especially in the proximity of sandy bays such as Carlingford and Belfast Loughs and Dundrum Bay, Co. Down; Blacksod Bay, Co. Mayo; and Portnoo and Bundoran, Co. Donegal. The largest wintering flock in Ireland, of about 70 birds, occurs at Glashagh and Ballyheirnan Bays, Co. Donegal.[265]

Long-tailed duck fossils discovered at Yarm Hill, Southwold, Suffolk, date from the Late Upper Pliocene to Early Pleistocene, found in the Norwich Crag deposits (c.2.1–1.7 my BP). However, Tyrberg reported that their identification had been rejected by Harrison as indeterminable. Other remains, found in separate layers, are from the Late Pleistocene/Late Glacial (13–10 ky BP) site at Creag nan Uamh cave, Sutherland. It is probable that they bred in these historic cooler times but as the climate warmed up they may have withdrawn towards the Arctic Circle. Yalden and Albarella (2008) have recorded Late Glacial fossils at Inchnadamph, Sutherland, as well as bones at Port Eynon, Cymru (Mesolithic); Wroxeter, Shropshire (Roman) and at Longthorpe, Cambridgeshire (Roman) and at Peel, Isle of Man (Post Mediaeval). They may have bred, very occasionally, over the past 200–300 years in Scotland.

It is claimed that eggs of breeding birds were collected from Shetland on several occasions – in 1848 and 1887. Eggs were collected in Orkney in 1911, and breeding allegedly occurred again in 1912 and 1926. Despite a 'strong suspicion' that they may have bred in the Western Isles during 1969, there is no clear evidence of breeding in Scotland since the eggs were found in Orkney in 1911. Their presence during the breeding season, but without proof of nesting, was recorded in 13 10-km squares during the *New Atlas* survey of 1989–91.

The drakes come into full breeding plumage in midwinter (Fig. 89). The head and neck are boldly patterned black and white with a brown spot behind and below the eye. The lower chest, back, wings and tail are dark or black-brown. The two elongated central tail feathers, a feature shared with only one other duck, the pintail, are 17–24 cm long, over half the length of the body. Known in North America as oldsquaws, because their calls are apparently reminiscent of chattering old Eskimo squaws, their voices travel great distances over the Arctic stillness. Their calls are almost impossible to describe in words – musical, continuous, somewhat reminiscent of the noise coming from a mixed kittiwake

FIG 89. Long-tailed duck, male in autumn/winter plumage. From September onwards the male becomes much whiter and the short bill develops a pink band.
(Alan Williams/NHPA)

FIG 90. Long-tailed duck, male in summer plumage. From about late April onwards the male develops his summer plumage, with a brown back, white-grey flanks and rear end and a grey/white head patch. The black scapulars are edged rufous-yellow, creating a scraggy appearance. The central pink band on the black bill is retained from the autumn, but eventually the whole bill becomes black during the summer. (Ken Kinsella)

and guillemot breeding colony with low-pitched kittiwake calls and subdued guillemot grunting. The call of the male has been described as a loud, resonant polysyllabic note, 'ahr-ahr-ahroulit'.

By April the drake has moulted the white feathers on his head and neck, replacing them with brown ones, and the long thin white scapulars are exchanged for shorter brown feathers (Fig. 90). This duller plumage, a functional eclipse, remains until July, when the scapulars are moulted again and the tail feathers replaced. The primaries are moulted, the drakes regaining their flight by the end of September.

When females arrive on the breeding grounds they have consumed about 40 per cent of the fat reserves they accumulated prior to spring migration. Egg production accounts for 69 per cent of the remaining reserves. It is thought that the females do not eat during incubation, but by the time of autumn migration they have regained the same amount of body fat as they had prior to spring migration.[266] They do not breed until they are 2 years old, and breeding success is largely influenced by predators. Mean clutch size in Iceland was 7.9 eggs over the period 1961–70, and hatching success of nests was 64.6 per cent.[267] In Manitoba 20.5 per cent of nests were destroyed by predators on the mainland, and 30.4 per cent on islands.[268] Warm Arctic temperatures have been shown to positively influence breeding success.[269] During a five-year Swedish study, 26–52 per cent of females had a brood, and there was a positive correlation between the proportion of females with broods and rodent abundance – high numbers of lemmings and voles kept the predators happy, with the result that they paid less attention to the ducks.[270] The mean annual survival of Icelandic-ringed adults has been estimated at 0.72, one of the highest of all ducks.

TABLE 63. Long-tailed duck: sites in Britain where the mean five-year peak exceeded 160 birds (National threshold). Another 20 sites held more than a mean peak count of 50 birds.

LOCATION	MEAN 5-YEAR PEAK 2002/03–2006/07	PEAK COUNT 2006/07
Moray Firth, Highland	7,575	10,878 (Feb)
Sound of Harris, Western Isles	365	—
South Uist West Coast, Western Isles	345	—
Scapa Flow, Shapinsay & Deer Sounds, Orkney	300	—
Firth of Forth, Lothian	284	213 (Feb)

TABLE 63. – *Cont.*

Loch Branahuie (Lewis), Western Isles	272	—
Branahuie Banks (Lewis), Western Isles	196	—
Hacosay, Bluemull and Colgrave Sounds, Shetland	193	—
Broad Bay (Lewis), Western Isles	186	—

TABLE 64. Long-tailed duck: sites in Ireland where the mean five-year peak exceeded 20 birds (National threshold).

LOCATION	MEAN 5-YEAR PEAK 1996/97–2000/01	PEAK COUNT 2000/01
Gweebarra Bay, Co. Donegal	52	—
Inishfree Bay, Co. Donegal	40	—
Belfast Lough, Co. Antrim	28	30
Drumcliff Bay Estuary, Co. Sligo	25	—

45. BLACK SCOTER *MELANITTA NIGRA* (**A**)

The drake has the distinction of being the only duck in the world with a completely black plumage, which has been described as 'boot-polish black' (Fig. 91). They do not pass through an annual eclipse plumage as most other drakes do, retaining more or less the same plumage throughout the year. Their feet are black – surf and velvet scoters have bright-red feet. The black scoter, *Melanitta nigra* (monotypic), has a low Arctic breeding distribution, generally between 60° and 70° N, extending east from Iceland, Britain and Ireland, Scandinavia, through Arctic Russia to western Alaska with some numbers breeding in Arctic Canada in the regions of Newfoundland, Labrador and Hudson's Bay. It occurs throughout northern Europe east through Arctic Russia to about 120° E. The American scoter, *Melanitta americana* (monotypic), no longer considered a subspecies, then takes over, breeding east to Newfoundland and Labrador.

The black scoter population consists of about 1.6 million birds, of which about three-quarters winter in the Baltic Sea. The European breeding segment of

FIG 91. Black scoter, male. The smallest scoter, and the male is the only all-black duck. On close view a small orange patch can be seen on the upper mandible. The female is brown with light cheeks contrasting with a darker crown. (Alan Williams/NHPA)

this population is small, estimated at 100,000–120,000 pairs, located principally in Russia west of the Urals, Norway, Sweden and Finland with smaller numbers in Iceland. Because of the difficulties of accurately counting these scoters, the problems raised by winter inter-site movements and the shortage of recoveries of ringed birds, much remains to be known. During winter they are entirely sea-going, forming compact flocks of black, buoyant, bobbing ducks. Every flock is worth close inspection for surf or velvet scoters that may be lurking among the flock.

British and Irish breeding birds moult in coastal waters, where they appear to join others from further afield in some huge gatherings. The largest numbers seem to be offshore in Liverpool Bay, especially the shallow area of Blackpool called Shell Flat, while over 20,000 have been counted regularly in Carmarthen Bay, Wales, and at sites off the east coast of Scotland and England – over 5,000 are regular off the Norfolk coast. European and Russian nesting scoter are well known for their remarkable moult migrations, travelling in their thousands – mostly adult males first – from late June to mid August from northwestern Siberia through the Baltic to moulting grounds principally off the coast of Jutland, the Netherlands, some locations along the British east coast and off western France. The numbers of moulting birds off Denmark and in the Baltic

Sea are small compared with the observed passage of birds through the Baltic, raising the question as to whether there are other, unknown moulting areas in the North Sea, Atlantic or elsewhere. In Ireland there is an intriguing westerly passage off Cape Clear, Co. Cork, from mid February to mid December, with highest numbers between the second half of June and the first half of August, seldom exceeding a total of 50 birds a day but once reaching 100.[271]

After their moult, from September onwards, many thousands migrate west from the Baltic to winter in shallow coastal waters (5–15 m deep) around Britain and Ireland. With improved counting and monitoring of British sites, the known size of the wintering population has been increased from 27,350 to 50,000–65,000 birds for the period 1990–99.[272] There were an estimated 23,190 wintering birds in Irish waters for the period 2000–04. Virtually nothing is known of their wintering ecology, or of intra-winter movements between sites. Winter immigrants join immature birds that have remained in British and Irish coastal waters during the summer. Bivalve molluscs – mainly blue mussels up to 4 cm long and cockles – form between 60 and 90 per cent of their diet. The molluscs are swallowed whole, and ground up in the bird's powerful gizzard. Eight recoveries of British-ringed breeding birds suggest that the population winters in British coastal waters rather than moving south to French, Iberian and northwest African waters, where large numbers of the European population congregate. The most important wintering areas for the European population, however, are in the western Baltic and the Kattegat, Denmark, where up to 940,000 birds have been counted.

The large beds of blue mussel in Dingle Bay, Co. Kerry, attract some of the largest congregations in Ireland. In mid September 2006 I watched upwards of 6,500 birds in the waters off Rossbehy sand dunes, where large rafts of ever-restless scoter moved around like large flocks of starlings, with groups of birds constantly lifting up off the water to join other flocks, leapfrogging other flocks in the process.

Black scoters are prone to dramatic declines in wintering numbers. Many thousands disappeared from traditional Irish east-coast sites after the severe winter of 1962/63, possibly because their mollusc feeding beds had been decimated during the harsh weather. Several thousand birds vanished from the coastline between Wexford, Co. Wexford, and Dundrum Bay, Co. Down, the next winter, and only a few hundred had returned by the following winter.[273] Black scoter frequenting the Moray Firth, Highland, declined from about 10,000 in the early 1970s to fewer than 2,300 in January 2000, then increased to just short of 8,000 in February 2004 but fell back to 1,908 in February 2007, according to WeBS.

Scoters are especially susceptible to oil pollution and have endured many oiling incidents, the most serious being the *Sea Empress* in mid February 1996, which created one of the worst ever oil-related bird kills in northwest Europe. Some 72,000 tonnes of oil spewed into the sea around southwest Wales, affecting 4,700 black scoters that had the misfortune to be present in the western parts of Carmarthen Bay. A minimum of 4,000 were killed outright. Numbers wintering in the bay have since recovered.

The black scoter is well represented by fossils from the Pleistocene late Cromerian interglacial period (c.470 ky BP) to the Holocene (10–0 ky BP) from twelve sites in Britain and Ireland, with later evidence from Iron Age deposits (700 BC – AD 43) in Somerset. Like so many other ducks, it was not proven as a breeding species in Britain until the nineteenth century, when it was found nesting in northeast Sutherland in 1855. Thereafter it expanded its range into nearby counties.

Within Britain and Ireland the black scoter is today a scarce breeder, clinging on by its proverbial eyelashes at its southernmost European breeding point, way outside its main nesting range. A comprehensive survey of Britain and Ireland in 1995 found 439 birds, based on which the British and Irish population was estimated at 195 pairs (100 in Ireland, 95 in Britain). In Ireland, three sites held 51 per cent of the population. In Britain, birds were spread over 61 sites in 23 10-km squares, all in Scotland. During the past 40 years the species has suffered both a population decline and a range contraction.

The first Irish breeding record was from Lower Lough Erne, Co. Fermanagh, in 1905, with the possibility of breeding there in 1904. Thereafter the population has been well followed. By 1915 at least five pairs were nesting, and in 1917 seven pairs bred, increasing steadily until 1952, when it was thought that there were about 50 pairs. Breeding peaked during 1967–74, when 137–167 pairs were present. A decline then set in, until they were extinct in Lough Erne by the early 1990s. Their decline may have been due to deterioration of water quality – from increased sewage, fertiliser and industrial inputs – reducing invertebrate food availability, or possibly also from predation by American mink and competition for food with coarse fish.[274] Some of the Erne birds may have redistributed themselves south to other locations in the Republic of Ireland, as indicated by a 1999 lake survey.

The total Irish population declined from 180 to 100 pairs between 1967 and 1981, and further to 80 pairs (pre-breeding population) in 1999 at five large lakes: Lough Corrib, Co. Galway (87 birds), Lough Ree, Co. Westmeath (82 birds), Loughs Conn and Cullin, Co. Mayo (30 birds) and a hitherto unknown site, Lough Arrow, Co. Leitrim (12 birds).[275] At least one pair bred in County Galway in 2007. It is possible that they may be on their way to becoming extinct in Ireland. More surveys are urgently required to determine their status. Irish nesting localities, mostly at calcareous lakes, are quite different from Scottish breeding sites at oligotrophic/mesotrophic waters. Rich food resources in Irish waters may be the extra inducement. In Scotland they have ceased to breed in Shetland, central Scotland, and Dumfries and Galloway. Historical data are lacking, but in the Flow Country numbers declined from some 50 pairs in 1988 to 35 pairs in 1995.[276] A recent RSPB/SNH update found only 52 breeding pairs in the whole of Scotland.[277]

Scottish and Irish (if any remain) breeding birds are under pressure during the nesting season from predation by American mink, red foxes, hooded crows and magpies, from food competition by fish, and from water pollution and afforestation of breeding habitats; and in winter they are liable to suffer from oil contamination when they congregate in compact rafts in shallow coastal waters.

Age of first breeding is 2–3 years, and the nest, constructed by the female, is concealed in dense vegetation, usually on an island or along a lake margin. Average clutch size of 35 Irish nests was 6.8, compared with 8.7 for 187 clutches in Iceland. Of 38 Irish nests only 16 (42 per cent) successfully hatched, hooded crows and magpies being the main predators. Hatching success from 159 nests studied in Iceland in the 1960s was considerably higher at 81.8 per cent (range 57.2–88.9). Most duckling mortality occurred within the first two weeks of life, and thereafter duckling survival rates to fledging varied greatly, from 20 to 60 per cent.[278] The mean annual survival rate for adults ringed in Iceland is 0.77. Recapture data of ıtwelve ringed birds in the White Sea suggested a mean annual survival rate for adults of 0.80.[279]

TABLE 65. Black scoter: sites in Britain where the mean five-year peak exceeded 500 birds (National threshold).

LOCATION	MEAN 5-YEAR PEAK 2002/03–2006/07	PEAK COUNT 2006/07
Carmarthen Bay, Dyfed	20,544	14,412 (Feb)
Moray Firth, Highland	5,871	1,908 (Feb)
North Norfolk Coast, Norfolk	4,792	4,960 (Dec)
Alt Estuary, Merseyside	2,915	3,288 (Feb)
Aberdeen Bay, Aberdeenshire	2,877	1,525 (May)
Firth of Forth, Lothian	1,669	576 (Feb)
Towyn to Llanddulas	1,548	1,800 (Sep)
Cardigan Bay, Gwynedd	1,235	(69) (Dec)
St Andrew's Bay, Fife	972	0
Durham Coast, Durham	685	(181) (Nov)
The Wash, Lincolnshire	684	1,810 (Feb)

In addition to the WeBS ground-count data, aerial surveys estimated 63,387 black scoter in Liverpool Bay in February/March 2007 and 13,477 in Carmarthen Bay in January 2007.

TABLE 66. Black scoter: sites in Ireland where the mean five-year peak exceeded 230 birds (National threshold).

LOCATION	MEAN 5-YEAR PEAK 1996/97–2000/01	PEAK COUNT 2000/01
Wexford Bay, Co. Wexford	4,188	5,760 (Jan)
Castlemaine Harbour & Rossbehy, Co. Kerry	2,423	1,000 (Jul)
Brandon Bay - Inner Brandon Bay, Co. Kerry	1,225	250 (Aug)
Donegal Bay, Co. Donegal	894	631 (Jan)
Nanny Estuary & shore, Co. Meath	829	463 (Mar)
Dundrum Bay, Co. Down	828*	—
The Mullet, Broadhaven & Blacksod Bays, Co. Mayo	449	238 (Feb)
Ballinskelligs Bay, Co. Kerry	449	—

46. AMERICAN SCOTER *MELANITTA AMERICANA* (A)

In comparison with the black scoter, the drake American scoter has a smoother head profile and a differently shaped bill – shorter, with a more hooked nail, lacking the basal knob and with a more extensive and brilliant orange-yellow patch on top (Fig. 92). The courtship call is also different. On the basis of these diagnostic differences the TSC of the BOURC recommended that two monotypic species be recognised – the black scoter, *Melanitta nigra*, and the American scoter, *Melanitta americana*. The breeding range of the American scoter that winter off the Atlantic coasts of North America is in eastern Canada, where there is a population of some 130,000–200,000 birds. The observations of American scoter in British waters are assumed to come from this population.

There are seven BBRC-accepted occurrences of the American scoter in British waters between 1950 and 2006. The first record was an adult male from Gosford Bay, Lothian, December 1987 to January 1988. WeBS 2004/05 recorded a

FIG 92. American scoter, courting group of males and females, New Jersey, USA. The male resembles the black scoter but has a conspicuous swollen orange-yellow bill with small black tip. The yellow bill base is evenly swollen and does not form a knob as in the black scoter. Females are almost indistinguishable from female black scoter. (Woodfall Wild Images/Photoshot. Marie Read/NHPA)

drake off Lavan Sands, Gwynedd, in March 2005, probably the same bird that has been appearing there each winter since early 1999. The same bird was probably the one recorded by WeBS as off Llanfairfechan Saltings, Gwynedd, in March 2006. There are no records from Ireland.

There are no reported fossils from Europe.

47. SURF SCOTER *MELANITTA PERSPICILLATA* (**A**)

This scoter is a regular vagrant from North America. They are the least numerous of scoters worldwide, with a declining population of 150,000–250,000 birds.[280] The male has a massive and bizarrely multi-coloured bill with white, red, yellow and black, and a conspicuous white patch on the nape, formed by elongate hair-like feathers (Figs 93 and 94). Another white patch, on the forehead, is greatly variable in size and shape. The head and bill shape are more eider-like than in the other scoters. The absence of a white wing patch separates it from the velvet scoter. The female can only be identified from other female scoters at close range, 200–250 m, when the pale brown head patches are conspicuous. Both sexes have bright-red legs and feet, like the velvet scoter. They breed in Alaska and northern Canada.

FIG 93. Surf scoter, male. Plumage similar to that of black scoter but has diagnostic white patches on head and nape. The bill is yellow and white. The female is brown with pale cheeks and nape. In flight like black scoter with no wing markings. (David Tomlinson/NHPA)

FIG 94. Surf scoter, male. The undersurfaces of the flight feathers are pale whitish but not so shiny as in the black scoter. The black-and-white head patterns are almost more conspicuous in flight. The legs are pink and black. (Woodfall Wild Images/ Photoshot. Marie Read/ NHPA)

The surf scoter is one of the most frequently seen Nearctic ducks in Europe, with many records from Britain and Ireland, followed by France, with fewer from Denmark, Norway, Finland, Iceland, the Netherlands and Sweden. Between 10 and 25 birds have been reported annually in British and Irish waters since 1984, mainly during the autumn and winter, with peaks in late October and early April. Single birds, sometimes two, seldom more than seven together, are often seen with other scoters, usually associating with velvet rather than black scoters. There are several records from May and June in Finland and Sweden, suggesting that these scoters, caught up with velvet scoters on the wintering grounds, are returning with them to the breeding grounds. Males are most frequently reported in Europe, as they are more easily identified.

Their apparent increasing frequency in Europe is probably due more to greater numbers of skilled birdwatchers than to a real increase in visiting birds. The majority of the 370 records accepted by the BBRC for 1950–2001 have been in Scotland, especially around Orkney and Shetland. The key site for observing surf scoter, however, is generally considered to be Ruddons Point, on the northern shore of the Firth of Forth, Fife.

Due to its frequency of occurrence the species is no longer considered for records by the BBRC as of 1 January 2002. Birds reported by WeBS 2004/05 were all from Scottish sites: three at Traigh Luskentyre, Harris (January), two at Culbin Bar, Inner Moray Firth (December), and a single drake wintering in the Firth of Forth. WeBS 2005/06 reported one at Findhorn Bay, Moray, and several in the Firth of Forth. They were recorded at three sites in Scotland during WeBS 2006/07.

In Ireland they were extremely rare up to 1965 but soon afterwards became an annual visitor. A total of 145 had been recorded to the end of 2006, with an annual average of three birds from 1987 to 1996. They have been most frequently recorded by I-WeBS along the sandbanks at Wexford Harbour, Co. Wexford. They have also been observed in Ballinskelligs Bay, Brandon Bay and Castlemaine Harbour/Rossbehy, Co. Kerry, in Donegal Bay and in Cork Harbour.

There are two fossil records from Britain – the only European records – from Scotland and Herefordshire, found in Late Pleistocene deposits. It is unusual to find fossils of Nearctic species in the Palaearctic, and it is worth noting that Tyrberg states that the identification of these fossils requires confirmation.

48. VELVET SCOTER *MELANITTA FUSCA* (A)

The velvet scoter (Fig. 95) is distinguished from the smaller black and surf
scoters by a white wing patch – not usually visible when the birds are sitting on
the water, but conspicuous in flight or when the birds are flapping their wings.
Their feet are red, as are those of the surf scoter, visible when the birds are
diving. The black bill has yellow or orange sides. They are often associated with
flocks of black scoter.

Three subspecies of the velvet scoter were formerly recognised, differing
in head and bill measurements. However, the TSC of the BOURC has
recommended the recognition of two species: the velvet scoter, *Melanitta fusca*
(monotypic), and the white-winged scoter, *Melanitta deglandi* (polytypic, with
subspecies *M. d. deglandi* and *M. d. stejnegeri*).[281]

FIG 95. Velvet scoter, two males. The largest of the three scoter in British and Irish
waters. Distinguished from the other two by white secondaries, conspicuous in flight,
but when the males are on water the white feathers may not be seen unless the plumage
is ruffled. Lower bill is yellow. (Roger Tidman/NHPA)

The velvet scoter breeds across northern Europe from Scandinavia east through Siberia to at least the Yenisey River at 90° E. The white-winged scoter (*M. d. stejnegeri*) then takes over from the velvet scoter, breeding further east in northern Russia and extending into east Asia, while the Pacific form (*M. d. deglandi*) breeds in North America from northwest Alaska east to Hudson Bay and south to Manitoba.

Velvet scoters are the least numerous of all European sea ducks. Their breeding populations are located in northern Norway, Sweden and Finland, and in the coastal zones of the Baltic. Velvet and black scoter have an overlap of their breeding range in central Scandinavia and western Siberia. They have been suspected, and stated with some authority,[282] to have bred in Scotland on various occasions, but the supporting evidence has not been considered adequate. During the 1988–91 fieldwork for the *New Atlas* they were recorded as present, with no evidence of breeding, in three 10-km squares, one in Scotland, one in northern England and the other in eastern England.

An estimated 1 million individuals comprise the Baltic and west European wintering population, and these are primarily found in Danish waters and the Baltic Sea. Large, previously unknown, numbers have recently been found in the Gulf of Pommern (c.285,000) and in the Gulf of Riga (c.137,000). Further birds are scattered around the margins of the North Sea and along the Atlantic coast as far south as northwest Africa. There were an estimated 3,000 birds wintering in British coastal waters during 1995–99. Today there are fewer, with a maximum of only 1,035 counted during WeBS 2006/07. They were recorded at 18 sites, nine of which were in Scotland and nine in England. Most records were of single birds. The bulk of the population is located almost entirely at three sites in east Scotland (Table 67).

There are two British recoveries of individuals ringed in Norway and Finland, but it is thought that birds from northern Russia may also winter in British and Irish coastal waters. Small numbers of moulters, mostly adults, are present, mixed with black scoters, at traditional British east-coast moulting sites from late summer onwards. These are joined by females and juveniles throughout August and September. Large numbers also moult in Danish coastal waters.

Velvet scoters are regular visitors, in small numbers, to Irish coastal waters, principally along the east coast, with 15–30 recorded each winter off Co. Meath – 29 were noted off Germanton in January 2001. Birds arrive off the east coast from about mid October and remain until April. Elsewhere, especially along the west coast, only small numbers are noted, usually ones and twos, rarely more than four birds together – though 16 were recorded off Castlegregory, Co. Kerry, in April 1977.

There are two fossil records from the Late Pleistocene/Late Glacial period (13–10 ky BP) from Sutherland and Derbyshire/Staffordshire and several bone records from the Mesolithic, Neolithic, Iron Age and Post Mediaeval periods (Yalden and Albarella 2008).

TABLE 67. Velvet scoter: sites in Britain where the mean five-year peak exceeded 30 birds (National threshold).

LOCATION	MEAN 5-YEAR PEAK 2002/03–2006/07	PEAK COUNT 2006/07
Moray Firth, Moray	1,935	743 (Dec)
Firth of Forth, Lothian	1,069	(926) (Nov)
St Andrew's Bay, Fife	230	0
Lunan Bay, Angus	130	2 (Jun)
Aberdeen Bay offshore, Aberdeenshire	52	—
Dee Mouth to Don Mouth, Aberdeenshire	33	(0)

TABLE 68. Velvet scoter: sites in Ireland that have supported peak counts of more than 2 birds during I-WeBS counts, 1994/95–2000/01.

LOCATION	MEAN 5-YEAR PEAK 1994/95–2000/01	PEAK COUNT 2000/01
Belfast Lough, Co. Down	7	4
Nanny Estuary and shore, Co. Meath	5	14
Liscannor Bay (Liscannor–Rinanoughter), Co. Clare	4	8
Cork Harbour, Co. Cork	4	4
Lough Foyle, Co. Derry	3	2
Tralee Bay, Lough Gill & Akeragh Lough, Co. Kerry	3	4
Donegal Bay, Co. Donegal	2	3

49. BUFFLEHEAD *BUCEPHALA ALBEOLA* (**A**)

This is a tiny, compact sea duck with a general resemblance to the goldeneye. The male (Fig. 96) is distinguished from the male goldeneye by a small band of white around the back of the head. The female has a narrow white oblong patch extending behind the eye. They breed in North America, in Alaska, western and southern Canada, with an estimated population of 1.4 million birds in 2004.[283] Like the goldeneye, they are hole-nesters in trees by pools, ponds and rivers.

The bufflehead is a very rare vagrant to western Europe. The BOURC reviewed 17 British pre-1958 records and accepted only one into Category A – a female or immature shot on the Great Pool on Tresco, Scilly, on 7 January 1920, 16 years before the first bird was brought to Europe from Connecticut for Jean Delacour's collection at Clères, Normandy. The Tresco bird was eventually stuffed and put on display at the Isles of Scilly Museum. There is one other pre-1950 record accepted by the BBRC. The first post-1950 occurrence was a male at Foxcote Reservoir, Buckinghamshire, observed from 28 February to 8 March 1961. Another male was at West Loch Bee, South Uist, Western Isles, 14–18 March 1980.

FIG 96. Bufflehead, male. Buffleheads are the smallest of all sea ducks, reminiscent of a small goldeneye and no larger than a Eurasian teal. Males have a black back and head with a large white patch covering the sides of the head and extending to the nape. The pale patch is much smaller on the female. (Bill Coster/NHPA)

A further nine records brought the total up to 13 birds accepted by the BBRC to the end of 2006. The numbers of buffleheads kept in captivity increased significantly after 1970, and the likelihood of seeing one of captive origin in the wild has become much greater.

The first Irish record, a female, was seen at the Gearagh, Co. Cork, 18 January to 8 March 1998. Another, a first-year male, was present at Lough Atedaun, Co. Clare, from 6 January to 25 February 2007.

There are no fossil records reported from Europe, as would be expected of a Nearctic species.

50. BARROW'S GOLDENEYE *BUCEPHALA ISLANDICA* (AE)

Easily overlooked and mistaken for common goldeneye, Barrow's is distinguished by its crescent-shaped, rather than round, white patch in front of the eye (Fig. 97). The head is glossed purple, rather than the green of the common goldeneye. The world population of this primarily Nearctic species has been estimated at 205,500–256,300 individuals, most breeding in western North America. Only 4,500 birds breed in northeast Canada and a further 1,500–1,800, declining, in Iceland.[284] The Icelandic birds are thought to be sedentary, isolated from the northeast Canadian birds, and concentrated (85–90 per cent of the population) in the Lake Myvatn/upper Laxá River areas. The northeast Canadian birds would be the most likely source of any genuine vagrants arriving in western Europe.

The first BBRC-accepted British record for the period 1950–2006 was of an adult male seen at the mouth of the River Irvine, Ayrshire, Scotland, on 4 November 1979. During its stay it was observed displaying to female goldeneyes and remained with a group of duck on the sea between Irvine and Ayr. Later it moved to a freshwater lake, where it remained until 28 December 1979. This was the first record where the probability of it being a wild bird outweighed the likelihood that it had escaped. Two further occurrences to the end of 2006 have been accepted by the BBRC. The first Barrow's goldeneye was hatched in Britain in 1911 from eggs brought from Iceland, but it died soon afterwards. Later, from about 1923 onwards, many were reared successfully from eggs transported from Iceland. But the birds did not breed easily, with the first success in 1937.[285]

The first Irish record accepted by the IRBC was a male observed on Quoile Pondage, Strangford Lough, Co. Down, 20 November to 11 December 2005. Presumably the same male returned to the Quoile Pondage from 4 November 2006 to 22 April 2007.

There are no reported fossils from Europe.

FIG 97. Barrow's goldeneye, male. Resembles common goldeneye but larger. Breeding males have a purple-glossed head and a white crescent, not a spot as in the common goldeneye. (Ken Kinsella)

FIG 98. Barrow's goldeneye, female. Very similar to female goldeneye, but with a darker head and a more yellow bill. (Ken Kinsella)

51. COMMON GOLDENEYE *BUCEPHALA CLANGULA* (**A**)

The common goldeneye (Fig. 99) has an extensive breeding range in North America, from where it stretches into and across northern Eurasia within the coniferous zone from 55° to 70° N. The European breeding population is concentrated in Finland (200,000–250,000 pairs) and Sweden (75,000–100,000 pairs). Western Russia and Norway hold more than 30,000 and 10,000 pairs respectively. It is a hole-nesting duck, typically of boreal forests, utilising both natural and abandoned black woodpecker nesting holes, preferably in older forests. The erection of numerous nest boxes (75,000+) in Swedish and Finnish forests encouraged the populations to expand significantly, fuelling a 50 per cent increase in wintering numbers in northwest Europe since the mid-1980s. In contrast, those wintering in central Europe have remained more or less stable over the past 20 years.

Some 1–1.3 million goldeneye winter in northwest Europe, chiefly in Denmark, in the western Baltic, along the south Norwegian coastline, and in the Netherlands. An estimated 24,900 wintered in Great Britain during the period 1995–1999, with a further estimated 9,665 in Ireland 1990–2004. Numbers in both countries showed a steady increase from the mid-1970s to the mid-1990s. Since then, numbers have fallen quite markedly to levels similar to those of the mid-1970s. Numbers at their largest haunt, Loughs Neagh and Beg, Northern Ireland, have been declining since 1990/91.

They occur in both freshwater and coastal habitats, but many of the latter were abandoned in the 1960s and 1970s when sewage discharges were discontinued. Our wintering birds originate, based on limited recovery of ringed birds, in Sweden (43 recoveries of birds either ringed in Sweden or ringed in Britain and recovered in Sweden), Finland (9), Norway (4), the Netherlands (1), Germany (1) and Russia (1).

The main wintering sites in these islands are Loughs Neagh and Beg, Northern Ireland, where numbers peaked close to 13,600 birds for the three winters 1991–93 but fell back to some 8,500 for the winter 2000/01, then declined further. The peak numbers for January 2006 were 2,780 birds. The large surface area of the loughs and a rich supply of aquatic invertebrates – predominantly caddis fly larvae, freshwater shrimps, water boatmen, common spire shell, probably the zebra mussel – and plant material, mainly seeds of pondweed, make this area very attractive to these diving ducks.

Fossil remains of common goldeneye occur in the Cromerian interglacial deposits (c.600–500 ky BP) at Boxgrove, Sussex, at West Runton, Norfolk,

(450–500 ky BP), and in deposits of more recent origin at Derbyshire Peak Caves, from the last glacial (13–10 ky BP). Fossils have also been found in Iron Age deposits (700 BC – AD 43) in Somerset and Lagore, Co. Meath (AD 750–950). The species may have nested historically in Britain during cooler periods, especially during the Little Ice Age (1550–1850) and possibly in Scotland during the nineteenth century – as suggested by numerous summering records, but without proof of actual nesting.

The first confirmed breeding in Britain took place in 1931, when a pair nested in a rabbit burrow near the salt marsh at Burton on the Dee Estuary, Cheshire. Breeding occurred again the following year. Because of the curious nesting site, the birds involved were possibly injured, unable to return to their native breeding areas.

The natural colonisation of Scotland – at the extreme western limit of the breeding range – commenced in 1970 when a pair bred at a site near Aviemore, and again in the following two years. By 1992 the total breeding population was more than 120 pairs, encouraged by the provision of over 700 nest boxes – the most important limiting factor for goldeneye is probably nest-hole availability. Goldeneye are now nesting away from the main area of colonisation. Breeding of feral birds, escaped from the WWT's Martin Mere reserve, has also occurred in Lancashire. A pair nested at Chew Valley Lake, Somerset, in the summer of 2008.[286]

FIG 99. Common goldeneye, male. Green gloss on head, round white spot in front of eye, less black on back than Barrow's goldeneye. (Laurie Campbell/NHPA)

The first confirmed Irish breeding was on Lough Neagh, Co. Antrim, in 2000, after many years of birds summering on the lough. Since then, there has been no further proven breeding, despite provision of nesting boxes in suitable breeding locations. Numbers summering on Lower Lough Erne, Co. Fermanagh, have been increasing in recent years and there is always the hope that they may breed there. Ringing recoveries of nine Scottish breeding birds indicate that this population winters within Great Britain, with birds travelling relatively short distances. One ringed Scottish bird has been recovered in Northern Ireland.

There is a lack of available published information on the breeding biology and population dynamics of the goldeneye in Britain, but more information is available from Canada. Adults are slow to be recruited into the breeding population, unusual for a small duck. Of 22 known-aged females (ringed as ducklings) in a British Columbia study, 36 per cent bred aged 2 years, 32 per cent aged 3 and 22 per cent aged 4 years. One female first bred in her fifth year, another in her sixth. Eggs are laid from early April onwards, with an average clutch size of 9–11. Egg dumping is not unusual, creating frequent double clutches. Mixed clutches, principally with common merganser and smew, have been recorded in Finland. Of 223 nests in the British Columbia study, 64 per cent hatched, most failures being due to female desertion during egg laying or incubation. Nest loss due to predation was relatively low at 12 per cent, reflecting the advantage of tree-hole nesting. This study found that mean brood size (based on 86 broods examined) decreased from 8.7 at hatching to 3.1 near fledging. The survival of young after leaving the nest averaged 36.5 per cent, and the average number of young reared per nesting female per year was 1.3.[287]

The lifetime reproductive success of 108 females in British Columbia, followed from their first breeding until the end of their lifespan, averaged 2.25 independent offspring. Productivity was skewed according to age: most females produced no fledged young, but a few – predominantly older birds – produced large numbers. Of 243 young that fledged in the years 1984–92, 76.1 per cent were produced by only 23.2 per cent of breeding females. The annual mean survival of breeding females, based on capture–recapture methods over nine years, was 0.61. Survival of females was much higher in western Germany – over a 20-year period with no hunting – at 0.83. The most important factor limiting the population in British Columbia, where most populations are considered stable, is probably nest-hole/cavity availability, especially in recent or historically cleared woodlands. The shortage of suitable nest sites not only restricts the number of breeding birds but also encourages intraspecific brood parasitism (egg dumping), which can reduce breeding success and thus adversely impact local population dynamics. The impact of hunting is thought to be small.[288]

TABLE 69. Common goldeneye: sites in Britain where the mean five-year peak exceeded 249 birds (National threshold).

LOCATION	MEAN 5-YEAR PEAK 2002/03–2006/07	PEAK COUNT 2006/07
Firth of Forth, Lothian	816	328 (Jan)
Inner Moray & Inverness Firth, Highland	727	221 (Feb)
Abberton Reservoir, Essex	472	478 (Feb)
Humber Estuary, Yorkshire	472	401 (Jan)
Inner Firth of Clyde, Dumbarton and Argyll	452	688 (Feb)
Rutland Water, Leicestershire	447	356 (Feb)
Loch Leven, Perth & Kinross	286	517 (Nov)
Hornsea Mere, E Yorkshire	282	91 (Dec)
Morecambe Bay, Lancashire	258	(191) (Feb)

TABLE 70. Common goldeneye: sites in Ireland where the mean five-year peak exceeded 95 birds (National threshold).

LOCATION	MEAN 5-YEAR PEAK 1996/97–2000/01	PEAK COUNT 2000/01
Loughs Neagh & Beg, Co. Armagh/Down/etc	4,483*	2,780 (Jan)*
Lower Lough Erne, Co. Fermanagh	259*	169 (Mar)*
Lough Sheelin, Co. Cavan	230	252 (Jan)
Lough Derg (Shannon), Co. Tipperary	197	23 (Jan)
Strangford Lough, Co. Down	196*	82 (Nov)*
Lough Ree, Co. Westmeath	185	123 (Jan)
Belfast Lough, Co. Antrim	180*	(108) (Jan)*
Lough Oughter complex, Co. Cavan	175	78 (Jan)
Malahide Estuary, Co. Dublin	170	164 (Feb)
Lough Swilly, Co. Donegal	159	113 (Feb)

TABLE 70. – *Cont.*

Wexford Harbour & Slobs, Co. Wexford	138	88 (Dec)
Upper Lough Erne, Co. Fermanagh	135	118 (Jan)
Lough Arrow, Co. Sligo	132	—
Larne Lough, Co. Antrim	110*	97 (Feb)*
Lough Money, Co. Down	113	128 (Jan)

52. SMEW *MERGELLUS ALBELLUS* (A)

The male smew, the smallest of the mergansers and only slightly larger than a teal, appears white, marked with black with a conspicuous black eye patch (Fig. 100). It cannot be mistaken for any other of our wintering duck. The female is generally grey, with a chestnut cap and white cheeks.

Smew have a wide breeding range extending eastwards from northern Norway, Sweden and Finland through Siberia to Kamchatka, 162° E, in the taiga and forest–tundra zones between 55° N and the Arctic Circle. The estimated breeding population in Fennoscandia is 1,050–2,100 pairs, with the largest numbers in Finland (1,000–2,000 pairs) and Sweden (250–350 pairs). They first bred in Norway in 1925, and there are now 10–20 pairs. There are much larger numbers in western Siberia (7,000–15,000 pairs). However, the latter population is likely to be even larger in view of the numbers wintering in northwest Europe, which have been estimated somewhat conservatively and uncertainly – due to difficulties of securing complete censuses – at 40,000 birds,[289] including 20,000–25,000 in the Baltic Sea, 10,000–20,000 in the Netherlands, principally on the Ijsselmeer and along the river Rhine. In December 1991 about 30,000 were discovered wintering at the Szecin Lagoon, on the Polish/German border on the southern shore of the Baltic Sea, necessitating an increase in the estimate of the northwest European wintering population.

There are other smew populations breeding in northern Russia (about 35,000 birds) – the separation point between these and the more westerly breeding population is unknown – that winter around the Black Sea and the eastern Mediterranean. Further east in Siberia another breeding population winters in central and southwest Asia and the Caspian, numbering about 30,000 birds.

Evacuation of the breeding grounds commences in early September, and by the end of October all birds have departed. Their main arrival in the North Sea and the Baltic is mid December or January, coinciding with cold weather further

FIG 100. Smew, male. A small 'sawbill' duck reminiscent of common goldeneye. Viewed from a distance, it looks all white with a black eye (loral mask). A closer view reveals a white crest with a black base and a black back. Almost always encountered on fresh water. (Alan Williams/NHPA)

east. The relatively few that travel on to Great Britain and Ireland each winter – some 370 each winter during the period 1995–99 but much fewer today – occur mainly in southeast England and East Anglia, but more around the southern margin of the Cambridgeshire Fens than in Norfolk and Suffolk. Peak numbers arrive in January. They are highly migratory, cold weather on the Continent driving additional birds, probably from the Netherlands, into England and Ireland. They are scarce visitors to Scotland (usually 15–20 birds each winter) and Wales. Numbers counted during WeBS 2006/07 were the lowest – maximum count 100 in February 2007 – since 1991/92 and fewer than half the number reported the previous year. Only one was recorded from Northern Ireland.

Formerly rare winter visitors to Ireland, with only 104 records between 1800 and 1949, mainly between November and March, smew have established themselves more recently as regular guests, particularly in the northern parts of the country. There were 30 individuals recorded in the Republic of Ireland alone during 1998, including an unprecedented flock of nine at the shallow, brackish wetland at Blanket Nook, Co. Donegal. Twenty were recorded in Ireland during 2003. In more recent winters small numbers – fewer than eleven birds – have been seen.

The winter habitat preferences of the smew are similar to those of the goldeneye and the common merganser. They favour fresh water, and are generally found where it is shallow, less than 3 m deep. Reservoirs, formerly important wintering sites in Britain, have become less important as smew have shifted to flooded gravel pits where nearly 66 per cent of wintering birds were found during WeBS 2000/01. They also appear, but less frequently, on brackish waters and in estuaries, visited for feeding purposes. They are, in general, highly mobile and restless duck, frequently shifting feeding and resting areas. During winter and early spring their food is mainly freshwater fish – young salmon and trout, minnows, roach, gudgeon, etc – supplemented with some insects, obtained by surface-diving, normally in water 1–4 m deep. They feed under ice provided that there is sufficient access. Like other mergansers, they poke their heads into the water before diving down to snatch their prey – a behaviour that conserves energy by preventing the bird setting off underwater unless prey is spotted first. When caught, the small fish are firmly clinched in the narrow slender bill, both mandibles edged with saw-like sharp teeth.

Fossils of smew have been recovered together with those of many other Anatidae, including the mandarin duck, from the Middle Pleistocene Cromerian interglacial deposits (c.470 ky BP) in West Runton Cave, Norfolk, and at five other Late Pleistocene (127–10 ky BP) sites in Britain, some with Holocene deposits (10–0 ky BP). One Irish Cave in Co. Sligo had fossils probably from the Holocene. Remains have also been found in East Anglian peatlands dating from the Neolithic/Bronze ages (6,000–700 BC).

They nest in tree holes, 10 m or more above the ground, throughout the taiga and forest–tundra zones. Their preferred habitats are broadleaf woodlands surrounding freshwater lakes, along flooded riversides and other wetland areas, especially backwaters and sheltered bays of larger rivers. Their distribution is closely associated to that of the black woodpecker, in whose holes they often nest. Nest boxes are also occupied. Nest sites are keenly contested, not only among smew but also with goldeneye, both species sometimes laying in the same nest site and resulting in a mixed brood being reared. They are known to occasionally hybridise in the wild with goldeneye. There is slender information on their breeding biology. Clutch size is 6–9 but up to 14 eggs has been recorded, probably a case of egg dumping by another female. Incubation by the female lasts 26–28 days. The fledging period is about ten weeks. The age of first breeding is thought to be 2 years.[290] There is no readily available information on breeding success or adult survival. Moulting flocks of males have been recorded in Siberia but not in Europe.

TABLE 71. Smew: sites in Britain where the mean five-year peak exceeded 5 birds. A further 12 sites exceeded the National threshold of 4 birds.

LOCATION	MEAN 5-YEAR PEAK 2002/03–2006/07	PEAK COUNT 2006/07
Wraysbury Gravel Pits, Berkshire	49	19 (Jan)
Cotswold Water Park (West), Gloucestershire	25	13 (Feb)
Dungeness Gravel Pits, Kent	20	17 (Feb)
Lee Valley Gravel Pits, Hertfordshire	15	7 (Jan)
Rye Harbour and Pett Level, E Sussex	14	3 (Jan)
Thorp Water Park, Surrey	12	3 (Jan)
Twyford Gravel Pits, Berkshire	12	—
Seaton Gravel Pits and River, Kent	8	1 (Feb)
Fen Drayton Gravel Pits, Cambridgeshire	8	3 (Dec)
Rutland Water, Leicestershire	8	5 (Feb)
Colne Valley Gravel Pits, Hertfordshire	7	8 (Feb)
Thrapston Gravel Pits, Northamptonshire	7	—
Little Paxton Gravel Pit, Cambridgeshire	7	4 (Jan)

TABLE 72. Smew: sites in Ireland that have supported smew during I-WeBS counts, 1996/97–2000/01.

LOCATION	MEAN 5-YEAR PEAK 1996/97–2000/01	PEAK COUNT 2000/01
Wexford Harbour and Slobs, Co. Wexford	18	2
Lough Oughter complex, Co. Cavan	10	1
Larne Lough, Co. Antrim	10	1
Lough Swilly, Co. Donegal	8	9

TABLE 72. – *Cont.*

Upper Lough Erne, Co. Fermanagh	4	4
Shannon & Fergus estuaries, Co. Limerick/Kerry/Clare	2	1
Parisee Lough, Co. Cavan	2	1
Lough Foyle, Co. Derry	2	1

53. HOODED MERGANSER
LOPHODYTES CUCULLATUS (AE)

This elegant merganser breeds in North America, mainly on the west coast of Canada and the USA, as far north as southern Alaska, and also in southeastern Canada and the eastern United States. The population is estimated at 270,000–385,000 birds. Although evidence from the Christmas Bird Counts and other sources suggests that the eastern population is increasing, with an estimated 80,000 birds, the species rarely occurs in Europe. The male is predominantly black and white with a fan-like erectile white crest surrounded by black (Fig. 101). The breast is white with two black bars, and the flanks are brownish. The female resembles a smaller and darker female red-breasted merganser.

Hooded mergansers are widely held in waterfowl collections. By 1997 some 51 keepers of waterfowl in Great Britain had 329 hooded mergansers, and 92 females produced fertile eggs. The National Waterfowl Census revealed that 206 young were hatched in Britain in 2001. This considerable potential source of escapees, coupled with the relative scarcity of birds in northeastern America, necessitates extreme care when assessing sightings of possible wild birds.

The hooded merganser was once placed in the BOU's Category B List, based on a record of a first-winter male shot in the Menai Straits, near Bangor, Gwynedd, in the winter of 1830/31. Following a review of the record in 1999, the merganser was relegated to Category E, being considered inadequately documented. This had been the only extant record for Great Britain, with most subsequent claims considered likely to have been escapes. A previously accepted British sight record of a female at Willen Lake, Buckinghamshire, on 28–29 December 1983, was reviewed in 1992 and considered to be probably an escape. There have been several other subsequent records including those at Newbiggin (2002) and Shetland (2006).[291] Presumably these will need to be reviewed in the light of the BOURC's announcement on page 246.

FIG 101. Hooded merganser, male displaying. Most of the male's courtship displays are associated with crest-raising. The flanks are reddish-brown. The breast is white with two black bars in front of the wing. (Alan Williams/NHPA)

A female, or immature, hooded merganser, of undeterminable age, seen and photographed at Oban Trumisgarry, North Uist, Outer Hebrides, from 23 October to 1 November 2000, was initially placed by the BOURC in Category D List ('a species that would otherwise appear in Category A except that there is reasonable doubt that they have ever occurred in a natural state'). Following a recent review of this record the BOURC announced in June 2008 that the species had been admitted to Category A of the British List. The BOURC stated that the

Oban Trumisgarry bird had occurred during a month of Atlantic depressions that brought 13 American wigeons, three ring-necked ducks, three lesser scaups and an inland surf scoter as vagrants from the Nearctic to the Palaearctic. Other documented records of genuine vagrants include four from the Azores since 2001, one from the Canaries and one from Iceland. However, the BOURC is of the opinion that most records in Britain involve birds of captive origin.

In Ireland the IRBC has accepted three records (of four individuals): a male and female shot in Cork Harbour, December 1878; one shot in the Shannon Estuary, off Ballylongford, Co. Kerry, January 1881; and an immature male seen at Acton Lake, Co. Armagh, on 21 December 1957. During I-WeBS counts one was seen on Kilbrean Lough, Co. Kerry, on 21 November 1996, and another was reported from Lough Leane, Co. Kerry, in January 1997,[292] but both were considered escapes.

There are no reported fossil records from Europe, following the pattern of other Nearctic duck species.

54. RED-BREASTED MERGANSER *MERGUS SERRATOR* (A)

The red-breasted merganser (Fig. 102) is one of the world's most successful ducks, measured by its circumpolar breeding distribution, which spans the northern tundra and boreal zones between 50° and 75° N. British and Irish breeding birds belong to the north, northwest and central European population of 170,000 birds that occur in east Greenland, Iceland, the Faeroes, Scandinavia, northwest Russia through Siberia and south to Denmark, the Netherlands, Germany, Poland and (since 1993) Normandy. The bulk of the breeding population is located in Finland (30,000–40,000 pairs), Norway (10,000–30,000 pairs) and Sweden (14,000–18,000 pairs). The birds breeding in west Greenland are sometimes assigned to a poorly defined subspecies, *Mergus serrator schioleri*, that may not deserve recognition. It is thought that the west Greenland population winters on the southwest coast of Greenland. The size of the west and east (nominate race) Greenland populations is estimated at 1,000–5,000 pairs. There are a further 250,000 birds in North America. There are fewer than 10,000 birds in western Siberia.

A curious feature of the red-breasted merganser is the asymmetrical nuchal crest – a transverse ridge on the palatine bones that runs against the grain of biological symmetry.

The wintering population in Great Britain was best estimated at 9,840 birds for the period 1995–99, while a further estimated 3,390 wintered in Ireland during 2000–04. Wintering numbers have been steadily declining since the

FIG 102. Red-breasted merganser, male. Colourful, with a dark green back, white collar and chestnut breast. Females have orange-brown heads. In flight the neck is long. Equally at home in marine and fresh waters. (Danny Green/NHPA)

mid-1990s, although numbers had risen from the early 1970s. Birds of the northernmost parts of the breeding range are migratory, while the southern populations are more or less sedentary. Immigrants arrive from September onwards, but it is not until mid or late October that birds from the northern areas – Norway, Sweden, Finland and northwest Russia – vacate their nesting grounds to head south and southwest to arrive first in the Baltic and then in Britain and Ireland. It has been suggested that most wintering birds on the east and south coasts of England, from the Wash southwards, are of Continental origin.[293] The recovery of ten Icelandic-ringed birds in Britain and Ireland between October and March supports the belief that some of the Icelandic breeding population (2,000–4,000 pairs)[294] winters mainly in Scotland, as well as in northern England and Ireland. One Icelandic-ringed bird has also been recovered from east Greenland and another from Denmark. Part of the east Greenland breeding population is thought – supported by another ring recovery – to migrate to Iceland, where some probably remain while others may travel on to Britain and Ireland.

The recovery of 16 of 196 adults ringed in Britain and Ireland shows that these undertake, in general, only local movements from their breeding grounds to nearby coastal areas to moult and winter. Males, having deserted the females after the onset of incubation, gather together with immatures and non-breeding birds at coastal locations during June and July to moult. Relatively large numbers of moulting birds congregate in Scotland at the Sound of Gigha off the Argyll coast and off Tentsmuir, Fife; in England at Lindisfarne, Northumberland; and in Ireland at Dundrum Bay, Co. Down, at the mouth of the Erne Estuary, Co. Donegal, off Clogher Head, Co. Louth, and off the north Dublin coast.

During winter, mergansers are almost exclusively coastal or marine, preferring estuaries, bays, brackish lagoons and shallow offshore waters. Here they generally occur in small flocks, feeding on small fish (10–15 cm), especially sticklebacks and gobies. They are entirely carnivorous, sometimes feeding cooperatively, herding and corralling small fish by diving in line or encircling them. Like other mergansers they 'snorkel' when fishing, placing their heads underwater first to locate prey before expending energy on diving and chasing the fish. When in fresh water they feed on salmon and trout fry, and this brings them into conflict with fishermen – for it has been claimed that over 1,000 young salmon are consumed by each duckling up to the time of fledging. Their overall impact on fish can be high. It was calculated that the average summer population of 131 ducklings reared on Windermere, Cumbria, would consume 2.6 tonnes of fish per year, mainly perch, if these ducklings ate the same amount of food as four experimental ducklings. Adults have been estimated to eat 200–250 g of fish, or 20–25 per cent of the average body weight, per day, requiring 15–20 average-sized fish, caught in 250–300 dives requiring 4–5 hours of foraging.

Fossil records show that the red-breasted merganser was present in Britain during the Middle Pleistocene Hoxnian period (c.270 ky BP) at Swanscombe, Kent, and the Cromerian interglacial period (c.500 ky BP) in Suffolk. It was also present in Middle Devensian deposits in the Lea Valley and at Merlin's Cave, Herefordshire (65–25 ky BP). Their bones also date from the Dark Ages (c. AD 400–1066). Remains of bones in peat and other deposits from the Mesolithic, Neolithic, Bronze and Iron Ages indicate that it was present in eastern England and a food item in those periods. Their bones have also been discovered at the lake dwellings at Lagore, Co. Meath (AD 750–950). They may well have been present in Britain and Ireland ever since then. They were mentioned by Ælfric the Grammarian (955–1020), English abbot and author, in his Glossary, compiled in c.998.

In Britain and Ireland there were estimated to be a minimum of 2,150 and 700 breeding pairs respectively during 1988–91. Their principal nesting areas are in the north and west, spread over a range of habitats, from sheltered lakes and large rivers to wild coastal zones. For more than 150 years the Scottish population has gradually been spreading east and south, first colonising northern England (Cumberland) in 1950, then three years later north Wales (Anglesey). Further range expansion has taken place since then. The Irish breeding population began to spread from the early twentieth century onwards – Co. Cork was colonised sometime around 1920, Co. Wexford in 1929, followed by Counties Longford, Antrim and Armagh, Co. Dublin in 1935, and more recently breeding was first proven in Co. Derry in 1955,[296] followed by two pairs breeding at Lough Beg, Co. Derry, in 1957, Since then, a small number have bred every year, with a maximum of five pairs in 1963.[297]

Most birds do not breed until their second year, many not until their third. The non-breeding proportion of adult females in Iceland in any given year is about 18 per cent.[298] The female selects her nest site on the ground in dense vegetation, close to the water's edge. Egg dumping was found to be fairly common – 4.5 per cent intraspecific and 19.1 per cent interspecific, most of the latter being subsequently deserted. In a Finnish study of 3,110 eggs laid over three years, 77 per cent hatched and of these 14 per cent young were reared. The average productivity of young per pair in the three years was 1.5, 2.0 and 0.7, so the losses were 84, 78 and 92 per cent. In Iceland annual productivity of flying young per female was estimated at 2.1.[299] There is no available published information on survival rates.

TABLE 73. Red-breasted merganser: sites in Britain where the mean five-year peak exceeded 130 birds. A further 9 sites exceeded the National threshold of 98 birds.

LOCATION	MEAN 5-YEAR PEAK 2002/03–2006/07	PEAK COUNT 2006/07
Firth of Forth, Lothian	588	347 (Oct)
Fleet and Wey, Dorset	384	284 (Feb)
Poole Harbour, Dorset	347	213 (Jan)
Moray Firth, Highland	292	211 (Oct)
Morecambe Bay, Lancashire	232	(118) (Mar)
Chichester Harbour, W Sussex	200	217 (Feb)
Lavan Sands, Gwynedd	184	81 (Aug)
Inner Firth of Clyde, Dumbarton & Argyll	174	195 (Aug)
Duddon Estuary, Cumbria	161	106 (Oct)

TABLE 73. – *Cont.*

Inner Loch Indaal, Islay	155	—
Langstone Harbour, Hampshire	152	159 (Dec)
Loch Ryan, Dumfries & Galloway	134	106 (Dec)

TABLE 74. Red-breasted merganser: sites in Ireland where the mean five-year peak exceeded 50 birds. A further seven sites exceeded the National threshold of 35 birds.

LOCATION	MEAN 5-YEAR PEAK 1996/97–2000/01	PEAK COUNT 2000/01
Inner Galway Bay, Co. Galway	250	247 (Nov)
Strangford Lough, Co. Down	243*	390 (Dec)*
Wexford Harbour & Slobs, Co. Wexford	206	61 (Oct)
Larne Lough, Co. Antrim	163*	196 (Sep)*
Dundalk Bay, Co. Louth	160	257 (Aug)
Belfast Lough, Co. Down	150*	110 (Feb)*
Lough Swilly, Co. Donegal	130	105 (Jan)
Cork Harbour, Co. Cork	119	64 (Dec)
Carlingford Lough, Co. Down	118*	171 (Aug)*
Lough Foyle, Co. Derry	83*	35 (Sep)*
Malahide Estuary, Co. Dublin	83	62 (Feb)
Clew Bay, Co. Mayo	73	105 (Jan)
Courtmacsherry Bay/ Broadstrand Bay/ Dunworley, Co. Cork	71	105 (Dec)
Outer Ards Shoreline, Co. Down	61*	108 (Mar)*
The Mullet, Broadhaven & Blacksod Bays, Co. Mayo	55	72 (Dec)
Dungarvan Harbour, Co. Waterford	54	—

55. COMMON MERGANSER *MERGUS MERGANSER* (A)

The common merganser, more familiar to us in Britain and Ireland as the goosander, resembles the smaller and darker red-breasted merganser but lacks the head crest, while the breast, flanks and underparts are white, more or less suffused with yellowish-pink (Fig. 103). The female is more difficult to separate from its cousin but has a sharp division between the chestnut fore-neck and the white chest, whereas in the red-breasted merganser the division is graduated and blurred. When in flight there is more white on the wings than displayed by the red-breasted merganser.

Their breeding range is more southern but overlaps that of the red-breasted merganser, extending through the Holarctic in the temperate and boreal zones between the Arctic Circle and 50° N. The nominate race, *Mergus merganser merganser*, breeds across northern Eurasia from Iceland, Britain, Ireland, northern Scandinavia, northern Russia and Siberia to the Bering Sea. Largest breeding numbers are in Finland (20,000–30,000 pairs), followed by Sweden (10,000–20,000 pairs). A curious outpost population of the nominate race (450–500 pairs) breeds in the Alps. Another race, *M. m. orientalis* (the form *M. m. comatus* is now considered to be synonymous with *orientalis*), breeds in the highlands of central Asia, while the North American form, *M. m. americanus*, breeds from coast to coast on that continent.

About 266,000 common mergansers winter in northwest and central Europe, originating from the more northerly parts of the breeding range.[300] British breeding birds would generate a wintering population of some 8,100 birds, to which should be added about 8,000 Continental visitors, to total 16,100 birds during the winter for the period 1995–99. The winter visitors are mostly found in southern Britain, arriving from northern Fennoscandia, northwest Russia, Germany and the Netherlands, as shown by the recovery of ringed birds. The Icelandic breeding population (100–300 pairs)[301] is sedentary, with no ring recoveries reported to date from Britain or Ireland. Very few common mergansers, perhaps some 10–20, spend the winter in Ireland. The WeBS annual index of wintering birds in Britain has been declining since 1997/98 but is now showing signs of levelling off and is back to the level of the mid-1980s.

The common merganser is controversial because of its predilection for salmon and trout. Small fish, usually less than 10 cm in length, constitute most of the diet, and the prey taken depends upon the habitat and availability of species. In freshwater habitats, preferably with water no deeper than 4 m, salmon, brown trout, eel, perch, minnow, grayling, pike, miller's thumb, dace, rudd, roach,

FIG 103. Common merganser, male. Similar shape to the red-breasted merganser but larger. Breeding males appear mostly white except for the black head and neck. The red bill is conspicuous. Long-bodied in flight, with white underparts and scapulars. (Alan Williams/NHPA)

barbell, bleak and carp are all taken. In coastal waters the prey includes gunnel, herring. cod, plaice andsand-eel. In certain locations at specific times common mergansers can have a detrimental impact on fish populations. In one Scottish study, during the summer, 124 common merganser stomachs contained mainly salmon (57.2 per cent by frequency), brown trout (9.7 per cent) and eels (14.5 per cent), other fish and insects etc making up the balance.[302] During the winter a wide variety of coarse fish is eaten.

The common merganser does not have a long fossil history in Britain, with relatively recent records coming from Somerset (12.5–9.3 ky BP) and Derbyshire from the Late Pleistocene/Upper Palaeolithic deposits at five different horizons (c.20 ky BP). Their bones have also been recovered from Iron Age (700 BC – AD 43) deposits in Somerset.[303] It is possible that it survived through the Middle Ages. There are records in the literature of common merganser in Britain from 1622 onwards.

The estimated British breeding population in 1993 was 2,900–3,600 pairs.[304] They are relatively sedentary (usually moving less than 150 km), apart from the extraordinary moult migration of males. Several ornithologists claimed that the common merganser had bred in Orkney sometime during the eighteenth century, on North Uist in 1858, South Uist in 1862 and in Perthshire from 1864 onwards, but it was not until 1871 that the first two breeding records – a nest with ten eggs in a hollow of a tree at Loch Ericht, Perthshire, and seven ducklings seen on Lough Awe, Argyll – were widely accepted. Thereafter it became increasingly recorded in summer in the west of Scotland, especially after a large winter influx of birds from the Continent in 1875–76. Breeding became more frequent and the range extended southwards until 1941, when England (Northumberland) was penetrated. Since then, it has spread further south, proving especially successful in the uplands of Wales, with one confirmed breeding pair in 1968–72 increasing to 10 in 1977 and 100 by 1985.[305] The species now breeds as far south as Devon and Cornwall. Exceptionally, it also bred in East Anglia in 2006 to at least 2008.[306] The common merganser also extended its breeding range southwards in Europe from 1850 onwards.

The first recorded breeding in Ireland was in Co. Donegal in 1969. It subsequently bred in the county for several years, but not since 1989 (Table 75). After that, wintering birds were found at a series of non-breeding sites over the years, revisiting a site for a few years and then fading out. The number of wintering common mergansers peaked at 23 on the River Foyle (Counties Donegal, Derry and Tyrone) in 1993. The only current wintering location is Lough Rath, south Donegal, where numbers peaked at ten in January 2001. These irregular sites give hope that a pair or two are breeding somewhere in Donegal – or at least that the pattern of immigration from Scotland, which no doubt gave rise to the original breeding pair in 1969, is still occurring. More recently a new breeding site has been established in Co. Wicklow, with one pair nesting in 1993, and in 2004 four, five or possibly six pairs bred, with four nest boxes being occupied. It is possible that the Wicklow birds originated in Wales, following the population expansion there. It is more than likely that breeding has taken place, or will take place, in some other counties – Mayo, Galway and Sligo are high on the list of candidates.

TABLE 75. Common merganser: summary of breeding and late spring/summering records in Ireland, 1969–2008.

YEAR	LOCATION	DETAILS
1969–71	Co. Donegal	1 pair bred at site x
1972–73	Co. Donegal	No breeding at site x
1974	Co. Donegal	1 pair bred at site x
	Co. Derry	Castlerock, 1 female 10/05 joined by a male on 11/05
1975	Co. Donegal	1 pair bred at site x
1976	Co. Donegal	1 pair bred at site x
	Co. Donegal	Blanket Nook, 1 female 22/05
1977	Co. Donegal	1 pair bred at site x. Up to 3 males + 2 females at site. Birds were seen at 3 or 4 other likely sites from winter 1977/78 to spring 1979 with no proof of breeding
1978	Co. Donegal	1 pair bred at site x. Average 5 young reared for 7 years. Max brood 13
	Co. Galway	Lough Corrib, 1 male 08/05
1979	Co. Donegal	Not breeding at site x where 2 pairs present
1980	Co. Donegal	Not breeding at site x where up to 5 birds present
	Co. Antrim	Shane's Castle, 1 female 01/04 and a pair 10/06. 1 female on 16/06 and 21/06 may have been the same birds
1981	Co. Donegal	Birds present at site x. 4 birds at another site, spring
1982	Co. Donegal	Birds not seen again at site x or elsewhere in county
	Co. Mayo	Doo Lough, 1 pair, 23/06
1983–89		No records of summering or breeding birds
1989	Co. Donegal	Bred
1990		No records of summering or breeding birds
1991	Cos. Armagh/Down	Lough Shark/Acton Lake. 1 female 04/11/90 to 02/12/90 & remained until 05/05/91

TABLE 75. – *Cont.*

1992	Co. Mayo	One male Lough Carrowmore 20/06, joined by female on 05/07
1993	Co. Wicklow	First breeding recorded
1994	Co. Wicklow	1 pair bred + 2 young, River Avonmore. Present Lough Tay May/June, max. 4 females on 01/06. Glendalough 25/05 to end June, with peak 1 male + 5 females on 14/05
1995	Co. Wicklow	Glendalough, 01/04 to 04/06, 1 male + max 4 females. Breeding strongly suspected at one site where female seen entering nesting hole
	Co. Armagh	L. Neagh, Oxford Isle. 1 pair. 15/02 & 19/04
1996	Co. Wicklow	1 pair bred + 3 young
1997	Co. Wicklow	Glendalough, Lough Tay, Lough Dan. Total 19 birds 13/04 to 03/05. Bred at Glendalough, adult female + 4–6 young; 14 birds 15/06
1998	Co. Wicklow	No evidence of successful breeding. Min of 9 at Glendalough
1999	Co. Wicklow	Lough Tay, 2 males + 2 females 30/04
2000	Co. Wicklow	Glendalough, bred. 3 females 31/04; 2 females/immatures 27/06. Lough Dan, 2 males + 1 female 15/04; 4 males + 1 female 21/05
2001	Co. Wicklow	No confirmed breeding
2002	Co. Wicklow	No confirmed breeding
2003	Co. Wicklow	3 nests with clutches of 14, 11 and 7 eggs. All successfully hatched
2004	Co. Wicklow	4 pairs nested in nest boxes with clutches 6, 11 and 12. A 1 or 2 pairs may have bred
2005	Co. Wicklow	1 to 2 pairs; 2 young
2006	Co. Wicklow	Breeding presumed
2007–08	Co. Wicklow	None of 9 special nest boxes used

Data from Irish Bird Reports; Northern Ireland Birdwatchers Association reports; Whilde, 1993; Hillis, 2006; R. Sheppard, personal communication.

Their preferred breeding habitats are clear freshwater lakes (where it is easy to spot prey), rivers, or ponds associated with the upper sections of rivers in forested areas (preferred habitat is broadleaf woodland). Tree holes made by black woodpeckers (but of course not in Britain or Ireland) or natural cavities – openings about 12 cm wide with an internal diameter of about 25 cm are ideal – are favoured nesting sites, but they will also breed, when trees are scarce, under boulders, in holes in banks or under bushes. Artificial nest boxes are popular nesting sites. Unlike the red-breasted merganser, the common merganser is solely an inland breeder.

Females do not breed until the age of 2 years, the average clutch size is 8–9 in Europe, and egg dumping is common when nest sites are few – up to 39 eggs have been found in one nest. Incubation normally lasts 28–35 days, a relatively long period, and the young are nidifugous and self-feeding, cared for by the mother and brooded at night when small. Hatching success is high, 91 per cent of 199 nests in Finland. Twenty per cent of the nests there were 'dump nests', and of 392 nesting attempts about 68 per cent of all eggs laid hatched.[307] Fledging period is 60–70 days, another relatively long time, and thus the female often deserts her brood before they fledge so that she can start her moult. One month is required for this, so many birds do not regain the power of flight until early October. In a Finnish study the average clutch size at hatching was 10.8, and the average number of young reared was 6.8 per pair.[308] The mean annual adult survival rate, based on recoveries of British- and Swedish-ringed birds wintering in Britain, is 0.60, lower than the calculated rates for two other members of the sea-duck tribe Mergini – long-tailed duck (0.72) and common scoter (0.77) – probably reflecting their conflict with fishing interests. The availability of food influences breeding success, and this may be responsible for an apparent four-year population cycle detected among British common mergansers.[309]

Male common mergansers, like so many other male ducks, desert their females once incubation has started, absenting themselves from the breeding grounds from May to October. Having gathered together on inland waters with one-year-old males from the end of May onwards, they undertake a remarkable northward moult migration in late summer, to four large fjords around Nordkapp, in the far north of Norway.[310] Prior to their return to Britain in October/November they join vast numbers, almost the entire European population of some 35,000 adult males, congregating in the Tana River estuary (70° 30' N), close to their moulting grounds. The direct flight line from Edinburgh (a theoretical median point) is 2,300 km, making the overall journey almost double that undertaken by pink-footed geese during their northerly moult migration. A small number of British adult males remain in the country to moult locally. The Norwegian moulted males return to Britain in October and November. Females, not so lucky and with less 'free' time to engage in such extensive movements, moult locally in Britain.

British breeders are partial migrants, moving only small distances to their wintering grounds from their natal areas and mostly remaining within a radius of 150 km of their breeding sites. Birds winter on both inland and coastal water habitats but more frequently on fresh water – lakes, gravel pits and large rivers.

TABLE 76. Common merganser: sites in Britain where the mean five-year peak exceeded 70 birds (National threshold 161).

LOCATION	MEAN 5-YEAR PEAK 2002/03–2006/07	PEAK COUNT 2006/07
Loch Lomond, Dumbarton & Argyll	(261)	(261) (Sep)
Tay Estuary, Fife	234	313 (Jul)
Tyninghame Estuary, Lothian	138	157 (Aug)
River Tweed, Kelso/Coldstream, Scottish Borders	108	74 (Dec)
Eccup Reservoir, W Yorkshire	105	82 (Nov)
Yetholm Loch, Scottish Borders	100	32 (Dec)
Castle Loch, Lochmaben, Dumfries & Galloway	98	85 (Nov)
Firth of Forth, Lothian	86	(60) (Jun)
Spittal to Cocklawburn, Northumberland	75	116 (Aug)
Tweed Estuary, Northumberland	74	123 (Aug)
Solway Firth, Cumbria	73	29 (Sep)

TABLE 77. Common merganser: sites in Ireland that have supported birds during WeBS and I-WeBS counts, 1994/95–2000/01.

LOCATION	NUMBER OF RECORDS 1994/95 – 2000/01	PEAK COUNT
Belfast Lough, Co. Down	20	1
Loughs Tay and Dan, Co. Wicklow	8	16
River Foyle, Co. Donegal	6	8
Lough Gowna complex, Co. Longford	3	2
Killineer Quarry, Drogheda, Co. Louth	3	1
Carrowmore Lake, Co. Mayo	2	2
Shannon & Fergus estuaries, Co. Limerick/Kerry/Clare	2	1
Dungarvan Harbour, Co. Waterford	2	3
Lough Conn, Co. Mayo	2	2

56. RUDDY DUCK OXYURA JAMAICENSIS (C1E*)

The ruddy duck is a shocking sight on first encounter, not resembling any other British or Irish breeding duck – short and dumpy with a tail cocked upright during display (but normally held horizontally) and possessing a broad bill, short neck and prominent head. The male in summer plumage has rich brown upper parts, breast and flanks contrasting with white cheeks and a black top to the head (Fig. 104). The underparts are whiter and the bill is bright blue. The female is overall brown in summer with a darker head cap and nape and paler cheeks. The bill is grey blue.

The ruddy duck is a native of North and Central America and the northern part of South America. The native population is more than 0.5 million birds.[311]

Ruddy ducks were first brought to Britain in the 1930s, and were kept in waterfowl collections.[312] In 1948 three pairs plus a drake were imported from Utah and Pennsylvania, USA, by the Wildfowl Trust, Slimbridge, and they bred the following year. The highly aquatic ducklings had to be left with their mothers because traditional hand rearing was not successful, and some evaded capture

FIG 104. Ruddy duck, male. An unmistakable duck – dumpy body shape and ruddy coloured, white face with black cap extending down the nape, and an often-erect black tail. During winter the plumage is grey with retained white face and black cap. Females are similar to male winter plumage but with a dark line on the cheek. Ruddy ducks seldom fly, and when they do they stay low over the water. (Mike Lane/NHPA)

'by diving extremely well', and so avoided pinioning. About 70 juveniles flew from Slimbridge between 1956 and 1963, most before or during the severe 1962/63 winter. The first record of wild breeding occurred at Chew Valley Lake, Somerset, in 1960, thus beginning one of the most successful colonisations of Britain by an alien bird. The subsequent populations in Britain and western Europe are all based on the very narrow genetic base of the seven Slimbridge birds.

In 1959 the ornithologist and aviculturalist Jean Delacour wrote that 'Ruddies are extremely quaint and interesting and should be kept more widely … they agree well with other ducks.'[313]

There are no known fossil remains of ruddy duck in Britain or Ireland, following the pattern of other Nearctic species.

As with other ducks, they are difficult to census, especially as they nest in small groups. Their breeding population is best assessed by winter counts and dividing by a factor of six.[314] From 1960 to 1980 numbers increased exponentially, slowing to 10 per cent per annum during the 1980s. By 1991 there were 3,400 wintering in Britain, representing 567 breeding pairs, based on January WeBS counts. By January 2000 wintering numbers had risen to an all-time high of 4,565 birds as determined by WeBS, equating to 761 breeding pairs. Numbers peaked in 2002/03. Following the introduction of a government control programme in 2002/03 numbers have fallen sharply in five subsequent winters. The 2006/07 index value was similar to that in 1985/86.

Ruddy ducks were slow to colonise Ireland. The first breeding (four young) was recorded in 1973 at Oxford Island NNR, Lough Neagh, Co. Armagh. In 1982 they dispersed from the site and spread to other breeding localities. By 1986 there were some 27–30 birds wintering at Portmore Lough, Co. Antrim, where numbers peaked at 206 in January 1996. The self-sustaining population in Northern Ireland was estimated at 20–30 pairs in 2002, but more recent studies in 2004 put the breeding population between 25 and 29 pairs spread between 14 locations. The first breeding in the Republic of Ireland was of a single pair in Co. Dublin (1992); subsequent breeding occurred in Co. Wexford (1993 and 2000) and Co. Tipperary (1998, two young).[315]

Their preferred breeding habitats are shallow freshwater marshes and ponds rich in emergent, floating and bottom vegetation and with stable water levels, a habitat generally associated more with grebes than with ducks. During winter they move to larger inland water bodies such as reservoirs and gravel pits. Their breeding season is longer than that of most wildfowl, from April to October – a hangover from the duck's near-tropical origins – allowing the rearing of two broods in a season. Most females attempt to breed at 1 year old, egg-dumping in other ruddy duck nests (in Wales there were 25 dump nests among 100 examined), then continuing to lay a full clutch in their own nest. In comparison with other similarly sized British ducks they lay the largest clutch in terms of total mass and weight – the average clutch represents 95 per cent of the female's body weight, compared with 78 per cent for the teal and 66 per cent for the garganey. Such large eggs ensure the ducklings are strong and robust at hatching. In North America clutch sizes are larger – the mean of 71 clutches in Iowa was 8.1 – and the total weight of the eggs can be more than three times the weight of the female. Mean clutch size in Britain for wild birds is 6.4 (range 3–11); the incubation period is relatively short, 23–26 days in the wild (USA), and the young can dive immediately on departing the nest. Nesting success is high in Great Britain: the estimated productivity rate per successful breeding female is 2.7 ducklings, and an assumed adult and juvenile survival rate of 0.7 and 0.6 respectively would account for rapid population growth. However, there is no available published information on adult survival rates. They are unique among British wildfowl in undergoing a complete pre-breeding moult, generally in February and March, on their wintering grounds.

They are omnivorous, feeding mainly on insect larvae and aquatic plant seeds gathered when surface-diving. The bottom ooze is strained while the bird swings its head from side to side as the bill is opened and closed rapidly. They will also graze underwater on the leaves of pondweed, tasselweed and eelgrass.[316] They are generally nocturnal feeders, but during the breeding season they will feed during the day.

Following the establishment of wild breeding populations in Great Britain they spread into continental Europe, initially occurring in countries closest to Britain. There is no evidence of transatlantic vagrants from North America travelling to Europe, based on comparisons of patterns of mitochondrial DNA of European and North American ruddy ducks.[317] Ruddy duck are now present in at least 21 western Palaearctic countries, with breeding attempts recorded in at least 12, including Iceland, and regular breeding attempts in five – France, Ireland, Morocco, the Netherlands and Spain.[318]

The arrival of ruddy ducks in Spain has led to ecological problems for the white-headed duck, a rare and globally threatened species. The genetic purity of the white-headed duck is threatened by interbreeding with the ruddy duck. If present trends of hybridisation – the hybrids are fertile – continue it is more than likely that the white-headed duck will be totally subsumed by the ruddy duck. DNA analysis shows that they are distinct species, separated by some 2–5 million years of evolution. This hybridisation is the greatest threat to the survival of the white-headed duck, according to the 1979 Bern Convention on European Wildlife and Natural Habitats. Moreover, the International White-headed Duck Action Plan (endorsed by the Commission of the European Union, the Bonn Convention and the African–Eurasian Waterbird Agreement) states that the extinction of the white-headed duck is only likely to be prevented if rapid action is taken to control ruddy ducks in Europe.

The global population of the white-headed duck is fewer than 15,000 birds, located mainly in central Asia, where there have been population declines due to habitat loss and hunting.[319] In western Europe the white-headed duck breeds only in western Spain (and Portugal?), forming a discrete and isolated population, not connected with the c.400 birds breeding across the Mediterranean in Tunisia and Algeria. There are separate small populations in eastern Europe. In Spain they came close to extinction in 1977 when only 22 birds remained due to hunting and habitat destruction. Protection measures by the Spanish government and voluntary organisations then assisted the population to increase to c.700 individuals by the mid-1990s.[320] There are now several hundred breeding pairs, and numbers are increasing. At El Hondo, Valencia, the breeding population increased from 4 pairs in 1994 to 190 pairs in 2000 and is still rising.[321] There are now estimated to be some 2,500 birds in Spain.

Britain is the suspected source of ruddy ducks on the Continent, and on the Spanish white-headed duck breeding grounds in particular. The pattern of occurrence of ruddy ducks in European countries is correlated with British population increases, having started only when the species was well established in Britain. Since 1996 flocks of 30–80 birds have migrated annually from Britain to winter at one site in northern France, demonstrating the duck's capacity to migrate southwards into Europe. Since 1983 up to 27 birds have arrived on migration in Spain annually, and 30 were seen there in January 1997, following cold weather in Britain and across northern Europe during December 1996. It is highly likely that British birds have been migrating to winter in Spain for several years.[322] However, there are no recoveries of British-ringed birds for proof.

The first hybrid ruddy x white-headed ducks were seen in Spain in 1991, and a control programme commenced. By 1994 most hybrids and ruddy ducks were dead. Between 1984 and May 2006 a total of 159 ruddy ducks and 65 hybrids were shot in Spain.

In 2003 the British government announced that the ruddy duck would be eradicated from the wild in Britain. The programme would fully respect Britain's obligations to maintain, as far as possible, the current diversity of bird species. The proposed action was supported by many conservation bodies, including the WWT and the RSPB, but attracted opposition from naturalists and animal welfare organisations who were concerned that it would cause disruption and cruelty, and cost too much. The five-year eradication programme will cost about £3.337 million, half of the money put up by EU LIFE Nature funding and the balance matched by the Department of Environment, Food and Rural Affairs (DEFRA). The control programme contract was awarded to the Central Science Laboratory, an Agency of DEFRA. The aim is to reduce ruddy duck numbers to below 175 individuals within 5–7 years, providing access to the 40 most important post-breeding and wintering sites in Britain is available from landowners. If necessary, powers of compulsory access will be invoked to ensure the programme's success. Three other European countries – France, Portugal and the Netherlands – have also instigated ruddy duck control programmes. Between September 2005, when the eradication programme began, and 15 January 2007 a total of 2,689 ruddy ducks had been shot in the UK. Coordinated population counts at the top 50 UK ruddy duck sites in December 2006 and January 2007 suggested that the national population had been reduced by approximately 2,000 birds.[323]

TABLE 78. Ruddy duck: sites in Britain where the mean five-year peak exceeded 150 birds (National threshold not yet set). Another 34 sites exceeded 30 birds.

LOCATION	MEAN 5-YEAR PEAK 2002/03–2006/07	PEAK COUNT 2006/07
Staines Reservoirs, Surrey	577	227 (Sep)
Abberton Reservoir, Essex	458	261 (Dec)
Hanningfield Reservoir, Essex	393	276 (Dec)
Chew Valley Lake, Somerset	348	(130) (Dec)
Dungeness Gravel Pits, Kent	242	189 (Dec)
Blagdon Lake, Somerset	210	85 (Nov)
Pitsford Reservoir, Northamptonshire	210	102 (Feb)
Rutland Water, Leicestershire	201	17 (Oct)
Hillfield Park Reservoir, Hertfordshire	198	263 (Oct)
Blithfield Reservoir, Staffordshire	170	23 (Dec)
Holme Pierrepont Gravel Pits, Nottinghamshire	153	106 (Jan)

TABLE 79. Ruddy duck: sites in Ireland that have supported more than 1 bird during WeBS and I-WeBS counts 1994/95–2000/01.

LOCATION	MEAN 5-YEAR PEAK 1994/95–2000/01	PEAK COUNT 1994/95–2000/01
Loughs Neagh & Beg, Co. Armagh/Down/etc	46	89
Broad Water Canal, Co. Antrim	14	31
Wexford Harbour and Slobs, Co. Wexford	14	4
Lough Eorna, Co. Tipperary	10	14
Clooney Lough (Castletown), Co. Meath	6	3
Hillsborough Forest Lake, Co. Down	2	3
Nanny Estuary and Shore, Co. Meath	2	2

CHAPTER 4

Social Behaviour

T HE COMPLEX BEHAVIOURAL STRATEGIES that have evolved in wildfowl have arisen to serve one critical objective – the survival of populations and their individual members. Much of this behaviour is instinctive, and has been crafted by natural selection to ensure the maximum productivity of young birds and breeding efficiency. Moreover, members of the Anatidae must not only be reproductively successful but should also maintain their genetic integrity. Thus courtship and sexual behaviour, especially among the ducks, have the purpose of avoiding the disadvantages of hybridisation.

The two big divisions of the Anatidae – the Anserinae (swans and geese) and the Anatinae (ducks) – have quite different strategies with regard to breeding (Table 80). Swans and geese generally pair for life, mature slowly and do not normally breed until aged two or three, sometimes four, years old. As a result, the Anserinae have limited opportunities for rapidly increasing their numbers. Moreover, as they are generally monogamous, gene flow is slow. They also have a tendency to return to breed in their natal areas, interbreeding with other members of their geographic group. All this facilitates adaptation to local conditions and the development of subspecies.

Most of the geese that winter in Britain and Ireland, such as the brant, greylag, white-fronted and bean geese, have well-marked subspecies or races, for the reasons given above. Even the visiting transatlantic greater and lesser Canada geese exhibit a range of subspecies. However, there is one important exception to this general rule – the barnacle goose. While the Greenland, Svalbard and Russian populations may be in the very early stages of developing subspecific characteristics, no plumage, morphological or genetic differences have yet been detected. The red-breasted goose, one of our rarest winter visitors, is also an

TABLE 80. Breeding and population characteristics of the Anatidae.

CHARACTERISTIC	SWANS AND GEESE	MOST DUCKS
Sexual dimorphism	No major differences	Males brightly coloured, females drab
Life span	Long	Short
Sexual maturity	2–3 years	First year
Duration of pair bond	Lifetime	One year
Clutch size	Small/medium	Large
Gene turnover	Slow	Fast
Overall fecundity	Low	High
Capacity for rapid population increase	Low	High

exception, in that it has such a small and geographically focused breeding population that subspeciation has not yet had a chance to evolve. In the case of the swans, both the species that visit Britain and Ireland in winter exhibit marked subspeciation on a global scale, though neither manifests any subspecific differences within the British and Irish wintering populations. Our wintering whooper swans come essentially from one population breeding in Iceland, while the tundra (Bewick's) swans that winter with us originate from a wide geographic range stretching eastwards across northern Russia.

WINTERING BEHAVIOUR

Wildfowl are particularly interesting among birds because most geese and many of the swans breed within the Arctic Circle. Once the breeding season is completed they must undertake arduous and extensive migrations southwards to escape the onset of harsh weather conditions that make food unavailable. Most swans and geese, together with their offspring, endure as family units from the hatching of the young to the next breeding season. Cohesiveness of families confers advantages upon young birds, as well as improving breeding success of the adults and adult survival. Hugh Boyd showed, in some pioneering work over 50 years ago, that amongst European white-fronted geese wintering at Slimbridge, Gloucestershire, large families that engaged in conflicts with other geese were the most successful in winning these battles, while smaller families were successful against adults without juveniles, and so on.[1] Thus within the wintering flock there was a social hierarchy, dominated by large families. This ensured that the large unified families secured the best feeding areas, resulting in better survival chances for the young and adults, together with enhanced breeding success the following summer.

With regard to ducks there is virtually no social cohesion of the family during the winter period. As a general rule the young are fully independent by the onset of winter.

The parents of successful goose and swan families are generally in better physical condition than adults without young that have been excluded from the best feeding areas. This is particularly important when it comes to establishing a breeding territory the following spring. In the case of the mute swan ferocious territorial fights between rival males, sometimes leading to the death of the weaker and smaller male, can take place during the defence of a territory in spring (Fig. 105). In these conflicts the swan in better physical condition as a result of better winter feeding is most likely to be the winner.

Some families remain together even in subsequent winters. Among Bewick's swans the young return to the breeding grounds with their parents, and up to 68 per cent of these young then associate with their parents after the breeding season, during the next winter, even if the parents have successfully bred. In other species the number of these 'carry-over' families is low. During my 47-year study of a wintering population of some 2,500 barnacle geese on the Inishkea Islands, Co. Mayo, the frequency of carry-over families as a proportion of successful families has been less than 3 per cent. Ducks, on the other hand, do not stay together as a family once the young have fledged.

Our wintering swans and geese could be compared, in a way, with elephants whose young stick together with their parents while being trained and instructed in survival strategies. The strong advantage of staying together as a family group means that, unlike most other birds, young geese and wild swans do not rely on instinct alone to guide them on migration in their first year, and they must learn the routes and strategies from their parents. Staying together has survival value not only for migration training but also on the wintering grounds, as discussed above. Parents are very protective of their young, and spend a great deal of time ensuring that they have access to the best available grazing. With regard to the barnacle geese that winter on the Inishkea Islands, as the winter progresses and food becomes scarcer the successful parents move their families off the islands to better feeding grounds on the mainland, leaving behind a population of geriatric and unsuccessful or non-breeding adults.

Most migratory geese and many ducks have a strong propensity to return to the same wintering areas in subsequent years. This can be regarded as an

FIG 105. Mute swans: territorial dispute. Mute swans can be extraordinarily aggressive towards interlopers in their breeding territory. Such fights can sometimes lead to the death of one of the swans. (Eric Soder/NHPA)

evolutionary response to the known availability of secure feeding as well as safe roosting areas. Returning to known winter sites will facilitate enhanced survival of the individuals concerned, and, moreover, breeding productivity will be improved. Winter site fidelity of the Greenland barnacle geese that visit the Inishkea Islands is very pronounced. The same individuals, identified by colour and numbered rings that can be read in the field, return winter after winter to the same fields on the two closely located islands of Inishkea North and Inishkea South. Young barnacle geese (1–2 years old) show a greater tendency than adults to wander to other wintering locations. Some males, having paired in Iceland during spring migration, will follow the female back to her own established wintering grounds. In contrast, for Bewick's swans the conflict of winter site loyalty, following pairing, is usually decided by the male, who returns to his traditional wintering area with his mate.[2]

Similar site fidelity has been shown to exist among Icelandic greylag geese wintering in Scotland, where observations of marked birds revealed that three-quarters of all resightings were of birds returning consecutively to the same or adjacent region, and about half of resighted geese recorded in four consecutive winters returned to the same region. There was no significant difference between age groups or sexes.[3] Other studies have shown that 76 per cent of pink-footed geese ringed at a Lancashire wintering site returned there the following winter.[4] There were no differences between the sexes, or between adults and young, in their return to the wintering grounds. For the Greenland white-fronted goose the resighting rate in subsequent winters on their premier Irish wintering haunt on the North Slob, Co. Wexford, was even higher at 86 per cent, though this may have been influenced by the species' specific feeding requirements.[5] No differences were found between the sexes with regard to site fidelity, but young birds in their second and third winters showed a greater tendency to move winter sites than would be expected by chance, due possibly to pair formation or the break-up of the family.

BREEDING BEHAVIOUR

Monogamy, whether long-term or seasonal, is the mating system of wildfowl. Among the swans and geese it is usually long-term. The divorce rate among geese and swans is extremely low. A survey of 919 pairings of Bewick's swans that were known to have ended showed there were no cases of divorce, while the annual divorce rates among whooper and mute swans were 0.7 and 5.8 per cent respectively during the same study period.[6] There are many advantages of monogamy. John Bowler found in his study of Bewick's swans that the dominance rank of the male in winter flocks affected the extent to which his female partner was able to build up fat reserves, as indicated by the abdominal profile of the female. Barnacle geese pairs that had been together many years were found to be feeding on the edges of flocks where feeding conditions were best, providing better opportunities for the females to build up essential body reserves for the forthcoming breeding season.[7] A high abdominal profile, indicating good body condition, at the end of the winter had a significant positive effect on the pair's breeding success. Moreover, established pairs of geese and swans spend less time and energy on courtship, which allows more time to be spent on feeding and improving body condition for the breeding season. In contrast, several ducks have a different strategy of annual monogamy, forming new pair bonds each winter season. As with swans and geese, the male's attendance with his mate during winter allows the female to build up good body reserves for the forthcoming breeding season. However, unlike the swans and geese the drake deserts his mate during the incubation period and takes no further role in the rearing of the family. The cryptic plumage of the female helps her to blend into her nest site, while the presence of a brightly coloured male would only draw attention to the incubating female.

Some ducks provide classic examples of avian polygamy or promiscuity, in contrast with most other birds where monogamous pair bonds endure through the breeding season while both parents nurture and provide for their young. Most ducks have precocial young that can easily fend for themselves almost immediately after hatching. Others nest near abundant food supplies where the female alone, with no assistance from the male, can guide the young to food supplies. Thus the role of the drake in such circumstances is very much reduced to his often ritualised courtship and subsequent copulation with the female. The great majority of drakes, having established strong pair bonds with their female partners, desert the females as soon as the clutch has been laid and incubation has started.

Courtship and pair formation

In his paper on the evolution of duck courtship, Paul Johnsgard discusses the value of the pre-nesting bond between male and female, and the courtship leading up to the bond.[8] If the male in most duck species will soon desert his female, what value is there in his often elaborate and high energy-consuming courtship behaviour?

Among most ducks the often brightly coloured males indulge in a series of elaborate displays, not only to attract a female but also to fend off other male competitors. Another important aspect of the ritualistic male displays is to ensure 'species recognition' from the female, to make sure they are mating with their own species. Thus the fundamental function of his displays is to maintain the reproductive isolation between closely related species. Otherwise a taxonomic nightmare would ensue, with interbreeding of closely related ducks with the eventual loss of a species in a sea of hybrids. Such a mess of jumbled genes can be found among some diving ducks, where there is a plethora of hybrids such as greater scaup x tufted duck, pochard x ferruginous duck, tufted duck x pochard, tufted duck x ring-necked duck and so on – a veritable nightmare for ornithologists!

In the case of mallard courtship, taken as a typical example among dabbling ducks, it is the female that chooses the male from several suitors. In most duck populations there is an excess of males to females, which puts the drake's

FIG 106. Mallard copulation. Copulation in all ducks takes place in water, and is generally preceded by both birds pumping their heads up and down while holding their bills horizontal. (Ernie Janes/NHPA)

courtship behaviour at a competitive premium – meaning that drakes with the most vigorous displays and brightest plumages have the best chance of securing a female partner and reproducing.

During mallard courtship, which may start in late autumn and continue until spring, one or more females are usually in the presence of a group of males. The drake initiates the courtship process by focusing his attention on one of the females and greets her by going through a series of general comfort movements such as drinking, preening behind his wing and body shaking. He follows these activities by a series of actions that include whistling as he stretches his neck vertically while at the same time lifting his tail and shifting his wings to expose the purple speculum (wing patch on the trailing edge). This is done as he presents himself in profile view to the female, thus ensuring maximum visual impact. He then swims, after pointing his bill straight at the female, head almost touching the water, past her, a behaviour described as 'nod-swimming'. He finally stretches his neck vertically while flicking it and simultaneously shaking his tail. This intense display is described as 'head-up-tail-up', and 'down-up', and at the same time the male is 'grunt-whistling', terms first used by the eminent ethologist Konrad Lorenz. The drake finishes off his courtship by stretching his neck high while orientating his blackish nape feathers towards the female. If she is interested she 'nod-swims', jerking forward towards the tail of the drake with inciting calls and movements. Other interested drakes are seen off by her sideways head movements. The female initiates copulation by movements and whistling. Mutual head pumping precedes copulation (Fig. 106).

The innate nature of drake displays reflects their genetic constitution just as plumage does, and together they characterise or define a species. As Paul Johnsgard has pointed out, the fascination of pair-forming behaviour in male ducks is not so much in their taxonomic applications but in understanding their obviously adaptive functions, such as maintaining reproductive isolation between closely related species.[9]

The different plumages, especially those of drakes, are enhanced by social courtship rituals, made more competitive by the surplus of males and the fact that it is the female that selects her mate. Not all drakes secure a female. When a drake is selected the female mallard follows closely behind, signifying a preference for him. She ultimately leads him back to her ancestral breeding spot, rather than the male leading her to his area. The switching of mates each year encourages gene flow and prevents the development of races or subspecies as found with many geese and swans. Because ducks have early sexual maturity, short-duration pair bonds and large clutch sizes, they have the capacity for rapid population increases, a characteristic not shared with swans and geese.

The basic courtship rituals displayed by mallard are found, often with modifications, among most other ducks, many of which are more exotically plumaged than the drake mallard. The courtship behaviours of four other ducks – the mandarin, common goldeneye, long-tailed duck and shelduck – exhibit some variations of mallard rituals and these will be discussed below.

The gaudily plumaged drake mandarin employs his brightly coloured plumage to maximum advantage during his somewhat aggressive courtship of the female. The male produces a nasal, whistling call during courtship display, whereas the female makes a high-pitched courtship call that sounds like 'keet'. The male also makes a high-pitched staccato bark, a barely audible whistle and, heard least often, a grunting sound similar to that of a wild pig. Courtship commences during the autumn and involves elaborate and complex movements. The male starts by performing comfort movements like the drake mallard – drinking, preening and body shaking. During the drinking and preening-behind-the-wing display, the drake lifts his ornamental sail feather while facing the female to expose the metallic blue outer vain feather that is normally hidden. While doing the characteristic 'head shake' the drake lowers his head to the water, then throws it up rapidly while shaking it and his tail feathers vigorously. The neck and crown rufous feathers are erected to add greater visual effect (Fig. 107). A more complex double display shake is also performed. As with the mallard, the female takes the initiative in choosing her mate by inciting behaviour towards the preferred male. She will initiate copulation by performing head-pumping movements, then extending prone on the water. The male

FIG 107. Mandarin duck: two males displaying. (Manfred Danegger/NHPA)

FIG 108. Pair bonds between mandarins are strong. If both birds survive to the next breeding season they re-form their old bond rather than forming new ones. Mandarins represent a symbol of devotion. (Ken Kinsella)

performs bill-dipping movements before mounting, and after copulation swims away from the female while orienting the back of his head in her direction. Unlike the mallard, drake mandarins are among the few duck species that guard the female and ducklings until they can fly.

If a pair of mandarins survives together through two breeding seasons they typically re-form the old bonds rather than finding new mates. For this reason the Chinese and Japanese regard mandarins as symbols of devotion, love and marital fidelity (Fig. 108).

male display

male and female display, including copulation

FIG 109. Common goldeneye courtship behaviour. From Johnsgard, *Handbook of Waterfowl Behavior* (Cornell University Press, 1965).

The common goldeneye, a more modestly plumaged species, has an array of courtship movements that make full use of its dark green head and striking large white spot between the upper mandible and bright yellow eye. Much of the courtship ritual (Fig. 109) is thought to have derived from hostile behaviour. The most striking sequence is the slow and fast head-throw-kick. The head is stretched upwards and rapidly thrown backwards to rest on the drake's back while he utters a very audible 'rrrt' noise (Fig. 110). At the same time both feet kick backwards, throwing up a shower of water as if he were a miniature paddle steamer. These head-throws have been timed by analysis of filmed birds, and it was found that the average time for the head-throw performance was 1.29 seconds.[10] I once watched upwards of 400 common goldeneye during early spring at the Ormoz accumulation lake, northeast Slovenia, where most of the birds were engaged in courtship display. The day was windless. The cacophony of their 'rrrt' calls, the seemingly violent head-throws and the thrashing of water made it a memorable encounter with wildfowl.

FIG 110. Common goldeneye male: head-throw display. Goldeneyes have one of the most spectacular and complex courtship behaviours of all ducks that breed in Britain and Ireland. The head-throw – there are three variants of this action – is perhaps the most dramatic part of this behaviour. (Alan Williams/NHPA)

The long-tailed duck, apart from being one of the most northerly-distributed of the Anatidae, is one of the most social and gregarious of ducks. They appear to spend more time than other ducks in the business of pair formation, while their loud eerie call, a polysyllabic 'ahr-ahr-ahroulit', or 'ow-ow-owdle-ow', echoes across the Arctic stillness. Unlike most other ducks, they do not become sexually mature until their second year.

Courtship commences in early summer and continues throughout winter, well into spring. Competition for a female can be intense; often a group of up to 15 males will encircle a female, all vying for her attention. The range of their courtship behaviour is remarkable. Robert Alison, who studied these ducks for many years in Arctic Canada, recorded the male performing at least a dozen different displays – lateral head-shaking, bill-tossing, rear-ending, porpoising, wing-flapping, body-shaking, parachute, breast, turning the back of the head, bill-dipping, steaming and neck-stretching displays.[11] There are frequent spectacular courtship flights and aerial displays during which the female is pursued by a group of males with much vocalisation. There is probably more aerial chasing and display in the courtship rituals of long-tailed ducks than in other ducks, and this might be related to a lower wing loading, which would

FIG 111. Long-tailed duck: male displaying to female, Norway. The classic head-throw and erect tail are essential elements in his courtship behaviour. (Jari Peltomaki/NHPA)

make complex aerial manoeuvres easier than for ducks with a high wing loading. The females, as part of their incitive behaviour, produce guttural calls while lifting their chins. The male's long tail is raised vertically during the tail-end display (Fig. 111), then his head and neck are lowered to the water as his legs kick backwards. Pair bonds are renewed annually, with females often remaining with their mate from the previous year, and appear strong.

In addition to the true ducks, the subfamily Anatinae includes the 14 species of sheldgeese and shelducks in the tribe Tadornini, and they in effect provide a transition or bridge between the true ducks and the true geese. Pair bonds appear to be fairly strong in sheldgeese, but less strong in shelducks. Unlike the geese, all the species in this tribe exhibit conspicuous courtship behaviour. The female incites the males to attack other males or females and then she selects her mate on the basis of how the male responded to her inciting (Fig. 112). On the return of the male from his attack he preens behind his wing on the side facing the female and she responds by preening behind her wing facing the male, which exposes her metallic speculum. This ritualised preening is a sexual display.

FIG 112. Common shelduck males fighting. These rival males are in dispute over a claim to a female during courtship. Disputes can also arise over the defence of an estuarine feeding territory, the size of which (ranging from 1,000 to 2,000 m²) is determined by the density of invertebrate prey. (Jari Peltomaki/NHPA)

FIG 113. Common shelduck courtship. From Johnsgard, *Handbook of Waterfowl Behavior* (Cornell University Press, 1965).

The courtship of geese and swans can be quite elaborate, despite the absence of marked plumage differences between the sexes. Jeff Black and Myrfyn Owen identified a series of well-defined steps that barnacle geese at WWT Slimbridge went through during pair formation. Much of the courtship behaviour of these geese is repeated by other geese with minor modifications. Initially a male tries to position himself between the female he is courting and other close potential suitors, so-called 'herding behaviour'. Then the male carries out a mock attack with outspread wings, running away from the female to attack imaginary neighbours. He returns to the female with a 'triumph display', during which both male and female face each other upright and perform a duet of cackling noises (Fig. 114). The male then extends his neck and head towards the female's head, whereupon she turns away before or after the male makes contact with his bill.[12]

It has often been stated that courtship and pair formation of geese takes place on the wintering grounds, but I have never observed it among the wintering flocks of barnacle geese on the Inishkea Islands, Co. Mayo, from the time the geese arrive in mid October to their departure in late April. I suspect

FIG 114. Four stages in the social behaviour of the barnacle goose. The social display during the pair formation process in geese involves (a) herding behaviour – the second stage in the pair formation process: the male attempts to position himself between the female and her nearest neighbours; (b) mock attack with wing display – the third stage in pairing process of new partners: male runs away from female to attack imaginary neighbours and returns to female, which joins in exaggerated triumph ceremony; (c) triumph ceremony posture when both male and female hold upright stance while emitting cackling vocalisations as a duet; and (d) triumph ceremony posture when male extends his head and neck toward female's head: female faces away before or after he makes contact with his bill. From Black and Owen (1988). (Artwork by Joe Blossom, reproduced with permission)

that courtship and pairing take place in the northern valleys of Iceland, where the geese spend less than a month feeding prior to departure for the breeding grounds in northeast Greenland. It is also possible that pair formation may take place on the breeding grounds, among two-year and older birds in non-breeding flocks or groups. A similar situation exists among Bewick's swans, which have been studied by Eileen Rees.[13] She found that in 40 years of watching individually identifiable Bewick's swans at Slimbridge, nearly 4,000 pairs were observed but there were no instances where both members of a pair were seen separately at

FIG 115. Whooper swan courtship: triumph display. This is one of the commonest social displays between courting whooper and other wild swans. The wing flapping and waving is accompanied by loud vocalisation. (Hellio & Van Ingen/NHPA)

Slimbridge in the winter prior to being first recorded together. She concluded that the swans paired elsewhere – possibly on the spring-migration staging areas, or on the breeding grounds, or during the summer in the non-breeding flocks.

Incubation and rearing of the young

The close bond between male and female in several species of geese is critical during the incubation period. Geese tend to nest in exposed sites and are vulnerable to attack from many different predators. On the other hand, ducks generally nest in concealing vegetation and are in less need of protection from predators. During the summer of 1985 my colleagues Michael Viney, Richard Nairn and Steve Newton studied the breeding behaviour of the barnacle goose in Ørsted Dal, Jameson Land, in northeast Greenland (Fig. 116). Here the geese breed on cliff ledges up to 150 m above the base of the cliff. The cliffs are inaccessible to the principal predator of the geese – Arctic Foxes – but glaucous gulls and ravens cruised along the cliffs in search of exposed or temporarily vacated nests. The goose incubated the eggs while the gander stood sentry-like, on or close to the nesting ledge. His presence was sufficient deterrent to ward off

FIG 116. Barnacle goose: cliff breeding habitat in northeast Greenland. (David Cabot)

any aerial predator attacks on the nest. During incubation the goose left the nest for short periods to feed on the nutrient-rich emerging vegetation on the valley floor. The number of feeding trips decreased as incubation progressed, with fewer trips prior to and after hatching. Incubating females spent approximately 3 per cent of their time away from the nest on feeding trips that lasted a mean duration of 37 minutes. In her absence the gander kept watch over the nest and prevented any predators stealing the eggs. The ganders were away three times more often and spent, on average, 44 minutes away from the incubating goose.

As incubation proceeded, the gander moved closer to the nest. After hatching, and some 42 hours later when the goslings were ready to jump off the cliff, the gander played an important role in stimulating the goose and goslings to leap off the ledge. The gander had intensive bouts of the characteristic pre-flight head-flicking, with intervals of craning his neck in the extremely erect position. The gander called frequently, made short flights to and from the nesting ledge and generally elevated the level of excitement. The behaviour intensified, and eventually the gander jumped off the nesting ledge, followed by the goose and hapless goslings. The goslings that remained on the ledge were called down by their parents from the base of the cliff. The goslings were then rounded up and led through the rather impenetrable boulder scree at the cliff base by both parents. On several occasions Arctic Foxes appeared, attracted by the goose clamour, and were harassed, without much success, by the gander and goose. Both parents then led the surviving goslings to the security of a pond or stream. Thereafter the family party remained intact. In other Arctic-nesting geese the gander also plays a critical role in the protection of the goose, the nest site and the goslings.

For most ducks the story is very different, with the female undertaking all the tasks of incubation and duckling rearing alone. In some ducks, such as the common eider, broods from different females come together to form a crèche of upwards of 100 ducklings, attended by several females. One advantage of such behaviour is that the risk of predation of the ducklings by gulls decreases with crèche size. A tight group of ducklings makes it hard for the gulls to pick off any individual.

The social cooperation shown by the common eider has clear survival advantages for the small ducklings. The same is true of the other types of social and reproductive behaviour discussed in this chapter – the various strategies for successful breeding, seasonal or lifelong monogamy, the survival and prospering of the family unit among swans and geese, the courtship rituals that serve among other things to prevent hybridisation among the ducks. All these behaviours, and many more, have evolved through the long process of natural selection, and they are part of what defines the Anatidae and ensures their survival as a very successful group of birds.

CHAPTER 5

Food and Feeding Ecology

THERE ARE MANY FACTORS THAT REGULATE a population (see Chapter 6), and among the many causes of mortality are predation, disease, starvation and hunting – but food is the key regulator of populations, and of the individual breeding success of all wildfowl. Swans, geese and ducks have a long evolutionary history of selecting their food according to the amount of energy they obtain from it in relation to the effort spent searching for it and consuming it. The key issue of 'profitability' – minimum effort for greatest gain of energy – has led to a range of diverse morphological adaptations, especially bill size and structure, for different feeding techniques. They have developed distinct feeding strategies designed to avoid competition by closely related wildfowl for the same food. The evolutionary driver in this instance has been the need to maximise food profitability. Wildfowl are also fortunate because their great mobility allows them to travel long distances rapidly in search of new food supplies when local resources have been exhausted or become unavailable due to freezing conditions, flooding, drought or sudden land-use change.

Many wildfowl move down a food energy and nutrient gradient as winter progresses. On arrival of the birds from the northerly breeding areas to their British and Irish wintering grounds, energy-rich foods are first consumed, and when these are exhausted ducks, geese and swans engage with lower-quality foods (Fig. 117). The feeding behaviour of some wildfowl, especially the geese, would appear to be extremely sophisticated in managing their resources by 'farming' grasslands and salt-marsh pastures to ensure maximum production of nutrients in fresh vegetation growth, especially during the spring when body reserves must be built up for the northward migration and the forthcoming

FIG 117. Dark-bellied brant geese feeding, East Mersea Island, Essex. When brant geese arrive from the Arctic they traditionally first feed on eelgrass growing on the estuarine mudflats. When the eelgrass is eaten out they switch to the less nutritious sea lettuce and then move on to graze salt-marsh grasses, as here. However, many geese short-circuit this sequence by feeding on improved grassland throughout the winter. (Alan Williams/NHPA)

breeding season. This strategy is part of managing the energy cycle. Because of their special needs, wildfowl are past masters at managing their energy cycle to meet their high energy demands. Thus they build up their body condition during spring and autumn to meet these stress peaks.

The basic feeding strategy of all wildfowl is to obtain as much energy as possible per unit time, and they adopt different tactics to achieve this objective.

FIG 118. Eurasian teal, male, feeding in shallow waters at Brownsea Island, Dorset. Teal are opportunistic feeders, feeding in waters generally less than 8 cm deep. During the summer they feed on aquatic insects, larvae, molluscs and crustaceans. (Melvin Grey/NHPA)

For example, wildfowl share out the food resources, as exemplified by a group of mostly dabbling, ducks – mallard, Eurasian teal (Fig. 118), northern pintail, northern shoveler, common shelduck, Eurasian wigeon and common goldeneye. These all share the same estuarine feeding habitat during the autumn and winter but avoid competition by feeding in different zones and on different foods. A study of the food they consumed in an estuary in southeast England showed that they partitioned out the food resources through different feeding habits and exploited, in general, their own food niches (Table 81).

TABLE 81. Estimated percentage consumption of food by wildfowl in a southeastern English estuary.

WILDFOWL	ESTIMATED PERCENTAGE PRINCIPAL FOOD EATEN BY VOLUME OF DIET					
	Algae	Vegetative plant parts	Seeds	Crustaceans	Small molluscs	Small insects
Mallard	—	—	75	10	—	—
Eurasian teal	—	—	10	—	75	5
Eurasian wigeon	40	50	—	—	—	—
Northern pintail	—	—	5	—	75	—
Northern shoveler	—	—	10	—	60	10
Common shelduck	5	—	—	—	80+	—
Common goldeneye	—	—	—	90	—	—

From Olney, 1965.

COMPETITIVE EXCLUSION AND ADAPTIVE RADIATION

As a group of closely related species sharing the same aquatic habitat, wildfowl show a remarkable adaptive ability to avoid competition for food, the most critical of all their resources. In the 1930s the Russian microbiologist Georgyi Gause, working on a laboratory culture of unicellular ciliate protozoans feeding on the same bacterial food, proposed the *competitive exclusion principle*, that two species that compete for the exact same resources cannot stably coexist.[1] One of the two competitors will always have a slight edge over the other which, in the long run, leads to the extinction of the other or an evolutionary shift of the inferior competitor towards a different ecological niche. The Anatidae are prime examples of Gause's principle in operation.

Competition for the same resource can be avoided by resource partitioning, ensuring that food is shared out equitably among all the closely related species living in the same habitat. Wildfowl are exemplary practitioners of this. Through adaptive radiation of bill structure and feeding habits, different wildfowl species are able to coexist, each exploiting its own food niche (Fig. 119). Long before humans started to cultivate agricultural crops, the wide range of wildfowl

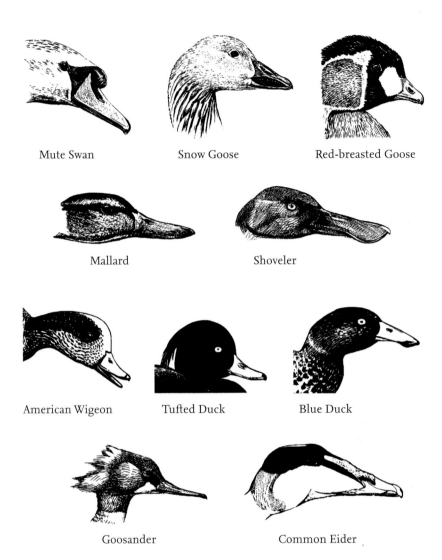

Mute Swan Snow Goose Red-breasted Goose

Mallard Shoveler

American Wigeon Tufted Duck Blue Duck

Goosander Common Eider

FIG 119. Adaptive radiation in wildfowl bill structure. Artwork by Joe Blossom, Mark Hume and Helen Shackleton. From J. Kear, *Ducks, Geese and Swans* (Oxford University Press, 2005). Reproduced with permission.

FIG 120. Mallard, female. Note the lamellae on the lower mandible. (Laurie Campbell/NHPA)

FIG 121. Northern shoveler: pair filter-feeding from water surface. (Joe Blossom/ NHPA)

feeding behaviours and different bill structures would have evolved, driven by intense selective pressure experienced at times of maximum food shortages during the winter.

The basic structure of the bill of wildfowl is broad and flattened with a series of serrations or transverse lamellae lining the mandibles. All Anatidae have one row of lamellae on the ventro-internal edge of the upper jaw. Many dabbling ducks, which depend on more efficient filtering mechanisms, have extra lamellae – a row on the dorso-lateral edge of the lower jaw and another on the lateral surface. Mallard, for example, have 36–54 lamellae on the upper jaw and 72–80 in the dorso-lateral row of the lower jaw (Fig. 120; see also Chapter 1, Fig. 4).[2]

The tongues of wildfowl are fleshy and thick, and many are covered with small rasp-like spiny protrusions endowing the tongue with a sandpaper-like quality somewhat akin to the tongue of a cow. When dabbling ducks are filter-feeding, the tongue works as a pump, pressed rapidly up and down against the palate. The downward action sucks liquid into the slightly open bill while the upward motion pushes the liquid out of the mouth through the fine lamellae, which filter off and trap minuscule plants and animals, similar to the feeding technique of baleen whales. The northern shoveler is the extreme example of a filter-feeder, possessing an enormous bill whose lamellae strain out the smallest food particles, in contrast to other dabbling duck such as the mallard and northern pintail, which extract much larger food morsels (Fig. 121). The most sophisticated filter-feeding ducks have a double layer of lamellae, twice as many as most of the diving ducks, which generally swallow their much larger prey – molluscs and other invertebrates – whole, and therefore have little need for filtering mechanisms.

Apart from surface-feeding, the two other major evolutionary trends in wildfowl feeding techniques are diving and grazing. Among the diving ducks, the bills of the piscivorous mergansers have evolved along different lines to those of the dabbling ducks – their bills are long and thin with a hooked terminal nail and tooth-like serrations on the mandibles, which are designed to strongly grip wriggling, slimy small fish. The dorsal surface of the tongue has two rows of barbs that facilitate the holding of the prey. Diving sea ducks such as the long-tailed duck, greater scaup, tufted duck and black scoter have carefully partitioned out their similar food resources – principally molluscs and crustaceans – and have evolved different preferential feeding and maximum diving depths. The long-tailed duck is capable of the deepest dive, travelling down to feed at a depth of 20 m (some have been recorded at 65 m in North America). Next is the black scoter, which can operate in depths of 10–15 m, then the tufted duck (7 m), while the greater scaup operates as a relatively shallow-water feeder, diving down to 5 m. The skull of a diving duck has fewer air spaces than that of other wildfowl, an adaptation that provides less buoyancy while avoiding the problems of changing pressures experienced at great depths.

Geese and swans specialise in grazing, while a few of the dabbling ducks such as Eurasian wigeon and Eurasian teal will also graze when opportunities present themselves. Geese have evolved more conical bills compared with other wildfowl, and their lamellae have developed into tooth-like structures that assist the biting, cutting or snapping of blades of grass and other vegetation. The larger and more massive goose bills, such as those of the greylag and white-fronted geese, facilitate the uprooting of rhizomes and other underground plant structures, while the petite goose bills, such as those of the red-breasted, barnacle and brant geese, are adapted more for precision and high-speed work – barnacle geese can manage up to 230 pecks a minute. Arctic-breeding geese all graze the tundra vegetation during summer, but it was during the critical winter months that they became specialised, over the course of evolution, to feed in different habitats, each focusing on their own niches.

Of the five geese regularly wintering in Britain and Ireland, brant are generally maritime, feeding on intertidal mudflats picking up eelgrass and algae, especially sea lettuce, or grazing salt-marsh vegetation, of which common saltmarsh-grass and sea plantain are favourite species. Barnacle geese, with one of the shortest goose bills facilitating precise pecking and some of the fastest pecking rates, specialise on small plants such as white clover and red fescue in maritime grasslands, especially in plantain swards on the western seaboards of Ireland and Scotland. The Greenland white-fronted goose historically fed on raised and blanket peatlands in Scotland and western and central Ireland, where they dug up bulbils and roots of various plants, particularly bog cotton (cottongrass) and white beak-sedge. The greylag goose fed in coastal and inland *Scirpus* marshes, where it excavated club-rush roots rich in energy reserves. The pink-footed goose historically fed on grasses on shifting estuarine salt marshes as well as on seeds of sedges and rushes in more permanent estuarine marshes. Today the historical niche specialisation has become somewhat blurred as geese now feed mostly in agricultural landscapes that offer up many new and nourishing food resources – reseeded and nitrogen-enriched grasslands, spilt grain (barley, wheat or oats), autumn stubbles, shoots of winter cereals, potatoes, turnips, swedes, carrots, sugar beet and other root crops.

Swans have massive bills, and their dextrous long necks allow them to feed on the submerged leaves, stems, roots and seeds of a wide range of aquatic plants. The mute swan is vegetarian, feeding not only on floating and submerged aquatic plants – principally pondweeds, stoneworts and water-milfoils – but also on emergent plants and seeds on the margins of waters. During winter eelgrass becomes an important food in brackish and estuarine waters. By 'up-ending', swans are able to increase the depth of their aquatic feeding by an extra 15–20 cm. Mute swans also feed on herbs and grasses on land, especially on improved grassland, and they will also occasionally eat sprouting cereals. Whooper and tundra swans are more adaptable in exploiting farmland crops, and in some instances feed extensively on crops. While leaves, stems, roots and seeds of fresh and brackish water plants formed the traditional diet of whooper swans, increasing numbers of birds are feeding on farmland and exploiting agricultural crops such as improved grassland, stubble grain, potatoes, winter cereals, sugar beet and even turnips. Tundra swans feed mostly on leaves, shoots, roots, rhizomes and tubers, usually in water less than 1 m deep, either by dipping the head and neck into the water or by up-ending. Like the whooper, they will graze in marshy or partially flooded pastures, where they dig and root up the energy-rich stolons and roots of plants.

A study of wintering Bewick's swans feeding on the Ouse Washes showed the birds preferring soft grasses – floating sweet-grass, creeping bent and marsh foxtail. The energy and starch-rich roots of marsh yellow-cress were another prominent item in the diet. They also fed on flood banks, taking white clover stolons and leaves of grasses such as perennial rye-grass and cock's-foot.[3] The large and heavy bills of swans, like those of geese, facilitate the uprooting of stolons, shoots, roots and rhizomes. But they are not just large blunt instruments, being capable of picking up small items such as spilt grain and delicately cropping small grasses.

The size and position of wildfowl feet also show adaptive radiation. Diving ducks such as the mergansers possess some of the largest feet relative to body size, allowing additional power and manoeuvrability while chasing small fish. As in many other diving ducks, their feet are located towards the end of the body, an adaptation facilitating extra swimming power. On land these ducks appear to walk uncomfortably, more or less forced to stand up more vertically than other wildfowl because of the position of their legs. Dabbling ducks, such as the mallard and Eurasian teal, represent a halfway house, their legs placed further forward, towards the duck's centre of gravity. On terra firma they look more comfortable walking, despite some waddling. The longer legs of geese are the most forward-positioned, almost at the centre of gravity, making for an easier terrestrial grazing life. The geese must be well balanced as they crop and pluck while moving through the grasses and herbs for durations of up to 15 hours a day.

FOOD SELECTION

In general, wildfowl seek out wetlands where nutrient levels are high. Wetlands that are showing moderate levels of eutrophication, whether from fertiliser runoff, sewage discharges or certain effluents from food-processing factories, often attract large numbers of wildfowl. The productivity of many invertebrates will have been stimulated, and these are most attractive high-energy foods for the carnivorous ducks. Similarly, geese and swans will seek out the high nutrient content of grasses in reseeded and well-fertilised fields. Special grass mixtures are cultivated in nature reserves to provide the most nutritious food for visiting wildfowl. For example, at the nature reserve at the WWT, Slimbridge, about half of the fields have been sown with perennial rye-grass, with the balance made up of red fescue and common bent. The fields are fertilised to provide maximum nitrogen content and palatability of the grasses for the wintering white-fronted geese and other wildfowl (Fig. 122).

FIG 122. Eurasian wigeon feeding on flooded grassland at the Wildfowl & Wetlands Trust, Slimbridge. (Richard Taylor Jones)

The nutrient content of food is just as critical to the wellbeing of the birds as it is for us. Proteins are needed for growth and maintenance, but for energy wildfowl need carbohydrates and fat. Carbohydrates, stored as glycogen in the liver and muscle tissues, can be mobilised relatively quickly but there is a limited supply of this energy. Fat is the most important energy reserve for wildfowl, hence the laying down of large fat reserves prior to spring and autumn migrations, when body weights of geese and swans can increase by up to 20 per cent. Fat can provide about 38 kJ/g energy, compared with about 18 kJ/g from proteins. When extracting energy from food, not all wildfowl are efficient converters. For example, the barnacle goose appears to extract about one-third of the energy from the grasses it feeds upon when grazing on small grasses in plantain sward communities along the west coast of Ireland (see discussion on energy budgets, p. 294).

Feeding habits and food selection have been more closely studied in geese than in other groups of wildfowl because they are larger and easier to observe. In general the diet of herbivores is relatively low in nitrogen and high in fibre. The challenge facing those wildfowl that are herbivores is to maximise the protein intake while minimising the fibre content. Large amounts of plant material have to be ingested before the bird can obtain sufficient energy and nutrients for all its needs. In the absence of a digestive system that can efficiently extract all the nutrients and proteins from the vegetation, geese spend virtually all their daylight hours feeding, and often feed also at night with bright moonlight.

To maximise their feeding efficiency, geese must select plant species with the highest nutrient content and the least fibre. And for each plant the geese must be capable of selecting leaves of the best quality from the less good parts – the basis of the optimal foraging theory. Greenland white-fronted geese, when feeding during their spring staging in Iceland, not only select the grass with the highest nitrogen content – timothy – but also are highly selective for the largest laminae (the middle, longest and youngest leaf), which contains the highest nutrient level, ignoring the smaller leaves on each plant.[4]

Many geese 'farm' their food to ensure sustainable productivity of grass containing high levels of protein (protein content is highly correlated with overall carbohydrate and energy content, and is also correlated with low levels of structural compounds – fibre – that increases the digestibility of the grass). For example, large numbers of brant geese feed on Dutch salt marshes during the spring staging period when they are rapidly building up their body reserves for the long migration northwards and preparing for the breeding season. Large numbers visit the marshes in a regular pattern, once every 3–5 days. The duration of the feeding visits was related to the time elapsed since the last visit, suggesting that the geese were responding to the regrowth of the vegetation, returning to the area only after adequate growth had occurred. Experimental clipping of one of their principal foods, the sea plantain, was carried out to simulate grazing by the geese. Light clipping promoted plantain growth, at a rate twice that of unclipped or ungrazed areas. The new growth was mostly confined to the upper shoots, with the effect of concentrating nutrients and nitrogen in these parts of the plant. Maximum productivity of new shoots occurred when the plantain was clipped every four days, removing about one-third of the plantain, which was exactly what the geese were observed doing.[5]

Flightless moulting greylag geese, feeding principally on common saltmarsh-grass on the island of Saltholm, Denmark, also farm their food by sequential harvesting. This encourages a sward of young, rapidly growing grass laminae (leaves) high in proteins, mobilised to support new feather growth. The young laminae also have low levels of structural fibre, which enhances the digestibility of the food and facilitates the assimilation of nitrogen by the geese. The geese sequentially grazed the saltmarsh-grass sward every 6–8 days, and examination of grass laminae in their oesophagus showed lamina length consistent with growth from clipping the grass every six days. Experimental clipping of the grass showed that average biomass and protein accumulation was highest at clipping intervals of nine days, and therefore the geese were re-grazing the saltmarsh-grass at shorter intervals than would have produced maximum benefit to them. They had struck a balance between the maximum number of harvests they could take while maintaining highest protein levels and overall biomass in the sward.[6]

There is some evidence that geese use the mechanical properties of grass leaves to select those that are beneficial in terms of protein and nutrient values. Nutrient content is positively correlated with water content and negatively with the amount of fibre. Thus if the geese chose the most fragile leaves they would gain the most nutritious bite. It has been suggested by Myrfyn Owen that when the goose grips a grass leaf, the tougher ones, with least nutritive value, would slip through the bill while the least fibrous ones, watery and nutrient-rich, would break off and be ingested by the goose.[7]

ENERGY BUDGETS

The amount of time spent feeding by wildfowl varies according to the energy, protein and carbohydrate values of the food as well as the availability of the food (Table 82). Herbivores such as the swans, geese and some dabbling ducks need to spend substantial amounts of time feeding on low-energy leafy vegetation. For example, some geese such as brant and Greenland white-fronted geese spend up to 95 per cent of daylight time feeding, and many geese will continue feeding at night if they are in a secure environment. Swans, generally free from predation, also feed at night. A herbivorous dabbling duck such as the Eurasian wigeon must feed for up to 56 per cent of a 24-hour day, while for the gadwall the figure is 64 per cent. As both these species are crepuscular, some feeding will also take place at night. The seed-eaters and omnivores spend less time feeding, as their foods are richer in energy. The mallard and the Eurasian teal spend approximately 35 and 42 per cent of the 24-hour day, respectively, engaged in feeding.[8]

TABLE 82. Energy, protein and carbohydrate values of different wildfowl foods. Availability refers to the ease with which available energy or nutrients are digested and absorbed. Feeding time refers to the time taken to fulfil daily minimum requirements when feeding on such food.

FOOD SOURCE	ENERGY (KCAL/G)	PROTEIN (%)	CARBOHYDRATE (%)	AVAILABILITY	FEEDING TIME
Animal	5.0	40–75	1–20	Low	High
Agricultural grains	5.0	9–25	35–80	High	Low
Seeds	4.5	9–15	35–60	Variable	Moderate
Tubers	4.0	15	75	Moderate–high	Low
Leafy vegetation	3.5	15–20	15–50	Variable	High

Data from Baldassare & Bolen, 1994.

Unlike other herbivores, geese, swans and many duck have only a limited capacity to break down and digest the large amounts of cellulose and plant fibres ingested. Bovines have large multi-chamber stomachs, including big rumens in which plant material can be stored and gradually broken down by special cellulose-digesting microorganisms. But wildfowl have no storage capacity and, anyway, would not want to carry extra weight because of flight problems. So their food is only partially digested as it passes relatively rapidly through the gizzard, intestine and out through the cloaca. Larger birds, and those with enlarged caeca, are able to digest some cellulose through microbial digestion. The digestion is limited in small geese because of their small body and gut and consequent short intestinal retention time. About half of the gross energy – relatively digestible carbohydrates – of green plants eaten by yearling lesser snow geese in Canada is in the cell wall. Research, based on feeding these geese pelleted alfalfa, has shown that they retain about 45 per cent of dietary cellulose, the highest level recorded among birds, and the rest passes through undigested. It would appear that the capacity for cellulose digestion in other geese is highly variable. For example, the Atlantic greater Canada goose, feeding on salt-marsh grasses, has been found to retain and digest about 30 per cent of the cellulose in the green plants consumed. No digestion of cellulose could be demonstrated in another *Branta* species, the black brant, while incubating barnacle geese have been shown to retain about 26 per cent of cellulose in their graminoid diet.[9]

The daily intake of food is related to the size of the duck, goose or swan, but as a general rule the daily dry-weight consumption of food is approximately 10 per cent of the bird's wet body weight.[10] Geese grazing on grass have to eat more of their high-fibre, low-nutrient grasses than fish-eating mergansers, who can satisfy their daily nutrient needs by snapping up several fish in half an hour. In one study it was discovered that when mute swans fed on low-energy sea lettuce in Sweden they consumed about 8 kg per bird per day to meet their daily food requirements.[11]

FIG 123. European white-fronted goose feeding. Grass forms most of the winter diet, and reseeded fields are preferred to old pastures. Rye-grass, meadow grass, Yorkshire-fog and creeping bent are the main grasses eaten on inland pastures. Different species are taken in the salt-marsh pastures. (Roger Tidman/NHPA)

Myrfyn Owen studied the food intake of the wintering European white-fronted geese at the New Grounds, Slimbridge. There the geese usually arrived at the feeding grounds 30 minutes before sunrise and left 30 minutes after sunset. On short days they spent over 90 per cent of their day feeding, the remaining time being devoted to other essential activities. During longer days they spent more time on the feeding grounds and rested for longer. Their feeding rate was extremely rapid and increased with time of day to a mean maximum of just over 130 pecks per minute. This allowed the food, which is digested on the roost, to accumulate in the oesophagus. The geese ate between 650 and 800 g of fresh food per day, over 25 per cent of their body weight. The rate of feeding increased to compensate for a decrease in the food supply towards the end of the winter. At times the geese ate clover stolons, but this is less efficient than grazing and was an infrequent activity. There were indications of food selection on a small scale, but Myrfyn Owen concluded that maintaining a high rate of food intake is more important to geese, which digest their food inefficiently, than selecting the most nutritious diet possible (Fig. 123). Juveniles fed faster, were less selective, and walked more quickly than the adults. They also spent less time alert for possible dangers. This probably means that young birds are at an advantage in terms of food intake and are able to increase their body weight in most winters.[12]

It is little wonder that these geese will switch to high-energy foods such as sugar beet, turnips, spilt grain and potatoes when available. The availability and procurement of food is perhaps the most critical issue for wildfowl. It is even more important for wildfowl than most other animals because of their long and arduous migrations. Those wildfowl that breed in the Arctic are faced with additional energy demands concerning egg formation and production, as well as the relatively long incubation periods when there is little time for feeding.

Wildfowl are faced with five major energy-stress periods during the year – winter, spring migration, breeding, moulting and autumn migration. Throughout the yearly cycle wildfowl obtain their energy from two sources, endogenous or internal body fats and proteins, and exogenous in the form of the food they eat. For each phase of the annual energy cycle, ducks, geese and swans adapt their feeding strategies according to their needs. In general they will only draw upon endogenous or body reserves when they are unable to obtain enough energy from feeding on exogenous sources. Endogenous energy draw-down occurs during the two migration periods, and during the incubation of the eggs.

When wildfowl arrive in their wintering areas they have 'burnt up' much of their fat reserves on the southward migration. Their winter feeding strategy is to rebuild these fat reserves and hold them until the spring migration northwards. However, this is not a constant process, for several geese and ducks show a midwinter decline in body weight. As spring approaches this is quickly made up, and most wildfowl show a significant build-up of body reserves and corresponding body-weight increase. During our study of Greenland barnacle goose we have weighed about 1,000 birds of all ages and sexes throughout the year, and we have found a significant increase in body weight from the end of March to the end of April, prior to the spring migration. This is particularly marked in females, both adult and immature, with body-weight increases of some 20–25 per cent over midwinter weights.

My colleague Brian West investigated the resting metabolic rate (RMR) of barnacle geese and studied their daily energy flux during winter on the Inishkea Islands, Co. Mayo. We had earlier established a positive correlation between winter temperatures (recorded at Belmullet Meteorological Station, some 17 km northeast of the islands) and subsequent breeding success in Greenland (see Chapter 6). It was suggested that the effect was mediated through the influence of temperature on the growth of grass on which the geese fed. Therefore it was of interest to investigate the effects of low temperature on the metabolism of the geese and to examine their energy budget on the wintering grounds. Their RMR was determined by indirect calorimetry in an open circuit system for two adult males. The results showed RMRs of 10 and 11 ml O^2/kg/min (i.e. 172 and 129 kcal per goose-day) in the thermoneutral zone. These results were in general conformity with other experimental results. Thus the average RMR of an average-weight goose from Inishkea was approximately 140 kcal per day. The critical temperature was 7 °C. Temperatures below this level may affect the geese by imposing upon them the necessity to expend energy on their thermoregulation. Mean monthly local meteorological records from Belmullet showed that winter temperatures frequently fell below 6 °C. It was calculated that a fall to 3 °C would cause an increase in RMR of about 20 per cent of the level of thermoneutrality.

Food consumption, faecal output and energy assimilation were measured, and showed that the calorific value of ingested food was 780 kcal per goose-day, with a faecal value of 530 kcal per goose-day. These results indicated that assimilation was only about 16 per cent of ingested food by weight, or 32 per cent by calorific value. The net amount of energy taken into the goose daily was 250 kcal. An energy budget was calculated for the average barnacle goose of weight 1.98 kg, feeding 9.7 hours a day and flying approximately 1 hour per day. Food intake supplied 780 kcal, droppings comprised an output of 530 kcal, existence metabolism consumed 170 kcal and flight 65 kcal, leaving a spare of 15 kcal. The geese, under normal conditions, are in a state of positive energy balance. The spare 15 kcal are essential to maintain body temperature if it falls below thermoneutrality, to restore body reserves after the autumn migration and for building up fat reserves for the spring migration to Iceland and on to Greenland. Thus these geese have a narrow margin for error in their energy budget. Temperatures below thermoneutrality, disturbance resulting in extra flights or shortage of food would reduce the energy budget to negativity, at least for certain periods during winter. This in turn could impair their ability to breed successfully.[13]

The northerly spring migration is probably the most energy-tasking phase in the life of wildfowl, especially for those that have to traverse long distances over the sea – light-bellied brant geese, Greenland and Svalbard barnacle geese, Greenland white-fronted goose, and to a lesser extent whooper swan, pink-footed goose and greylag goose. Also included are a small group of ducks that only have to travel to Iceland, a much less onerous trip than to Greenland and Arctic Canada. Other wildfowl, migrating over land, can set down if weather conditions become difficult. On land they can feed for several days, replenishing lost body reserves while waiting for the weather to improve. Those flying over the sea can touch down to rest, but there are no refuelling possibilities, and at the same time their energy reserves will be declining, albeit slowly.

Until recently we knew little about the behaviour of these 'over-water' migrants, the assumption being that they flew without landing until they reached their destinations. Satellite tracking (see Chapter 6) has shown that whooper swans and Greenland barnacle geese can be blown off course by adverse winds and, with declining body reserves, settle on the sea, where they often perish. During the spring of 2008 one whooper swan and one barnacle goose, both satellite-tagged in Ireland, were blown off course by strong northeast winds while on their way to Iceland, settled on the water and died. Whether these birds were travelling by themselves or in small groups is unknown. It is more than likely that each satellite-tagged bird represented a small flock of birds that would have perished also. Such studies help us to appreciate how dangerous and energy-taxing these over-water migrations are for many wildfowl.

More detailed information on the behaviour of whooper swans migrating between Iceland and Britain or Ireland was obtained by Pennycuick and colleagues from the analysis of ten satellite-tagged swans in relation to detailed weather and astronomical data.[14] Height profiles for four northbound and three southbound swans showed that two of the birds flew continuously for most of the sea crossing, with one reaching 1,856 m above sea level, the maximum height recorded. The others flew low and often landed on the water, sometimes for prolonged periods. The sea crossings took from 12.7 to 101 hours to complete. The birds continued their sea crossings provided that the visibility was more than 2 km and the altitude above the horizon of either the sun or the moon was higher than –4°, otherwise they remained on the water. Calculations based on flight performance indicated that an amount of fat equivalent to 25 per cent of the lean mass of the female would have been sufficient for the crossing, with some in reserve so the female would arrive in Iceland with a little extra reserve fat. The situation with a large male was estimated to have been more marginal. Little or no excess fat would have been available to power their flights from sea level to the heights recorded for some of the swans.[15] These findings underscore the critical importance for the swans, and indeed for all wildfowl, of building up body reserves prior to the spring migration northwards.

During the breeding season the greatest energy demands on female geese and swans come from egg formation and incubation. These are the 'capital' breeders (see Chapter 6), drawing down their stored fat, proteins and minerals. Some geese, such as the lesser snow and barnacle geese, arrive on the breeding grounds and lay their eggs almost immediately and only feed occasionally during incubation. Others, such as the Canadian-breeding brant geese, may feed for a couple of weeks on emerging vegetation before laying and incubating. Ducks, on the other hand, spend more time than geese and swans on their breeding grounds building up their fat reserves, something that may be due to greater availability of food at lower latitudes, where most ducks breed. Food is less abundant in more northern latitudes at the beginning of the breeding season.

FIG 124. Adult whooper swan, Iceland: initial growth of new primary flight feathers. (David Cabot)

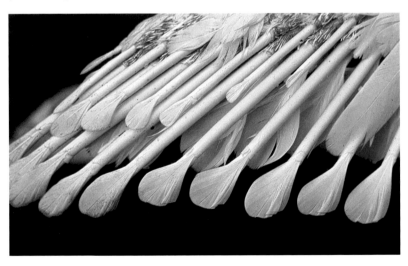

During the energy-demanding post-breeding moult of swans and geese up to 25 per cent of their body weight can be lost and then regained with the growth of new flight feathers. It would appear that most wildfowl draw upon their fat reserves to supply the energy required for the moult (Fig. 124).

Over the course of evolution the various species of swans, geese and ducks have become supremely adapted to a wide range of different ecological niches, exploiting different food resources and employing different feeding strategies. Nonetheless, there are several pressure points during the year when the availability of food, and competition for limited supplies, are critical – in particular the winter period, the northward spring migration, the breeding season, the post-breeding moult and autumn migration. As a most successful group of birds, wildfowl have adopted various strategies to deal with these issues, and in addition their continued success, as judged by their distribution, range and generally increasing numbers, especially as winter visitors to Britain and Ireland, has very much been dependent upon their flexibility to adapt to and exploit new food resources, especially those offered up by changing agricultural practices.

CHAPTER 6

Population Dynamics

P OPULATION DYNAMICS CONCERNS the fluctuating size and composition of any given population of animals or plants in space and time, and the factors that regulate these changes. There are four key issues that are part of the regulatory process, and in the case of wildfowl these can be defined as follows: *recruitment* refers to the number of birds born into the population and departing from the breeding grounds in good condition; *mortality* means the number of birds dying in the population; *immigration* is the number of birds arriving into the population from another geographic area; and *emigration* is the number of birds moving out of the population and going elsewhere (Fig. 125).

In a stable population the mortality rate is balanced by the number of births, rather than the other way around as formerly thought. If recruitment exceeds mortality then the population will increase. Conversely, if mortality exceeds recruitment the population declines. The mechanisms that control these processes are extremely complex, often not well understood, despite more information being available on wildfowl populations than for most other groups of animals.

For long-lived birds such as swans and geese, small shifts in adult survival rates have a far greater impact in reducing or increasing numbers in a population than a decline or increase of breeding success. Because of this, the impact of shooting and hunting as a key regulator of numbers has long been debated. One school of thought claims that shooting is a form of *compensatory* mortality, taking out mainly immatures, inexperienced adults, the weak and the sick that would have died anyway under natural circumstances. If this were not the case, and shooting of a particular species ceased, then numbers in that population should increase. In such cases shooting is an *additive* form of

FIG 125. Dark-bellied brant geese, Langstone Harbour, Hampshire. The number of birds in the population is regulated by recruitment, mortality, immigration and emigration. This is a classic 'boom or bust' species, with wild swings of productivity ranging from total breeding failure some years to over 50 per cent young birds in the winter flocks in other years. (Guy Edwardes/NHPA)

mortality. Evidence to support additive mortality is provided by the numerical performance of several different populations of geese. The Svalbard population of barnacle geese wintering on the Solway Firth numbered some 300 birds in the late 1940s. The geese were partly protected from shooting in the UK from 1954 and in Svalbard the next year, and the Caerlaverock National Nature Reserve was established three years later. Shooting in Norway and Svalbard was prohibited in 1961/62. The population responded by steadily increasing each year to reach 29,815 birds counted in the Solway Firth in November 2007.[1] This dramatic population growth was due to reduced adult mortality following the shooting ban rather than to any change in the recruitment rate.[2] The Greenland white-fronted goose population responded in a similar manner. In 1982 there were some 16,000–17,000 birds in the population. Shooting moratoria were introduced in Scotland (1981) and Ireland (1982), and by the spring of 1999 numbers had more than doubled to 35,573 birds, a direct response to the decline in adult mortality brought about by the cessation of shooting. Adult mortality rates were high, at 30–40 per cent in the 1940s and 1950s,[3] compared with 21.5 per cent today (2002).[4] However, since peaking in 1999 numbers have declined to 24,804 birds in spring 2006, almost certainly due to reduced breeding success rather than increased mortality rates.

Swans and geese respond markedly to small shifts in adult mortality rates because of their biological and demographic characteristics – they are long-lived, have delayed sexual maturity, and generally lay small clutches of eggs. In many species only a small proportion of adults breed successfully in any given year, so that the number of young in the autumn flocks may comprise 5–10 per cent of the population. Ducks, on the other hand, especially the dabbling ducks, are shorter-lived, breed generally the year after hatching, and lay large clutches and produce large numbers of young – which may comprise up to 50 per cent of the autumn population. Thus the impact of shooting as a factor elevating adult mortality rates is quite different in ducks compared with geese and swans, because of the different biological characteristics.

Natural populations are frequently held in check by the availability of a particular resource, generally food. As a population increases, the numbers of individuals begin to exceed the capacity of the resource. Increased mortality occurs, disproportionately among young birds, with the result that fewer are recruited into the breeding population and numbers then decline if mortality rates exceed recruitment levels. This type of mortality is *density-dependent*, severest when numbers are highest and least when numbers are low. Immigration and emigration to and from the population from other geographically separated populations can provide some alleviation, but these options are much reduced if the population is already occupying its entire available habitat.

In order to better understand the way the four basic factors control population dynamics one needs to know more about the underlying issues that affect recruitment and mortality rates, as well as those that have an effect on the movements of birds in and out of the population.

Within the lifetime of a swan, goose or duck there are critical moments when the birds need to successfully complete certain actions to enable them to reproduce successfully, to survive and avoid mortality – body conditioning of females in late spring; spring migration; incubation, hatching and early chick care; post-breeding moult; autumn migration. Within this overarching framework there are more specific factors affecting both recruitment and mortality.

In a recent review of wildfowl population dynamics, Tony Fox identified eight key factors affecting recruitment and eight affecting mortality.[5]

RECRUITMENT

Recruitment factors are:
1   female condition;
2   body reserves and food supplies at point of laying;
3   parasites;
4   mate performance;
5   weather;
6   predation of eggs and young and anti-predator behaviour;
7   effects of age and sex;
8   availability of nesting sites and brood-rearing sites.

Female condition, body reserves and food supplies

Geese and swans have evolved strategies for the management of their body reserves for successful breeding that are very different from those of the dabbling ducks. They arrive in their Arctic breeding grounds stocked up with accumulated fats and proteins, built up during the final three or four weeks feeding on the wintering grounds prior to migrating northwards. The reserves are topped up on the spring staging areas. Female geese do not generally feed on arrival in the breeding grounds, although there is evidence that some – the lesser snow goose in Canada and the Greenland white-fronted goose in west Greenland – feed intensively on arrival to boost their protein and fat reserves.[6] Most female geese and swans mobilise energy from their stored reserves for egg production (which is a large physiological drain on body reserves – the weight of an average clutch of greylag, pink-footed and barnacle goose eggs represents 30.6, 23.5 and 26.5 per cent of body weight respectively) and for incubation and care of the young to fledging. Hence geese and wild swans are known as 'capital breeders', as they draw down on accumulated reserves. The energy demands on breeding female geese are such that by the end of incubation a female lesser snow goose may have lost up to 40 per cent of the body weight she had on arrival in the breeding grounds, while the male loses up to 20 per cent of his arrival weight.[7] Similar results have been recorded for barnacle geese.[8] Goose and swan eggs are large in relation to their body size and are loaded with a high-energy content, providing a 'kick-start' for the young, which leave the nest often within a few hours of hatching. Numerous studies have shown positive correlations between good female body condition – evaluated visually by differing abdominal profiles – at the end of the winter period and successful breeding, something that poultry and duck/goose farmers have known for centuries.

Most ducks, in contrast to geese and swans, build up their body condition on or near the breeding grounds, the females indulging in binge feeding during egg laying. They are thus known as 'income breeders'. The nidifugous ducklings depend more on immediately available food – generally chironomid midge larvae – than on accumulated reserves in the egg. The breeding success of most dabbling ducks is very much tied to the availability and abundance of midges and other insects just before, during and after hatching of the ducklings.

Parasites

Heavy loads of parasites – generally feather lice (Fig. 126), feather mites or internal parasites (helminths) – can affect body condition of females and hence their breeding success. Similarly, heavy infestations of parasites on young birds, transferred from their mother, can affect their survival. There is little or no information on the impact of parasites on the breeding success of swans, geese and ducks. This may suggest that parasite loading is not a problem. Indeed, it is rather unusual to come across adult geese carrying heavy infestations of feather lice, possibly because if the infestation was too high the bird would die in a short time and not be recorded. During the ringing of approximately 900 adult and juvenile barnacle geese in the Inishkea Islands, Co. Mayo, between 1961 and 2009, I came across only three geese with excessive burdens of lice. All were emaciated and significantly below average weight. One adult female caught in early February weighed only 1.45 kg (average of ten other females caught at the same time was 1.7 kg) and was found dead on the islands about a month later. In 1985

FIG 126. Feather louse, Anaticola sp., on the feather of a duck. These lice have a remarkable capacity for hanging on to a feather and are extremely difficult to dislodge. (Image Quest 3-D/ NHPA)

and 1987 we caught almost 800 adult, yearling and juvenile geese on the breeding grounds in northeast Greenland, and none was infested with excessive numbers of lice or carrying a heavy burden of feather mites.

Mate performance

Most wildfowl are monogamous, ducks generally for one season only, but geese and swans more often for life. Typically the male duck deserts the female once laying commences, playing no further role in nest protection or rearing the young. Clearly the performance of her mate has no role to play in the breeding success of the duck. On the other hand the male goose or swan makes a positive contribution to the breeding performance of the pair, participating in nest protection, brood rearing and defence of the family during autumn migration as well as during the winter period. Paired geese are more successful in obtaining better feeding on the wintering grounds and hence facilitating the body-conditioning of the female, essential to her subsequent successful breeding in the Arctic. If there was no advantage to breeding success then there would be a higher level of divorce among geese or swans.

Weather

Bad weather will affect the growth and availability of food on the wintering grounds and spring staging sites for geese and swans, preventing the birds from building up their necessary body reserves. Adverse weather conditions may also result in non-breeding seasons for many Arctic geese – delayed snow-melt rendering nesting sites unavailable, or severe weather coinciding with the onset of egg laying, preventing laying or destroying the eggs. In wetlands, drought will affect the productivity of the insects that are essential for successful breeding by dabbling duck, both at the time of laying and for the subsequent survival of young ducklings.

Predation of eggs and young, and anti-predator behaviour

Wildfowl are viewed by predators as hefty chunks of tasty meat, and their large, often numerous eggs are rewarding targets for polar bears, arctic foxes, arctic skuas, gyrfalcons, glaucous gulls and ravens in the Arctic. In temperate regions the red fox, mink, raven, other corvids and various gull species are the principal predators. Nest losses to predators can be considerable; for example 74 per cent of light-bellied brant goose nests in Svalbard were predated by polar bears.[9]

The threat of nest predation is underscored by the large number of anti-predator breeding strategies adopted – some geese nesting on vertical cliffs, others on islands, several duck species in tree holes and others hidden in

FIG 127. Arctic Foxes are significant predators of Arctic-breeding wildfowl, such as this female common eider. (Anna Henly/NHPA)

vegetation. Some ducks, such as eiders, sit tight in protective concealment, hoping the predator will overlook them, only bursting from cover at the very last moment (Fig. 127). Other wildfowl have developed nesting relationships with birds of prey, breeding close to gyrfalcons (barnacle geese) or to rough-legged buzzards, peregrine falcons and snowy owls (red-breasted geese). The birds of prey afford anti-predator protection to the geese (especially against arctic foxes) while the geese alert the birds of prey to approaching predators. Some highly dense colonies of geese benefit from predator swamping, minimising damage caused by predators.

Effects of age and sex

Breeding success in geese increases with age, and the most productive period for female geese is generally between the ages of 7 and 12 years – though after that it starts to decline. Evidence from various duck species is similar, but with earlier peaks in productivity. The age and experience of the male in the defence of the territory, nest site and young is also a factor in breeding success.

Availability of nesting sites and brood-rearing sites

There is some evidence that the Icelandic breeding populations of greylag and pink-footed geese, and the Svalbard barnacle geese, may at times suffer from a lack of suitable nesting sites and brood-rearing areas, as indicated by an increasing proportion of unsuccessful breeding adults (breeding birds currently make up less than 10 per cent of the Svalbard barnacle goose population, whereas 50 years ago it was closer to 40 per cent).[10] On the other hand the availability of nesting sites and brood-rearing areas for barnacle geese in northeast Greenland does not appear to be a restricting factor for the breeding success of the population. However, there is increasing competition for food on the moulting grounds between barnacle and pink-footed geese.

It is difficult to unravel the significance of each of these eight factors in the process of recruitment of Arctic-nesting geese, and even more difficult for ducks. It is likely, however, that good body condition of arriving geese and swans in the Arctic breeding grounds is a prerequiste for successful breeding. After their arrival, weather conditions, such as delayed snow-melt, may possibly be the main factor controlling breeding success. Losses during the egg stage due to poor nest protection by the adults are a further major cause of reduced productivity.[11]

MORTALITY

With regard to factors affecting mortality, the following are considered significant:

1   predation;
2   food availability and starvation;
3   weather;
4   parasites;
5   disease;
6   human-induced factors (shooting, collisions, poisoning etc);
7   density-dependent factors;
8   age and sex effects.

Predation

As mentioned earlier, predation of adults of breeding age has a far greater impact on wildfowl populations than the loss by predation of eggs and young. The latter is extremely variable, depending upon the location of nest sites and the abundance of predators. Depending upon nest cover and the number of predators the loss of eggs and/or the mortality of young can be as high as 100 per cent in many cases. Mortality among Arctic-nesting geese can be influenced by the abundance of alternative prey for the predators. For example, a correlation has been demonstrated between nesting success of brant geese and the abundance or lack of abundance of rodents on the breeding grounds. The geese bred successfully in years with an abundance of rodents, and unsuccessfully when rodents were scarce. When lemmings are hard to find, the principal predators, arctic fox and pomarine skua, switch their attention from their normal lemming prey to the eggs and young of the geese. These predator/prey swings are thought to be responsible for the large variations in productivity noticed on the wintering grounds, where the proportion of young birds in the winter flocks can vary from 0 to 50 per cent.[12]

Food availability and starvation

Food availability can be a critical matter at certain periods of the year. During February–March most wildfowl experience their lowest body weights, and their fat reserves are much reduced. During the winter 1999–2000 there was a massive mortality of an estimated 21,000 common eiders – the highest figure recorded since 1980 – in the Dutch Wadden Sea, and lower numbers dead in the German Wadden Sea, with mortality peaking in March/April. The wintering population was approximately 120,000. Adults made up about one-third of all dead birds, and of these about one-third were females. Investigations revealed that the birds could not survive an infection carried by a regularly occurring intestinal parasite, the thorny-headed intestinal worm *Profilicollis botulus*, contracted principally by eating its intermediate host, the shore crab. It was concluded that food shortages were responsible, and it was hypothesised that overfishing of cockles and mussels – principal food of the eiders – in the Wadden Sea in the early 1990s had reduced the food resources.[13] Other possible causes of mortality were examined – oil pollution, poisoning with contaminants, viral or bacterial infection, and immune system deficiency – and were ruled out.[14] While this was a dramatic incident, there are many other cases on a much smaller scale of starvation due to lack of food during extreme weather conditions.

Female geese can starve to death if they had been unable to build up enough body reserves to carry themselves through the Arctic incubation period. Food shortages at other critical points in wildfowl life cycles can also lead to elevated mortality rates. For example, if wildfowl are unable to accumulate enough fat prior to the southward autumnal migration then these birds are at greater risk of dying than the birds that were able to accumulate the full complement. The losses of young barnacle geese on autumn migration from Svalbard to the Solway Firth in 1986 were unusually high, at 33 per cent, because of high densities of the geese on their staging grounds, where there were inadequate food supplies.[15]

Weather

Weather can have direct or indirect impacts on mortality. Cataclysmic events such as tornadoes or violent storms will directly kill wildfowl, but its most important role is in controlling the production of food, critical to the survival of the birds. Wildfowl that breed in the Arctic Circle migrate south after the breeding season to escape sub-zero temperatures. Large population shifts of these birds, when in the more temperate latitudes of Europe, occur when temperatures there drop below zero Celsius as waters freeze up and food becomes unavailable. If low temperatures persist, as in the winters of 1946/47 and 1962/63, significant mortalities of adult birds occur that impact the breeding populations the following summer. Differing mortalities among wildfowl will occur – those with big bodies and large fat reserves can endure longer than the smaller wildfowl. Specialist feeders such as the dabbling duck, and especially Eurasian teal, can be hardest hit when their feeding wetlands are frozen over for long periods. As they can only withstand three or four days without food they often undertake spectacular migrations in search of new feeding grounds.

Results from the satellite-tracking of adult swans and geese travelling north and south between their Arctic breeding grounds and Britain and Ireland have shown that some birds can be affected by strong winds, getting blown off course and disappearing, suggesting that the bird had perished. Such a bird could be alone or part of a flock travelling with it. It is impossible to quantify the extent of this weather-related mortality on migration, but we know it does happen.

Parasites

There is little evidence to show that parasites directly cause significant mortality among wildfowl. Their indirect impact could be of greater significance in lowering the host's tolerance to food shortages, adverse weather and other stress factors – which are more easily handled by the bird if it is in good health, as was probably the case with the mass mortality of eiders mentioned above. However, as with mortality due to adverse weather on migration, the evidence of death or impairment by parasites is extremely hard to gather because birds can die in remote areas or fall into the sea.

Disease

Bacterial, viral and fungal diseases can cause dramatic large-scale mortalities. In North America, the bacterium responsible for avian cholera killed up to one-third of all ducks concentrated in shallow lakes of the Texas Panhandle area during 1949/50. The smaller wildfowl, especially the green-winged teal, were more susceptible than larger species such as Canada geese.[16] Large mortalities of waterfowl have been caused by the indirect toxic effects of botulism (ingestion of the neurotoxin produced by the bacterium *Clostridium botulinum*) in North America, where up to 4–5 million ducks have perished. Duck plague is an acute, highly contagious herpesvirus disease of ducks, geese and swans. Avian influenza and duck plague (duck viral enteritis or DVE) are also deadly to waterfowl populations. Again in North America, the 1973 duck plague outbreak at the Lake Andes National Wildlife Refuge in South Dakota killed an estimated 40 per cent of 100,000 mallard and 3 per cent of 9,000 Canada geese wintering on the refuge and the nearby Missouri River. The outbreak was the first major epizootic of this disease ever reported in free-flying wild waterfowl.

The impact of disease on waterfowl populations appears to have been more pronounced in North America, where densities of populations are often much higher than in Europe. Similar to the questions concerning the role of parasites affecting mortality, the long-term impacts of disease on populations are unclear.

Human-induced factors

The long-term impact of shooting on wildfowl populations is difficult to determine (Fig. 128). For small populations such as the Greenland white-fronted goose and the Svalbard barnacle goose population the banning of shooting was marked by substantial population increases. For the larger duck populations it is difficult to disentangle the impacts of shooting and other factors that may influence population dynamics. The German anti-hunting group Komittee gegen den Vogelmord has estimated that the 650,000 shotgun licence holders registered in Great Britain shoot approximately 16,000 pink-footed geese, 16,000 greylag geese, 25,000 Canada geese, 527,000 Eurasian wigeon, 212,000 Eurasian teal, 200,000 mallard, 105,000 tufted duck, 101,000 common pochard, 40,000 northern pintail, 18,000 gadwall and 12,000 northern shoveler each year.[17] Added to these figures should be those birds that were not killed directly but 'crippled', leading to their reduced survival – which in some cases can result in an additional 20 per cent mortality. Large wildfowl such as geese and swans, which have a particularly high wing loading, lack the quick manoeuvrability of the small ducks, and find it harder to avoid collisions with man-made structures – which can be responsible for heightened levels of mortality. For example, in 1967 Malcolm Ogilvie showed that over half the mortality in mute swans in Britain was due to collision with overhead power lines, while human-induced mortality accounted for 85 per cent of all mute swan deaths.[18]

FIG 128. Wildfowler in Kent, midwinter. Mortality of breeding *adults* is of far greater significance to the population dynamics of wildfowl than the loss of *first-winter* birds from shooting. (David Tipling/NHPA)

Density-dependent factors

For years there has been a circular argument about the impact of mortality inflicted by shooting, as mentioned at the beginning of this chapter. Many argue that shooting is a form of *compensatory* mortality, and that the birds shot would have been destined to die anyway from sickness or disease. Moreover, the removal of birds from a population by shooting would reduce competition for an essential resource such as food in winter and thereby assist a higher survival of birds than if population numbers were higher. If this shooting mortality was below a certain threshold then there would be no long-term impacts on the population. If shooting mortality was high this would be *additive* mortality, on top of the naturally occurring mortality, and the population would decline. The argument for compensatory mortality is dependent upon a linkage between natural mortality and population size. Thus such mortality becomes density-dependent.

When wildfowl populations are controlled by density-dependent factors, with a large annual production of young birds, then the surplus birds can be harvested by shooting. Many wildfowl studies, especially concerning ducks, have shown that when the populations are shot there is reduced natural mortality in the population. However, for the larger and Arctic-based breeding geese the contrary is probably true. Their low and relatively constant level of natural mortality does not provide much room for compensatory mortality when the population is shot.

The greater snow goose in North America is among the most numerous of all geese in the world, with a population size of 7.56 million birds. A study of survival rates and population dynamics over a 30-year period (1970–98) concluded that hunting mortality had the most important impact on population dynamics, and in the absence of density-dependent effects hunting could be used to limit the growth of this population. During the study the population increased tenfold. This growth could not be explained by changes in reproductive rates, which were similar over the three decades – overall mean of 26 ± 3 per cent young in autumn flocks – with no evidence of density-dependent effects. Adult survival did not differ between the periods of rapid population increase and those when there was no population growth. Adult harvest rates were much higher during the period of no population growth than before or after. Reduced survival due to increased hunting mortality is thought to have brought about stagnation of population growth.[19]

Age and sex effects

Young and inexperienced wildfowl suffer a higher mortality rate than adults. In the case of a long-lived species such as the mute swan, fledged young in their first year of life endure a 59 per cent mortality, reducing to 32 per cent in their second year and further declining to 20 per cent for adult birds.[20] Very little of this mortality is caused by hunting. For quarry species proportionately larger numbers of young birds are shot than adults due to their need to disperse more widely in search of food. For larger wildfowl such as the snow goose, mortality during their first year from shooting was 59 per cent, compared with 25 per cent among older geese.[21] Interestingly, in the case of protected populations of geese, such as the Svalbard population of barnacle geese, the difference between first-year and adult mortality rates is much less.[22] Finally, young birds suffer higher mortality during hard weather conditions or during food shortages.

Immigration and emigration are the two other major processes in population dynamics. To a certain degree they provide elasticity to populations. When the number of birds in any one population increases to exceed the carrying capacity of, say, food resources or nest-site availability, then emigration can reduce pressure on these resources, with birds moving to another geographically separated population of the same species. Conversely, immigrants can arrive to join a declining population from one that is being overshot or is suffering from resource depletion. In general there is little immigration or emigration among goose and swan populations, and they often appear to be closed and quite discrete. The situation among ducks is less clear but almost certainly involves higher levels of both immigration and emigration.

COLLECTING AND INTERPRETING THE DATA

Ornithologists, in common with many other field biologists working on population dynamics, are repeatedly tormented by uncertainties – how precise are the data, and do they reflect accurately what is going on within the population? For example, has the total population been counted accurately? Are the methods used to calculate mortality and survival rates producing dependable results? Is there sufficient information on the movements and migrations of individuals in and out of the population? How closed or open is the population? To what extent are productivity data, such as the number of first-winter birds in the wintering flocks of wildfowl, skewed by the non-random mixing of birds? Is the sampling extensive enough? What about observer bias? What are the best times for annual population assessments, and for determination of breeding success and the proportion of first-winter birds?

Good estimates of the total number of individuals in a population, particularly for the larger wildfowl such as the swans and geese, are now available thanks to extensive networks of amateur and professional ornithologists, international cooperation and the use of aerial surveys. During the winter wildfowl are generally to be found in specific and well-known sites, enabling entire populations to be censused simultaneously, either by coordinated ground counts or by aerial census, or a combination of both. More problematic is obtaining reliable estimates during the breeding season, when the birds are usually thinly spread out over vast geographic areas. Estimates of breeding populations that extend over such huge areas can be made by aerial-survey random transects, verified by ground truthing, the results from which can then be extrapolated for the whole breeding habitat.

Studies on breeding biology, carried out often in remote places difficult of access, are needed to determine the factors affecting birth rates and productivity. Some of the key factors that require to be established are the pre-breeding condition of birds, especially nesting females; weather conditions on the breeding grounds; competition for nesting sites; predation of nests; hatching success; mortality and survival rates of chicks before and after leaving the nest but prior to fledging; nesting success (proportion of nests raising at least one chick); competition among young birds for food during the period of rapid growth to fledging. As the availability and quality of food are key factors in density-dependent population regulation, studies are also required on the feeding ecology and activity budgets of young and adult wildfowl, not only on the breeding grounds but also in the autumn and spring staging locations, as well as on the wintering grounds.

A long-established method of estimating the summer's breeding success or productivity among geese and swans, without expending large budgets on travelling to the breeding grounds, is to record the numbers of adults and first-winter birds, identified by plumage differences, in randomly selected sample units of 50 birds in the wintering flocks. The proportion of first-winter birds, expressed as a percentage of all birds in the population, indicates breeding success that summer. The reliability of these sample counts is based on the assumption of random mixing of the whole population throughout its wintering range and the random distribution of families throughout the flocks, assumptions known to be flawed. For example, families of geese are more frequently found on the edges of flocks; there is a higher proportion of successful families among the first flocks of geese to arrive on their wintering grounds in the autumn; successful families tend to disengage themselves from the main wintering flocks at the back end of the winter, when food shortages occur in certain habitats, to seek better feeding grounds elsewhere. Mean brood size of families, another key population statistic, is also assessed on the wintering grounds – and the same issues arise as for the assessment of the proportion of young birds in the flocks.

For several species of swans and geese it is possible to count all the members in the population. When the proportion of young birds in these winter flocks has been calculated and their number subtracted from the total population, the residue of adults and subadults can be compared with figures from the previous year to determine the number that have survived. The data collected provide not only an estimate of productivity but also an estimate of the mortality or survival rates of adults (plus subadults) over one year, both key statistics for understanding population dynamics. Such calculations provide best results for so-called 'closed populations' when all the birds are counted. When applied to an 'open population', where immigration and emigration are active, then the results are not very dependable. However, long time series of counts extending over, say, a continuous period of 30 years or more will smooth out inconsistencies.

A fundamental research tool in the study of wildfowl population dynamics is the leg-ring or band (Fig. 129). Traditionally metal, each is inscribed with a unique number and a return address to which the ring should be sent if the bird is shot, found dead or captured. The reported recovery of rings, together with finding details, provides basic information on migration and movements. The age and sex of the bird, the ringing and finding locations, and causes of mortality can also be established. Mortality rates for different age cohorts – first-year, second-year, older, etc – can also be calculated from a series of ring recoveries over a period of years. Again these sources of information are open to bias – for example, shooting pressures differ from region to region, and the return of rings is very much influenced by cultural considerations ranging from lack of interest to fear of being prosecuted if the rings are returned.

FIG 129. Whooper swans, caught as moulting adults in Iceland, and now waiting to be ringed, weighed and measured before they are released again. (David Cabot)

The advent of tough, two-ply laminated polyvinyl plastic (PVC) rings in the 1960s opened up a new era of research in population dynamics. These rings, commonly called Darvics, are made of calendered unplasticised PVC foil, laminated under heat and pressure. Each ring carries a unique alphabetic or numeric code, and can be white, yellow, blue, etc, providing an almost infinite number of combinations. Up to three alphabetic or numeric digits are normally etched through one of the laminations, endowing each ringed bird with a unique 'licence plate' (Fig. 130). The rings can be read at a distance of up to 600 m, depending upon light conditions, optical quality of the telescope and experience of the observer. Thus Darvic-ringed wildfowl can be visually 'recovered' for the rest of their lives, often at many different geographic locations over long time periods, without the bird being physically caught again. This is not only good for

FIG 130. Darvic and coloured rings on barnacle goose. This goose –Darvic O/BDJ left and B/B/m right tarsus – was originally ringed on the Inishkea Islands, Co. Mayo, as a first-winter male on 8 January 1972. Here it has been retrapped during the annual moult in northeast Greenland, July 1984. It was then recorded again in two subsequent winters on the Inishkea Islands, until the end of March 1986. Its field-readable 'licence plate' had allowed it to be visually recorded many times without ever being caught again. (David Cabot)

the wildfowl, as additional physical trapping trauma is avoided, but also beneficial for the wildfowl catcher, who expends enormous amounts of time and energy capturing birds whether by duck decoy, cage traps, rocket-propelled or cannon nets, mist nets or many other ingenious methods.

The advantages of Darvic rings over traditional markings are enormous. If there is good observer coverage of the species at its various wintering haunts then continuous observations of individuals can be made. The age of pairing, first successful breeding and reproductive performance during the lifetime of a goose or swan can be easily tracked. Divorce rates can be monitored, inter-site movements followed and more dependable mortality rates can be calculated compared with calculations based on the recovery of metal rings. Individually marked birds can be monitored during studies of wildfowl energetics, especially the relationship between body condition (as indicated by abdominal body profile) and subsequent breeding success. In summary, the tracking of these individually ringed birds over time provides vital information on the productivity during the individual's lifetime, mortality and survival rates, migrations and movements.

Darvic rings are easy to read on wildfowl such as barnacle geese that graze on closely cropped grass sward, or on brant geese that feed while walking on a muddy shore. But on birds ambulating in longer vegetation, such as the white-fronted goose and the other grey geese, or those that spend much of their time in

FIG 131. Greater snow geese and one small Canada goose, south of Eureka, Canada, 4 July 2007. Coloured alphanumeric neck collars have been used on many snow geese, and on a number of other wildfowl species. (Alyn Walsh)

water, such as the whooper swan, leg-rings are much more difficult to read. To overcome these visual-recapture difficulties special Darvic neck-bands, engraved with a unique alphabetic or numeric code as with leg-rings, were developed and have been successfully used on geese and swans (Fig. 131). It is possible to read these neck-bands at distances of up to 800 m.

Tracking the movements and migrations of wildfowl by satellite telemetry provides sophisticated insights into individual behaviour in a way that no other marking system can. There are many different types of transmitters. A frequently used system employs a small (30 or 45 g) solar-powered Argos/GPS transmitter (often called a PTT, platform terminal transmitter), sprouting a short wire antenna, attached to the back of the goose, duck or swan by a knicker-elastic harness (Fig. 132). The transmitter is programmed to send signals at specific times, according to what information is seasonally required, to a polar-orbiting NOAA satellite. Sensors measure temperature, its own battery voltage and animal activity, and there is also a twelve-channel GPS receiver that senses altitude,

FIG 132. Satellite transmitter on the back of a light-bellied brant goose. Each transmitter is powered by miniature solar panels. The short aerial assists the transmission of data to the orbiting NOAA satellite. Each tarsus carries a different coloured Darvic ring to facilitate field identification of the bird. (Alyn Walsh)

heading and speed. A receiving ground station downloads the signals, and the data are then provided online to the researcher. The exact geographic positions of the bird, to within ± 18 m, can be established. From these data and measurements, even the bird's energy consumption and heart rate can also be calculated.

Within Britain and Ireland satellite transmitters have produced remarkable results. Large-bodied long-distance migrants have been the main species studied – whooper swans, light-bellied brant geese, Greenland white-fronted geese, and the Svalbard population of barnacle geese; and recently (April 2008) Greenland-breeding barnacle geese that winter on the Inishkea Islands, Co. Mayo, have been fitted with satellite transmitters. Movements of these birds can be viewed at **www.wwt.org.uk/research/tracking/maps.asp**. Details that can be seen on the web-site include the migration flight line of a specific goose, the date and time of its transmission, its geographic coordinates, flight compass direction, speed and altitude. Then, when the goose has reached its breeding or wintering grounds, more information can be obtained about its local movements.

While satellite tracking is providing new and exciting information, it is basic research methods and techniques that have provided good information for a better understanding of the population dynamics of three well-known wildfowl – the mute swan, barnacle goose and mallard. These species have been chosen as they are well-known exemplars representing the three major wildfowl groups – swans, geese and ducks. Moreover, each has been subject to detailed studies for many years.

MUTE SWAN

The mute swan (Fig. 133) is the largest and heaviest flying wildfowl in the world. The male's average weight is 11.8 kg, and the eggs – average weight 340 g – are the weightiest of all wildfowl eggs. Their large size, conspicuous nests and easily studied breeding biology make them ideal subjects for the study of population dynamics.

It is one of the most widely distributed wildfowl in Britain and Ireland, found predominantly in the lowlands, rarely occurring above 300 m. Most favoured habitats are rivers and streams (36 per cent of nests during a 1983 survey), lakes and pools (26 per cent of nests) and canals and drains (21 per cent of nests). Because the birds are more or less sedentary, the populations in Scotland, England, Wales and Ireland are relatively discrete, facilitating the study of their population dynamics.

FIG 133. Already an impressive size, the mute swan can make itself even larger during territorial disputes by raising its neck feathers and elevating its wings. About 15 per cent of its time during the day is spent preening. (Ken Kinsella)

There have been various attempts, mostly incomplete, to census the breeding population at a national level (Table 83). The results show that overall the population remained relatively stable from 1955 to 1983, suffering a setback, estimated at 25 per cent, during the hard winters of 1961/62 and 1962/63, from which it recovered. During the 1970s and 1980s numbers in the major lowland river systems such as the Thames, Trent and Warwickshire Avon declined, partly in response to drainage impacts but thought to be principally because of poisoning by ingestion of anglers' lead fishing weights and, to a lesser extent, spent gun-shot, mistakenly taken by the swans for grit.

TABLE 83. Mute swans breeding and wintering in Great Britain, 1955–2002.

PERIOD	CENSUS METHOD	BIRDS	BREEDING PAIRS	NON-BREEDING BIRDS
1955 and 1956	Breeding survey	19,900–21,600	3,550–4,000	12,800–13,600
1961	Breeding survey	c.19,000	(29.4%)	(70.6%)
1978	Breeding survey revision	c.17,630	c.3,115	11,400
1983	Breeding survey WeBS	18,900	c.3,150	12,600
1988–92: 5-year mean	Winter survey	25,750	—	—
1988–91	Breeding survey	c.27,000	—	—
1990	Breeding survey	25,800	—	—
1995–99: 5-year mean	WeBS + extrapolation	c.37,500	—	—
2002	Breeding survey	31,700	6,150	19,400

Data from Campbell, 1960; Eltringham, 1963; Ogilvie, 1981; Owen *et al.*, 1986; Delany *et al.*, 1992; Gibbons *et al.*, 1993; Kirby, 1995; Kershaw & Cranswick, 2003; Ward *et al.*, 2004.

Lead is a non-specific toxin affecting most bodily systems, including the haematological, muscular and nervous systems. Acute poisoning can follow the ingestion of ten or more lead shot, or fewer of anglers' lead fishing weights, with death occurring within days. The annual estimated weight of lead fired into all habitats in Britain in 1990 was 2,000 tonnes, of which 160 tonnes went specifically into wetlands and was available to mute swans and other wildfowl. In Ireland the comparative figures were 153 and 46 tonnes respectively.[23]

Some swans died from direct poisoning, others had impaired breeding success. In Britain, public awareness and the introduction first of voluntary codes concerning the use of lead fishing weights in 1982, followed by legislation that banned the sale and use of lead weights in England and Wales from 1 January 1987 (but not Scotland, where voluntary codes were implemented), has greatly improved the situation.[24] In addition, legislation was introduced in

1999 making it illegal in England to shoot certain species of wildfowl with lead shot, and to use lead shot below the high tide mark or in areas of International importance for wildfowl.[25] Similar restrictions came into effect in Wales in September 2000, but there is no parallel legislation in Scotland or in Ireland.

It is likely that the incidence of all forms of lead poisoning in Britain has declined further over the past 15 years. The apparent 39 per cent increase in the mute swan population between 1985 and 1996 was almost certainly facilitated by a decline in lead poisoning in addition to a series of mild winters, resulting in reduced mortality of both adults and immatures. There has been a notable increase in the size of non-breeding flocks in urban areas, which are to a large extent dependent upon supplementary feeding provided by the public during the winter. In Ireland the lead-poisoning situation is more serious than in Britain now. Almost 70 per cent of all dead mute swans found up to the early 1990s had died as a result of lead poisoning.[26]

Since the mid-1980s numbers of mute swans have progressively increased. The 1990s witnessed a remarkable 45 per cent increase in numbers, based on a breeding survey in 1990 and the five-year mean from WeBS counts 1995–99. The annual indices of birds wintering in Great Britain, calculated from WeBS counts, show an almost continuous upward trend, with a few minor blips (1992/93 and 1993/94), since the winter of 1985/86. This rapid population increase is confirmed by the results of surveys organised by the British Trust for Ornithology (BTO), whose Common Birds Census (CBC) and Waterways Bird Survey (WBS) have monitored mute swans since 1966.[27] Overall the mute swan population in Britain and the Isle of Man increased by 23 per cent over the period 1990 to 2002, a slower rate than in the 1980s. In the past five or so years, since 2002/03, numbers have been more stable, and in 2006/07 they showed a slight decline, but this was within the expected range of fluctuation. Numbers in Northern Ireland at WeBS-monitored sites have declined rather dramatically since 1999/2000.

Numbers in Ireland have never been satisfactorily censused. An estimate of 5,000–6,000 birds was produced for the early 1970s, later updated to 7,000.[28] In the late 1980s there was an estimated 10,000 birds, extrapolated from data collected by Ralph Sheppard during the winter counts 1984/85 to 1986/87.[29] The estimated 19,000–20,000 breeding birds for 1988–91, based on extrapolation from data obtained for the *New Atlas*, is considered unrealistically high.[30] A more rational figure, based on I-WeBS and WeBS counts for 1999/2000–2003/04 and subjected to an extrapolation multiplier of 1.65 – derived from a study in Britain[31] – to incorporate uncounted and dispersed swans on small wetlands, canals and other water bodies not covered by I-WeBS, produced a population of 11,440 birds.[32] The figure of 21,100 birds quoted in the 2005 publication *Ireland's Wetlands and their Waterbirds* was a mistake.[33]

BTO surveys of the breeding performance of British mute swans have shown little change since the 1960s, apart from a decline in mean failure rate of eggs (Fig. 134). Some resources, almost certainly food in some locations, are becoming scarce. If the total numbers continue to rise at the rate recorded during the 1990s then it would be expected that density-dependent factors will probably suppress breeding performance, with a decline in productivity and recruitment of young birds into the breeding population.

FIG 134. Productivity changes for mute swan in Britain 1966–2006. From S. R. Baillie *et al.*, Breeding birds in the wider countryside: their conservation status 2007 (BTO, 2007). Reproduced with permission.

Variable	Mean annual sample size	Trend	Modelled in first year	Modelled in 2004	Change	Comment
Clutch size	19 clutches	linear decline	5.79 eggs	5.25 eggs	-9.3%	small sample
Brood size	33 broods	None				
Daily failure rate (eggs)	26 eggs	linear increase	0.72% nests/day	2.02% nests/day	180.6%	small sample
Daily failure rate (chicks)	20 chicks	None				small sample
Laying date	11	None				small sample

Changes in mean clutch size, mean brood size, egg stage nest failure, chick stage nest failure rate and laying dates.

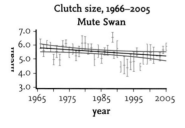

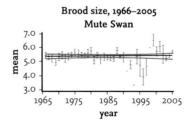

FIG 134. – *Cont.*

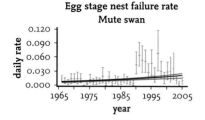

Egg stage nest failure rate
Mute swan

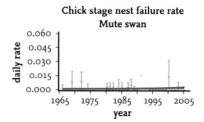

Chick stage nest failure rate
Mute swan

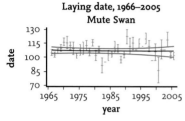

Laying date, 1966–2005
Mute Swan

Immigration and emigration are important elements of population dynamics, as discussed earlier. If there is little or no movement of birds in and out of the local, regional or national populations then their dynamics are easier to unravel. Fortunately the mute swan falls into the category of 'little movement'. The median natal dispersal distance from 307 British and Irish ringing recoveries is 14 km.[34] Malcolm Ogilvie analysed the recovery of some 2,156 swans that had been ringed in Britain and recovered by 1966. Most (70.2 per cent) had travelled less than 16 km from the place of ringing (usually following the line of a watercourse), and only 46 (2.1 per cent) had travelled more than 80 km, some of which included moult migrants.[35] There was no evidence to support regular migrations overseas. However, a small number of birds ringed in Sweden, Denmark and Holland were recovered in southeast England during the severe winter 1962/63, and it is likely that similar movements occur during other periods of hard weather – a total of 13 ringed abroad have been recovered in Britain, mostly under cold weather conditions. Additional evidence to support these hard-weather immigrations is provided by 43 swans ringed mostly in southeast England during cold winters and their subsequent recovery during spring and summer on their return to Holland, Germany, southwest Sweden and northern France.[36]

Irish-ringed mute swans move greater distances than their British cousins. It has been argued that higher survival rates of Irish swans lead to more competition and a consequent shortage of breeding territories, thus the need for immature swans to travel further from their natal areas in search of breeding territories. The movements of 227 swans ringed at the Lough, Cork, revealed 77 per cent moving between 16 km and 48 km, with a median distance travelled of 30 km. Eight birds moved more than 80 km, including one which went 460 km across the Irish Sea to Staffordshire. Birds in their second year travelled the most, and the greatest cumulative distance, while there was little movement of swans older than four years.[37] There is some movement of immature Scottish birds, mainly from the Uists in the Outer Hebrides to Northern Ireland and the Irish Republic – Counties Antrim, Donegal and Derry – as evidenced by 14 recoveries up to 1988.[38] There has been no evidence of return movements of these birds. There have been fewer than ten recoveries of British ringed birds in Ireland, mostly on the east coast. A disproportionate number have come from birds ringed on the Isle of Man. Despite the low numbers of birds moving from one population to another there is probably sufficient gene flow to prevent subspeciation.

The imperative for all animals is to beget more of their own. The age of first breeding is a critical issue in population dynamics – the longer it is delayed the greater the need to produce sufficient young that will survive until they enter the breeding population and replace their parents. As with other large long-lived birds, mute swans do not breed successfully until they are about four or five years old. Studies during the 1960s in the Oxford area, carried out by Chris Perrins and colleagues at the Edward Grey Institute of Field Ornithology, found that the annual adult survival rate was 82 per cent – i.e. 18 per cent of the adults died per year, meaning that within each pair 0.36 adults died per year on average.[39] For the population to remain stable, therefore, every year 0.36 offspring from each pair had to enter the breeding population in their fourth year. The Oxford study found that 0.43 young survived to their fourth year (in more recent years the figure has risen to 0.54), providing the population with a healthy margin of recruitment, and a valuable buffer if incidents of exceptional mortality, such as a severe winter, occurred. However, if the adults did not breed until their fifth year only 0.32 young birds would survive until then, and be available for recruitment. As this recruitment rate was less than the adult mortality at the time, the population would slowly decline unless the mortality was balanced by immigration. Matters become more complex due to the great variation of age of first breeding – figures from the Oxford study showed that 10 per cent of adults bred at age three years, 37 per cent at age four years, 53 per cent at age five years and 71 per cent aged six years. Recent information from the long-term Abbotsbury study showed that the mean age at first breeding for males was 4.61 years, and for females 4.31 years.[40]

Pairing generally takes place during the winter and spring, mainly within the non-breeding flocks composed of birds aged 1–4 years old. Courtship is a slow process, ensuring a close bond between the birds. During pre-copulatory behaviour both birds dip their heads under water almost simultaneously, following which they rub their heads on their backs or sides, or preen. As the process continues their movements become synchronised, each swan behaving as if it was a mirror image of the other. The male then mounts the female and afterwards the necks are held erect again with their bills pointing upwards at first, then downwards. Preening and bathing then follow. Mute swans mate more frequently than necessary just to fertilise the eggs, probably because it strengthens the bond between the birds.

Mute swans are fabled for their devotion to each other. Clive Minton studied the fates of more than 100 individually marked swans in Staffordshire in 1961–67 and found that 85 per cent of paired breeding swans retained the same mate, if it was still alive, from year to year. Divorce occurred in less than 3 per cent of successful breeders and 9 per cent of failed breeders. Non-breeding pairs were less stable, with only 75 per cent retaining the same mate. These low rates of change reflect the selective advantages of fidelity. Most mute swans retain the same breeding site from year to year. Only 2 per cent of surviving pairs moved their territories more than 8 km from their previous nesting site.[41]

Territory size is variable, depending upon the local feeding ecology and swan numbers. The average linear territory size on some of the best-quality rivers around Oxford is 2.5–3 km, while on the river Thames outside the Oxford area it is about 15 km. Although normally solitary breeders, extraordinarily high nesting densities can be encountered in coastal lagoons that are rich in food resources. For example at Abbotsbury at the west end of the Fleet – a 14 km long stretch of tidal inlet with a declining salinity content towards Abbotsbury behind Chesil Bank in Dorset – some 150 pairs nest in close proximity, with a mere 2–20 m between nests (Fig. 135). This high-density nesting is made possible by the protection from many of the hazards facing breeding birds in other locations. There are also large quantities of food available – especially eelgrass and tasselweed.

Other instances of high-density nesting are generally spasmodic, possibly involving a high proportion of young birds, trial-breeding for the first time. In Ireland I once found 43 nests on a one-hectare island at Our Lady's Island Lake, Co. Wexford, on 13 May 1961. The average clutch size was 4.9. Two hundred and sixty-five swans were present on the lake then, compared with 348 at the end of the previous November. A week later the number of nests had increased to 59, but all the earlier nests showed evidence of predation by mammals, possibly rats or mink, and it is unlikely that any of the 59 pairs bred successfully. During the previous summer, 50 swans had been recorded on the lake, but only one pair bred successfully. In subsequent summers, also, only one pair bred, with between

FIG 135. Mute swans at the Abbotsbury swannery, Dorset. (Guy Edwardes/NHPA)

12 and 50 swans present during the breeding season. In 1987 I came across a similar nesting explosion on Inch Lough, Co. Donegal, where I found 42 nests on a small islet, less than half a hectare in extent. Such breeding densities had not previously been recorded in the lough – nor subsequently. These outbursts of high-density nesting are most likely encouraged by sudden availability of abundant food supplies.

Under normal circumstances the mute swan is one of the most territorial of all birds, defending its 'patch' throughout the year, their aggressive behaviour towards other swans intensifying during the nesting period. The male's behaviour during incubation is often dramatic, with outstretched flapping wings accompanied by vigorous hissing. The ferocity of the defence is unparalleled in other birds and is difficult to explain. It may have evolved when the swan was a truly wild species in continental Europe, subject to predation by wolves, brown bears and other large mammals. Forceful aggression by the swan would have been necessary to ward off these attacks.

Within the population a relatively large proportion – up to 30 per cent – of *pairs* in Staffordshire that defended territories did not breed in any given year.[42] In another study, in Dublin, 54 per cent of all the *individual* swans aged five years did not attempt to breed.[43] While such a high proportion of non-breeders might seem a waste of an opportunity to obey the biological imperative, there are reasons for this, probably related to density-dependent factors. During a study of the Abbotsbury swans (1976–2000) Chris Perrins and colleagues found that intermittent non-breeding by adult birds – known as 'skippers' – accounted for the loss of 400 bird years of potential breeding, or an average of 9 (range 2–28) per cent per year.[44] Skipping is also widespread among Arctic-breeding geese (see barnacle goose, p. 336). With generally low levels of adult mortality and consequent high longevity and a potentially long breeding life, there is no need for large wildfowl to breed every year. This intermittent non-breeding of mature adult 'skippers' could be viewed as a part of an adaptive strategy in which these birds are spared the potential costs of reproduction with an expected enhancement of their survival rates. The 'skippers' may also have a higher probability of reproducing in subsequent years. One might also view intermittent breeding as a method of maximising lifetime reproductive success in which an individual would pick a year in which its chances of breeding successfully would be greatest.

Avian egg and clutch sizes are determined both by inheritance and by environmental factors. David Lack argued that the average clutch size in waterfowl varies inversely with the relative size of the egg and has evolved in relation to the availability of food for the female around the time of laying.[45]

The mean clutch size of the mute swan in six studies in Scotland and England ranged from 4.8 to 6.9 eggs (Table 84) – a relatively small clutch compared with most other wildfowl, where sizes of 11–14 are not unusual.[46]

On completion of incubation, carried out solely by the female, during which she may lose up to 33 per cent of her body weight, the nidifugous cygnets leave the nest within 24–48 hours of hatching. Hatching success is quite variable, with nest failure rates ranging from 29 to 49 per cent depending upon location and circumstances. The commonest causes of failure are human destruction of eggs and flooding of nests. If clutches are lost early on in the season many of the swans will lay a second clutch, albeit generally a smaller one.

Most cygnets are light grey with white underparts. However, some may have an all-white plumage. These are the so-called Polish cygnets, a variety, or morph, of the mute swan. In addition, Polish cygnets have pale, almost pink legs – not the usual black – a colour they retain for life. Originally thought to be a different species, they were erroneously accorded the scientific name *Cygnus immutabilis* after they were first encountered on the river Trent, Staffordshire, in 1686.[47] It was later realised that Polish swans derived from birds imported to Britain from the Baltic states and eastern Europe, where in some locations they constitute up to 20 per cent of the population. Within Europe the lowest proportion of Polish swans occurs in Britain (1 per cent) and the highest (76 per cent) in the Göttingen region of Germany, while in Poland the proportion of breeding Polish swans varied from 1.8 to 8.3 per cent of 336 breeding pairs examined.[48] The genes controlling the two morphs are located on the sex chromosome. Male birds have two matching sex chromosomes, while females have only one sex chromosome. So the female cygnets with the Polish gene (recessive to the grey gene) are always white as it cannot be overridden by the dominant grey gene. As a consequence many more females (about 26 per cent) are of the Polish form than males (about 10 per cent).

Both adults remain with the cygnets throughout the summer, initially assisting their brood by rooting up vegetation outside the reach of the cygnets' shorter necks. The great length and flexibility of the neck is due to the presence of 25 cervical vertebrae (swans have more than 60 vertebrae altogether), more than any other animal, even the giraffe, which like all mammals has only seven vertebrae in its neck. The additional flexibility provides the swan with a successful adaptation to foraging aquatic vegetation in preferred water depths of 0.5–1.2 m. Apart from its function as a feeding instrument, the dextrous neck is used to great effect during courtship and other behavioural ceremonies.

The cygnets stay with their parents until at least September, when most of them are able to move, or fly, away from their parents voluntarily, or are chased away, to join the non-breeding flocks. However, a few young will remain with their parents until the following spring, as is the case with geese as well as whooper and Bewick's swans.

While the cygnets are still small the adults go through their annual moult in their own territory, commencing at the end of July or early August. Primary and secondary flight feathers are shed together, making the swans flightless for a period of 4–7 weeks, depending upon local circumstances. To ensure that the cygnets retain some protection from one parent, the male and female stagger their moults. Generally the female commences first, the male waiting until her new flight feathers are well advanced.[49] When there are no cygnets to protect, the adults gather together with other mute swans – see below – and shed their feathers simultaneously. The moult is geared to the most advantageous period of the year when the weather is generally warmest and food is at peak production. This allows the moulting birds to replace the considerable drain of internal energy resources and sustain the metabolic activity associated with new feather growth. It has been estimated that the complete plumage of a bird may represent some 20–30 per cent of the total lean dry body mass of a bird.[50] The energy required to regenerate the moulted feathers results in a body-weight loss of some 5–10 per cent, depending upon locality. In one Danish study it was found that a mute swan's primary feathers grow at a rate of some 6–7 mm per day to reach their full length of 400 mm after 67 days.[51] Average primary-feather growth rate has been recorded at 6.1 mm per day at Berwick-upon-Tweed.[52] The swans can fly, however, 3–4 weeks before their flight feathers are fully grown.

The survival of the cygnets and immatures determines the recruitment rate of new birds into the population. Survival rates are variable, ranging from 41–68 per cent during the first year to 75–90 per cent in the third year, according to local circumstances (Table 84). Adult survival rates are naturally much higher, because by their third year the birds are more experienced at finding food and avoiding hazards and other types of mortality; nationally they are in the range 74–87 per cent,[53] very similar to the 77–90 per cent found in the studies summarised in Table 84. The high mean adult survival rate of 94 per cent noted for the Abbotsbury population during earlier studies has been recalculated at 85 per cent, based on more recent work.[54]

As the national population of mute swans in Britain remained more or less stable between 1955 and 1983, with dips during the hard winters, the number of young surviving per pair to breed must have *equalled* twice the adult mortality. In a stable population with an average annual adult mortality rate of 18 per cent an average of 0.36 young per pair (0.18 x 2) would need to survive to the breeding age of four years old, as explained above.

TABLE 84. Some demographic features of Scottish and English mute swan populations.

AREA AND STUDY PERIOD	HEBRIDES 1978–82	ABBOTSBURY 1969–80	MIDLANDS 1961–78
Clutch size	6.1	4.8	6.6
% nests lost	30	38	49
Brood size at hatching [a]	*	*	2.6
Brood size at fledging	1.8	(1.9)	1.9
Annual survival rate [b]			
To 1st year	1.04	+	0.79
To 2nd year	0.78	+	0.53
To 3rd year	0.59	+	0.37
To 4th year	0.44	+	0.28
Adult survival	0.90	0.94	0.82
Balance per annum [c]	0.24	(0.82)	− 0.08

AREA AND STUDY PERIOD	OXFORD 1 1960s–80s	OXFORD 2 1960s–80s	LOWER THAMES 1979–84
Clutch size	6.0	6.9	6.8
% nests lost	*	14	6
Brood size at hatching [a]	4.0	3.8	3.4
Brood size at fledging	2.0	2.8	1.7
Annual survival rate [b]			
To 1st year	1.3	1.03	0.65
To 2nd year	0.89	0.69	0.45
To 3rd year	0.67	0.46	0.31
To 4th year	0.43	0.31	*
Adult survival	0.82	0.82	0.77
Balance per annum [c]	0.07	− 0.05	− 0.15

Data from Perrins, 1991.

[a] Includes failed nests.

[b] Number of cygnets per pair that survive to June the following year.

TABLE 84. – *Cont.*

^c The difference between the number of cygnets per pair surviving to breeding age
and the number of adults dying per pair per year.

+ Not available on a per brood basis. Survival of first-year individuals from September
to the following June was about 68 per cent; thereafter about 90 per cent per annum.

* Not available.

For the next 19 years to 2002, as the British national population was
significantly expanding, survival of young birds to recruitment into the
population as breeding birds must have *exceeded* twice the adult mortality rate.
This could have come about by (1) increased juvenile survival – fewer predators,
less human interference, more available food, mild winters, etc – or (2) reduced
adult mortality – no or reduced lead poisoning, mild winters, more food being
provided by the public, etc – or (3) more adults breeding at an earlier age.

The results from six study areas (Table 84) showed high adult survival rates in
the Hebrides and at Abbotsbury, both populations holding their own and slightly
increasing, while the Oxford, Midlands and Lower Thames populations
experienced declines of 70 per cent or more between the early 1960s and mid-
1980s. The losses would have been larger but for immigration, thus emphasising
its role in population dynamics. While reproductive and adult survival rates are
the key elements in the balance of numbers, the various studies showed that
populations can remain more or less stable with adult annual mortality of
between 82 and 94 per cent, suggesting that there is a surplus of available young
birds waiting 'in the wings' to move into the population and take their positions
as mature breeders.

The consequences of a small *increase* in adult mortality for long-lived species
such as swans and geese are considerable. For example, a 1 per cent reduction on
a 95 per cent adult survival rate will require a disproportionate increase in the
numbers of young from 0.1 to 0.12 per pair – a 20 per cent increase – required to
survive in order to maintain numbers.[55]

Chris Perrins concluded from his comparative study in 1991 that mute swans
can maintain stable populations with a wide range of different demographic
characteristics in which adult survival rates ranged from 94 per cent to as low as
82 per cent per annum or, put another way, when adult losses varied from 6 to 18
per cent. Such flexibility is biologically advantageous, as it allows swan
populations to maintain their numbers in the face of occasional severe weather
conditions and intermittent episodes of mortality brought about by disease, as
well as exceptional mortality, which in the case of the mute swan is mostly
caused by human activities.

BARNACLE GOOSE

Unlike the mute swan and mallard populations, the numbers of the Greenland breeding population of the barnacle goose show little evidence, as yet, of being subject to density-dependent factors. The barnacle goose population breeding in Svalbard, on the other hand, is subject to density-dependent population control factors that have become more pronounced in recent years as increasing numbers have brought about intensification of competition for food resources. Both populations have increased dramatically over the past 50 years or so (Fig. 136). The Greenland population expanded from 8,300 birds in 1959 to 70,501 in March 2008.[56] The Svalbard population rose somewhat similarly, from 3,000–4,000 birds in the 1960s to 29,815 in November 2007.[57] Most of the wintering Greenland birds are found on Islay, where there has been an estimated annual increase of 6 per cent since the 1970s, compared with a 2.7 per cent annual rate of increase for the Irish wintering population and 3.2 per cent for Scottish, non-Islay, wintering birds.

FIG 136. Greenland barnacle goose population size, 1959–2003, derived from aerial surveys (dotted lines) and ground counts (solid line, Islay only). From J. Worden *et al.*, The Greenland population of the barnacle goose *Branta leucopsis* in Britain and Ireland 1956/57 to 2002/03 (WWT/JNCC, 2004). Reproduced with permission.

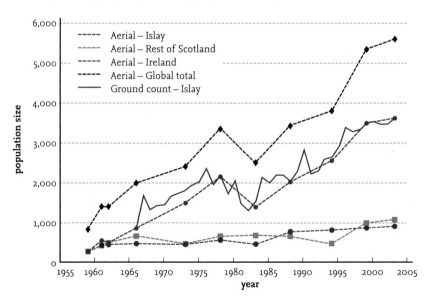

Shooting mortality held down both populations historically to the point where they were considered to be at dangerously low levels in the late 1950s.[58] When shooting was banned, at the same time as nature reserves were being created, numbers took off without any density-dependent factors restraining the increases. Shooting had been responsible for most of the known adult mortality, and when it ceased adult survival rates increased dramatically, allowing increased breeding capacity and recruitment of young birds into the population. Food resources were also abundant on the wintering grounds and in the spring and autumn staging areas, and breeding sites were virtually unlimited.

Now that numbers in the Greenland population have risen to their highest levels ever, it might be expected that the population would begin to be controlled by density-dependent factors. With regard to those wintering on Islay there have been statistically significant declines in the *proportion* of breeding birds and *productivity* of birds since 1995, while there has also been an almost significant (at the 5 per cent level) decline in the proportion of juveniles in the winter flocks.[59] Analysis of population counts on Islay using the Pollard randomised test showed that the Islay population exhibited a density-dependent decline for the period 1966–78, but over a longer period, 1966–2003, there was no evidence of such a decline.[60] This was confirmed by another statistical test, developed by Dennis and Taper.[61] On the other hand, variations in weather have been shown to affect breeding performance and recruitment rates of young birds into the breeding population. In the early 1990s Fox and Gitay analysed the annual fluctuations in the breeding success of barnacle geese wintering on Islay, as reflected in the percentage of juveniles in the wintering flocks. They found the number of successful breeding pairs to be directly related to the size of the breeding population, and concluded that it was highly unlikely that density-dependent factors were operating on the population. Correlations between breeding success and the previous winter weather conditions at Tiree (closest meteorological station to Islay), northern Iceland (where the geese spend about one month staging before moving to Greenland), and Mesters Vig, northeast Greenland (close to the breeding grounds), showed that 60 per cent of the variation in breeding success could be explained by early spring weather conditions in Scotland, spring and early summer conditions in Iceland during the staging period, and conditions in Greenland on arrival.[62] These findings supported some work that Brian West and I did 18 years earlier on the barnacle goose population wintering on the Inishkea Islands, Co. Mayo, which showed that winter temperatures close to the islands (at Belmullet, 17 km northeast) were correlated with subsequent goose productivity on the breeding grounds. Mild winters allowed good

FIG 137. Barnacle goose: a mature adult, with very clear white tips to the wing coverts. (Jari Peltomaki/NHPA)

growth of grasses – the main food resource of the geese – allowing the birds to build up greater critical energy reserves, indicated by body weight, than was possible in winters with lower temperatures and consequently less growth of grass.[63]

With regard to the Svalbard population, on the other hand, it has been clearly shown that declines in fecundity and in the survival of young birds, thus affecting recruitment of young birds into the breeding population, *are* operating. Myrfyn Owen and Jeff Black have shown that the 3,000 km autumn migration from Svalbard to the Solway Firth is the most hazardous part of the goose's life cycle, and most deaths during this period are probably the result of inadequate fat reserves for the migration. There is competition between adults and young birds for food during the rearing and fattening periods on the breeding grounds. In some years considerable numbers of young birds fail to complete the migration. Based on the numbers of geese ringed in Svalbard in 1986, some 35 per cent of the young failed to reach the wintering grounds (i.e. a 35 per cent mortality rate). Goslings that were hatched late in the season and that had low body weights at the age of 3–5 weeks suffered higher mortality. Differences in survival rates were found among the geese according to the different breeding locations where habitat quality and density of geese varied.[64] It was also established that average breeding success fell as numbers in the population increased and competition for food resources intensified. But brood size did not decline, as a smaller proportion of successful breeding adults were contributing to the productivity of the population.

With my colleagues Brian West and Maurice Cassidy I have closely followed the population dynamics of the Greenland birds, both on their Greenland breeding grounds (over three summers) and on the wintering haunts, principally on the Inishkea Islands, Co. Mayo, for the past 48 years, qualifying the project as one of the longest goose monitoring programmes in western Europe. Steve Percival and others have been studying the dynamics of Greenland birds wintering on Islay, Scotland, and have also followed the geese to their Icelandic staging grounds. Myrfyn Owen and Jeff Black, and more recently Larry Griffin, together with colleagues from the University of Grøningen in the Netherlands, and the Norwegian Polar Institute, have been following the fortunes of the Svalbard population on their breeding grounds, at their autumn and spring staging areas, as well as in their winter quarters on the Solway Firth. Valuable new information on the migration and movements of the population has been gathered by the fitting of GPS satellite transmitters to the geese. For the purposes of this chapter only the Greenland breeding population will be considered in detail (Fig. 138).

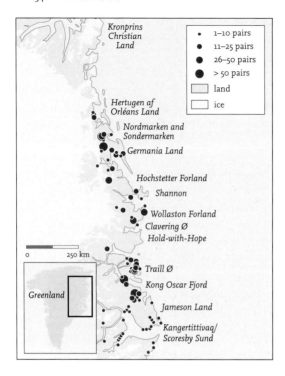

Kronprins
Christian
Land

•	1–10 pairs
●	11–25 pairs
⬤	26–50 pairs
⬤	> 50 pairs
▭	land
▭	ice

Hertugen af
Orléans Land

Nordmarken and
Sondermarken

Germania Land

Hochstetter Forland

Shannon

Wollaston Forland

Clavering Ø

Hold-with-Hope

0   250 km

Greenland

Traill Ø

Kong Oscar Fjord

Jameson Land

Kangertittivaq/
Scoresby Sund

FIG 138. Distribution and approximate size of barnacle goose colonies in northeast Greenland. In some areas broods have been observed but the colonies not located, for example at Hold-with-Hope. From J. Madsen *et al.*, *Goose Populations of the Western Palearctic* (Wetlands International & National Environmental Research Institute, Denmark, 1999). Reproduced with permission.

The Greenland population breeds on the east and northeast coasts of Greenland from Scoresby Sund north to Hertugen af Orleans Land, a distance of some 900 km. The coastline is indented by long fjords and glaciated valleys in a rugged, barren landscape. During the summer the coastal strip, glacial valleys and fjords thaw out to support a rich Arctic vegetation that provides essential food to the geese from their arrival at the end of May to their departure in August. The geese breed colonially, mainly on cliff ledges and rock outcrops standing high above coastal plains or on the sides of valleys. Colony size is usually small, ranging from a few pairs to up to 150. A typical nest will be located near the top of a 50–100 m sheer cliff, with a further 100–300 m of boulder scree leading down to the valley bottom.

A typical breeding area in Greenland is the valley of Ørsted Dal, Jameson Land (Fig. 139). It is about 43 km from its head to the sea and about 6 km wide in its lower section. It is a classic glaciated valley with a broad U shape. The walls of the valley are formed by upstanding cliffs – sandstones and shales with basalt intrusions spreading out horizontally through the sandstone – that have been eroded to form massive scree slopes at their feet (Fig. 140). The cliff walls on

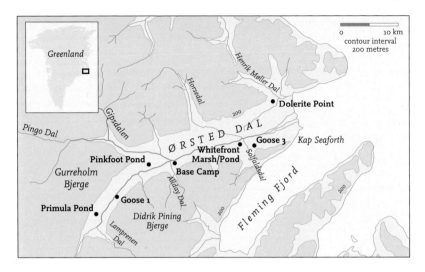

FIG 139. Ørsted Dal, northeast Greenland, the site of several barnacle goose breeding colonies on the cliffs that rise up from the valley floor. From D. Cabot *et al.*, *Biological Expedition to Jameson Land, Greenland 1984* (Barnacle Books, 1984).

FIG 140. Ørsted Dal cliffs. These vertical cliffs rise some 200 m above the valley floor and provide safe and secure nesting sites for barnacle geese. (David Cabot)

which the geese nest give the valley an atmosphere like an amphitheatre, cut off from the surrounding mountain ranges. The central and dominant feature is the main river, which has superimposed its fluvial features on the glacial moraines. In the lower part of the valley the river broadens out into a series of braided channels up to 1 km wide, which become swollen with melt-water in June and July.

In Ørsted Dal a total of 201 pairs bred in 1984, located in nine colonies, with a mean of 22.3 pairs per colony (range 3–50). The mean estimated height above the valley floor was 200 m (range 80–300 m) and the mean height above the scree was estimated at 39 m (range 20–70 m).[65] Some 800 km further north in Nordmarken, during 1987, seven colonies held a total of 116 pairs, with a mean of 16.6 (range 3–33). The mean estimated height above the valley floor was 133 m (range 80–200 m) and mean height above the scree was 47 m (range 30–80 m).[66]

The geese nest on cliffs to avoid predation by the arctic foxes that roam the flat tundra landscape below. It is not unusual to find a gyrfalcon nesting either in, or in close proximity to, a colony. The presence of the falcon discourages reconnoitring glaucous gulls and ravens, predators of goose nests. There are also

FIG 141. White-phase gyrfalcon feeding its young. The nest is in close proximity to a small colony of nesting barnacle geese. Several small goslings were observed being snatched off the cliffs by the gyrfalcon. (David Cabot)

many eyes in the goose breeding colony to alert the gyrfalcon to any potential danger. For the geese, the downside of this association is that the falcons take some of the barnacle goslings, snatching them off the cliff ledges as 'hot gosling takeaways'. However, the advantages of this cohabitation must be mutual for goose and falcon (Fig. 141).

The barnacle goose's nest site (Fig. 142) presents problems for the goslings when they have to leap off the cliffs to the ground below and then travel with their parents to the security of nearby lakes, where they undergo rapid growth until they fledge. Until relatively recently it was not known exactly how the cliff-nesting barnacles got their young down safely from the nests. In his book *Wild Geese*, Malcolm Ogilvie refers to published accounts of adult barnacles carrying goslings down to the ground either in their bills or on their backs.[67] The objections

FIG 142. Barnacle goose nest. A flat platform on the cliff face is usually selected for the nest site. The nest is rudely constructed with goose droppings and a large number of down feathers plucked from the breast of the female, which exposes part of the goose's skin as a brood patch and allows immediate body-heat transfer to the eggs as she incubates them. When she departs the nest for a brief feeding session in the valley below she arranges the feathers over the eggs to keep them warm and out of sight of predators. The male usually remains on guard near the nest. (David Cabot)

to these methods of transport were reviewed by Ogilvie, who concluded that a free fall or bouncing down by stages was possible without killing the goslings. Such behaviour had already been described for cliff-nesting Canada geese[68] and, of course, it is a common phenomenon in some cliff-nesting auks, although here the flightless young are about three weeks old and have been well fed on the ledges by their parents. The first systematic observations of this amazing spectacle of free-falling goslings were made during our 1984 expedition to Jameson Land, when jumping chicks were captured in the documentary film *Valley of the Geese*, produced for Irish television (RTE).[69]

Continuous 24-hour observations made on nests in Ørsted Dal showed that on average incubating females spent 3 per cent of their time away from the nest with a mean trip duration of 37 minutes. The number of feeding trips declined as hatching began. Limited observations suggested that the goslings spent about 42 hours on the nesting ledge after hatching and before the jump. In 1987, in Germania Land, we found the mean time spent before departure from the nesting ledge was 41.3 hours (range 28–62), based on observations made on eleven nests. Of 94 goslings observed to jump from a total of 30 nests at Kap Seaforth, Ørsted Dal, in 1984, 26 were lost in the scree, 13 were taken by foxes and two by glaucous gulls, representing an overall loss of 43.6 per cent. Of 41 goslings hatching from 12 nests in Nordmarken in 1987, 16 were taken by foxes, two by gyrfalcons and one each was lost in the scree and fell out of the nest, a loss of 48.8 per cent. The combined overall loss of 135 goslings, from prior to jumping to the age of two weeks in the security of ponds or lakes, was 45.2 per cent.[70]

The mean loss of young, as measured by comparing brood sizes on the lakes in northeast Greenland and later on the Inishkea Islands, was 23 per cent in 1984, 3 per cent in 1987 and 17 per cent for the two years combined (Table 85). This is markedly less than that recorded in the Svalbard population in 1986, possibly due to differences in density-dependent factors on the breeding grounds.

Once the goslings have survived the jump from the nest and have reached the comparative safety of the tundra lakes, they must spend 40–50 days fledging, and all the while they are at risk from Arctic Foxes and glaucous gulls, and are competing for food with other goose families (Fig. 143). Additional mortality will be incurred during the migration from Greenland to Iceland and from some shooting as they rest, for about a month, on their staging grounds in lowland marshes in southeast Iceland. The onward migration to Scotland and Ireland will also take its toll, and further losses will then be incurred on the wintering grounds, where there is again competition for food. Another critical point is the ability of a breeding female to accumulate sufficient body reserves on the wintering grounds and at the spring staging areas, ensuring good physiological

TABLE 85. Breeding performance of barnacle geese as measured from nests in northeast Greenland to wintering grounds on Inishkea, Co. Mayo, 1984 and 1987.

	ØRSTED DAL (1984)	NORDMARKEN (1987)	COMBINED (1984 + 1987)
Clutch size range	2–6 (n = 30)	2–6 (n = 12)	2–6 (n = 42)
Mean clutch size	3.57 (n = 30)	4.16 (n = 12)	3.7 (n = 42)
Mean brood size prior to jump	3.13 (n = 31)	3.42 (n = 12)	3.2 (n = 43)
Mean brood size (c.2 weeks old) in lakes	2.40 (n = 50)	2.33 (n = 18)	2.4 (n = 68)
Mean brood size, winter (October to December), Inishkea Islands, Co. Mayo	1.86 (n = 122)	2.26 (n = 85)	2.0 (n = 207)

condition to withstand the final leg of migration to northeast Greenland and to get through the energy-demanding breeding season.

The physiological demands on the female are considerable. First there is egg production, for which she must draw on her body reserves (a full clutch represents 26 per cent of the female's body weight), and then she must withstand an incubation period of some 25–26 days, during which she eats little or no food. Studies on four captive breeding, free-flying females at the Wildfowl & Wetlands Trust at Slimbridge showed a mean weight loss of 90 g per day during laying and subsequently 26 g per day during incubation.[71] Thus an average female of 2.5 kg body weight might have to endure a weight loss of 1 kg, or 40 per cent of her weight, for these two critical activities. Such a loss can lead to death of the female while on the nest under adverse weather conditions towards the end of incubation, as has been found in the snow goose in Canada.[72]

The annual energy cycle of the barnacle goose follows a regular pattern. Soon after their arrival back on their wintering grounds on the Inishkea Islands they replenish their energy reserves, depleted during the breeding season and on migration from Greenland via Iceland. Initially they feed by rooting and grubbing up white clover stolons, rich in energy and easily digested. When these are exhausted the geese switch to the grasses red fescue and smooth

FIG 143. An alert barnacle goose mother watches over three goslings while they feed. After jumping from the cliff-ledge nest sites the goslings are taken to the safety of a nearby small lake. (Joe Blossom/NHPA)

meadow-grass, which are plucked more delicately, but at a great speed, from the short sward.

It is probable that the geese selectively graze or 'farm' areas of the grass swards at critical times of the year, to encourage the growth of rapidly growing grass shoots with a high protein content. Lamina (leaf) extension rates and protein content in grazed grass shoots are greater than in ungrazed grass even without the beneficial effects of fertilisation by goose droppings.[73] Thus the geese, by controlled grazing of their swards, are maximising available nitrogen content and digestibility of the grass. Body weights remain more or less stable during the first part of winter, often decreasing during the second half, especially when temperatures fall below 5 °C, when grass will no longer grow. Many barnacle geese are confined to low-grade feeding habitats, fearsome of moving to lusher pastures where there are human and other disturbances such as illegal shooting. On the Inishkea Islands it is the family parties that leave the islands first when food resources become scarce, especially in February and March. These successful parents take their broods to better feeding areas on the mainland and elsewhere, leaving behind the failed and non-breeders.

Increasing spring daylight and rising temperatures stimulate grass growth, the first flushes rich in proteins that are easily digested. Body reserves, indicated by body weight, increase rapidly – especially among females and first-winter birds – throughout April until their departure towards the end of the month, first to Iceland, where they stop in the northern valleys for about a month and top up their energy reserves, while some unpaired adults engage in courtship behaviour, before moving north again to their breeding cliffs in Greenland. It makes biological sense to arrive already paired, fertilised and ready to lay eggs, so that the breeding season can be fitted into the short Greenland summer.

The southward migration losses have not yet been calculated. The geese are legally protected in Greenland from 1 June to 15 August but nonetheless many are shot, especially in the Scoresby Sund region during the summer. The estimated kill by Inuit hunters is 500–1,000 barnacle and pink-footed geese (both species lumped together) each year during the 1980s.[74] In Iceland barnacles are legally protected from 15 March to 1 September, but recoveries of ringed birds show that the law is not always respected. Figures published by the Icelandic Wildlife Management Institute show the following barnacle goose kills: 1995, 1,876; 1996, 1,619; 1997, 2,629; 1998, 2,283; 1999, 1,376; 2000, 1,412.[75]

Protection from shooting was provided in Scotland in 1954 but a special Order in Council, made in 1955, permitted shooting between 1 December and 31 January on all Scottish islands west of longitude 5° W. This order was apparently made to facilitate one 'well placed' individual on Islay.[76] To begin with, about 200 birds were shot annually from the island population of some 5,000. Numbers killed rose to some 1,500 from a declining island population of some 13,000–18,000. Total protection was afforded to the geese under the Wildlife and Countryside Act 1981, but limited shooting on Islay continued under licences issued by the Scottish Office Agriculture, Environment and Fisheries Department. The licences were granted to protect crops from 'serious agricultural damage' by the geese. Over the period 1982–91 a mean of 792 (range 447–1,365) geese were shot annually, representing some 5.3 per cent of the birds then wintering on the island. Today there is reduced shooting (about 500 per winter from 2000) since the introduction of a scheme of payments to farmers based on a fixed sum per goose deemed to be causing damage. In Ireland the barnacle goose has been legally protected since 1976, although it was earlier protected at its principal haunt on the Inishkea Islands, Co. Mayo, where 50 per cent of the Irish wintering population occurred, from 1965 onwards by Game Birds Protection Orders made under the Game Preservation Act 1930.

With regard to the overall mortality from shooting of immature and adult barnacles in Greenland, Iceland and Scotland, the figures quoted above suggest an average annual kill of some 2,250 birds in the 1990s out of a total population of about 36,000 geese, a mortality of 6.3 per cent, representing nearly half of the total estimated annual mortality (see below).

Summer breeding success of the population is normally assessed on the wintering grounds by sample age-ratio counts – the proportion of first-winter birds in random samples of 50 birds, the convention for many years. Regular counting is carried out on their two principal wintering grounds, on Islay since 1958 and on the Inishkea Islands since 1961. On Islay the proportion of young birds in the winter flocks was a mean of 14 per cent for the 20-year period 1961–80, while on Inishkea it has been lower at 6.9 per cent over a 45-year period 1963–2007 (Fig. 144).[77]

FIG 144. Proportion of first-winter birds on Inishkea and Islay for breeding years 1969–2002. From J. Worden *et al.*, The Greenland population of the barnacle goose *Branta leucopsis* in Britain and Ireland 1956/57 to 2002/03 (WWT/JNCC, 2004). Reproduced with permission.

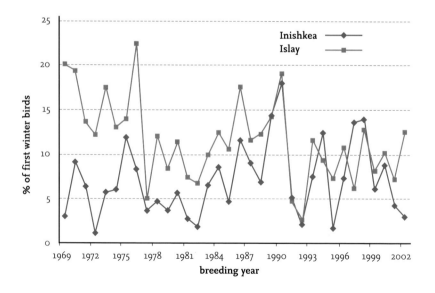

While age-ratio counts provide a key statistic for understanding population dynamics, they are subject to many potential sources of error, as discussed earlier in this chapter, including inconsistency between different observers, the timing of counts during winter, difficulty of distinguishing young birds from adults as the winter progresses due to progressive moulting, and other factors.

The second key winter statistic is mean brood size of successful adults. The number of goslings parents bring back to the wintering grounds is positively correlated with the proportion of first-winter birds in the winter flocks.

The data on the proportion of first-winter birds and mean brood size, along with total population counts, provide the basis for a model of the structure of the overall population. Any short-term anomalies arising from the open nature of the Inishkea wintering population, during which geese move to and away from the islands, will be smoothed out by the long run of continuous data. Taken over a long period the data can also be used to calculate mean annual mortality rates. During the period 1961–2005 the average structure of the population was approximately 6.9 per cent young birds in their first winter, the balance of 93.1 per cent being made up of geese more than one year old. Of these approximately 7.3 per cent were successful breeders, leaving a huge residue (85.8 per cent) that either did not attempt to breed – 'skippers' – or were unsuccessful breeders.

The large proportion of non-breeders and unsuccessful breeders determined on the wintering grounds is consistent with several observations made on the northeast Greenland breeding grounds.[78] In 1956, an expedition found that approximately 98 per cent of adults (including some immature birds) either did not breed or bred unsuccessfully, and only six successful breeding pairs (broods of three, three and five, plus twelve young that were taken to represent three pairs) were found among 340 pairs. In 1961 and 1963 approximately 89 per cent of 1,634 geese recorded were unsuccessful in producing young birds. In 1974 91 per cent of 2,178 geese observed did not attempt to breed or failed to rear young.

Thus the Greenland barnacle population is characterised by an unusually large proportion of non-breeding or unsuccessful adults, and low rates of productivity and mortality. The incidence of non-breeding is not so high in the Svalbard population, where each year between 11 and 26 per cent of the adults do not establish breeding territories, while 49 per cent of females and 35 per cent of adult males of a 1972 cohort died without recruiting young into the next generation and only 15 per cent of the birds contributed half the next generation's recruits.[79]

Mortality from shooting was formerly high in certain localities when the barnacle was a quarry species. Now protected throughout Britain and Ireland, overall mortality rates have declined to one of the lowest levels of all geese wintering in these islands. Using population census data, almost exclusively from Islay over the wintering periods 1985/86 to 1994/95, the annual adult survival rate was calculated at 86 per cent or, conversely, an annual mortality rate of 14 per cent.[80] A more reliable method, based on the non-return of one bird of a pair of individually marked geese and involving 603 'pair years', gave a figure of 83 per cent survival, an annual mortality rate of 17 per cent.[81] An even higher rate of survival of 92 per cent, or 8 per cent annual mortality, was calculated from population census data from the Inishkea Islands for the years 1962–2003.[82] However, we know that such estimates are subject to error due to the open nature of the population, with immigration and emigration throughout the winter, both on Inishkea and on Islay. An alternative estimate of annual mortality, based on annual resightings or loss of individually marked geese ringed on the Inishkea Islands, was 13 per cent, close to Islay's 17 per cent (individually marked birds) and 14 per cent (gross population counts).[83] Annual survival rates for adults and juveniles, once they have arrived back on Islay, are not significantly different.

More recent work carried out by Sarah Walley at Exeter University utilised a dataset based on 558 Inishkea Darvic-ringed adult geese, with 5,680 subsequent visual sightings between 1976 and 2006 used in the analysis. Using the capture–mark–recapture analysis programme MARK, she found there was no difference in mortality rates between males and females. Those that had been recorded at more than one wintering site over different wintering years had a survival probability of 0.91 (Table 86).[84]

TABLE 86. Percentage annual adult mortality rates at Islay, Argyll, and the Inishkea Islands, Co. Mayo.

METHOD OF CALCULATION	ANNUAL ADULT MORTALITY (%)	
	ISLAY, ARGYLL, 1985–94	INISHKEA, CO. MAYO 1962–2003
Resightings of ringed birds	17	13
Resightings of ringed birds (Walley)	—	9
Population counts	14	8

The establishment of accurate survival/mortality rates for different age cohorts of the barnacle geese is critical for the construction of a population dynamics model. But because survival/mortality and recruitment rates are constantly changing over time due to many different factors, coupled with the fact that the proportion of the mature geese successfully breeding varies from year to year, the construction of such models becomes something of a nightmare. However, what we do know is that mortality rates of the adults are relatively low compared with other goose species, somewhere between 8 and 13 per cent, and that the proportion of successful parents is similarly low, in the order of 7 per cent. Meanwhile, the overall population of Greenland barnacle geese has been increasing at the rate of some 4.5 per cent per annum over the past 50 years without any apparent density-dependent population checks as experienced by the Svalbard population. We have a mass of data on the individual breeding performance of individuals over their lifetime. These data show very spasmodic breeding success of the individuals. Hopefully within the next five years we will be able to better understand and model the population dynamics of this fascinating goose.

MALLARD

Mallard (Fig. 145), one of the most abundant and hunted duck in Britain and Ireland, are able to withstand considerable hunting pressures and high adult mortality rates to hold their overall population at a relatively stable level. Density-dependent population regulating factors have been demonstrated controlling the numbers in the population. These factors will operate most forcefully when shooting pressures do not remove the surplus ducks from the population. At present the environmental carrying capacity for mallard in Britain and Ireland would appear to have been reached. The index of wintering numbers in Britain, as determined by WeBS, has shown a slow decline since the early 1980s. The British maximum fell around 10 per cent from 2005/06 to 2006/07, its lowest level since 1977/78. Reasons for the slow decline are complex and include few winter immigrants, poor breeding success, fewer released birds and fewer cold-weather aggregations.[85]

Five key density-dependent factors concerning mallard population regulation were identified in a 16-year study carried out in Britain by David Hill:[86]

1 predation of nests;
2 mortality of chicks due to competition for food or space associated with territorial or other aggressive interactions;
3 loss of adults and juveniles through shooting during the autumn;
4 loss of adults and juveniles during the autumn and winter, probably due to competition for food;
5 reduced recruitment to territorial populations through competition for food or space, associated with territorial or other aggressive interactions.

FIG 145. This fine drake mallard is engaged in a leg stretch, a classic comfort movement. (Eric Soder/NHPA)

Of the above, the survival of the ducklings during their first two weeks of life, when they are feeding on emerging aquatic invertebrates, was the key factor determining total numbers of young birds in the autumn. During the first month after hatching in artificially created lakes in southern Britain, ducklings were found to spend 50 per cent of their time feeding, and within their first two weeks 80 per cent of this foraging time was spent chasing or picking up insects from either the surface of the water or lake-side vegetation.[87] Feeding experiments with newly hatched ducklings in an oligotrophic flooded gravel pit in Buckinghamshire showed a strong correlation between the growth of ducklings during their first four days and the number of invertebrates taken and total amount of protein eaten.[88] If large numbers of young birds are produced, and the survival of these is high, it was found that a greater proportion of birds are unable to establish breeding territories the following spring through excessive competition.[89] However, mortality of birds over the wintering period was also regulated in a density-dependent manner – the more birds there are in a specific locality the less food is available and the greater is the mortality.

Density-dependent factors can be modified by unpredictable variables such as fluctuating numbers of wildfowl – local and resident birds can be augmented by other mallard arriving either as hand-reared birds turned out for shooting or as genuine migrants, which may originate outside the country. During migratory movements large numbers may shift from a particular feeding area as food is eaten out. When food becomes sparse during the winter months there can be more localised, rather than true migratory movements. Thus these birds escape the density-dependent factors that were beginning to exert themselves for that specific locality. But escape from one locality and transferring to another feeding ground may compound such factors in the new location.

The clutch size is variable but normally 9–12 eggs. In a study of 180 mallard nests at Decoy Wood, Slimbridge, during 1961–63, the average size of early clutches was 12.6 eggs, later clutches 9.9 eggs. Hatching success of 2,293 eggs of wild nesting mallard at Slimbridge was 82.4 per cent, while the number of successful nests (hatching at least one egg) was 88.7 per cent.[90] In another study at Chew Valley Lake, north Somerset, 1957–62, the mean brood size of 80–140 nests was 6.9 (range 4.9–7.9) and the number of young reared per successful female was 4.7.[91] Broods from clutches of just under 9 eggs on a Buckinghamshire gravel pit declined from 6.5 at three days to just over 2 at fledging, representing a survival rate of 27 per cent when total brood losses were taken into account (Fig. 146). At Sevenoaks, Kent, in a gravel pit reserve managed specially for ducks, production per breeding pair varied between 0.8 and 5.3 young, with a mean of 3.3.[92] Using data from the national breeding waterfowl survey of Britain in 1980,

FIG 146. A brood of nine mallard ducklings will probably be reduced to two or three by the time they fledge. (Ernie Janes/NHPA)

a productivity of 2.7 young per pair was calculated.[93] The number of young will be further reduced throughout the autumn and winter by mortality rates greater than those experienced by adults, to a level of 1–1.8 per pre-breeding adult.

Estimates of the overall breeding success of mallard can also be obtained by studying the ratio of juvenile to adult wings collected from birds shot. Wings were collected in Britain over a 15-year period, 1966–80, and a high productivity of young birds was established – 64.3 per cent young birds in the winter flocks. This was the highest productivity figure of nine species of duck (six dabbling and three diving ducks) studied. However, these data almost certainly exaggerate the proportion of young birds, which are more likely to be shot than older ones.

Generally speaking, of all mallard eggs laid, fewer than half (range 30–50 per cent) will hatch or produce young birds to fledging (50–60 days after hatching). Those that do survive to fledging will be further reduced by mortality, at an approximate rate of 70 per cent, before they reach one year old, the time of first breeding. Thus only a tiny proportion of all eggs laid will come through to produce an adult bird ready to breed. But to maintain a stable population each pair of mallard would only need to produce, on average, one young bird per year that will survive to breed.

In the 1980s David Hill calculated that the maximum sustainable yield (the numbers of birds that could be killed) from mallard populations in England was 29 per cent of the *post-breeding* population.[94] It is hard to reconcile this with an annual adult mortality in northwest Europe of 48 per cent as calculated by Hugh Boyd, who also concluded that the mallard is not capable

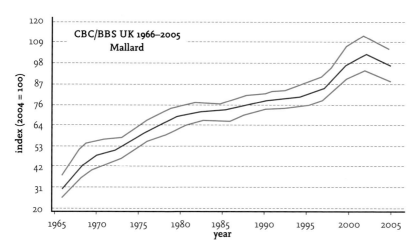

FIG 147. Breeding population changes for mallard in the UK 1966–2005. From S. R. Baillie *et al.*, Breeding birds in the wider countryside: their conservation status 2007 (BTO, 2007). Reproduced with permission.

of sustaining its population if adult losses exceed a rate of approximately 55 per cent. The mortality rate for younger birds is much higher, estimated by Boyd for birds in their first year after fledging at about 69 per cent.[95] Another study estimated mortality rates in north Somerset at 57 per cent for adults and 76 per cent for first-year birds over the period 1948–59.[96] Other calculations of mortality rates by Hohn in the 1940s gave an annual mean adult loss of 65.3 per cent during the first year after ringing, with an average length of further survival after ringing of 1 year and 2 months. Mallards ringed as young had a mortality rate of 88.2 per cent during their first year of life, with an average period of survival of 4.5 months after ringing.[97]

With such an apparent difference between the estimated productivity (64 per cent young in winter flocks) and mortality rates (48 per cent by Boyd) one would have expected the mallard population to have increased over the period 1966–2005, which it did, according to the BTO's Common Birds Census and Breeding Bird Survey results (Fig. 147). The breeding population steadily increased from the mid-1960s until 1996 and from then onwards to 2002, the increase accelerated with the overall assessment of the long-term trend of a rapid increase. There has been a decline since 2003 that continued to 2006. Large-scale releases of hand-reared birds are thought to have been partly behind the population increases.

FIG 148. Mallard drakes exhibit a high level of aggressiveness when fighting over mates, territory and food. Fighting birds frequently grab each other by the back of the neck. (Bill Coster/NHPA)

However, the full annual story is more complicated, because winter populations, according to the annual indices prepared from data obtained from WeBS counts in Britain during September to March, have been in a slow continuous decline since the beginning of the 1980s. Numbers rose marginally in 1998/89, but thereafter continued their decline to the latest WeBS figures for 2006/07.[98]

Five key density-dependent factors have already been mentioned above. With regard to productivity of the breeding stock, the following four factors would also be operating: (1) emigration from crowded areas, reducing competition for nest sites and food; (2) an increasing number of non-breeding adults; (3) reduced hatching success through interference; and (4) reduced rearing success through competition for food (Fig. 148). With regard to mortality inflicted by shooting, if it is below the threshold level for holding the population in a stable situation then numbers will be controlled by natural mortality operating through the density-dependent mechanisms already discussed.

The overwinter loss in Britain is density-dependent, i.e. the more birds present in a particular area in September the more die or leave the area.[99] Thus mallard numbers wintering in Britain are now limited by habitat availability, whereas for other duck species such as gadwall, northern shoveler, Eurasian teal and Eurasian wigeon this is not the case, as shown by the fact that populations over the long term (25 years) have increased.

As the movements and migrations of mallard can have such negative or positive impacts in population regulation, information on these variables is essential for a better understanding of the population dynamics. British and Irish breeding mallard are mostly sedentary. The majority of recoveries of birds ringed in these islands as juveniles and adults during the breeding season (May to August) show little emigration, with most birds recovered within 20 km of the ringing location after breeding. Movements of hand-reared mallard are less extensive than those performed by wild birds. In Britain 80 per cent of recoveries were within a 10 km radius of the ringing location.[100] At Carton Estate, Co. Kildare, 738 hand-reared pulli and 60 adult mallard were ringed in July 1967. By August 1977 some 84 had been recovered, of which 68 per cent had been shot within a 10 km radius of Carton.[101] Despite being of comfort to the wildfowlers who reared and released the birds, the addition or 'leakage' of these into the wild population raises issues of the introduction of possibly undesirable non-wild genes into the population. The introduction of these additional birds also intensifies the density-dependent factors operating on the wild population.

There is an increase in the number of mallard in Britain and Ireland from the autumn onwards, as shown by results from WeBS and I-WeBS. Recoveries of ringed birds suggest that up to 75 per cent of our winter population is made up of immigrants from the Continent. This is based on mallard ringed during the winter in Britain and Ireland, with 638 out of 863 recoveries coming from the Continent during the breeding season. These birds came from Fennoscandia, Russia, Poland, Denmark, Germany, the Netherlands, Belgium and France. The decline in the numbers wintering in Britain and Ireland may be due to a reduction in the number of continental immigrants. During the 1950s and 1960s the proportion of British and Irish winter-ringed mallard recovered on the Continent was above 50 per cent. This had fallen to less than 25 per cent by the 1980s.[102] The decline in the number of winter immigrants could be associated

FIG 149. There is an increase in the number of mallard in Britain and Ireland from the autumn onwards. (R Sorensen & J Olsen/NHPA)

with the reasons that are behind the decline of Bewick's swans and European white-fronted geese wintering in these islands.

Recoveries of British- and Irish-ringed birds from Poland, Denmark and Germany show a significant imbalance of males (75 per cent of all recoveries), due to abmigration – males that have paired up with 'foreign' wintering females and are subsequently 'dragged' out of Britain to the female's country of origin. Some Icelandic birds, from an estimated breeding population of 5,000 pairs, also winter in Britain and Ireland, as indicated by ringing recoveries.

CONCLUSION

In this chapter some aspects of the population dynamics of three contrasting species of wildfowl have been presented. The key issue raised has been the role played by density-dependent effects in the mute swan, barnacle goose and mallard. For each species complex factors are at work controlling the populations, and some are density-dependent. Both the mute swan and the barnacle goose are 'capital breeders', which impacts on their feeding ecology in a different way to that of the mallard, an 'income breeder'. Mallard would have a more flexible approach than geese and swans towards preparation of their body reserves for breeding.

The mute swan can accommodate variations in mean annual adult mortality rates between 6 and 18 per cent while maintaining a stable population. When adult mortality rates are at the high end there are sufficient reserves of immature birds waiting in the wings to enter the population, either locally or as immigrants, to balance any deficit of lost adults. A high proportion of swans could also start breeding early, in their third year if necessary. A large amount of breeding potential, which could be triggered into action, also resides with the mature but non-breeding 'skippers'. The reduction of breeding productivity noted in the CBC and WBS surveys – small clutch sizes and higher rates of egg and chick 'failures' – suggests that the population is beginning to be affected by density-dependent factors. It might be expected that breeding productivity will decline further if overall population numbers continue to rise.

The case of the Greenland-breeding barnacle goose is somewhat the same but different in many details. There is no evidence, as yet, of density-dependent regulation despite the continued growth of the population. However, if the population continues to increase at the rate it has been doing then density-dependent factors will inevitably start to regulate the populations. The Svalbard breeding population is already regulated by density-dependent factors, principally concerning the availability of food to young birds.

The mallard is a more complex case, and different from the mute swan and barnacle goose. Large numbers of hand-reared birds are annually added to the population each summer, but it has been clearly shown that recruitment rates of young birds into the population, thus affecting total numbers, are controlled by density-dependent factors operating during the first two weeks of the ducklings' lives as they compete for food resources. The balance between recruitment and mortality is also complicated by the large numbers of continental winter immigrants and the effects of abmigration.

CHAPTER 7

Wildfowl Conservation

BOUT 60 YEARS AGO THE STATUS and distribution of many wintering wildfowl in the UK and Ireland was very different to that of today. Many species were scarce, and more were struggling for their survival. Several were suffering from excessive shooting pressure, but more importantly their specialist wetland habitats were under threat from drainage for flooding relief, land reclamation for agriculture, other development activities and pollution. There were few wildfowl refuges and sanctuaries where the birds were secure from shooting and other disturbances, and where they could feed on their particular foods undisturbed.

The shift in the fortunes of wintering wildfowl, and many of the early successes in wildfowl conservation in Britain and Ireland, arose from the educational and scientific endeavours of Sir Peter Scott and his colleagues in the Wildfowl & Wetlands Trust, originally established in 1946 as the Wildfowl Trust on the banks of the River Severn at Slimbridge, Gloucestershire. The extensive collections of birds both at Slimbridge and later at other WWT centres were visited by many thousands of people, providing close encounters with wildfowl that were not generally available in the wild (Figs 150 and 151). Peter Scott emerged as the patron saint of wildfowl through his work on radio and television, and in print. He stimulated enormous public interest in wildfowl and the issues concerning their conservation, not only in the UK and Ireland but also worldwide.

A more enlightened approach by hunters gradually evolved, while new national and local wildfowl reserves were established by government, local authorities and, more recently, by County Naturalists' Trusts. Worked-out gravel pits provided opportunities for the creation of new wildfowl habitats, as did the development of new reservoirs, amenity lakes and ponds throughout the UK.

FIG 150. Mute swans, whooper swans and other wildfowl being fed at the WWT Centre at Caerlaverlock, Dumfriesshire. (Joe Blossom/NHPA)

FIG 151. WWT Welney Wildfowl Reserve, part of the Ouse Washes system. The area is an SPA as well as an SAC and a Ramsar site. The WWT established its wetland centre here in 1970 and now manages 250 hectares of wetlands. (Martin Senior)

The major beneficiaries of these habitats were the dabbling ducks – northern shoveler, garganey, gadwall and Eurasian teal – and among the diving duck smew and tufted duck. Egyptian geese, greater Canada geese, the re-established population of greylag geese and the naturalised population of barnacle geese also found safe and secure nesting habitats in these wetlands. Ironically it was the success of these and other wildfowl species under a more conservation-conscious society that was to lead to problems of conflict later.

ENVIRONMENTAL CONFLICTS

The increase in numbers of many wildfowl, especially the swans and geese, has given rise to conflicts with agriculture to the point where many geese are now regarded as pests in some localities and are subject to control measures. The issue has been exacerbated by a decline in the availability of traditional feeding habitats and the discovery by geese and swans of new and more nutritious agricultural crops. Many of these issues were discussed at an important international workshop on *Farmers and Waterfowl* held in the Netherlands in 1991.[1]

A classic case is the pink-footed goose. Its traditional main winter habitat is thought to have been salt marsh, but from the late nineteenth century the geese moved inland to feed on farmland. In recent decades birds have fed on valuable agricultural crops, such as fertilised grassland and cereals, and have frequently been accused of reducing crop yields and puddling soils. In autumn, when they feed on fields containing post-harvest root crops, such as potatoes and waste sugar beet, they do no harm, but during midwinter and spring, when these sources have been exhausted, and when the birds need to improve their body condition, they graze on growing cereals and come into direct competition with livestock for the spring growth of grass.

With regard to Greenland barnacle geese, salt marshes, coastal pastures and islands were traditionally selected as favoured feeding areas, but more recently the requirement for short-cropped sward has been met by intensively managed grasslands. The geese feed on grasses, herbs, leaves, white clover stolons and seeds, as well as barley and oat stubbles, spilt grain and under-sown grass. Over recent years there has been an increase in the use of agricultural fields as feeding grounds. Most conflict occurs on Islay and several of the other inhabited islands off the north and west coasts of Scotland. In response to these increasing agricultural conflicts Scottish Natural Heritage (SNH) established Goose Management Schemes on Islay and on South Walls, Orkney, in 1993. Farmers now receive payments from SNH related to goose damage. The increasing numbers of barnacle geese in the Lissadell area, Co. Sligo, are beginning to cause some anxiety among farmers.

The West Atlantic light-bellied brant goose was traditionally an intertidal feeder, dependent upon sea grasses, algae and salt-marsh plants including fescues and saltmarsh-grass. Inland feeding was first noted in Ireland and Iceland during the mid-1970s, and since then feeding on grasslands has increased steadily, especially in east and southeast Ireland, with 25 per cent of the population spending a large proportion of its time foraging on managed grasslands. In Dublin, light-bellied brant geese can be seen feeding on one of their most bizarre sites, inland parks and playing fields (Fig. 152). In a few areas, most notably on the Wexford Slobs, Co. Wexford, Dungarvan Harbour, Co. Waterford, and Strangford Lough, Co. Down, the geese feed on cereal crops, both waste in autumn stubbles and spring seed, and on waste potatoes. Interestingly, however, they return to the salt marshes to feed prior to their spring migration.

FIG 152. West Atlantic light-bellied brant geese feeding on a rugby pitch, Dublin. (David Cabot)

Introduced species can also give rise to problems. For example, there are about 90,000 greater Canada geese in Britain and their numbers are increasing by 9 per cent each year. They were first introduced in Britain during the seventeenth century to embellish wildfowl collections, and to provide food and hunting. Large numbers of these geese can disperse the breeding avifauna of some lowland freshwater ecosystems and may contribute to water eutrophication and ground erosion. They can also be agricultural pests. The situation in Ireland is not so acute as the goose population has not reached a critical threshold prior to explosive growth. In the African–Eurasian Waterbird Agreement's draft conservation guidelines on avoidance of introductions of non-native migratory waterbird species, greater Canada geese are listed as being of medium biodiversity risk, as 'negative impacts on biodiversity are little understood.'[2] Similar issues arise with the feral greylag goose population, which is also increasing at a rapid rate, especially in southern England.

The daily intake of fish by the sawbills – the red-breasted merganser and common merganser – has been calculated to be in the order of 20–33 per cent of their body weight. Red-breasted mergansers appear to select salmon parr to smolts, as they like to eat smaller fish. It has been calculated that adults consume 200–250 g of fish a day. On Windermere, Cumbria, the average summer population of red-breasted mergansers consumes 2.6 tonnes of several different fish species per year.[3] See Chapter 3 for further details.

CURRENT TRENDS IN WINTERING WILDFOWL IN BRITAIN AND IRELAND

Numbers of wintering ducks, geese and swans in the UK have, overall, increased greatly over the last three decades. Numbers rose steadily from the mid-1970s to the late 1990s as wildfowl populations responded to improved protection of wetlands internationally, better regulation of hunting and changes in agricultural practices. From 2000 numbers have on average stabilised, and during the winter of 2006/07 they experienced a decrease – though it is too early to say if this was a temporary blip or the beginning of a downward trend.[4] For Ireland the picture is less clear, due to the absence of long-term data.

Long-term (25 years) and short-term (10 years) trends in the numbers of wintering wildfowl in the UK have been derived from data collected by WeBS and the National Swan and Goose monitoring programme, as presented in the most recent national report (2007) on *The State of the UK's Birds*. Only short-term trends (9 years) are available for Ireland (Table 87).[5]

TABLE 87. Trends in the numbers of wintering wildfowl in the UK and Ireland.

SPECIES/ SUBSPECIES/ POPULATION	PERCENTAGE LONG-TERM TREND (25 YEARS) UK	PERCENTAGE SHORT-TERM TREND (10 YEARS) UK	PERCENTAGE SHORT-TERM TREND (9 YEARS) IRELAND
Mute swan	111	22	−1
Bewick's swan	12	−30	*
Whooper swan	270	124	3
Pink-footed goose	238	19	—
European white-fronted goose	−60	−56	—
Greenland white-fronted goose	n/a	−20	−2
Icelandic greylag goose	−1	−6	2
Northwest Scotland greylag goose	n/a	81	—
Re-established greylag goose	900	92	—
Canada goose	178	37	—
Greenland barnacle goose	n/a	41	6
Svalbard barnacle goose	217	62	—
Dark-bellied brant goose	26	−27	—
West Atlantic light-bellied brant goose	n/a	14	6
Svalbard light-bellied brant goose	210	92	—
Common shelduck	−11	−13	1
Eurasian wigeon	71	9	−3
Gadwall	396	52	0
Eurasian teal	62	23	0
Mallard	−30	−12	−2
Northern pintail	−4	18	−2
Northern shoveler	57	26	−3
Common pochard	−39	−41	−7
Tufted duck	2	5	8
Greater scaup	−6	42	—

TABLE 87. – *Cont.*

Common eider	−29	−3	—
Common goldeneye	−1	−26	−6
Red-breasted merganser	−1	−36	−3
Common merganser	8	−30	—
Ruddy duck	443	56	—

Data from Eaton *et al.*, 2008; Lynas *et al.*, 2007. Long-term trends (25 years) are the percentage changes between the smoothed index values for 1979/80 and 2004/05. Short-term (10 years) trends are the percentage changes between the smoothed values for 1994/95 and 2004/05. * = no data available as too few sites. National monitoring of Greenland white-fronted geese, Northwest Scotland greylag geese, Greenland barnacle geese, West Atlantic light-bellied brant geese started later than for other species, so only 10-year trends are shown.

Our winter visiting wildfowl are only one side of the equation; the other is the contribution made by our national breeding populations. Therefore it is important to know how the breeding populations are faring.

CURRENT TRENDS IN BREEDING WILDFOWL IN THE UK

The breeding trends of six common wildfowl species in the UK have been monitored since 1970 by the BTO (Table 88), initially under the Waterways Bird Survey (WBS) and more recently by the Breeding Bird Survey (BBS).[6]

TABLE 88. Trends in the UK breeding populations of six wildfowl species.

SPECIES	PERCENTAGE LONG–TERM TREND (1970–2006)	PERCENTAGE BBS TREND (1994–2007)
Mute swan	151 [a]	0
Greylag goose	n/a	220
Canada goose	n/a	149
Shelduck	220 [a]	27
Mallard	98	27
Tufted duck	15 [b]	67

Data from Eaton *et al.*, 2008. BBS, Breeding Bird Survey.

[a] The trend during the period covered solely by the Common Birds Census

TABLE 88. – *Cont.*

(prior to 1994) may be unrepresentative of the UK due to geographical or habitat-related bias.

b Long-term trend 1975–2006.

It is clear that none of these six species is of conservation concern. On the contrary, the opposite could be said for the Canada and greylag geese, which have almost reached pest levels in some UK locations. However, it is interesting that while the number of wintering mallard in the UK is declining, for reasons discussed in Chapter 6, the UK breeding population is holding its own. It may not be a coincidence that mallard, shelduck and tufted duck have the largest duck breeding populations in the UK and Ireland while at the same time they seem to be prospering the most successfully of all ducks. Other dabbling ducks – Eurasian teal, northern pintail, Eurasian wigeon, common pochard, northern shoveler – all have small and vulnerable breeding populations. For example, there are *c.*11–51 pairs of pintail in the UK and 30–40 in Ireland, and the teal breeding population is *c.*1,500–2,600 pairs in the UK and 350–555 in Ireland. During the winter some 30,000 pintail visit the UK and 1,235 winter in Ireland, while some 192,000 teal winter in the UK and a further 45,000 in Ireland. Thus the contribution that our breeding ducks make to the overall wintering populations in these islands is small. While we might be able manage our small breeding populations to some degree, when it comes to the number of birds wintering in these islands we are very much at the mercy of factors outside our control.

How should we set our conservation priorities? What diversity and abundance of ducks, geese and swans are we looking for in Britain and Ireland? What numbers and species and races should we aspire to host during the winter, or indeed as breeding birds? Where would we like them to be distributed? What is the best way to manage them? Provision of protected natural habitats, creation of new habitats by physical means, or changing agricultural practices? Restriction of shooting by shorter hunting seasons, or by the introduction of bag limits set in relation to the previous season's breeding success? Should we do more to protect the breeding habitats of our breeding duck rather than focusing on looking after our many winter visitors (Fig. 153)? Winter visitors can be fickle – already the numbers of European white-fronted geese, Bewick's swans and dark-bellied brant are declining because of 'short stopping' on the European mainland, something outside our control. If global warming is holding back Arctic and northern breeding species we may be left with our small native breeding populations of duck as our only wintering wildfowl.

FIG 153. Lady's Island Lake, Co. Wexford. Located in southeast Ireland, this 466 ha shallow brackish coastal lagoon with a shingle/sand barrier has one of the highest breeding densities of wildfowl in Ireland, including gadwall, garganey and northern shoveler. There is also a feral greylag goose breeding population. Recent years have seen reduced wintering wildfowl numbers, attributed to a decline of tasselweed. (Alyn Walsh)

Apart from attempting to manage our indigenous breeding populations and winter visitors there are questions that arise from introduced and feral populations – not only the Canada and greylag geese mentioned above but also the snow goose, Egyptian goose, and of course ruddy duck. The ecological ramifications of these 'new' wildfowl are big. They interbreed with other closely related species to produce hybrids that are often fertile. Hybrid offspring are usually conspicuous. But shuffling the genes can sometimes be less obvious – if, for example, feral greylags breed with migrant birds from Iceland or with the native Scottish population. Is it possible that undesirable genes could be introduced to 'wild' birds that may alter their migration patterns and other types of behaviour? Or is this just the process of evolution, the creation of variation upon which natural selection will get to work? This was certainly not behind the thinking of the UK ruddy duck eradication programme (because of the potential threat to Spanish breeding white-headed ducks). If ruddy ducks, why not also eliminate other introduced wildfowl species that may disturb the genetics of closely related family members?

In Table 89 a distinction is drawn between the conservation status of resident breeding populations and winter visitors. The evaluation criteria are tortuous but necessary to tease out those species on the Amber List.

CONSERVATION STATUS OF WILDFOWL IN BRITAIN AND IRELAND

Leading governmental and non-governmental conservation organisations in the UK recently reviewed the bird populations of conservation concern in *The Population Status of Birds of Conservation Concern in the UK 2002–2007*.[7] A similar review was carried out in Ireland in 2007.[8] The results from both reviews are incorporated into Table 89. Species were classified for inclusion onto one of three lists: **Red** (high conservation concern), **Amber** (medium conservation concern) and **Green** (those that fulfil none of the Red or Amber criteria):

- **Red List (high conservation concern).** The criteria for inclusion are: (i) globally threatened according to the criteria of the International Union for the Conservation of Nature (IUCN); (ii) historical population decline in the UK during 1800–1995; (iii) rapid (> 50 per cent) decline in UK breeding populations; and (iv) rapid contraction of UK breeding range over last 25 years.
- **Amber List (medium conservation concern):** those wildfowl with an unfavourable conservation status in Europe; those whose population has declined historically but has made a substantial recent recovery; rare breeders; and those with internationally important or localised populations.
- **Green List:** those that fulfil none of the above criteria.

The black scoter is the only breeding wildfowl species that qualifies for the Red List, on account of the rapid (> 50 per cent) contraction of its UK and Irish breeding range over the past 25 years.

Qualification for inclusion in the Amber List (Table 89) is based on the following criteria:

HDrec: Historical population decline during 1800–1995, but recovering population size has more than doubled over the last 25 years.

BDMp: Moderate (25–49 per cent) decline in UK or Irish breeding population over the last 25 years.

BDMr: Moderate (25–49 per cent) contraction of UK or Irish breeding range over the last 25 years.

WDMp: Moderate (25–49 per cent) decline in UK or Irish non-breeding population over the last 25 years.

SPEC 2 or 3: Species with unfavourable conservation status in Europe (SPEC = Species of European Conservation Concern), as determined by the European Commission specialist working groups.

BR: Five-year mean of 1–300 breeding pairs in UK or Ireland.

BL: ≥ 50 per cent of UK or Irish breeding population in 10 or fewer sites, but not BR.

WL: ≥ 50 per cent of UK or Irish non-breeding population in 10 or fewer sites.

BI: ≥ 20 per cent of European breeding population in UK or Ireland.

WI: ≥ 20 per cent of northwest European non-breeding population in UK or Ireland.

TABLE 89. Amber list of wildfowl in the UK and Ireland.

SPECIES	HDrec	BDMp	BDMr	WDMp	SPEC 2 or 3	BR	BL	WL	BI	WI
Mute swan					Ir				UK	Ir
Bewick's swan					UK Ir			UK Ir		UK
Whooper swan				UK Ir				UK Ir		UK Ir
Bean goose								UK		
Pink-footed goose								UK		UK
White-fronted goose			E (UK)					UK Ir		G (UK)
Greylag goose						UK		UK Ir		UK
Barnacle goose					UK Ir			UK Ir		UK
Brant goose					UK r			UK Ir		UK Ir
Common shelduck								UK Ir		UK
Eurasian wigeon								UK Ir		UK
Gadwall					UK Ir	Ir	UK	Ir		UK
Eurasian teal	Ir									UK

TABLE 89. – *Cont.*

SPECIES	HDrec	BDMp	BDMr	WDMp	SPEC 2 or 3	BR	BL	WL	BI	WI
Northern pintail					UK Ir	UK Ir		UK Ir		UK
Garganey					UK Ir	UK Ir				
Northern shoveler						Ir				UK
Common pochard					Ir	Ir		Ir		UK
Tufted duck					Ir	Ir		Ir		
Greater scaup					UK Ir	UK Ir		UK Ir		
Common eider								UK Ir		
Long-tailed duck							UK			
Velvet scoter					UK Ir			UK		
Common goldeneye						UK Ir		UK Ir		
Common merganser						Ir				

UK, United Kingdom; Ir, Ireland; E, European race of white-fronted goose; G, Greenland race of white-fronted goose.

UK NATIONAL BIODIVERSITY PLAN (NBP)

In response to the Convention on Biological Diversity, signed at the Rio Earth Summit in 1992, the UK Government has prepared a National Biodiversity Plan (NBP) to protect its biological resources, embracing many thousands of plant and animal species including wildfowl. The plan identifies priority species and subspecies, and sets out conservation targets for them. Separate NBPs have been prepared for Wales, Scotland and Northern Ireland by their respective Executives. The NBP documents are quite remarkable not only for their concepts, language and graphic designs, but for integrating nature in an overall land-use planning context, rather than treating species or subspecies from a stand-alone position – which is, unfortunately, often the case with more traditional conservation planning. Species Action Plans (SAPs) have been published for Red List species such as the breeding population of black scoter.[9] The Scottish Executive has prepared its own SAP for the Greenland white-fronted goose because of the important guardian role Scotland plays for the wintering geese. The various NBPs are reviewed on a regular basis by relevant Government agencies, advised by stakeholder groups. These national plans with associated SAPs have great potential to secure conservation objectives for a wide range of flora and fauna. The plans are transparent, well presented and educative instruments in themselves, and they provide genuine stakeholder participation.

In Ireland the National Parks and Wildlife Service (NPWS) of the Department of the Environment, Heritage and Local Government launched the NBP in April 2002.[10] Like its UK counterpart, it provides a framework for the conservation of biological resources and contains a commitment to 91 actions including the preparation of SAPs. So far, the corncrake is the only bird species for which an SAP has been prepared.

One swan, three geese and two diving ducks were identified as priority species in the UK NBP in 1995, based on one or more of the criteria below, and they remain on the priority list as of June 2007:

a species or subspecies designated as being at risk of extinction in Europe;
b species or subspecies that have declined in the UK by at least 50 per cent over the past 25 years (severe decline);
c species or subspecies for which there are other valid reasons for qualification including a lack of recovery from the decline that led to the inclusion on the UK BAP priorities in 1995.

The NBP priority species are:
- Bewick's swan (a)
- European white-fronted goose (a)
- Greenland white-fronted goose (b)
- Dark-bellied brant goose (a)
- Greater scaup (b)
- Black scoter (b and c)

Species of high conservation concern (Red List)

Black scoter

The black scoter is a nationally threatened breeding species in the UK. It is the only species of breeding waterfowl on the Red List, because of its small and declining breeding population. The UK Government has therefore prepared an SAP for the black scoter with Scottish Natural Heritage as the official government contact point and RSPB and WWT as joint lead partners.[11] A national survey of

UK breeding black scoters in 2007 found that the population had fallen by 45 per cent since the previous survey in 1995, to just 52 breeding pairs. The population on Islay has virtually disappeared, and there are few birds left on Tayside, with the result that the species is more or less restricted to a few large lochs in the Inverness Glens and smaller lochs scattered across the Caithness and Sutherland Flows. The rate of decline since 1995 – 4.4 per cent a year – is one of the most severe recorded for a UK bird in recent years and, given its tiny size, we are in danger of losing the UK breeding population of black scoters. Research into the cause of this decline is required urgently if it is not to join other species on the 'black list' of birds that have become extinct as breeding species in the UK.[12] Implementation of the black scoter SAP is overseen by a steering group comprising governmental and non-governmental conservation organisations, local authorities and landowners, chaired by WWT.[13]

The species is extinct in Northern Ireland. In the Republic of Ireland breeding numbers declined by 44 per cent from 1967 to an estimated 50 pairs in 1999. It is possible that if it is not now (2008) extinct only a very few pairs may remain. The main threats to the survival of the black scoter breeding in Scotland come from their principal terrestrial predator, the feral mink. Mink kill nesting adults and young scoters. Many nesting areas and sites in northern Scotland have been obliterated by new coniferous plantations. The water run-off from these afforested areas has increased the acidity in nearby lakes, to the detriment of the quality and quantity of scoter food. The birds are also vulnerable to coastal oil pollution during the winter. Climate change may also be a factor contributing to the black scoter declines in Ireland and Scotland.

The black scoter SAP has the following objectives:

- in Scotland, increase the breeding population to at least 100 pairs by 2008;
- in Scotland, maintain at least the existing breeding range;
- regain black scoter as a breeding species in Northern Ireland;
- maintain the current range and distribution of moulting black scoters;
- maintain the current range and distribution of wintering black scoters.

The inclusion of the black scoter on the Red List raises some questions about priorities and conservation policy. There are an estimated 1.6 million black scoters in western Siberia, Scandinavia and Iceland and the population is considered stable. It is not a species under global or even national threat outside these islands. In Scotland and Ireland they are at the southern extremity of their breeding range. It can be difficult for some northern species to hold on to these southern outposts, especially if climate change is a factor influencing breeding redistribution. In other words, is the black scoter doomed as a breeding species in Scotland and Ireland, on its way out? If it is, can we justify our effort to halt its decline? Should we not rather be devoting scarce financial and manpower resources to other wildfowl that stand a better chance of remaining and improving their status as breeding species in the UK and Ireland? Eurasian teal, Eurasian wigeon, northern shoveler, northern pintail and common pochard might be better bets for SAPs. These are, of course, Amber List species – but don't they deserve more? By the time criterion (b) – see above – qualifies a species to be red-listed it is perhaps too late to attempt to arrest the decline and turn the population around.

Species of moderate conservation concern with declining wintering populations (Amber List)

Not all the 24 amber-listed wildfowl species and subspecies will be discussed here. I will focus on the five species/populations that have been identified as priority species in the UK's NBP.

Bewick's swan

The decline in numbers wintering in the UK and Ireland is probably due to 'short stopping' of the swans on the Continent, attracted by better food and feeding conditions. The annual index, calculated from WeBS data, peaked in 1996/97, since when numbers have been in decline. During 2006/07 the British maximum numbers were half those of the previous winter and the lowest for 30 years (Fig. 154). The relatively few severe winters on the Continent in recent years have also allowed the swans to stay on the European mainland without pushing westwards. Global warming may be a significant factor in the Bewick's swans 'short stopping'. However there is some evidence that the overall breeding population may be declining, and this could be a contributory factor.[14] There would seem to be very little that we can do to encourage more Bewick's swans to winter in these islands other than praying for severe continental winters.

European white-fronted goose

As with the Bewick's swan, the decline of the European white-fronted goose as a winter visitor to the UK is probably a case of 'short stopping', the geese preferring to winter on the Continent. The annual index and trend computed from WeBS shows a dramatic decline since 1969/70. During 2006/07 numbers fell by around 70 per cent to their lowest level so far. On the other hand, the flyway population (1 million birds) is in a healthy, stable state. In the western parts of Britain, including the most important wintering site at Slimbridge, numbers have been declining in recent years, with several sites being abandoned. No sites

FIG 154. Wildfowl on the Ouse Washes at Welney, Norfolk. During the winter of 2006/07 this single site held up to 99 per cent of the total British wintering population of Bewick's swans. (Alan Williams/NHPA)

FIG 155. Roundstone Bog complex, Co. Galway: traditional haunt of the Greenland white-fronted goose. (Robert Thompson/NHPA)

in the UK support internationally important numbers of these geese. Hunting is the most significant cause of mortality for this species in the Western Palaearctic, and it remains a popular quarry for hunters throughout its wintering range. The 2006/07 winter flocks had 16.7 per cent young and the average brood size was 1.9, both lower than the average for the past ten years. In view of the hunting pressure in Europe the population would need to be more productive to counterbalance shooting mortality. Again, as with the case of the Bewick's swan, there would appear little that we can do to encourage a larger wintering population in the UK, if the declining numbers are due to 'short stopping'.

Greenland white-fronted goose
The world population peaked at approximately 35,600 birds in the spring of 1999, and since then it has been in steady decline, falling to some 24,800 birds in spring 2006 at the time of the last complete census. Low breeding success during recent years (an average of 10.6 per cent young birds in the winter flocks 2006/07, almost half the normal productivity for the past 15 years) has been blamed for the decline. There are some indications, however, that for the total population the rate of decline may be slowing down. Competition for food and breeding sites in west Greenland from recently arrived and more aggressive Canada geese may be the key to declining breeding success. Shooting of passage birds in Iceland was banned from the autumn of 2006. The annual bag in Iceland prior to 2007 was approximately 3,000 geese, enough to seriously impact the population, which was already struggling with reduced breeding success. Traditional feeding occurred on bogland habitats in the UK and Ireland (Fig. 155), but in recent years the geese have increasingly shifted onto intensively managed grassland, especially in the most important wintering areas in Ireland (Wexford Slobs) and in Scotland (Islay). Goose management schemes were initiated on Islay in 1992/93 by Scottish Natural Heritage to alleviate the conflict that had arisen due to damage to agricultural crops through goose grazing.

Scottish Natural Heritage included the goose as a priority species in its SAP under the NBP in January 2007. It was prioritised for management action because of its significant decline and because it is the focus of conflicts where coexistence is difficult to achieve. The five-year SAP aims to:
- halt the decline in the Greenland white-fronted goose population by 2010;
- maintain and, where possible, enhance the wintering range of the Greenland white-fronted goose in Scotland.

The actions envisaged to achieve the above objectives are:
- contribute to the updating and implementation of a management plan ('Flyway Plan') which covers the United Kingdom, Ireland, Iceland and Greenland (the plan was first drawn up in 1992 but never ratified);
- continue to develop and implement local goose management schemes;
- continue the comprehensive census programme across Scotland, and ensure that results are properly disseminated.

As the world population of this goose winters in the UK and Ireland alone, and the species is not yet subject to any 'short stopping', we can possibly assist the geese while they are with us by implementing practical goose management schemes at a local level. This is a project that could positively assist the conservation of this goose.

FIG 156. Brant geese silhouetted against the moon as they fly to roost. (Bill Coster/NHPA)

Dark-bellied brant goose

Since peaking in 1993/94, the annual index of the dark-bellied brant goose, as calculated from WeBS data, declined until winter 2003/04, since when it has increased notably in the subsequent three winters (Fig. 156). During 2006/07 the maximum counted British wintering population was 5 per cent higher than in the previous year and the highest since 2000/01. The decline in the numbers wintering in the UK and throughout the whole flyway population (314,000 in the early 1990s and then down to 200,000 in 2002) is related to a series of poor breeding seasons since the early 1990s. The mortality rate for the population has been estimated at 15 per cent, and unless productivity of young birds exceeds this by a good margin then the population will once again decline.

Following the rapid population growth in the mid-1970s the geese started to move inland from coastal areas to feed on grassland, winter cereals and oilseed rape. On their autumn arrival in the UK the geese travel through a series of food habitats – first they crop eelgrass and the seaweed *Enteromorpha* on the mudflats and in shallow estuarine and coastal waters, then grasses in the salt marsh, and finally inland to the richer agricultural foods. During the spring return to the breeding grounds they exploit fresh growth in the salt marshes. In the UK, conflict with agriculture arises in Norfolk, Suffolk, Essex and along the south coast of England when the geese forage on winter cereals and oilseed rape. To lessen the conflict locally, nature reserves are managed for these birds, providing alternative feeding areas, often in combination with scaring operations outside the reserve.

Greater scaup

There are probably fewer than five pairs breeding spasmodically in northern Scotland. There were two known breeding occurrences in Northern Ireland during the late 1990s. It is probably our rarest breeding duck. It is not clear what conservation actions could assist this species in the UK and Ireland. The preparation of an SAP should clarify the issues.

With regard to the numbers visiting Britain and Ireland, the annual index and trend of wintering greater scaup in the UK has more or less remained stable since the steep decline after 1973/74. The decline seen in the past few years is within the range of fluctuation over this period. The west European flyway population is stable at about 310,000 birds, although decreases (due to unknown causes) have been noted in northwest Europe.

COOPERATION BETWEEN EUROPEAN UNION STATES

Both Britain and Ireland are special places for wildfowl. We are at the end of major flyways of waterfowl migrating southeast, south and southwest for the winter from Canada, Greenland, Iceland, northern and central Europe, as well as from the Arctic extending from northern Norway eastwards into Russia and Siberia. And during severe weather conditions on the Continent large numbers of wildfowl are driven west and southwest to the UK and Ireland to escape the grip of freezing conditions that make feeding almost impossible. In spring and summer, also, smaller numbers of other wildfowl species come from Europe and Africa to breed in these islands.

Because birds migrate long distances, traversing many different states, it is not sufficient to protect them over just part of their range. At the administrative and political levels, more than anything else a key EU Directive on Wild Birds (79/409/EEC) – adopted in 1979 and now applicable in all EU states – obliged member states to provide stricter protection for all wild birds, especially for those classified as endangered in Europe. The Wild Birds Directive identifies, in its Annex 1, species that are rare, in danger of extinction or vulnerable to changes

FIG 157. Martin Mere, Lancashire. Part of a former lakeland and coastal area extending to some 1,300 ha of the Lancashire coastal plain during the seventeenth century, Martin Mere SPA covers 119 ha. Notable species here are whooper and Bewick's swans, pink-footed geese and northern pintail. (Richard Taylor Jones)

in habitat and that need protection. The wildfowl included in Annex 1 are Bewick's swan, whooper swan, Greenland white-fronted goose, lesser white-fronted goose, barnacle goose, red-breasted goose, ruddy shelduck, marbled duck, ferruginous duck, Steller's eider, smew and white-headed duck. The Directive requires member states to designate Special Protection Areas (SPAs) for the listed rare and vulnerable species, for regularly occurring migratory species, such as ducks, geese and waders, and for wetlands, especially those of International importance, which attract large numbers of migratory birds each year (Fig. 157). The objective is to protect birds at their breeding, feeding, roosting and wintering areas. The establishment of a network of important sites for wildfowl and other birds is mandatory. While many SPAs have coincided with existing designated national nature reserves and other protected area designations, there is no doubt that, without the Wild Birds Directive and the 'encouragement' of the EU to provide effective protection for species and habitats, Ireland, the UK and most other EU member states would have been less enthusiastic in establishing SPAs.

The Habitats Directive (92/43/EEC), adopted in 1992 and now applicable to all EU states, provides for the creation of Special Areas for Conservation (SACs), many of which, while not strictly established for the protection of wildfowl, protect habitats of European significance that are, *inter alia*, of great importance to wildfowl, especially a wide diversity of wetlands that are important as feeding areas. The value of these two directives is enhanced by the legal procedures available to the EU Commission, whereby member states can be taken to the European Court and punished as well as being politically embarrassed if they fail to implement provisions in the two directives.

Under the Wild Birds Directive an Internationally important site qualifies if 1 per cent of the population of a species uses the site, or if more than 20,000 birds regularly use the site. The UK has designated 256 SPAs, covering 1.61 million hectares, of which approximately half are wildfowl wetlands (Table 90). The SPA network is of crucial importance for the protection of wildfowl both in the UK and in Ireland. In the Republic of Ireland a total of 131 SPAs, covering 0.28 million hectares, had been designated to December 2008 (Fig. 158). A further 25 sites will soon be designated.[15] The declared SACs and SPAs make up the largest coherent network of protected sites in the world.[16] There is no doubt that the creation of a network of SPAs and SACs has played a significant role in the conservation of wildfowl on national and European scales. The legal enforcement powers of the EU Commission to ensure member states create a sufficient number of sites, and to ensure that they are properly protected, has undoubtedly made the Natura 2000 network a great success. None of the conventions and agreements discussed below is supported with such powers of enforcement.

FIG 158. North Slob, Co. Wexford. The Wexford Wildfowl Refuge covers 194 ha of a total of 1,000 ha of reclaimed estuarine mud that is now empoldered farmland. The Refuge is an SPA as well as a Ramsar site. This is the world's most important winter site for nearly a third of the world population of the Greenland white-fronted goose. (Alyn Walsh)

TABLE 90. Special Protection Areas in the UK as at 25 September 2008.

| COUNTRY | CLASSIFIED SPAS | | POTENTIAL SPAS |
	NUMBER OF SITES	SITE AREA (HA)	NUMBER OF SITES
England	78	671,436	2
England/Scotland	1	43,637	0
England/Wales	2	37,748	1
Northern Ireland	14	108,204	2
Scotland	144	626,780	3
Wales	17	123,007	0
United Kingdom	**256**	**1,610,812**	**8**

From **www.jncc.gov.uk/page-1399**. Accessed 26 December 2008.

INTERNATIONAL CONVENTIONS AND AGREEMENTS

There are several international conventions and agreements that are beneficial to the conservation of wildfowl, and they will only be briefly mentioned here. The Ramsar Convention, exclusively aimed at the protection of wildfowl wetlands, is the most important.

The Bern Convention
The Convention on the Conservation of European Wildlife and Natural Habitats (the Bern Convention) was adopted in Bern, Switzerland in 1979, and came into force in 1982. Its principal aims are to ensure the conservation and protection of over 500 wild plant and more than 1,000 animal species and their natural habitats. Obligations are placed on the contracting parties, but without serious penalties for non-compliance.[17] The European Community implemented the Bern Convention through the adoption of EU Directive 79/409/EEC.

The Bonn Convention
On the wider conservation scale the Convention on the Conservation of Migratory Species of Wild Animals (also known as CMS or the Bonn Convention) aims to conserve terrestrial, marine and avian migratory species throughout their range. It is an intergovernmental treaty (**www.cms.int/about/treaties.htm**), concluded under the aegis of the United Nations Environment Programme, concerned with the conservation of wildlife and habitats on a global scale.[18]

The African–Eurasian Waterbird Agreement (AEWA)
The largest agreement developed so far under CMS auspices, the African–Eurasian Waterbird Agreement (AEWA) focuses on migratory waterbirds. It was concluded in 1995 in The Hague, and came into force in November 1999. AEWA adopts a unique flyway approach to waterbird conservation, focusing on 235 species ecologically dependent on wetlands for at least part of their annual cycle, including not only wildfowl but also many species of pelicans, storks, flamingos, waders, terns and gulls.[19]

The Ramsar Convention
The Ramsar Convention on Wetlands, signed in Ramsar, Iran, in 1971, is an intergovernmental treaty to protect wetlands. The 156 contracting parties have designated 1,676 wetlands covering some 150 million hectares.[20] There is a high

degree of overlap between Ramsar sites and SPAs. There are currently
146 designated Ramsar sites in the UK (Table 91), and 45 sites in the Republic
of Ireland with a surface area of 66,994 ha as of December 2008 (Fig. 159).

TABLE 91. Designated and proposed Ramsar sites in the UK as at 31 August 2007.

COUNTRY	DESIGNATED		PROPOSED
	NUMBER OF SITES	SITE AREA (HA)	NUMBER OF SITES
England	66	317,212	3
England/Scotland	1	43,637	0
England/Wales	3	39,336	0
Northern Ireland	19	88,093	4
Scotland	50	283,083	0
Wales	7	11,366	0
United Kingdom	**146**	**782,727**	**7**

From **www.jncc.gov.uk/page-161**. Accessed 26 December 2008.

FIG 159. Inner Galway Bay, Co. Galway. Part of a Ramsar site of some 11,905 ha,
consisting of the shallow sheltered part of a large sea bay with many intertidal inlets and
sheltered bays separated by low ridges of glacial deposits. This is an important wintering
site for light-bellied brant geese, Eurasian wigeon, Eurasian teal, northern shoveler, mute
swan and red-breasted merganser (nearly 7 per cent of the national population).
(David Cabot)

CONCLUSION

In summary, wildfowl have generally prospered well during the past 30 years. Increased public interest and concern, coupled with improving knowledge of the status, distribution and changing fortunes of geese, ducks and swans, better research information and results from various monitoring programmes, have provided a political and scientific stimulus for the relevant governmental institutions in both the UK and Ireland to take positive conservation action. The EU Birds and Habitat Directives have both been important 'drivers' in the struggle to better manage European wildfowl populations, especially through the Commission's encouragement of the UK and Irish governments. However, not all issues of wildfowl conservation have been resolved.

We need constant review and clearer definitions of what our conservation objectives should be. We need to review the criteria employed to identify endangered wildfowl. By the time some criteria have identified an endangered or red-listed species it may well be too late to arrest the decline. Years ago a friend told me that we shouldn't be trying to save a species that was on its way out, such as the red-necked phalarope in Ireland (now gone, despite excellent management efforts funded by the EU Life programme and BirdWatch Ireland) and the black scoter in Scotland (now on its way out, which may be related to global warming, among other threats). He said we should be looking at relatively common wildfowl, and he drew an analogy with common birds such as the house sparrow – they were extremely numerous at the time of our discussions and in no apparent danger. He said we should be preparing conservation programmes for them. He was right, but at the time few were prepared to listen. The house sparrow is now a red-listed species of high conservation concern.

Perhaps we need more lateral thinking, and even heretical thoughts. Perhaps we should start pondering the possible demise of our indigenous populations of teal, shoveler and pochard. For wintering wildfowl perhaps we should focus more on those for which we can provide practical management schemes within the UK and Ireland, and cease to worry about the 'short stoppers'. Wildfowl populations are extraordinarily dynamic in most aspects of their lives. We need to be equally dynamic in our approaches to their needs. We need to develop our techniques for monitoring their populations, movements and migrations, we need a better understanding of the population dynamics of individual species, and, overall, we need a continuous review of the effectiveness of conservation actions that have been undertaken. The exciting aspect of all this is the role that individuals can play. Without the vast army of volunteers who participate in collecting essential WeBS and I-WeBS data, and without the active participation of the non-governmental conservation organisations, we would never have reached the point where we are now. So get involved with WeBS or I-WeBS and other relevant field work, and join a conservation organisation to support its activities and to provide more membership muscle power in negotiation with sometimes slow-moving government agencies.

British Ornithologists' Union (BOU) and Irish Rare Birds Committee (IRBC) Lists of Wildfowl Recorded in Britain and Ireland

A total of 56 species of wildfowl on the British and Irish Lists (Categories A, B, C) are detailed below, with information on Category E status where relevant. I have taken the liberty of adding (1) the lesser Canada goose and (2) the muscovy duck, as both are under review by the BOU's Records Committee (BOURC) and/or the IRBC, and there is a good possibility that both may be upgraded, to Category A and Category C1 respectively. The 56 species listed here have been recorded in the UK as of 23 July 2008 and in Ireland up to the end of August 2008 (apart from the lesser Canada goose and muscovy duck) as regular winter visitors, vagrants or breeding species – whether naturally occurring or as non-indigenous escapes from wildfowl collections in self-sustaining wild populations.[1]

In 1997 the BOU categorisation of species recorded in Britain was revised to assist protection under national wildlife legislation, especially of naturalised species. Category C was expanded to allow species with different histories to be distinguished, Category D was reduced in scope, and a Category E was introduced to enable local and national recorders to monitor escaped species. These categories have also been adopted by the IRBC. A new Category F was established in 2007 to deal with historical records from AD 1800 back to 700,000 BP. The current categories are as follows:

A: Species that have been recorded in an apparently natural state at least once since 1 January 1950.

B: Species that were recorded in an apparently natural state at least once between 1 January 1800 and 31 December 1949, but have not been recorded subsequently.

C: Species that, although introduced, now derive from the resulting self-sustaining populations.

C1: *Naturalised introduced species* – species that have occurred *only* as a result of introduction.

C2: *Naturalised established species* – species with established populations resulting from introduction by man, but which also occur in an apparently natural state.

C3: *Naturalised re-established species* – species with populations successfully re-established by man in areas of former occurrence.

C4: *Naturalised feral species* – domesticated species with populations established in the wild.

C5: *Vagrant naturalised species* – species from established naturalised populations abroad.

C6: *Former naturalised species* – species formerly placed in C1 whose naturalised populations are either no longer self-sustaining or are considered extinct.

D: Species that would otherwise appear in Category A except that there is reasonable doubt that they have ever occurred in a natural state. Species placed in Category D only form no part of the British List and are not included in the species totals.

E: Species that have been recorded as introductions, human-assisted transportees or escapees from captivity, and whose breeding populations (if any) are thought not to be self-sustaining. Species that occur only in Category E form no part of the British or Irish List. In the list below, an E indicates the existence of a Category E population of the species in addition to its membership of Category A, B or C. Where birds of known or presumed captive origin have bred in the wild in Britain or Ireland, this is designated E*.

The classification of the Anseriformes used here follows that proposed by Livezey in 1986 and later refined in 1997.[2] Under this classification 55 genera and 173 species have been identified. The way in which the wildfowl have been arranged by Livezey is intended to reflect their evolution as revealed by cladistic analysis of their morphological characters. It is possible that this classification may be modified in future years with further molecular research. But in the meantime Livezey's classification has been adopted with some minor modifications by at least three recent major texts.[3] Here I have used Livezey's classification of families, subfamilies and tribes, but within each tribe I have followed the familiar BOU order of species[4] (as used in Chapter 3).

I have used the agreed International English names (Gill & Wright) for the listed species. In addition to the BOU/IRBC Category codes, each species (or in some cases each subspecies) is assigned one or more of the following BOU status codes:

RB – resident breeder
HB – hybrid breeder
MB – migrant breeder
WM – winter migrant
NB – naturalised breeder
PM – passage migrant
CB – casual breeder
SM – scarce migrant
FB – former breeder
V – vagrant

ORDER ANSERIFORMES

Family Anhimidae (screamers)
Genera 2
Species 3
Recorded in Britain/Ireland 0

Family Anseranatidae (magpie goose)
Genera 1
Species 1
Recorded in Britain/Ireland 0

Family Anatidae
Subfamily Dendrocygninae

Tribe Dendrocygnini (whistling ducks)
Genera 1
Species 8
Recorded in Britain/Ireland 0

Tribe Thalassornithini (white-backed duck)
Genera 1
Species 1
Recorded in Britain/Ireland 0

Subfamily Anserinae (geese and swans)

Tribe Cereopsini (musk duck)
Genera 1
Species 1
Recorded in Britain/Ireland 0

Tribe Anserini (true geese)
Genera 3
Species 16
Recorded in Britain/Ireland 11

- Bean Goose *Anser fabalis* **AE**; **WM** (*fabalis* & *rossicus*)
- Pink-footed Goose *Anser brachyrhynchus* **AE***; **WM**
- Greater White-fronted Goose *Anser albifrons* **AE***; **WM**
- Lesser White-fronted Goose *Anser erythropus* **AE*** (**E*** Britain only); **V**
- Greylag Goose *Anser anser* **AC2C4E***; **RB**, **NB** & **WM**
- Snow Goose *Anser caerulescens* **AC2E***; **V** (*caerulescens* & *atlanticus*)
- Greater Canada Goose *Branta canadensis* **AC2E*** (**A** Ireland only); **V**
- Lesser Canada Goose *Branta hutchinsii* **C2E***; **WM**. Under review by
  BOURC and IRBC for consideration as category A in Britain and Ireland
- Barnacle Goose *Branta leucopsis* **AC2E***; **WM**
- Brant Goose *Branta bernicla* **AE**; **WM** (*hrota* & *bernicla*) and **SM** (*nigricans*)
- Red-breasted Goose *Branta ruficollis* **AE*** (Britain only); **V**

Tribe Cygnini (swans)
Genera 3
Species 8
Recorded in Britain/Ireland 3

- Mute Swan *Cygnus olor* **AC2**; **RB**
- Tundra Swan *Cygnus columbianus* **A**; **WM** (*bewickii*) and **V** (*columbianus*)
- Whooper Swan *Cygnus cygnus* **AE***; **CB** and **WM**

Subfamily Stictonettinae (Freckled duck)
Genera 1
Species 1
Recorded in Britain/Ireland 0

Subfamily Tadorninae

Tribe Plectopterini (spur-winged goose and comb ducks)
Genera 2
Species 3
Recorded in Britain/Ireland 0

Tribe Tadornini (shelducks and sheldgeese)
Genera 6
Species 15
Recorded in Britain/Ireland 3

- Egyptian Goose *Alopochen aegyptiaca* **C1E*** (Britain only); **NB**
- Ruddy Shelduck *Tadorna ferruginea* **BDE*** (**E*** Britain only); **V**
- Common Shelduck *Tadorna tadorna* **A**; **MB**, **RB** & **WM**

Tribe Merganettini (torrent and steamer ducks)
Genera 3
Species 6
Recorded in Britain/Ireland 0

Subfamily Anatinae (true ducks)

Tribe Malacorhynchini (pink-eared duck and Salvadori's duck)
Genera 2
Species 2
Recorded in Britain/Ireland 0

Tribe Anatini (dabbling or surface-feeding ducks)
Genera 11
Species 60
Recorded in Britain/Ireland 13

- Muscovy Duck *Cairina moschatta* **E*** (Britain only). Under review by BOURC for consideration as Category **C1**
- Mandarin Duck *Aix galericulata* **C1E***; **NB**
- Eurasian Wigeon *Anas penelope* **AE***; **RB** and **WM**
- American Wigeon *Anas americana* **AE**; **SM**
- Gadwall *Anas strepera* **AC2**; **NB**, **RB**, **MB** and **WM**

- Eurasian Teal *Anas crecca* **AC2**; **RB**, **WM** and **PM**
- Green-winged Teal *Anas carolinensis* **A**; **SM**
- Mallard *Anas platyrhynchos* **AC2C4E***; **RB**, **NB**, **FB** and **WM**
- American Black Duck *Anas rubripes* **A**; **V** & **HB**
- Northern Pintail *Anas acuta* **A**; **RB** or **MB**, and **WM**
- Garganey *Anas querquedula* **A**; **MB** & **PM**
- Blue-winged Teal *Anas discors* **AE**; **V** & **HB**
- Northern Shoveler *Anas clypeata* **A**; **MB**, **WM** & **PM**

Tribe Aythyini (diving ducks – pochards and scaup)
Genera 4
Species 17
Recorded in Britain/Ireland 9

- Red-crested Pochard *Netta rufina* **AC2E*** (**E*** Britain only); **NB** & **SM**
- Canvasback *Aythya valisineria* **AE** (Britain only); **V**
- Common Pochard *Aythya ferina* **AE***; **MB** or **RB**; **WM** and **PM**
- Redhead *Aythya americana* **AE**; **V**
- Ring-necked Duck *Aythya collaris* **AE**; **SM**
- Ferruginous Duck *Aythya nyroca* **AE**; **SM**
- Tufted Duck *Aythya fuligula* **A**; **RB**, **WM** & **PM**
- Greater Scaup *Aythya marila* **A**; **CB**, **WM** and **PM** (*marila*)
- Lesser Scaup *Aythya affinis* **A**; **V**

Tribe Mergini (sea ducks)
Genera 10
Species 22
Recorded in Britain/Ireland 16

- Common Eider *Somateria mollissima* **A**; **RB** and **WM** (*mollissima*); **V**
  (*borealis*)
- King Eider *Somateria spectabilis* **A**; **SM**
- Steller's Eider *Polysticta stelleri* **A** (Britain only); **V**
- Harlequin Duck *Histrionicus histrionicus* **A** (Britain only); **V**
- Long-tailed Duck *Clangula hyemalis* **A**; **CB** and **WM**
- Black Scoter *Melanitta nigra* **A**; **RB** or **MB**, **WM** and **PM**
- American Scoter *Melanitta americana* **A** (Britain only); **V**
- Surf Scoter *Melanitta perspicillata* **A**; **SM**
- Velvet Scoter *Melanitta fusca* **A**; **WM** & **PM**

- Bufflehead *Bucephala albeola* **A**; **V**
- Barrow's Goldeneye *Bucephala islandica* **AE**; **V**
- Common Goldeneye *Bucephala clangula* **A**; **RB**, **WM** and **PM**
- Smew *Mergellus albellus* **A**; **WM**
- Hooded Merganser *Lophodytes cucullatus* **AE**; **V**
- Red-breasted Merganser *Mergus serrator* **A**; **RB** and **WM**
- Common Merganser *Mergus merganser* **A**; **RB** and **WM**

Tribe Oxyurini (Stiff-tailed ducks)
Genera 4
Species 9
Recorded in Britain/Ireland 1

- Ruddy Duck *Oxyura jamaicensis* **C1E***; **NB**

Non-Native and Non-Self-Supporting Feral Wildfowl Recorded in Britain and Ireland

This Appendix lists non-native and non-self-supporting feral populations of ducks, geese and swans in Britain and Ireland as recorded by WeBS reports 2001/02–2006/07. Supplementary information has been incorporated from the BOU's 2005 report on changes to Category C of the British List (Dudley, 2005). The species listed in this appendix form no part of the official British and Irish Lists, with most falling into Category E. It should be noted that some of the species recorded may not be free-flying but wing-clipped or pinioned. Those species that nest with their own kind and are known or presumed to have originated from a captive origin are marked **E***.

All occurrences of the wildfowl listed below relate to escapes from captivity, and all records relate to Britain unless otherwise stated. It is possible that other Category **D** and **E** species are at large in Britain and Ireland in addition to those listed below. The list that follows is based only on WeBS and I-WeBS reports, and on information obtained in the BOU report mentioned above.

Fulvous Whistling Duck *Dendrocygna bicolor* (**E**). Tropical America, Africa and Indian subcontinent. One at Godmanchester Gravel Pit, Cambridgeshire (September 2003); two at Chichester Harbour, Sussex (February 2004); one at Walland Marsh, Kent (April–June 2004); four at Chichester Gravel Pits, Sussex (November 2006).

Lesser Whistling Duck *Dendrocygna javanica* (**E**). Tropical Asia and East Indies. Single, Poole Harbour, Dorset (September 2006 and January 2007). Only previous WeBS record Severn Estuary, Gloucestershire, in 1994/95.

FIG 160. Fulvous whistling duck. (Joe Blossom/NHPA)

Swan Goose *Anser cygnoides* (**E***). East Asia. The domesticated version of the swan goose, known as the Chinese goose, was reported from 16 sites in 2001/02 and 10 in 2002/03. Peak numbers in 2004/05 were double those of the previous winter. In 2006/07 maximum number was 17 at eight British sites, with Diss Mere, Suffolk, holding largest number, up to five throughout the year. Peaks of four and three at Ellesmere Lakes and Oerley Reservoir, Staffordshire. respectively. One in Northern Ireland, Outer Ards shoreline, Co. Down.

FIG 161. Swan goose. (Ann & Steve Toon/NHPA)

Bar-headed Goose *Anser indicus* (**E***). South Asia. Peak of 28 at 45 sites throughout Britain 2006/07. Singles in Northern Ireland (Belfast Lough) and Channel Islands. Highest count at Deben Estuary, Suffolk (12 in October 2006), followed by Kilmardinny Loch, Dunbarton/Argyll (four throughout year) and Blenheim Park, Oxfordshire (three in July/August). Very few breeding attempts but some evidence suggests that they are slowly becoming more established. One to two pairs bred in 2001 and up to five pairs in 2002.

Ross's Goose *Anser rossii* (**DE***). Central Arctic Canada. Singles reported from seven sites in 2001/02 and five in 2002/03. Recorded from five sites in 2004/05 – two on Tees Estuary, Cleveland (July); one at Tyninghame Estuary, Lothians (August); one between Ardrossan and West Kilbride, Ayrshire & Arran (September/October). One at Orwell Estuary, Suffolk, and at Hamford Water, Essex, was probably the same bird. During 2006/07 only two birds at Skiffkey Fen, north Norfolk coast (September 2006) – regular in the area since 2002/03.

FIG 162. Bar-headed goose. (Ken Kinsella)

FIG 163. Ross's goose. (Ken Kinsella)

FIG 164. Emperor goose. (Bill Coster/NHPA)

FIG 165. Hawaiian goose. (Ann & Steve Toon/NHPA)

Emperor Goose *Anser canagicus* (**E***). Alaska and northeastern Siberia.
Total 22 birds during 2006/07, with a peak count of 21 at South Walney Island,
Morecambe Bay, Lancashire. Singles at Derwent Water, Cumbria (July 2006) and
Lackford Lakes Nature Reserve, Suffolk (October 2006). Has occasionally bred –
two pairs bred at South Walney Island, and one pair in Surrey.

Hawaiian Goose *Branta sandvicensis* (**no classification**). Hawaiian Islands.
Singles at Lower Derwent Ings, Yorkshire (1996/97), and Harewood Lake, West
Yorkshire (2003/04). One, Leisure Lakes, Lancashire (January 2006).

Coscoroba Swan *Coscoroba coscoroba* (**E**). Southern South America and
Falkland Islands. One, Burton Marsh, Dee Estuary (November 2005). Second ever
WeBS record since one on River Usk, south Wales (2000/01).

FIG 166. Coscoroba swan.
(Ken Kinsella)

Black Swan *Cygnus atratus* (**E***). Australia and New Zealand. Increasing
numbers and sites recorded by WeBS from 1992 (13 birds at eight sites) to 2006
(52 birds at 73 sites). Peak counts during 2006/07 were at Abberton Reservoir,
Essex (eight, August), Arnot Park Lake, Nottinghamshire (seven, November), and
at Ramsbury Lake, Wiltshire (six, March). Four were in Northern Ireland (two at
Loughs Neagh and Beg and a further two at Strangford Lough). Nine widely
scattered breeding pairs (with nine broods) across the length of Britain from
Orkney to Devon in 2001, up from four breeding and three non-breeding pairs
recorded in seven counties during 2000. Only two breeding pairs – only one
young seen – in 2002, in Greater Manchester and Sussex.

FIG 167. Black swan. (Dave Watts/NHPA)

Black-necked Swan *Cygnus melanocoryphus* (**E**). Southern South America and Falkland Islands. The first ever WeBS record was of four at Ramsbury Lake, Wiltshire (October 2004). Two at Ramsbury Lake during October 2006.

Cape Shelduck or **South African Shelduck** *Tadorna cana* (**E**). Southern Africa. Recorded in 2003/04 from Mersey Estuary, Cheshire, and Ellesmere Lakes, Shropshire. In 2004 there were singles at Doddington Pool, Cheshire (July); the Dee Estuary (September) and Colne Estuary, Essex (October). Three at Cley Marsh, north Norfolk coast (October 2005); one at Crosslanes, Shropshire (March 2006).

Australian Shelduck *Tadorna tadornoides* (**E**). Southern Australia. One, Benacre Broad, Suffolk, September 2000.

FIG 168. Black-necked swan. (Haroldo Palo Jr/NHPA)

FIG 169. Australian shelduck. (Daniel Zupanc/NHPA)

FIG 170. Paradise shelduck, male. (Mark Bowler/NHPA)

FIG 171. Orinoco goose. (Jean-Louis le Moigne/NHPA)

Paradise Shelduck *Tadorna variegata* (**E**). New Zealand. One, Par Sands Pools and St Andrews Road, Cornwall (summer 2003); probably the same bird throughout 2004/05.

Orinoco Goose *Neochen jubata* (**E**). South America. One, Roath Park Lake, Glamorgan (October and December 2005). First time recorded by WeBS.

Magellan Goose or **Upland Goose** *Chloephaga picta* (**E***). Southern South America and Falkland Islands. One, Merryton Ponds, Strathclyde (March 2000, from 1998/99). One, location not specified (September 2001 to March 2003). One, Auchlochan Pond, Lanarkshire (April 2004).

FIG 172. Magellan goose, Tierra del Fuego. (Martin Harvey/NHPA)

FIG 173. Wood duck. (Ken Kinsella)

FIG 174. Chiloe wigeon. (Ken Kinsella)

Wood Duck or **Carolina Duck** *Aix sponsa* (**E***). North America. Maximum of eight birds at ten sites in 2006/07. Highest total six birds throughout the year at Stanton Lake, Wiltshire. First WeBS record for Northern Ireland at Belfast Lough, March 2006. Breeding of birds of captive origin has occasionally been recorded.

Chiloe Wigeon *Anas sibilatrix* (**E**). Southern South America and Falkland Islands. Singles in July, September and December 2003/04. During 2004/05 singles at Harewood Lake, West Yorkshire (July and August), Blagdon Lake, Somerset (June), and the Dee Estuary (August). Two at Blagdon Lake (July 2005); two at Man Sands Ley, Devon (September 2005); one at Camel Estuary, Cornwall (June 2005). During 2006/07 two at Otter Estuary, Devon (September), and singles reported from four other sites in Britain.

Falcated Duck or **Falcated Teal** *Anas falcata* (**DE**). Eastern Asia. One, Minsmere, Suffolk, June 2002.

FIG 175. Falcated duck. (Ernie Janes/NHPA)

FIG 176. Baikal teal. (Ken Kinsella)

Baikal Teal *Anas formosa* (**DE**). Eastern Asia. One, Minsmere, Suffolk, December 2001. As announced in the BOURC's April 2007 report (*Ibis* **149**, 625–54), all British records of the Baikal teal are now under review in the light of the discovery of stable-isotope-based evidence for vagrancy to western Europe (Denmark, November 2005). One was shot at Crome, Co. Fermanagh, on 13 January 1967.

Speckled Teal *Anas flavirostris* (**E**). South America. Total of four birds in 2002/03: two at Bramshill Park Lake, Hampshire (December–January), and singles at Woburn Park, Bedfordshire (September), and on the Orwell Estuary, Suffolk (November). Two at Woburn Park in May 2004. Two at Bramshill Park Lake, November 2004 to February 2005 – seen here annually since early 1998. One at Elton Reservoir, Lancashire (October 2006), and another at Belvide Reservoir, Staffordshire (November 2006).

FIG 177. Speckled teal. (Laurie Campbell/NHPA)

FIG 178. Cape teal. (Ken Kinsella)

Cape Teal *Anas capensis* (**E**). Sub-Saharan Africa. One, Stanton Lake, Wiltshire (March 2004).

Chestnut Teal *Anas castanea* (**E**). Southern Australia. Two, Liden Lagoon, Wiltshire (October 2003; one in January 2004). During 2004/05 there were singles on the north Norfolk coast (November) and Scotney Pit and Dungeness Gravel Pits, Kent (June 2005). Two at Liden Lagoon in August 2005.

Yellow-billed Pintail *Anas georgica* (**E**). South America, Falkland Islands and South Georgia. Single, Dee Estuary, England/Wales (August 2002).

FIG 179. Chestnut teal. (Patrick Fagot/NHPA)

FIG 180. Yellow-billed pintail. (Roger Tidman/ NHPA)

White-cheeked Pintail or **Bahama Pintail** *Anas bahamensis* (**E**). West Indies, Galapagos Islands and South America. Recorded almost every year since 1993. Four singles, 2002. Maximum of ten birds, 2003/04. During 2004/05 recorded at four sites. During 2005/06 there were two at Stanton Lake, Wiltshire, in August, with singles in May and June, and one at Doddington Pool, Cheshire (February–June).

FIG 181. White-cheeked pintail. (Ken Kinsella)

FIG 182. Red-billed teal. (James Warwick/NHPA)

Red-billed Teal *Anas erythrorhyncha* (**E**). Southern and eastern Africa. Nine together at Harrow Lodge Park, Greater London (April 2002), and a single at Harewood Lake, West Yorkshire (July 2002). Two, January 2004.

Silver Teal *Anas versicolor* (**E**). South America. Two, Connaught Water, Essex (November 2002), and singles at Dee Estuary, England/Wales (October 2001), and in the Thames Estuary, Essex (August 2002).

Cinnamon Teal *Anas cyanoptera* (**E***). North and South America. One, Frensham Little Pond, Surrey (September and October 2002). One at Lower Windrush Valley Gravel Pits, Oxfordshire (January 2004).

FIG 183. Silver teal. (Bill Coster/ NHPA)

FIG 184. Cinnamon teal. (N. A. Callow/ NHPA)

FIG 185. Red shoveler
(Ken Kinsella)

FIG 186. Ringed teal. (Ann & Steve Toon/NHPA)

Red Shoveler *Anas platalea* (**E**). Southern South America. One at Connaught Water, Essex (October 2001).

Ringed Teal *Callonetta leucophrys* (**E**). South America. Two on Warren Pond, Epping Forest, London (October 2001); singles on Taw–Torridge Estuary, Devon (December 2001); Port Meadow, Oxfordshire (March 2002); Hanningfield Reservoir, Essex and Stanley Park Lakes, Liverpool (autumn 2002), and the Cotswold Water Park East, Gloucestershire & Oxfordshire and Mote Park, Kent (February 2003). One at Liden Lagoon, Wiltshire (June 2004). Maximum of three 2003/04 with singles at Hanningfield Reservoir; Cresswell Pond, Northumberland; Outwood Swan Sanctuary, Surrey, and Cotswold Water Park East. During 2005/06 singles at Liden Lagoon (July–August), Vyne Floods, Hampshire (October and December), and Coate Water, Wiltshire (February and March). During 2006/07 singles were present at six sites, at two of the above and four new sites.

Maned Duck *Chenonetta jubata* (**E**). Australia. One, Petworth Park Lakes, West Sussex (March 2003).

FIG 187. Maned duck. (A.N.T. Photo Library/NHPA)

FIG 188. Marbled duck. (Mike Lane/NHPA)

Marbled Duck *Marmaronetta angustirostris* (**DE**). Mediterranean and western Asia. Single birds during 2006/07 – first time ever recorded by WeBS – at Christchurch Harbour, Dorset (September/October), and Holland Marshes, Essex (December). There is always the outside possibility that genuine vagrants could reach Britain and Ireland from southern Europe.

New Zealand Scaup *Aythya novaeseelandiae* (**E**). New Zealand. One, Connaught Water, Essex (January to March and November 2002; also April, October and December 2004). One, Chew Valley Lake, Somerset (September and November 2004).

FIG 189. New Zealand scaup. (David Tomlinson/NHPA)

FIG 190. Rosybill.
(Ken Kinsella)

FIG 191. White-headed duck. (Melvin Grey/NHPA)

White-headed Duck *Oxyura leucocephala* (**DE**). Mediterranean and western Asia. Singles at Little Paxton Gravel Pits, Cambridgeshire (September 2003); Chew Valley Lake, Somerset (October 2003). One at Tees Estuary, Cleveland, at Dormans Pool (September 2004), and at Saltholm Pools (October 2004). One at Hilfield Park Reservoir, Hertfordshire (January/February 2005 and August to November 2005).

Rosybill or **Rosy-billed Pochard** *Netta peposaca* (**E**). South America. One, north Norfolk coast (April 2002).

Argentine Bluebill *Oxyura vittata* (**E**). Southern South America. One, Colwick Country Park, Nottinghamshire (March 2000); one, Melton Country Park, Leicestershire (September 2000, 2001/02, and July/August 2003). Probably the same bird at Netherfield Gravel Pits, Nottinghamshire (September/October 2004 and April, July and October 2005).

Endnotes

Chapter 1

1   Benton *et al.*, 2005.
2   Howard, 1964.
3   Delacour & Mayr, 1945; Johnsgard, 1978.
4   Livezey, 1986, 1997.
5   Amman, 1937

Chapter 2

1   Armstrong, 1958, p. 225.
2   Heron-Allen, 1928.
3   O'Meara, 1982.
4   Vincent of Beauvais. *Speculum Naturae*. Book xvii, p. 40.
5   Armstrong, 1958, pp. 225–6.
6   Gerard, 1633, pp. 1587–9.
7   Hyde, D. (1940). *The Children of Lir.* Talbot Press, Dublin. pp. 37–8.
8   Ó hÓgáin, D. (1990). *Myth, Legend and Romance*. Ryan Publishing, London. p. 272.
9   Payne-Gallwey, 1886.
10 Whitaker, 1918.
11 Cook, 1960.
12 Fox, 1986.

13 Ucko & Dimbleby, 1969.
14 Wood-Gush, 1985.
15 Hansen, 2002.
16 Kear, 1990.
17 Ashton & Ashton, 1999.
18 Delacour, 1964.
19 Kear, 1990, pp. 27–8.
20 Moubray, 1854.
21 Kear, 1990.
22 Darwin, C. (1883). *The Variation of Animals and Plants Under Domestication*, 2nd edn. Appleton & Co, New York. Vol. 2, pp. 295–6.
23 Palmer, 1976, Vol. 3, p. 279.

Chapter 3

1   Dudley *et al.*, 2006; Irish Rare Birds Committee, 2006. In addition to the 53 species in the published version of the British List, this chapter includes hooded merganser (already on the Irish List, and added to the British List in June 2008), lesser Canada goose and muscovy duck (both under review).

2 Austin *et al.*, 2008.

3 Crowe, 2005.

4 Kershaw & Cranswick, 2003; Crowe *et al.*, 2008.

5 Scott & Rose, 1996; Hagemeijer & Blair, 1997; Madsen *et al.*, 1999; BirdLife International, 2004; Delany & Scott, 2006.

6 US Fish and Wildlife Service, 2008.

7 Wernham *et al.*, 2002.

8 Fisher, 1966; Holloway, 1996; Gibbons *et al.*, 1993.

9 Ussher & Warren, 1900.

10 Tyrberg, 1998, with updates at web.telia.com/~u11502098/pleistocene.html; Stelfox, 1938.

11 Cramp & Simmons, 1977; Boyd, 1962.

12 Hillis, 2005, 2005, 2007.

13 Gill & Wright, 2006; British Ornithologists' Union Records Committee, 2007.

14 Ticehurst, 1957.

15 Van der Molen, J., Van Dijck, B. (1999). *Holocene tidal and wave-driven sand transport in the southern North Sea and the evolution of the Dutch coast. The non-steady state of the inner shelf and shoreline, Hawaii, 9–12 November 1999. IGCP Project 437.*

16 Esselink & Beekman, 1991.

17 Northcote, E. M. (1981). Size differences between limb bones of recent and subfossil mute swans, *Cygnus olor. Journal of Archaeological Science.* **8**, 89–98.

18 Whitmore, 1974.

19 Ticehurst, 1957.

20 Ticehurst, 1957.

21 Thompson, 1851.

22 Scharff *et al.*, (1918). The exploration of Castlepook Cave, County Cork. *Proceedings of the Royal Irish Academy* **35** (B), 3, 68.

23 Smith, C. (1750). *Ancient and Present State of the County and City of Cork.* A. Reilly for the author, Dublin.

24 O'Donoghue *et al.*, 1992.

25 Ogilvie, 1972.

26 Minton, 1971.

27 Coleman *et al.*, 2002.

28 Ward *et al.*, 2004.

29 Ogilvie, 1972; Ruger *et al.*, 1986.

30 Sheppard, 1993.

31 Kershaw & Cranswick, 2003.

32 Sangster *et al.*, 1997; Association of European Records and Rarities Committees, 2003.

33 Evans & Sladen, 1980.

34 Beekman, 1997.

35 Dirksen & Beekman, 1991.

36 Beekman, 1997.

37 Beekman, 1997; Ogilvie, 1969.

38 Worden, J. (2006) *Goose News* **5**, 8–10.

39 Sheppard, 1993.

40 Newth, J. & Rees, E. (2008) *Goose News* **7**, 11.

41 Colhoun *et al.*, 2000.

42 Laubek, 1995.

43 Hawkins, 1986.

44 Syroechkovsky *et al.*, 2002.

45 Bart *et al.*, 1991.

46 Evans, 1979.

47 Nichols *et al.*, 1992.

48 Evans, 1979

49 Boyd & Eltringham, 1962.

[50] Cranswick et al., 2002.
[51] Garðarsson, 1991; Laubek, 1998; Crowe, 2005.
[52] Pennycuick et al., 1996.
[53] Brazil, 2003.
[54] Hutchinson, 1989.
[55] Brazil, 2003.
[56] Haapanen, 1991; Rees et al., 1991.
[57] Brazil, 2003.
[58] Haapanen et al., 1973a, 1973b; Haapanen, 1991; Rees et al., 1991.
[59] Haapanen, 1991.
[60] Einarsson, 1996, quoted in Brazil, 2003.
[61] M. A. Ogilvie, quoted in Cramp & Simmons, 1977.
[62] Association of European Records and Rarities Committees, 2003.
[63] Ogilvie, 1978.
[64] Allen, L. (2006) Goose News 5, 13; Hearn, R. (2007) Goose News 6, 15–16; Reed, J. (2008) Goose News 7, 14.
[65] Parslow-Otsu & Kjeldsen, 1992.
[66] Worden, J. (2006) Goose News 5, 8–10; Hearn, R. (2007) Goose News 6, 15–16; Reed, J. (2008) Goose News 7, 14.
[67] Eriksson & Henricsson, 1990.
[68] Madsen et al., 1999.
[69] Tveit, 1984.
[70] Madsen et al., 1999.
[71] Boertmann, 1994.
[72] Madsen et al., 1999.
[73] Mitchell, 2008.
[74] Scott & Fisher, 1953.
[75] Fox et al., 1989.
[76] Bell et al.,1995.
[77] Pettifor & Rowcliffe, 1995.
[78] Boertmann & Glahder, 1999.
[79] Cabot et al., 1988.
[80] Boertmann & Glahder, 1999.
[81] Madsen & Mortensen, 1987.
[82] Madsen et al., 1999.
[83] Owen, 1976.
[84] Shimmings, 2003.
[85] Dalgety & Scott, 1948.
[86] Fox & Stroud, 2002.
[87] Fox & Francis, 2003, 2004.
[88] Fox, 2002.
[89] M. Fredriksen & A. D. Fox, quoted in Fox & Stroud, 2002.
[90] Kehoe, C. 2006. Racial identification and assessment in Britain: a report from the RIACT subcommittee. British Birds 99, 619–45.
[91] Bulletin of the British Ornithologists' Club (1901) 12, 80–1.
[92] www3.hi.is/~yannk/photos75-00.html. Accessed 30 November 2008.
[93] Swann et al., 2005.
[94] Boland & Crowe, 2008.
[95] Icelandic Wildlife Institute, quoted in Cranswick et al., 2005.
[96] Mitchell, 2008.
[97] Madsen et al., 1999; Meek, E. (2008), Goose News 7, 6–7.
[98] Jensen, 2006.
[99] Rehfisch et al., 2002.
[100] Merne, 1986.
[101] Cranswick et al., 2005; Wildfowl & Wetlands Trust press release, 25 August 2004.
[102] Dudley, 2005.
[103] Banks et al., 2005.
[104] Paxinos et al., 2002.

105 Buffon, 1754.
106 Madsen *et al.*, 1999.
107 Rehfisch *et al.*, 2002.
108 Thomas, 1977.
109 S. Dudley,
personal communication;
P. Milne,
personal communication.
110 Dudley, 2005.
111 Percival, 1992.
112 Ebbing *et al.*, 1991.
113 Owen & Black, 1991.
114 Slatkin, 1987.
115 Black *et al.*, 2007.
116 A. Walsh,
personal communication.
117 Griffin, L. (2008). *Goose News* **7**, 17.
118 Boyd, 1961.
119 Owen *et al.*, 1987.
120 Black *et al.*, 2007.
121 Dudley, 2005.
122 Ebbing, 2004.
123 Clausen *et al.*, 1998; Uspenski & Tomkovich, 1987; Hort, 1995.
124 Clausen & Bustnes, 1998.
125 Boyd, 1962; Madsen *et al.*, 1999.
126 Hall, C. & Colhoun, K. (2008). *Goose News* **7**, 18–19.
127 Cabot, 1965–75; Ó Bríain, 1989.
128 Clausen, 2007.
129 Garner & Millington, 2001.
130 Maltby-Prevett *et al.*, 1975.
131 Shields, 1990.
132 McDowell, 2002.
133 Martin, 2002.
134 Madsen *et al.*, 1999.
135 Black & Madsen, 1993.
136 Perkov, 2006.
137 Madsen *et al.*, 1999.
138 Ray, 1678.
139 Lever, 1977.
140 Sutherland & Allport, 1991.
141 Kershaw & Cranswick, 2003; Banks *et al.*, 2008.
142 Deane, 1954.
143 Thompson, 1851.
144 Deane, 1954.
145 Musgrove *et al.* 2007; Hagemeijer & Blair, 1997.
146 Dudley, 2005.
147 Delany *et al.*, 2001.
148 A. Musgrove,
personal communication.
149 Owen *et al.*, 1986.
150 A. Musgrove,
personal communication.
151 Anders *et al.*, in press.
152 Patterson *et al.*, 1974.
153 Kear, 1990.
154 S. Dudley,
personal communication.
155 Dudley, 2005.
156 Savage, 1952.
157 Mathers, 1996.
158 P. Milne,
personal communication;
P. Smiddy,
personal communication.
159 Lever, 1977.
160 Davies & Baggott, 1989.
161 Gibbons *et al.*, 1993.
162 Harradine, 1985.
163 A. Musgrove,
personal communication.
164 Hildén, 1964.
165 Bell & Mitchell, 1966.
166 Banks *et al.*, 2006.
167 Koskimies, 1993.

[168] Gilissen *et al.*, 2002.
[169] Martin, 1993.
[170] Fox, 1988.
[171] Dudley, 2005.
[172] Lynas *et al.*, 2007; Hillis, 2007.
[173] Serie & Swanson, 1976.
[174] Afton & Paulus, 1992.
[175] Duncan, 1986.
[176] Szymczak & Rexstad, 1991.
[177] Cabot, 2004.
[178] Ogilvie, 1983a.
[179] Hildén, 1964.
[180] Tamisier, 1971.
[181] Owen *et al.*, 1986.
[182] A. Musgrove, personal communication.
[183] McKinney et al., 1990.
[184] Harradine, 1985.
[185] O. J. Merne, quoted in Hutchinson, 1987.
[186] Todd, 1997.
[187] Thompson, 1851.
[188] Davidson, 1987.
[189] Hill, 1984a.
[190] Hill, 1984b.
[191] Kear, 1961.
[192] Phillips & Wright, 1993.
[193] Evarts & Williams, 1987.
[194] Austin & Miller, 1995.
[195] Garðarsson, 1975.
[196] Ogilvie & the Rare Breeding Birds Panel, 2000.
[197] McDowell, 2002.
[198] Hildén, 1964.
[199] Duncan, 1986.
[200] Reinecker, 1987; Hestbeck, 1993.
[201] Todd, 1997.
[202] Martin, 1993.
[203] Fokin *et al.*, 2000.
[204] BirdLife International/European Bird Census Council, 2000.
[205] Martin, 1993, p. 94.
[206] Delacour & Scott, 1956, vol. 2, p. 167.
[207] Stone *et al.*, 1997.
[208] Lynas *et al.*, 2007.
[209] Ruttledge, 1980.
[210] McDowell, 2002.
[211] Fokin *et al.*, 2000.
[212] Martin, 1993.
[213] A. Musgrove, personal communication.
[214] Martin, 1993.
[215] Monval & Pirot, 1989.
[216] Koskimies, 1993.
[217] Hildén, 1964.
[218] Newton, I., in Cramp & Simmons, 1977.
[219] Wainright, 1967.
[220] Vickery & Nudds, 1984.
[221] DuBowy, 1988.
[222] Dudley, 2005.
[223] Delacour & Scott, 1956, vol. 3, p. 60.
[224] Maclean *et al.*, 2005.
[225] Delacour & Scott, 1956, vol. 3, p. 65.
[226] Lack, 1986.
[227] Delany *et al.*, 2001.
[228] Maclean *et al.*, 2007.
[229] Hildén, 1964; Havlín, 1966; Hill, 1982.
[230] Hildén, 1964.
[231] Owen *et al.*, 1986, p. 432.
[232] Martin, 1993.
[233] Hildén, 1964.
[234] Bengtson, 1972a.
[235] Delacour & Scott, 1956, vol. 3, p. 84.
[236] Johnsgard, 1978, p. 313.
[237] Livezey, 1995.

[238] Tiedermann & Noer, 1998.

[239] Goudie *et al.*, 2000; Garner & Farrelly, 2005.

[240] Garner & Farrelly, 2005.

[241] Kelly, P.A. 2003. Posting dated 13/10/03 on IBN-L@Listerv.heanet.ie. Accessed 14 October 2003.

[242] Carter, 1995.

[243] Murray & Cabot, 2002.

[244] Hutchinson, 1989.

[245] Parker & Holm, 1990.

[246] Hildén, 1964.

[247] Milne, 1965.

[248] Coulson, 1984.

[249] Boertmann, 1994.

[250] BirdLife International, 2004.

[251] BirdLife International, 2004.

[252] Martin, 1993.

[253] Thomas & Robert, 2002; Garðarsson & Þórarinsson, 2003.

[254] F. Cooke and students, per H. Boyd, personal communication.

[255] A. Garðarsson, quoted in Scott & Rose, 1996.

[256] Bengtson, 1972b.

[257] Garðarsson & Einarsson, in press.

[258] Robertson *et al.*, 2000.

[259] Gains & Fitzner, 1987.

[260] Tucker, B. W., in Witherby *et al.*, 1938–42, vol. III, p. 319.

[261] Koskimies, 1993; Boertmann, 1994.

[262] Kirby *et al.*, 1993.

[263] S. Pihl, quoted in Scott & Rose, 1996.

[264] Author estimate, 2008; Crowe, 2005

[265] Garner & Farrelly, 2005.

[266] Petersen & Ellarson, 1979; Leafloor *et al.*, 1996.

[267] Bengtson, 1972a.

[268] Alison, 1975.

[269] Boyd, 1996.

[270] Pehrsson, 1986.

[271] Sharrock, 1973.

[272] Kirby *et al.*, 1993; Cranswick, 2003.

[273] Hutchinson, 1989.

[274] McDowell, 2002.

[275] Tierney *et al.*, 2000.

[276] Underhill *et al.*, 1998.

[277] A. Musgrove, personal communication.

[278] Bengtson, 1972a.

[279] Bianki, 1992.

[280] Sea Duck Joint Venture Management Board, 2001. *Sea Duck Joint Venture Strategic Plan: 2001–2006*. Quoted in Delany & Scott, 2006.

[281] Sangster *et al.*, 2005.

[282] Atkinson-Willes, 1963, p. 295.

[283] Sea Duck Joint Venture, 2004.

[284] Robert *et al.*, 2000; Ingadóttir, 2000; Delany *et al.*, 2006.

[285] Delacour & Scott, 1956, vol. 3, p. 186.

[286] www.cvlbirding.co.uk/log book/2008june.html; A Musgrove, personal communication.

[287] Eadie *et al.*, 1995.

[288] Ludwichowski *et al.*, 2002; Milonoff *et al.*, 2002; Eadie *et al.*, 1995.

[289] Delany *et al.*, 2001.

[290] P. Olney, in Kear, 2005, p. 743.

[291] *British Birds* 2003, **96**, 606; *British Birds* 2007, **100**, 752.
[292] O. Crowe, personal communication.
[293] Lack, 1986.
[294] Ingadóttir, 2000.
[295] Atkinson & Hewitt, 1978; Miller, 1996.
[296] Dove, 1956.
[297] McDowell, 2002.
[298] Bengtson, 1972a.
[299] Hildén, 1964.
[300] Delany *et al.*, 2001.
[301] Ingadóttir, 2000.
[302] Mills, 1962.
[303] Martin, 1993, p. 168.
[304] Crick *et al.*, 2004.
[305] Tyler, 1985.
[306] A. Musgrove, personal communication.
[307] Eriksson & Nittylä, 1985.
[308] Linkola, 1962.
[309] Kirby *et al.*, 1995.
[310] Little & Furness, 1985.
[311] DEFRA, 2007.
[312] Lever, 1987.
[313] Delacour & Scott, 1956, vol. 3, p. 231.
[314] Owen *et al.*, 1986, p. 462.
[315] Culbert & Furphy, 1978; Wells & Smiddy, 1995; Allen *et al.*, 2006.
[316] Owen *et al.*, 1986.
[317] Muñoz-Fuentes *et al.*, 2006.
[318] DEFRA, 2007.
[319] Hess, 2007.
[320] A. Green, in Scott & Rose, 1996.
[321] Green & Baz, 2001.
[322] DEFRA, 2007.
[323] DEFRA, 2007.

Chapter 4

[1] Boyd, 1953.
[2] Rees, 1987.
[3] Swann & Brockway, 2007.
[4] Fox *et al.*, 1994.
[5] Warren *et al.*, 1992.
[6] Rees *et al.*, 1996.
[7] Black *et al.*, 1996.
[8] Johnsgard, 1968.
[9] Johnsgard, 1968.
[10] Dane *et al.*, 1959.
[11] Alison, 1975.
[12] Black & Owen, 1988.
[13] Rees, 2006.

Chapter 5

[1] Gause, 1934.
[2] Lüttschwager, 1955.
[3] Owen & Cadbury, 1975.
[4] Kristiansen *et al.*, 2000.
[5] Prins *et al.*, 1980.
[6] Fox & Kahlert, 2003.
[7] Owen, 1980, p. 145.
[8] Owen & Black, 1990.
[9] Buchsbaum *et al.*, 1986; Sedinger *et al.*, 1989, 1995; Prop & Vulink, 1992.
[10] Sincock, 1962.
[11] Mathiasson, 1973.
[12] Owen, 1972.
[13] B. West, 1972. Observations on the resting metabolic rate of barnacle geese and their daily energy flux during winter. Unpublished report, Dublin.
[14] Pennycuick *et al.*, 1999.
[15] Pennycuick *et al.*, 1996.

Chapter 6

1   Austin *et al.*, 2008.
2   Owen & Norderhaug, 1977.
3   Boyd, 1958.
4   Fox & Stroud, 2002.
5   Fox, 2005.
6   Ganter & Cooke, 1996; Fox & Madsen, 1981.
7   Ankney & MacInnes, 1978.
8   Owen, 1980, p. 164.
9   Madsen *et al.*, 1989.
10 Owen, 1980, p. 172; L. Griffin, personal communication.
11 Owen, 1980, pp. 172–3.
12 Summers & Underhill, 1987.
13 Campuysen *et al.*, 2002.
14 van den Berk *et al.*, 2001.
15 Owen & Black, 1989a.
16 Petrides & Bryant, 1951.
17 *Independent* newspaper, 15 August 2006.
18 Ogilvie, 1967.
19 Menu *et al.*, 2002.
20 Coleman & Minton, 1980.
21 Boyd, 1976.
22 Owen, 1982.
23 Pain, 1992.
24 Sears & Hunt, 1991.
25 The Environmental Protection (Restriction of Use of Lead Shot) (England) Regulations (SI No. 2170).
26 O'Halloran *et al.*, 1991.
27 Crick *et al.*, 2004.
28 Ogilvie, 1981; Ruger *et al.*, 1986.
29 Sheppard, 1993; Rose *et al.*, 2002.
30 Gibbons *et al.*, 1993; O. Crowe, personal communication.
31 Kershaw & Cranswick, 2003.
32 O. Crowe, personal communication.
33 Crowe, 2005; O. Crowe, personal communication.
34 Wernham *et al.*, 2002.
35 Ogilvie, 1967.
36 Wernham *et al.*, 2002.
37 O'Halloran *et al.*, 1995.
38 Hutchinson, 1989.
39 Perrins & Reynolds, 1967.
40 McCleery *et al.*, 2002.
41 Minton, 1968.
42 Minton, 1968.
43 Collins, 1991.
44 McCleery *et al.*, 2002.
45 Lack, 1967.
46 Perrins & Reynolds, 1967.
47 Plot, 1686.
48 Kear, 1972; Latzel & Scherner, 1985; Weiloch & Czapulak, 1991.
49 Kear, 1972.
50 Jenni & Winkler, 1994.
51 Mathiasson, 1973.
52 Coleman *et al.*, 2002.
53 Bacon & Perrins, 1991.
54 McCleery *et al.*, 2002.
55 McCleery *et al.*, 2002.
56 Walsh & Crowe, 2008.
57 Austin *et al.*, 2008.
58 Boyd, 1961.
59 Trinder *et al.*, 2004.
60 Pollard *et al.*, 1987; Trinder *et al.*, 2004.
61 Dennis & Taper, 1994.
62 Fox & Gitay, 1991.
63 Cabot & West, 1973.
64 Owen & Black, 1989a.
65 Cabot *et al.*, 1984.
66 Cabot *et al.*, 1987.

[67] Ogilvie, 1978.

[68] Kondla, 1973.

[69] Cabot, D., *et al.* 1984. *op cit.*

[70] Cabot *et al.*, 1984, 1987.

[71] Lessells *et al.*, 1979.

[72] Harvey, 1971.

[73] Fox *et al.*, 1998.

[74] Born, E. W. (1983). Catch and distribution of marine mammals and seabirds in the Scoresby Sund area (East Greenland), Danbiu Aps (in Danish with English summary).

[75] www.ust.is/Veidistjornun/ Almennt/Veiditolur. Barnacle goose is *helsingi* in Icelandic.

[76] Madsen *et al.*, 1999.

[77] Ogilvie, 1983b; D. Cabot, unpublished data from Inishkea Islands, Co. Mayo.

[78] Goodhart & Wright, 1958; Marris & Ogilvie, 1962; Hall & Waddington, 1966; Ferns & Green, 1975.

[79] Owen & Black, 1989b.

[80] Pettifor *et al.*, 1996.

[81] Percival, 1992.

[82] Cabot & West, 1983; survival figure subsequently updated to 2003.

[83] D. Cabot, unpublished data.

[84] Walley, 2008.

[85] Austin *et al.*, 2008.

[86] Hill, 1984c.

[87] Robinson *et al.*, 2002.

[88] Street, 1978.

[89] Hill, 1984c.

[90] Ogilvie, 1964.

[91] Boyd & King, 1964.

[92] Hill, 1982.

[93] Tuite & Owen, 1984.

[94] Hill, 1984c.

[95] Boyd, 1962.

[96] Boyd & King, 1960.

[97] Hohn, 1948.

[98] Austin *et al.*, 2008.

[99] Hill, 1984c.

[100] Matthews, 1965.

[101] Cabot, 1977.

[102] Wernham *et al.*, 2002.

Chapter 7

[1] Roomen & Madsen, 1992.

[2] www.unep-aewa.org. Accessed 26 December 2008.

[3] Atkinson & Hewitt, 1978.

[4] Eaton *et al.*, 2008.

[5] Eaton *et al.*, 2008., Lynas *et al.*, 2007.

[6] Eaton *et al.*, 2008.

[7] Gregory *et al.*, 2002.

[8] Lynas *et al.*, 2007.

[9] uk bap website. www.ukbap.org.uk. Accessed 26 December 2008.

[10] www.npws.ie/en/Biodiversity/ Ireland/NationalBiodiversityPlan. Accessed 26 December 2008.

[11] Species Action Plan: common scoter. www.ukbap.org.uk/UKPlans.aspx?ID=444. Accessed 26 December 2008.

[12] Eaton *et al.*, 2008.

[13] www.wwt.org.uk/downloads/ 446/common_scoter_bap.html. Accessed 26 December 2008.

[14] R. Hearn, in Eaton *et al.*, 2008.

[15] www.npws.ie/en/ProtectedSites/ SpecialProtectionAreasSPAs. Accessed 26 December 2008.

[16] www.natura.org. Accessed 26 December 2008.

[17] www.jncc.gov.uk/page-1364.
Accessed 26 December 2008.

[18] www.cms.int/about/intro.htm.
Accessed 26 December 2008.

[19] www.unep-aewa.org/about/intro-
duction.htm.
Accessed 26 December 2008.

[20] www.ramsar.org.
Accessed 26 December 2008.

Bibliography

Afton, A. D. & Paulus, S. L. (1992).
Incubation and brood care.
In: Batt, B. D. J., Afton, A. D.,
Anderson, M. G. *et al.*, eds,
*The Ecology and Management of
Breeding Waterfowl.* University of
Minnesota Press, Minneapolis,
pp. 62–108.

Alison, R. M. (1975). *Breeding Biology
and Behavior of the Oldsquaw
(Clangula hyemalis L.).*
Ornithological Monographs 18.
American Ornithologists' Union,
Tampa, Florida.

Allen, D., Mellon, C. & Looney, D.
(2006). Ruddy duck *Oxyura
jamaicensis* in Northern Ireland.
Irish Birds **8**, 41–50.

Amman, G.A. (1937). Number of
contour feathers in *Cygnus*
and *Xanthocephalus. Auk* **54**,
201–2.

**Anders, N. R., Churchyard, T. &
Hiddink, J. G.** (in press). Predation
of the shelduck *Tadorna tadorna* on

the mud snail *Hydrobia ulvae.
Aquatic Ecology.*
DOI 10.1007/s10452-008-9216-5.

Ankney, C. D. & Macinnes, C. D.
(1978). Nutrient reserves and
reproductive performance of
female lesser snow geese. *Auk* **95**,
459–71.

Armstrong, E. A. (1958). *The Folklore of
Birds.* Collins, London.

Ashton, C. & Ashton, M., eds. (1999).
British Waterfowl Standards.
Senecio Press, Charlbury.

**Association of European Records and
Rarities Committees** (2003).
Taxonomic Recommendations.
www.aerc.eu/DOCS/AERCTAC.pdf.
Accessed 17 December 2008.

Atkinson, K. M. & Hewitt, D. P. (1978).
A note on the food consumption
of the red-breasted merganser.
Wildfowl **29**, 87–91.

Atkinson-Willes, G. L., ed. (1963).
Wildfowl in Great Britain. HMSO,
London.

Austin, G. E., Collier, M. P., Calbrade, N. A., Hall, C. & Musgrove, A. J. (2008). *Waterbirds in the UK 2006/07: the Wetland Bird Survey*. BTO/WWT/RSPB/JNCC, Thetford.

Austin, J. E. & Miller, M. R. (1995). Northern pintail (*Anas acuta*). In: Poole, A. & Gill, F., eds, *The Birds of North America*, No. 163. Academy of Natural Sciences, Philadelphia, and American Ornithologists' Union, Washington, DC.

Bacon, P. J. & Perrins, C. M. (1991). Long-term population studies: the mute swan. In: Bell. B. D., ed. *20th International Ornithological Congress*. New Zealand Ornithological Trust Board, Wellington, New Zealand, pp. 1500–13.

Baillie, S. R., Marchant, J. H., Crick, H. Q. P. *et al.* (2007). Breeding birds in the wider countryside: their conservation status 2007. BTO Research Report 487. BTO, Thetford. www.bto.org/birdtrends. Accessed 17 December 2008.

Baldassarre, G. A. & Bolen, E. G. (1994). *Waterfowl Ecology and Management*. Wiley, New York.

Banks, A., Collier, M., Austin, G., Hearn, R. & Musgrove, A. (2006). *Waterbirds in the UK 2004/05: the Wetland Bird Survey*. BTO/WWT/RSPB/JNCC, Thetford.

Banks, A. N., Wright, L. J., Maclean, I. M. D. *et al.* (2008) Second review of the status of introduced non-native waterbird species in the area of African–Eurasian Waterbird Agreement. BTO Research Report 489. BTO, Thetford.

Banks, R. C., Cicero, C., Dunn, J. L. *et al.* (2005). Forty-fifth supplement to the American Ornithologists' Union Check-list of North American Birds. *Auk* **121**, 985–95.

Bart, J., Limpert, R., Earnst, S. *et al.* (1991). Demography of eastern population Tundra Swans *Cygnus columbianus columbianus*. In: Sears & Bacon, 1991, pp. 178–84.

Beekman, J. H. (1997). International census of the north-west European Bewick's swan population, January 1990 and 1995. *Swan Specialist Group Newsletter* **6**, 7–9.

Bell, M. & Mitchell, C. (1966). Survival in surface feeding ducks. Unpublished report. Wildfowl & Wetlands Trust, Slimbridge.

Bell, M. V., Mitchell, C. R., Fox, A. D. & Stewart, A. (1995). Survival estimates of pink-footed geese *Anser brachyrhynchus*: 1987–1993. Report to Joint Nature Conservation Committee. Wildfowl & Wetlands Trust, Slimbridge.

Bengtson, S.-A. (1972a). Reproduction and fluctuations in the size of duck populations at Lake Mývatn, Iceland. *Oikos* **23**, 35–58.

Bengtson, S. A. (1972b). The breeding ecology of the harlequin duck

Histrionicus histrionicus (L.) in Iceland. *Ornis Scandinavica* **3**, 1–19.

Benton, M. J., Cook, E. & Hooker, J. J. (2005). *Mesozoic and Tertiary Fossil Mammals and Birds of Great Britain.* Geological Conservation Review Series 32. Joint Nature Conservation Committee, Peterborough, 8–10.

Bianki, V. (1992). Sea ducks of the White Sea. *IWRB Seaduck Bulletin* **2**, 23–9.

BirdLife International (2004). *Birds in Europe: Population Estimates, Trends and Conservation Status.* BirdLife Conservation series 12. BirdLife International, Cambridge.

BirdLife International/European Bird Census Council (2000). *European Bird Populations: Estimates and Trends.* BirdLife International Conservation Series 10. BirdLife International, Cambridge.

Black, J. M. & Madsen, J. (1993). Red-breasted goose: research and conservation needs. *IWRB Goose Research Group Bulletin* **4**, 8–15.

Black, J. M. & Owen, M. (1988). Variations in pair bond and agonistic behaviors in barnacle geese on the wintering grounds. In: Weller, M., ed., *Waterfowl in Winters.* University of Minnesota Press, Minneapolis, pp. 39–57.

Black, J. M., Choudhury, S. & Owen, M. (1996). Do barnacle geese benefit from long term monogamy? In: Black, J. M., ed., *Partnerships in Birds: the Study of Monogamy.* Oxford University Press, Oxford, pp. 91–117.

Black, J. M., Prop, J. & Larsson, K. (2007). *Wild Goose Dilemmas.* Branta Press, Grøningen.

Boertmann, D. (1994). *An Annotated Checklist to the Birds of Greenland.* Medelelser om Grønland, Bioscience 38. Danish Polar Centre, Copenhagen.

Boertmann, D. & Glahder, C. (1999). Grønlandske gåsebestande: en oversigt. Danmarks Miljøundersøgelser. DMU, Københaven (with English summary).

Boland, H. & Crowe, O. (2008). An assessment of the distribution range of greylag (Icelandic-breeding and feral populations) in Ireland. Interim report to the National Parks & Wildlife Service and the Environment & Heritage Service. BirdWatch Ireland, Wicklow.

Boyd, H. (1953). On encounters between wild white-fronted geese in winter flocks, *Behaviour* **5**, 85–129.

Boyd, H. (1958). The survival of white-fronted geese (*Anser albifrons flavirostris*) ringed in Greenland. *Dansk Ornithologisk Forenings Tidsskrift* **52**, 1–8.

Boyd, H. (1961). The number of barnacle geese in Europe in 1959–1960. *Wildfowl* **12**, 116–24.

Boyd, H. (1962). Population dynamics and the exploitation of ducks and geese. In: Le Cren, E. D. & Holdgate, M. W., eds, *The Exploitation of Natural Animal Populations*. Blackwell Scientific Publications, Oxford, pp. 85–95.

Boyd, H. (1976). Estimates of total numbers in the Hudson Bay population of lesser snow goose 1964–73. *Canadian Wildlife Service Progress Notes* **63**.

Boyd, H. (1996). Arctic temperatures and the long-tailed ducks shot in eastern North America. *Wildlife Biology* **2**, 113–17.

Boyd, H. & Eltringham, S. K. (1962). The whooper swan in Great Britain. *Bird Study* **9**, 217–41.

Boyd, H. & King, B. (1960). A breeding population of the mallard. *Wildfowl* **11**, 137–43.

Boyd, H. & King, B. (1964). Effects of a severe winter on ducks breeding in north Somerset. *Wildfowl* **15**, 47–50.

Boyd, H. & Ogilvie, M. A. (1961). The distribution of mallard ringed in southern Britain. *Wildfowl* **12**, 125–36.

Brazil, M. (2003).*The Whooper Swan*. T. & A. D. Poyser, London.

British Ornithologists' Union Records Committee (2007). 35th Report. *Ibis* **149**, 652–4.

Buchsbaum, R., Wilson, J. & Valiela, I. (1986). Digestibility of plant constituents by Canada geese and Atlantic brant. *Ecology* **67**, 386–93.

Button G. L. (1754). *Histoire Naturelle Générale et Particulière*. Paris.

Cabot, D. (1965–75). The status and distribution of the pale-bellied brent goose (*Branta b. hrota*) in Ireland. *Irish Wildfowl Conservancy Publications* **1**, **2**, **6**, **10**; and unpublished reports (1973–75).

Cabot, D. (1977). Movements and migration of the mallard in Ireland. *Irish Birds* **1**, 37–45.

Cabot, D. (2004). *Guide to Irish Birds*. HarperCollins, London.

Cabot, D. & West, B. (1973). Population dynamics of barnacle geese *Branta leucopsis* in Ireland. *Proceedings of the Royal Irish Academy* **73B**, 415–43.

Cabot, D. & West, B. (1983). Studies on the population of barnacle geese *Branta leucopsis* wintering on the Inishkea Islands, Co. Mayo. 1. Population dynamics 1961–1983. *Irish Birds* **2**, 318–36.

Cabot, D., Nairn, R. & Viney, M. (1984). *Biological Expedition to Jameson Land, Greenland 1984*. Barnacle Books, Dublin.

Cabot, D., Goodwillie, R. & Viney, M. (1988). *Irish Expedition to North-East Greenland 1987*. Barnacle Books, Dublin.

Campbell, B. (1960). The mute swan census in England and Wales 1955–56. *Bird Study* **7**, 208–23.

Campuysen, C. J., Berrevoets, C. M., Cremer, H. J. W. M. *et al.* (2002). Mass mortality of common eiders (*Somateria mollissima*) in the Dutch Wadden Sea, winter 1999/2000: starvation in a commercially exploited wetland of international importance. *Biological Conservation* **106**, 303–17.

Carter, S. P., ed. (1995). British Birds in 1991–92: the conservation and monitoring review. BTO and JNCC, Thetford.

Clausen, P. (2007). Light-bellied brent geese crossing 'borders' – but how many. *Goose News* **6**, 8–9.

Clausen, P. & Bustnes, J. O. (1998). Flyways of the North Atlantic light-bellied brent geese *Branta bernicla hrota* reassessed by satellite telemetry. *Norsk Polarinstitutt Skrifter* **200**, 227–43.

Clausen, P., Madsen, J., Percvial, S. & Anderson, G. O. A. (1998). Population development and changes in winter site use by the Svalbard light-bellied brent goose 1980–1994. *Biological Conservation* **84**, 157–65.

Coleman, A. E. & Minton, C. D. T. (1980). Mortality of mute swan progeny in an area of south Staffordshire. *Wildfowl* **31**, 22–8.

Coleman, J. T., Spray, C. J., Percival, S. M., Rickeard, A. T. & Yeoman, P. (2002). The dynamics of a flock of mute swans at Berwick-upon-Tweed with particular reference to the effects of age, sex, social status and body condition on molt. *Waterbirds* **25** (Special Publication 1), 346–51.

Colhoun, K., McElwaine, J. G., Cranswick, P. A., Enlander, I. & Merne, O. J. (2000). Numbers and distribution of whooper *Cygnus cygnus* and Bewick's *C. columbianus bewickii* swans in Ireland: results from the International Swan Census, January 2000. *Irish Birds* **6**, 485–94.

Collier, M., Banks, A., Austin, G. et al. (2005). *Waterbirds in the UK 2003/04: the Wetland Bird Survey.* BTO/WWT/RSPB/JNCC, Thetford.

Collins, R. (1991). Breeding performance of an Irish mute swan *Cygnus olor* population. In: Sears & Bacon, 1991, pp. 144–50.

Cook, W. A. (1960). The number of ducks caught in Borough Fen Decoy 1776–1959. *Wildfowl* **11**, 118–22.

Coulson, J. C. (1984). The population dynamics of the eider *Somateria mollissima* and evidence of extensive non-breeding by adult ducks. *Ibis* **126**, 525–43.

Cramp, S. & Simmons, K. E. L., eds (1977). *The Birds of the Western Palearctic.* Vol.1. Oxford University Press, Oxford.

Cranswick, P. A. (2003). Status and distribution of common scoter *Melanitta nigra* and velvet scoter *M. fusca* in the United Kingdom. In: *Western Palearctic Scoter Flyway Review: Proceedings of the Seaduck Specialist Group meeting at Fuglesø, Jutland 2000.* NERI Technical Report, pp. 59–65.

Cranswick, P. A., Bowler, J. M., Delany, S. N. et al. (1996). Numbers of whooper swans *Cygnus cygnus* in Iceland, Ireland

and Britain in January 1995: results of the International Whooper Swan Census. *Wildfowl* **47**, 17–30.

Cranswick, P. A., Colhoun, K., Einarsson, O. *et al.* (2002). The status and distribution of the Icelandic whooper swan population: results of the International Whooper Swan Census 2000. *Waterbirds* **25** (Special Publication 1), 37–48.

Cranswick, P. A., Worden, J., Ward, R. *et al.* (2005). *The Wetland Bird Survey 2001–03: Wildfowl & Wader Counts.* BTO/WWT/RSPB/JNCC, Thetford.

Crick, H. Q. P., Marchant, J. H., Noble, D. G. *et al.* (2004). Breeding birds in the wider countryside: their conservation status 2003. BTO Research Report 353. BTO, Thetford.

Crowe, O. (2005). *Ireland's Wetlands and Their Waterbirds: Status and Distribution.* BirdWatch Ireland, Newcastle, Co. Wicklow.

Crowe, O., Austin, G. E., Colhoun, K. *et al.* (2008). Estimates and trends of waterbird numbers wintering in Ireland, 1994/95 to 2003/04. *Bird Study* **55**, 66–77.

Culbert, R. W., & Furphy, J. S. (1978). The ruddy duck in Lough Neagh, Co. Antrim. *Irish Birds* **1**, 234–6.

Dalgety, C. T. & Scott, P. (1948). A new race of the white-fronted goose. *Bulletin of the British Ornithologists' Club* **68**, 109–21.

Dane, B., Walcott, C. & Drury, W. H. (1959). The form and duration of the display actions of the goldeneye (*Bucephala clangula*). *Behaviour* **14**, 265–81.

Davidson, R. (1987). Breeding birds of Lough Neagh, 1987. Unpublished report, Craigavon.

Davies, A. K. & Baggott, G. K. (1989). Egg-laying, incubation and intra-specific nest parasitism by the mandarin duck. *Bird Study* **36**, 115–22.

Deane, C. D. (1954). *Handbook of the Birds of Northern Ireland.* Ulster Museum, Belfast.

DEFRA (Department for Environment, Food and Rural Affairs) (2007). Eradication of ruddy ducks in the UK to protect the white-headed duck. www.nonnativespecies.org/Ruddy_Duck. Accessed 17 December 2008.

Delacour, J. (1964). *Waterfowl of the World.* Country Life, London. Volume 4, pp. 157–9.

Delacour, J. & Mayr, E. (1945). The family Anatidae. *Wilson Bulletin* **57**, 3–55.

Delacour, J. & Scott, P. (1956). *The Waterfowl of the World.* Country Life, London.

Delany, S. & Scott, D. A., eds (2006). *Waterbird Population Estimates,* 4th edn. Wetlands International, Wageningen.

Delany, S., Greenwood, J. & Kirby, J. S. (1992). National mute swan survey. Unpublished Report to JNCC.

Delany S. N., Reyes, C., Hubert, E. et al. (2001). *Results from the International Waterbird Census in the Western Palearctic and Southwest Asia 1995 and 1996.* Wetlands International Publication 54. Wetlands International, Wageningen.

Dennis, B. & Taper, M. L. (1994). Density dependence in time series of observations of natural populations: Estimation and testing. *Ecological monographs* **64**, 205–24.

Dirksen, S. & Beekman, J. H. (1991). Population size, breeding success and the distribution of Bewick's swans *Cygnus columbianus bewickii* wintering in Europe in 1986–87. In: Sears & Bacon, 1991, pp. 120–4.

Dove, R. S. (1956). Birds of Magilligan Strand. *Irish Naturalists' Journal* **12**, 53.

DuBowy, P. J. (1988). Waterfowl communities and seasonal environments: temporal variability in interspecific competition. *Ecology* **69**, 1439–53.

Dudley, S. P. (2005). Changes to Category C of the British List. *Ibis* **147**, 803–20.

Dudley, S. P., Gee, M., Kehoe, C., Melling, T. M. and the British Ornithologists' Union Records Committee (BOURC) (2006). The British List: a checklist of the birds of Britain (7th edition). *Ibis* **148**, 526–63.

Duncan, D. C. (1986). Survival of dabbling duck broods on prairie impoundments in south-eastern Alberta. *Canadian Field-Naturalist* **100**, 110–13.

Eadie, J. M., Mallory. M. L. & Lumsden, H. G. (1995). Common goldeneye (*Bucephala clangula*). In: Poole, A. & Gill, F., eds, *The Birds of North America*, No. 170. Academy of Natural Sciences, Philadelphia, and American Ornithologists' Union, Washington, DC.

Eaton, M. A., Balmer, D., Burton, N. et al. (2008). *The State of the UK's Birds 2007.* RSPB, BTO, WWT, CCW, EHS, NE and SNH, Sandy.

Ebbing, B. S. (2004). Onderzoek naar het broedsuccess van Zwartbuikrotganzen [Unravelling the breeding success of dark-bellied brent geese]. *Limosa* **77**, 71–8.

Ebbing, B. S., van Biezen, J. B. & van der Voet, H. (1991). Estimation of annual adult survival rates of Barnacle geese *Branta leucopsis* using multiple resightings of marked individuals. *Ardea* **79**, 73–112.

Einarsson, Ó. (1996). Breeding biology of the whooper swan and factors affecting its breeding success, with notes on its social dynamics and life cycle in the wintering range. Unpublished PhD thesis, University of Bristol.

Eltringham, S. K. (1963). The British population of the mute swan in 1961. *Bird Study* **10**, 10–28.

Eriksson, K. & Nittylä, J. (1985). Breeding performance of the goosander *Mergus merganser* in the archipelago of the Gulf of Finland. *Ornis Fennica* **62**, 153–7.

Eriksson, P. & Henricsson, T. (1990). Sädgåsen *Anser fabalis* i Asele lappmark. *Vår Fågelvärld* **49**, 7–14 (in Swedish with English summary).

Esselink, H. & Beekman, J. H. (1991). Between year variation and causes of mortality in the non-breeding population of the Mute Swan *Cygnus olor* in the Netherlands, with special reference to hunting. In: Sears & Bacon, 1991, pp. 110–19.

Evans, M. E. (1979). Aspects of the life-cycle of the Bewick's swan based on the recognition of individuals at a wintering site. *Bird Study* **26**, 149–62.

Evans, M. E. & Sladen, W. J. L. (1980). A comparative analysis of the bill markings of whistling and Bewick's swans and out-of-range occurrences of the two taxa. *Auk* **97**, 697–703.

Evarts, S. & Williams, C. J. (1987). Multiple paternity in wild populations of mallards. *Auk* **104**, 597–602.

Ferns, P. N. & Green, G. H. (1975). Observations of pink-footed and barnacle geese in the Kong Oscar Fjord region of north-east Greenland, 1974. *Wildfowl* **26**, 131–8.

Fisher, J. (1966). *The Shell Bird Book*. Ebury Press and Michael Joseph, London.

Fokin, S., Kuzyakin, V., Kalchreuter, H. & Kirby, J. (2000). *The Garganey in the Former USSR: a Compilation of Life-History Information*. Wetlands International, Wageningen.

Fox, A. D. (1988). Breeding status of the gadwall in Britain and Ireland. *British Birds* **81**, 51–66.

Fox, A. D. (2002). The Greenland White-fronted Goose Study census network. *Goose News* **1**, 11–13.

Fox, A. D. (2005). Population dynamics. In: Kear, 2005, pp. 132–51.

Fox, A. D. & Francis, I. S., eds (2003). Report of the 2001/2002 National Census of Greenland White-fronted Geese in Britain. Final report, September 2003. Greenland White-fronted Goose Study.

Fox, A. D. & Francis, I. S., eds (2004). Report of the 2002/2003 National Census of Greenland White-fronted Geese in Britain. Final report, April 2004. Greenland White-fronted Goose Study.

Fox, A. D. & Francis, I. S., eds (2007). Report of the 2006/2007 National Census of Greenland White-fronted Geese in Britain. Final report, September 2007. Kalø, Denmark.

Fox, A. D. & Gitay, H. (1991). Breeding success in Greenland barnacle geese *Branta leucopsis* wintering on Islay, Scotland. *Ardea* **79**, 359–64.

Fox, A. D. & Kahlert, J (2003) Repeated grazing of a saltmarsh by moulting greylag geese *Anser anser*: does sequential harvesting optimise biomass or protein gain? *Journal of Avian Biology* **34**, 89–96.

Fox, A. D. & Madsen, J. (1981). The pre-nesting behaviour of the Greenland white-fronted goose *Anser albifrons flavirostris*. *Wildfowl* **32**, 48–52.

Fox, A. D. & Stroud, D. A. (2002). *Anser albifrons flavirostris* Greenland white-fronted Goose. *BWP Update* **4**, 65–88.

Fox, A. D., Gitay, H., Owen, M., Salmon, D. G. & Ogilvie, M. A. (1989). Population dynamics of Icelandic-nesting geese 1960–1987. *Ornis Scandinavica* **20**, 289–97.

Fox, A. D., Mitchell, C., Stewart, A. *et al.* (1994). Winter movements and site fidelity of pink-footed geese *Anser brachyrhynchus* ringed in Britain with particular emphasis on those marked in Lancashire. *Bird Study* **41**, 221–34.

Fox, A. D., Kristiansen, J. N., Stroud, D. A. & Boyd, H. (1998). The effects of simulated spring goose grazing on the growth rate and protein content of *Phleum pratense* leaves. *Oecologia* **116**, 154–9.

Fox, J. B. (1986). Kellyville decoy and its catches. *Irish Birds* **3**, 245–54.

Gains, W. L. & Fitzner, R. E. (1987). Winter diet of the harlequin duck at Sequim Bay, Puget Sound, Washington. *Northwest Science* **61**, 213–15.

Ganter, B. & Cooke, F. (1996). Pre-incubation feeding activities and energy budgets of snow geese: can food on the breeding grounds affect fecundity? *Oecologia* **106**, 153–6.

Garðarsson, A. (1991). Movements of whooper swans *Cygnus cygnus* neckbanded in Iceland. In: Sears & Bacon, 1991, pp. 189–94.

Garðarsson, A. (1975). Islenskir votlendisfuglar [The birds of Icelandic wetlands]. *Rit Landverndar* **4**, 100–34 (in Icelandic with English summary).

Garðarsson, A. & Einarsson, Á. (in press). Relationships among food, reproductive success and density of harlequin ducks on the River Laxá at Mývatn, Iceland (1975–2002). In: Robertson, G. J. & Thomas. P.W., eds, *Harlequin Ducks in the Northwest Atlantic*. Canadian Wildlife Service Occasional Paper.

Garðarsson, A. & þórarinsson, þ. L. (2003). Utbreiðsla og fjöldi straumandar á Íslandi að vetrarlagi [Distribution and numbers of harlequin ducks wintering in Iceland]. *Bliki* **23**, 5–20 (in Icelandic with English summary).

Garner, M. & Farrelly, W. (2005). Eiders in Ireland: rare forms worth finding. *Birds Ireland*. www.birdsireland.com/pages/site_pages/features/eider/eider.html. Accessed 17 December 2008.

Garner, M. & Millington, R. (2001). Grey-bellied brant and the Dundrum conundrum. *Birding World* **14**, 151–5.

Gause, G. F. (1934). *The Struggle for Existence*. William & Wilkins, Baltimore.

Gerard, J. (1633). *The Herbal or General History of Plants*. The complete 1633 Edition as revised and enlarged by Thomas Johnson. 1975. Dover Publications, New York.

Gibbons, D. W., Reid, J. B. & Chapman, R. A. (1993). *The New Atlas of Breeding Birds in Britain & Ireland: 1988–1991*. Poyser, London.

Gilissen, N., Haanstra, L., Delany S., Boere, G. & Hagemeijer, W. (2002). *Numbers and Distribution of Wintering Waterbirds in the Western Palearctic and Southwest Asia 1997, 1998 and 1999: Results from the International Waterfowl Census*. Wetlands International Global Series 11. Wetlands International, Wageningen.

Gill, F. & Wright, M. (2006). *Birds of the World: Recommended English Names*. A. & C. Black, London.

Goodhart, J & Wright, T. (1958). North-East Greenland Expedition 1956. *Wildfowl* **9**, 180–90.

Goudie, R. I., Robertson, G. L & Reed, A. (2000). Common eider (*Somateria mollissima*). In: Poole, A & Gill, F., eds, *The Birds of North America*, No. 564. The Birds of North America, Inc., Philadelphia, PA.

Gregory, R. D., Wilkinson, N. I., Noble, D. G. *et al.* (2002). The population status of birds in the United Kingdom, Channel Islands and the Isle of Man: an analysis of conversation concern 2002–2007. *British Birds* **95**, 410–50.

Green, A. & Baz, H. (2001). *Oxyura leucocephala* white-headed duck. *BWP Update* **3**, 79–90.

Haapanen, A. (1991). Whooper swan *Cygnus c. cygnus* population dynamics in Finland. In: Sears & Bacon, 1991, pp. 137–41.

Haapanen, A., Helminen, M. & Suomalainen, H. K. (1973a). The spring arrival and breeding phrenology of the whooper swan in Finland. *Finnish Game Research* **33**, 33–8.

Haapanen, A., Helminen, M. & Suomalainen, H. K. (1973b). Population growth and breeding biology of the whooper swan in Finland in 1950–1970. *Finnish Game Research* **33**, 39–60.

Hagemeijer, E. J. M. & Blair, M. J., eds (1997). *The EBCC Atlas of European Breeding Birds: Their Distribution and Abundance*. T. & A. D. Poyser, London.

Hall, A. B. & Waddington, R. N. (1966). The breeding birds of Ørsted Dal, East Greenland, 1963. *Dansk Ornitologisk Forenings Tidsskrift* **60**, 186–97.

Hansen, K. (2002). *A Farewell to Greenland Wildlife*. Bære Dygighed & Gads Forlag, Copenhagen.

Harradine, J. (1985). Duck shooting in the United Kingdom. *Wildfowl* **36**, 81–94.

Harvey, J. M. (1971). Factors affecting blue goose nesting success. *Canadian Journal of Zoology* **49**, 223–34.

Havlín, J. (1966). Breeding seasons and success of pochard and tufted duck in Czechoslovakia. *Bird Study* **13**, 306–10.

Hawkins, L. L. (1986). Nesting behaviour of male and female whistling swans and implications of male incubation. *Wildfowl* **37**, 5–27.

Heron-Allen, E. (1928). *Barnacles in Nature and Myth*. Oxford University Press, London.

Hess, P. (2007). Notes and news: ruddy duck hybrids. *Birding* (March/April), 34.

Hestbeck, J. (1993). Survival of northern pintails banded during winter in North America, 1950–1988. *Journal of Wildlife Management* **57**, 590–7.

Hildén, O. (1964). Ecology of duck populations in the island group of Valassaaret, Gulf of Bothnia. *Annales Zoologici Fennici* **1**, 153–279.

Hill, D. A. (1982). The comparative population ecology of mallard and tufted duck. Unpublished DPhil thesis, University of Oxford.

Hill, D. A. (1984a). Factors affecting nest success in the mallard and tufted duck. *Ornis Scandinavica* **15**, 115–22.

Hill, D. A. (1984b). Clutch predation in relation to nest density in mallard and tufted duck. *Wildfowl* **35**, 151–6.

Hill, D. A. (1984c). Population regulation in the mallard *Anas platyrhynchos* L. *Journal of Animal Ecology* **53**, 192–202.

Hillis, J. P. (2005). Rare breeding birds in Ireland. *Irish Birds* **7**, 539–48.

Hillis, J. P. (2006). Rare Irish breeding birds. *Irish Birds* **8**, 97–106.

Hillis, J. P. (2007). Rare breeding birds in Ireland 2005 and 2006. *Irish Birds* **8**, 249–62.

Hohn, E. O. (1948). Mortality of adult and young mallards. *British Birds* **41**, 233–5.

Holloway, S. (1996). The *Historical Atlas of Breeding Birds in Britain and Ireland 1875–1900*. T. & A. D. Poyser, London.

Hort, C. (1995). Brent geese in north easternmost Greenland. *Dansk Ornitologisk Forenings Tidsskrift* **89**, 89–91.

Howard, H. (1964). Fossil Anseriformes. In: Delacour, J., *Waterfowl of the World*. Country Life, London, Vol. 4, 233–326.

Hutchinson, C. D. (1989). *Birds in Ireland*. T. & A. D. Poyser, Calton.

Ingadóttir, Á., ed. (2000). *Válisti 2: Fuglar [Red list 2: Birds]*. Náttúrufræðistofnun Íslands, Reykjavik (in Icelandic with English summary).

Irish Rare Birds Committee (2006). The Irish List. IRBC, Dublin. www.irbc.ie. Accessed 17 December 2008.

Jenni, L. & Winkler, R. (1994). *Moult and Ageing of European Passerines.* Academic Press, London.

Jensen, J.-K. (2006). Greylag geese in the Faeroe Islands. *Goose News* **5,** 7.

Johnsgard, P. A. (1965). *Handbook of Waterfowl Behavior.* Cornell University Press, Ithaca, New York.

Johnsgard, P. A. (1968). The evolution of duck courtship. *Natural History* **77,** 58–63.

Johnsgard, P. A. (1978). *Ducks, Geese, and Swans of the World.* University of Nebraska Press, Lincoln.

Kear, J. (1961). Early sexual maturity in the mallard. *British Birds* **54,** 427–9.

Kear, J. (1972). Reproduction and family life. In: Scott, P. & the Wildfowl Trust. *The Swans.* Michael Joseph, London.

Kear, J. (1990). *Man and Wildfowl.* T. & A. D. Poyser, London.

Kear, J., ed. (2005). *Ducks, Geese and Swans.* Oxford University Press, Oxford.

Kershaw, M. & Cranswick, P. A. (2003). Numbers of wintering waterbirds in Great Britain 1994/95–1998/99. I. Wildfowl and selected waterbirds. *Biological Conservation* **111,** 91–104.

Kirby, J. S. (1995). Winter population estimates for selected waterfowl species in Britain. *Biological Conservation* **73,** 189–98.

Kirby, J. S., Rees, E. C., Merne, O. J. & Garðarsson, A. (1992). International census of whooper swans *Cygnus cygnus* in Britain, Ireland and Iceland: January 1991. *Wildfowl* **43,** 20–6.

Kirby, J. S., Evans, R. J. & Fox, A. D. (1993). Wintering seaducks in Britain and Ireland: populations, threats, conservation and research priorities. *Aquatic Conservation: Marine and Freshwater Ecosystems* **3,** 105–37.

Kirby, J. S., Salmon, D. G., Atkinson-Willes, G. L. & Cranswick, P. A. (1995). Index numbers for waterbird populations. III. Long-term trends in the abundance of wintering wildfowl in Great Britain, 1996/67–1991/2. *Journal of Applied Ecology* **32,** 536–51.

Kondla, N. G. (1973). Canada goose goslings leaving cliff nest. *Auk* **90,** 890.

Koskimies, P. (1993). Population sizes and recent trends of breeding birds in the Nordic countries. Report from a working group under the Nordic Council of Ministers. Vesi-ja ympäristöhallitus, Helsinki.

Kristiansen, J. N., Fox, A. D. & Nachman, G. (2000). Does size matter? Maximising nutrient and biomass intake by shoot size selection amongst herbivorous geese. *Ardea* **88,** 119–25.

Lack, D. (1967). The significance of clutch-size in waterfowl. *Wildfowl* **18,** 125–8.

Lack, P. (1986). *The Atlas of Wintering Birds in Britain and Ireland* T. & A. D. Poyser, Calton.

Latzel, G. & Scherner, E. R. (1985). Der Brutbestand des Höckerschwans (*Cygnus olor*) im Stadtkreis Wolfsburg. *Vogelk. Ber. aus Niedersachsen* **17**, 1–13.

Laubek, B. (1995). Habitat use by whooper swans *Cygnus cygnus* and Bewick's swans *Cygnus columbianus bewickii* wintering in Denmark: increasing agricultural conflicts. *Wildfowl* **46**, 8–15.

Laubek, B. (1998). The northwest European whooper swan (*Cygnus cygnus*) population: ecological and management aspects of an expanding waterfowl population. Unpublished PhD thesis, University of Aarhus, Denmark.

Leafloor, J. O., Thompson, J. E. & Ankney, C. D. (1996). Body mass and carcass composition of fall migrant Oldsquaws. *Wilson Bulletin* **108**, 567–72.

Lessells, C. M., Sibly, R., Owen, M. & Ellis, S. (1979). Weights of female barnacle geese during breeding. *Wildfowl* **30**, 72–4.

Lever, C. (1977). *The Naturalised Animals of the British Isles*. Hutchinson, London.

Lever, C. (1987). *Naturalised Birds of the World*. Harlow, Longman, London.

Linkola, P. (1962). Havaintoja sorsalintujen lisääntymistuloksesta Keski-Hämessä [Notes on the breeding success of ducks in central Häme]. *Suomen Riitsa* **15**, 157–74 (in Finnish with English translation).

Little, B. & Furness, R. W. (1985). Long-distance moult migration by British goosanders *Mergus merganser*. *Ringing & Migration* **6**, 77–82.

Livezey, B. C. (1986). A phylogenetic analysis of recent anseriform genera using morphological characters. *Auk* **103**, 737–54.

Livezey, B. C. (1995). Physiology and evolutionary ecology of modern seaducks (Anatidae: Mergini). *Condor* **97**, 233–55.

Livezey, B. C. (1997). A phylogenetic classification of waterfowl (Aves: Anseriformes), including selected fossil species. *Annals of the Carnegie Museum* **66**, 455–94.

Ludwichowski, I., Barker, R. & Bräger, S. (2002). Nesting area fidelity and survival of female common goldeneyes *Bucephala clangula*: are they density-dependent? *Ibis* **144**, 452–60.

Lüttschwager, J. (1955). Lamellenzahl an Entenschnabeln. *Bonner Zoologische Beiträge* **6**, 90–4.

Lynas, P., Newton, S. F. & Robson, J. A. (2007). The status of birds in Ireland: an analysis of conservation concern 2008–2013. *Irish Birds* **8**, 149–66.

McDowell, W. M. (2002). *A History of the Birds of Northern Ireland*. Unpublished CD ROM. Belfast.

McKinney, F. B., Buitron, D. & Derrickson, S. R. (1990). Persistent quacking in dabbling ducks: a predator-luring signal? *Wildfowl* **41**, 92–8.

Maclean, I. M. D., Austin, G. E., Mellan, H. J. & Girling, T. (2005). WeBS Alerts 2003/04: changes in numbers of wintering waterbirds in the United Kingdom, its constituent countries, Special Protection Areas (SPAs) and Sites of Special Scientific Interest (SSSIs). BTO Research Report 416 to the WeBS Partnership. BTO, Thetford.

Maclean, I. M. D., Burton, N. H. K. & Austin, G. E. (2007). Declines in over-wintering diving ducks at Lough Neagh and Lough Beg: comparisons of within site, regional, national and European trends. BTO Research Report 432. BTO, Thetford.

McCleery, R. H., Perrins, C. M., Wheeler, D. & Groves, S. (2002). Population structure, survival rates and productivity of mute swans breeding in a colony at Abbotsbury, Dorset, England. *Waterbirds* **25** (Special Publication 1), 192–201.

Madge, S. & Burn, H. (1988). *Wildfowl: an Identification Guide to the Ducks, Geese and Swans of the World.* Christopher Helm, London.

Madsen, J. & Mortensen, C. E. (1987). Habitat exploitation and interspecific competition of moulting geese in Jameson Land, East Greenland. *Ibis* **129**, 25–44.

Madsen, J., Brenballe, T. & Mehlum, F. (1989). Study of the breeding ecology and behaviour of the Svalbard population of the light-bellied brent goose *Branta bernicla hrota. Polar Research* **7**, 1–21.

Madsen, J., Cracknell, G. & Fox, A. D., eds (1999). *Goose Populations of the Western Palearctic: a Review of Status and Distribution.* Wetlands International Publication 48. Wetlands International, Wageningen, the Netherlands; National Environmental Research Institute, Rønde, Denmark.

Maltby-Prevett, L. S., Boyd, H. & Heyland, J. D. (1975). Observations in Iceland and northwestern Europe of brant from Queen Elizabeth Island, N.W.T., Canada. *Bird Banding* **46**, 155–61.

Marris, R. & Ogilvie, M. A. (1962). The ringing of barnacle geese in Greenland. *Wildfowl* **13**, 53–64.

Martin, B. P. (1993). *Wildfowl of the British Isles and North-West Europe.* David & Charles, Newton Abbot.

Martin, J. (2002). From the Rarities Committee's files: unusual brent geese in Norfolk and Hampshire. *British Birds* **95**, 129–36.

Mathers, R. G. (1996). Abundance of a naturalized population of mandarin duck *Aix galericulata* (L.) and the habitat suitability in the Shimna valley, Co. Down, Northern Ireland. *Irish Naturalists' Journal* **25**, 280–5.

Matthews, G. V. T. (1965). Artificial propagation of wildfowl. *National Game Council of Ireland Report* 1965, 63–6.

Mathiasson, S. (1973). A moulting population of non-breeding mute swans with special reference to flight-feather moult, feeding ecology and habitat selection. *Wildfowl* **24**, 43–53.

Menu, S., Gauthier, G. & Reed, A. (2002). Changes in survival rates and population dynamics of greater snow geese over a 30-year period: implications for hunting regulations. *Journal of Applied Ecology* **39**, 91–102.

Merne, O. J. (1986). Greylag geese in Ireland, March 1986. *Irish Birds* **3**, 207–14.

Miller, J. B. (1996). Red-breasted mergansers in an urban winter habitat. *Journal of Field Ornithology* **67**, 477–83.

Mills, D. H. (1962). The goosander and red-breasted merganser as predators of salmon in Scottish waters. *Freshwater and Salmon Fisheries Research* **29**.

Milne, H. (1965). Seasonal movements and distribution of eiders in the northeast. *Bird Study* **12**, 170–80.

Milne, P. & McAdams, D. G. (2008). Irish rare bird report 2006. www.irbc.ie/reports/report2006.php. Accessed 17 December 2008.

Milonoff, M., Pöysä, H. & Runko, P. (2002). Reproductive performance of common goldeneye *Bucephala clangula* females in relation to age and life span. *Ibis* **144**, 585–92.

Minton, C. (1968). Pairing and breeding mute swans. *Wildfowl* **19**, 41–60.

Minton, C. D. T. (1971). Mute swan flocks. *Wildfowl* **22**, 71–88.

Mitchell, C. (2008). The Icelandic-breeding goose census 2007. *Goose News* **7**, 13–14.

Mitchell, C., Walsh, A., Hall, C. & Crowe, O. (2008). Greenland barnacle geese *Branta leucopsis* in Britain and Ireland: results of the international census, spring 2008. Wildfowl & Wetlands Trust, Slimbridge.

Monval. J.-Y. & Pirot, J.-Y. (1989). *Results of the IWRB International Wildfowl Census 1967–1986.* IWRB Special Publication 8. International Waterfowl & Wetlands Research Bureau, Slimbridge.

Moubray, B. (1854). *Moubray's Treatise on Domestic and Ornamental Poultry.* A Hall, Virtue, London.

Muñoz-Fuentes, V., Green, A. J., Sorenson, M. D., Negro, J. J. & Vilà, C. (2006). The ruddy duck *Oxyura jamaicensis* in Europe: natural colonization or human introduction?. *Molecular Ecology* **15**, 1441–53.

Murray, T. & Cabot, D. (2002). Eider *Somateria mollissima*: a new breeding species in County Mayo. *Irish Birds* **7**, 139–40.

Musgrove, A., Pollitt, M., Hall, C. *et al.* (2001). *The Wetland Bird Survey 1999–2000: Wildfowl and Wader Counts.* BTO/WWT/RSPB/JNCC, Thetford.

Musgrove, A., Collier, M., Banks, A. *et al.* (2007). *Waterbirds in the UK 2005/06: the Wetland Bird Survey.* BTO/WWT/RSPB/JNCC, Thetford.

Nichols, J .D. Bart, J., Limpert, R. J., Sladen, W. J. L. & Hines, E. (1992). Annual survival rates of adult and immature eastern population Tundra swans. *Journal of Wildlife Management* **56**, 485–94.

Ó Bríain, M. (1989). The social organisation, population ecology and distribution of Light-bellied Brent Geese (*Branta bernicula hrota*) wintering in Ireland. Unpublished PhD thesis, National University of Ireland.

O'Donoghue, P. D., O'Halloran, J., Bacon, P. J., Smiddy, P. & Cross, T. F. (1992). The population genetics of the mute swan *Cygnus olor* in Ireland. *Wildfowl* **43**, 5–11.

Ogilvie, M. A. (1964). A nesting study of mallard in Berkeley New Decoy, Slimbridge. *Wildfowl* **15**, 84–8.

Ogilvie, M. A. (1967). Population changes and mortality of the mute swan in Britain. *Wildfowl* **18**, 64–73.

Ogilvie, M. A. (1969). Bewick's swans in Britain and Ireland during 1956–69. *British Birds* **62**, 505–22.

Ogilvie, M. A. (1972). Distribution, numbers and migration. In: Scott, P. & The Wildfowl Trust. *The Swans.* Michael Joseph, London.

Ogilvie, M. A. (1978). *Wild Geese* T. & A. D. Poyser, Berkamsted.

Ogilvie, M. A. (1981). The mute swan in Britain, 1978. *Bird Study* **28**, 87–106.

Ogilvie, M. A. (1983a). A migration study of the teal (*Anas crecca*) in Europe using ringing recoveries. Unpublished PhD thesis, University of Bristol.

Ogilvie, M. A. (1983b). Wildfowl of Islay. *Proceedings of the Royal Society of Edinburgh* **83B**, 229–47.

Ogilvie, M. A. & the Rare Breeding Birds Panel (2000). Rare breeding birds in the United Kingdom in 1998. *British Birds* **93**, 358–93.

O'Halloran, J., Myers, A. A. & Duggan, P. F. (1991). Lead poisoning in mute swans *Cygnus olor* in Ireland: a review. In: Sears & Bacon, 1991, pp. 389–95.

O'Halloran, J., Smiddy, P. & Irwin, S. (1995). Movements of mute swans in south-west Ireland. *Irish Birds* **5**, 295–8.

Olney, P. (1965). The autumn and winter feeding of certain sympatric ducks. *Transactions of the Congress of the International Union of Game Biologists* **6**, 309–22.

O'Meara, J. J. (1982). Translator. *Giraldus Cambrensis [Gerald of Wales]. The History and Topography of Ireland [Topographia Hiberniae].* Humanities Press, Atlantic Highlands, NY.

Owen, M. (1972). Some factors affecting food intake and selection in white-fronted geese. *Journal of Animal Ecology* **41**, 79–92.

Owen, M. (1976). The selection of winter food by white-fronted geese. *Journal of Applied Ecology* **13**, 715–29.

Owen, M. (1980). *Wild Geese of the World*. Batsford, London.

Owen, M. (1982). Population dynamics of Svalbard barnacle geese 1970–80: the rate, pattern and causes of mortality determined by individual marking. *Aquila* **89**, 229–57.

Owen, M. & Black, J. M. (1989a). Factors affecting the survival of barnacle geese on migration from the breeding grounds. *Journal of Animal Ecology* **58**, 603–18.

Owen, M. & Black, J. M. (1989b). Barnacle goose. In: Newton, I., ed., *Lifetime Reproductive Success in Birds*. Blackwell, Oxford, pp. 349–62.

Owen, M. & Black, J. M. (1990). *Waterfowl Ecology*. Blackie, Glasgow.

Owen, M. & Black, J. M. (1991). The importance of migration mortality in non-passerine birds. In: Perrins, C. M., Lebreton, J.-D. & Hirons, G. J. M., eds, *Bird Population Studies, Relevant to Conservation and Management*. Oxford University Press, Oxford, pp. 360–72.

Owen, M. & Cadbury, C. J. (1975). The ecology and mortality of swans on the Ouse Washes. *Wildfowl* **26**, 31–42.

Owen, M. & Norderhaug, M. (1977). The population dynamics of barnacle geese *Branta leucopis* breeding in Svalbard 1948–1976. *Ornis Scandinavica* **8**, 161–74.

Owen, M., Atkinson-Willes, G. L. & Salmon, D. G. (1986). *Wildfowl in Great Britain*. Cambridge University Press, Cambridge.

Owen, M., Black, J. M., Agger, M. C. & Campbell, C. R. G. (1987). The use of the Solway Firth by an increasing population of barnacle geese in relation to changes in refuge management. *Biological Conservation* **39**, 63–81.

Pain, D. J. (1992). Lead poisoning in waterfowl: summary of national reports. In: Pain, D. J., ed., *Lead Poisoning in Waterfowl*. Proceedings of an IWRB Workshop, Brussels, Belgium, 13–15 June 1991. IWRB Special Publication No. 16. International Waterfowl & Wetlands Research Bureau, Slimbridge.

Palmer, R. S., ed. (1976). *Handbook of North American Birds*. Yale University Press, New Haven.

Parker, H. & Holm, H. (1990). Patterns of nutrient and energy in female common eiders nesting in the high arctic. *Auk* **107**, 660–8.

Parslow-Otsu, M. & Kjeldsen, J. P. (1992). Laplandske sædgæs i Nordvestjylland. *Dansk Ornithologisk Forenings Tidsskrift* **86**, 104–6.

Patterson, I. J., Young, C. M. & Tompa, F. S. (1974). The shelduck population of the Ythan estuary, Aberdeenshire. *Wildfowl* **25**, 16–28.

Paxinos, E. E., James, H. F., Olson, S. L. *et al.* (2002). mtDNA from fossils reveals a radiation of Hawaiian geese recently derived from the Canada goose (*Branta canadensis*). *Proceedings of the National Academy of Sciences of the USA* **99**, 1399–404.

Payne-Gallwey, R. (1886). *The Book of Duck Decoys: Their Construction, Management and History.* Van Voorst, London.

Pehrsson, O. (1986). Duckling production of the oldsquaw in relation to spring weather and small-rodent fluctuations. *Canadian Journal of Zoology* **64**, 1835–41.

Pennycuick, C. J., Einarsson, O., Bradbury, T. A. M. & Owen, M. (1996). Migrating whooper swans (*Cygnus cygnus*): satellite tracks and flight performance calculations. *Journal of Avian Biology* **27**, 118–34.

Pennycuick, C. J., Bradbury, T. A. M., Eirnarsson, O. & Owen, M. (1999). Response to weather and light conditions of migrating whooper swans *Cygnus cygnus* and flying height profiles, observed with the Argos satellite system. *Ibis* **141**, 434–43.

Percival, S. (1992). Population modelling of barnacle geese on Islay. Unpublished report to Scottish Natural Heritage.

Perkov, N. (2006). Physical condition and age structure of red-breasted geese wintering at Durankulak Lake, Bulgaria, February 2005. *TWSG News* **15**, 70–2.

Perrins, C. M. (1991). Constraints on the demographic parameters of bird populations. In: Perrins, C. M., Lebreton, J.-D. & Hirons, G. J. M., eds, *Bird Population Studies.* Oxford University Press, Oxford, pp. 190–206.

Perrins, C. M. & Reynolds, C. M. (1967). A preliminary study of the mute swan, *Cygnus olor. Wildfowl* **18**, 74–84.

Petersen, S. R. & Ellarson, R. S. (1979). Changes in Oldsquaw weight. *Wilson Bulletin* **91**, 288–300.

Petrides, G. A. & Bryant, C. R. (1951). An analysis of the 1949–50 fowl cholera epizootic in Texas Panhandle waterfowl. *Transactions of the North American Wildlife Conference* **16**, 193–216.

Pettifor, R. & Rowcliffe, J. M. (1995). Population viability analysis of Icelandic/Greenlandic Pink-footed Geese. Report to Scottish Natural Heritage. Wildfowl & Wetlands Trust, Slimbridge.

Pettifor, R. A., Percival, S. M. & Rowcliffe, J. M. (1996). Greenland barnacle geese: collation and statistical analysis of data and population viability analysis. Unpublished report to Scottish Natural Heritage.

Phillips, V. E & Wright, R. M. (1993). The differences in behaviour and feeding success of tame mallard ducklings *Anas platyrhynchos* in the presence of high and low fish populations at a gravel pit site, with reference to wild brood distribution. *Wildfowl* **44**, 69–74.

Plot, R. (1686). *The Natural History of Staffordshire*. Oxford.

Pollard, E., Lachine, K. H. & Rothery, P. (1987). The detection of density dependence from a series of annual censuses. *Ecology* **68**, 2046–55.

Pollitt, M., Hall, C., Holloway, S. *et al.* (2003). *The Wetland Bird Survey 2000–01: Wildfowl and Wader Counts*. BTO/WWT/RSPB/JNCC, Thetford.

Prins, H. H. T., Ydenberg, R. C. & Drent, R. H. (1980). The interaction of brent geese *Branta bernicla* and sea plantain *Plantago maritima* during spring staging: field observations and experiments. *Acta Botanica Neerlandica* **29**, 585–96.

Prop, J. & Vulink, T. (1992). Digestion by barnacle geese in the annual cycle: the interplay between retention time and food quality. *Functional Ecology* **6**, 180–9.

Ray, J. (1678). *The Ornithology of Francis Willoughby, translated into English and enlarged*. London.

Rees, E. C. (1987). Conflict of choice within pairs of Bewick's swans regarding their migratory movements to and from the wintering grounds. *Animal Behaviour* **35**, 1685–93.

Rees, E. (2006). *Bewick's Swans*. T. & A. D. Poyser, London.

Rees, E. C., Black, J. M., Spray, C. J. & Thorisson, S. (1991). The breeding success of whooper swans *Cygnus cygnus* nesting in upland and lowland regions in Iceland: a preliminary analysis. In: Sears & Bacon, 1991, p. 187.

Rees, E. C., Lievesley, P., Pettifor, R. A. & Perrins, C. (1996). Mate fidelity in swans: an interspecific comparison. In: Black, J. M., ed., *Partnerships in Birds: the Study of Monogamy*. Oxford University Press, Oxford, pp. 118–37.

Rehfisch, M. M., Austin, G. E., Holloway, S. J., Allan, J. R. & O'Connell, M. (2002). An approach to the assessment of change in the numbers of Canada geese *Branta canadensis* and Greylag geese *Anser anser* in southern Britain. *Bird Study* **49**, 50–9.

Reinecker, W. C. (1987). Survival and band recovery rate estimates of northern pintail banded in California, 1948–1979. *California Fish and Game* **73**, 230–7.

Robert, M., Bordage, D., Savard, J.-P. L., Fitzgerald, D. & Morneau, F. (2000). The breeding range of the Barrow's goldeneye in north east America. *Wilson Bulletin* **112**, 1–7.

Robertson, G. J., Cooke, F., Goudie, R. L. & Boyd, W. S. (2000). Spacing patterns, mating systems, and winter philopatry in harlequin ducks. *Auk* **117**, 299–307.

Robinson, J. A., Culzac, L. G. & Aldridge, N. S. (2002). Age-related changes in the habitat use and behaviour of mallard *Anas platyrhynchos* broods at artificially created lakes in southern Britain. *Wildfowl* **53**, 107–18.

Roomen, M. V. & Madsen, J., eds (1992). *Waterfowl and Agriculture: Review and Future Perspective of the Crop Damage Conflict in Europe.* IWRB Special Publication 21. International Waterfowl & Wetlands Research Bureau, Slimbridge.

Rose, P. M., Scott, D. A. & Delany, S., eds (2002). *Waterbird Population Estimates,* 3rd edn. Wetlands International Global Series 12. Wetlands International, Wageningen.

Ruger, A., Prentice, C. & Owen, M. (1986). *Results of the IWRB International Waterfowl Census 1967–1983.* IWRB Special Publication 6. International Waterfowl & Wetlands Research Bureau, Slimbridge.

Ruttledge, R. F. (1980). *A List of the Birds of Ireland.* National Museum of Ireland, Dublin.

Salmon, D. G. & Black, J. M. (1986). The January 1986 whooper swan census in Britain, Ireland and Iceland. *Wildfowl* **37**, 172–4.

Sangster, G., Hazevoet, C. J., van den Berg, A. B. & Roselaar, C. S. (1997). Dutch avifaunal list: taxonomic changes in 1977–97. *Dutch Birding* **19**, 21–8.

Sangster, G., Collinson, J. M., Helbig, A. J., Knox, A. G. & Parkin, D. T. (2005). Taxonomic recommendations for British birds. *Ibis* **147**, 821–6.

Savage, C. (1952). *The Mandarin Duck.* A. & C. Black, London.

Scott, D. A. (1982). Problems in the management of waterfowl populations. In: Scott, D. A. & Smart, M., eds, *Proceedings of the 2nd Technical Meeting on Western Palearctic Migratory Bird Management, Paris, 1979.* IWRB, Slimbridge, pp. 89–106.

Scott, D. A. & Rose, P. M. (1996). *Atlas of Anatidae Populations in Africa and Western Eurasia.* Wetlands International Publication 41. Wetlands International, Wageningen.

Scott, P. & Fisher, J. (1953). *A Thousand Geese.* Collins, London.

Sea Duck Joint Venture (2004). *Sea Duck Information Series: Bufflehead.* SDJV, Anchorage, AK. www.seaduckjv.org. Accessed 17 December 2008.

Sears, J. & Bacon, P. J., eds (1991). Proceedings of the Third IWRB International Swan Symposium, Oxford 1989. *Wildfowl* Supplement 1.

Sears, J. & Hunt, A. (1991). Lead poisoning in mute swans, *Cygnus olor*, in England. In: Sears & Bacon, 1991, pp. 383–8.

Sedinger, J. S., White, R. G., Mann, F. E., Burris, F. A. & Kedrowski, R. A. (1989). Apparent metabolizability of alfalfa components by yearling Pacific black brant. *Journal of Wildlife Management* **53**, 726–34.

Sedinger, J. S., White, R. G. & Hupp, J. (1995). Metabolizability and portioning of energy and protein in green plants by yearling lesser snow geese. *Condor* **97**, 116–22.

Serie, J. R. & Swanson, G. A. (1976). Feeding ecology of breeding gadwalls on saline wetlands. *Journal of Wildlife Management* **40**, 69–81.

Sharrock, J. T. R. (1973). *The Natural History of Cape Clear Island.* T. & A. D. Poyser, Berkhamsted.

Sheppard, R. (1993). *Ireland's Wetland Wealth: the Birdlife of the Estuaries, Lakes, Coasts, Rivers, Bogs and Turloughs of Ireland.* IWC, Dublin.

Shields, G. F. (1990). Analysis of mitochondrial DNA of Pacific brant (*Branta bernicla nigricans*). *Auk* **107**, 620–3.

Shimmings, P. (2003). The occurrence of Greenland white-fronted geese *Anser albifrons flavirostris* in Norway. In: Fox & Francis, 2003, pp. 5–14.

Sincock, J. L. (1962). Estimating consumption of food by wintering wildfowl populations. *Proceedings of the Southeastern Association of Game and Fish Commissioners* **16**, 217–21.

Slatkin, M. (1987). Gene flow and the geographic structure of natural populations. *Science* **236**, 787–92.

Stelfox, A. W. (1938). The birds of Lagore about one thousand years ago. *Irish Naturalists' Journal* **7**, 37–43.

Stone, B. H., Sears, J., Cranswick, P. A. et al. (1997). Population estimates of birds in Britain and in the United Kingdom. *British Birds* **90**, 1–22.

Street, M. (1978). The role of insects in the diet of mallard ducklings: an experimental approach. *Wildfowl* **29**, 93–100.

Summers, R. W. & Underhill, L. G. (1987). Factors related to the breeding production of brent geese *Branta b. bernicla* and waders (Charadrii) on the Taimyr Peninsula. *Bird Study* **34**, 161–71.

Sutherland, W. T. & Allport, G. A. (1991).The distribution and ecology of naturalised Egyptian geese *Alopochen aegyptiacus* in Britain. *Bird Study* **38**, 128–34.

Swann, R. L. & Brockway, I. K. (2007). Site fidelity of Icelandic greylag geese between winters. *Ringing & Migration* **23**, 238–42.

Swann, R. L., Brockway, I., Frederiksen, M. et al. (2005). The within-winter movements and site fidelity of Icelandic greylag geese *Anser anser*. *Bird Study* **52**, 25–36.

Syroechkovsky, E. V., Litvin, K. E. & Gurtovaya, E. N. (2002). Nesting ecology of Bewick's swans on Vaygach Island, Russia. *Waterbirds* **25** (Special Publication 1), 221–6.

Szymczak, M. R. & Rexstad, E. A. (1991). Harvest distribution and survival of a gadwall population, *Journal of Wildlife Management* **55**, 592–600.

Tamisier, A. (1971). Régime alimentaire des sarcelles d'hiver *Anas c. crecca* L. en Camargue. *Alauda* **39**, 262–311.

Thomas, C. B. (1977). The mortality of Yorkshire Canada geese. *Wildfowl* **28**, 35–47.

Thomas, P. W. & Robert, M. (2002). COSEWIC status report on the eastern Canadian harlequin duck (*Histrionicus histrionicus*). Report prepared for the Committee on the Status of Endangered Wildlife in Canada (COSEWIC), Ottawa, Ontario.

Thompson, W. (1851). *The Natural History of Ireland.* Vol. III. Reeve and Benham, London.

Ticehurst, N. (1957). *The Mute Swan in England: its History, and the Ancient Custom of Swan Keeping.* Cleaver-Hume Press, London.

Tiedermann, R. & Noer, H. (1998). Geographic partitioning of mitochondral DNA patterns in European Eiders *Somateria mollissima. Hereditas* **128**, 159–66.

Tierney, T. D., Dunne, J. & Callahan, T. (2000). The common scoter *Melanitta nigra nigra* breeding in Ireland: range expansion or site relocation? *Irish Birds* **6**, 447–52.

Todd, F. S. (1997). *Handbook of Waterfowl Identification.* Ibis, Vista, CA.

Tuite, C. H. & Owen, M. (1984). Breeding waterfowl on British inland waters in 1980. *Wildfowl* **35**, 157–72.

Tveit, G. (1984). Autumn migration, wintering areas and survival of bean geese *Anser fabalis* marked on the moulting grounds in Finnmark, North Norway. *Swedish Wildlife Research* **13**, 73–82.

Tyler, S. J. (1985). The wintering and breeding status of goosanders in Wales. Unpublished RSPB report.

Tyrberg, T. (1998). *Pleistocene Birds of the Palearctic: a Catalogue.* Publications of the Nuttall Ornithological Club, 27. Cambridge, MA.

Ucko, P. J. & Dimbleby, G. W., eds (1969). *The Domestication and Exploitation of Plants and Animals.* Duckworth, London.

Underhill, M. C., Gittings, T., Callaghan, D. A. *et al.* (1998). Status and distribution of breeding common scoters *Melanitta nigra nigra* in Britain and Ireland in 1995. *Bird Study* **45**, 146–56.

US Fish and Wildlife Service (2008). *Waterfowl Population Status, 2008.* Department of the Interior, Washington, DC.

Uspenski, S. M. & Tomkovich, P. S. (1987). The birds of Franz Josef Land and their protection. *Polar Geography & Geology* **11**, 221–3.

Ussher, R. J. & Warren, R. (1900). *The Birds of Ireland.* Gurney and Jackson, London.

van den Berk, V. M., Dirksen, S. & Poot, M. J. M. (2001). Mortality of eiders in the Dutch Wadden Sea 1999/2000: the search for the cause of mass mortality of eiders in the Dutch Wadden Sea. *Wadden Sea Newsletter* **1**, Special issue on eider mortality. Common Wadden Sea Secretariat, Wilmshaven.

Vickery, W. L. & Nudds, T. D. (1984). Detection of density-dependent effects in annual duck censuses. *Ecology* **65**, 96–104.

Wainright, C. B. (1967). Results of wildfowl ringing at Abberton Reservoir, Essex, 1949–1966. *Wildfowl* **18**, 28–35.

Walley, S. (2008). How climate and other variables have influenced the survival of Greenland barnacle geese. Unpublished manuscript, Centre for Ecology and Conservation, University of Exeter.

Walsh, A. J. & Crowe, O. (2008). Barnacle geese *Branta leucopsis* in Ireland spring 2008. *Irish Birds* **8**, 430–2.

Ward, R., Cranswick, P. A., Kershaw, M., *et al.* (2004) *National Mute Swan Census 2002.* WWT, Slimbridge.

Warren, S. M., Fox, A. D., Walsh, A., Merne, O. & Wilson, H. J. (1992). Wintering site interchange amongst Greenland white-fronted geese *Anser albifrons flavirostris* captured at the Wexford Slobs, Ireland. *Bird Study* **39**, 186–94.

Weiloch, M. & Czapulak, A. (1991). *Cygnus olor immutabilis* in Poland. In: Sears & Bacon, 1991, pp. 304–9.

Wells, J. H. & Smiddy, P. (1995). The status of the ruddy duck in Ireland. *Irish Birds* **5**, 279–84.

Wernham, C., Toms, M., Marchant, J., Clark, J., Siriwardena, G. & Baillie, S., eds. (2002). *The Migration Atlas: Movements of the Birds of Britain and Ireland.* T. & A. D. Poyser, London.

Whilde, T. (1993). *Threatened Mammals, Birds, Amphibians and Fish in Ireland. Irish Red Data Book 2: Vertebrates.* HMSO, Belfast.

Whitaker, J. (1918). *British Duck Decoys of To-Day.* Burlington, London.

Whitmore, S. B. (1974). *Swans of the World.* David & Charles, Newton Abbot.

Witherby, H. F., Jourdain, F. C. R., Ticehurst, N. F. & Tucker, B. W. (1938–42). *The Handbook of British Birds.* Witherby, London.

Wood-Gush, D. G. M. (1985). Domestication. In: Campbell, B. & Lack, E., eds, *A Dictionary of Birds.* T. & A. D. Poyser, Calton.

Worden, J., Mitchell, C. R., Merne, O. J. & Cranswick, P. A. (2004a). Greenland Barnacle Geese *Branta leucopsis* in Britain and Ireland: results of the international census March 2003. WWT, Slimbridge.

Worden, J., Cabot, D., Merne, O., Ogilvie, M. & Rowell, H. (2004b). The Greenland population of the barnacle goose *Branta leucopsis* in Britain and Ireland 1956/57 to 2002/03. WWT/JNCC, Slimbridge.

Yalden, D. W. & Albarella, U. (2008). *The History of British Birds.* Oxford University Press.

Index

The New Naturalist Library